LOVE

LOVE

BY MARGARET PERRON WITH
MARY KATHRYN LOVE
AND JULIEANNE CARVER

To Shannon
Thank you for sharing
in our story!
With love,
Julieanne Carver

■ HAZELDEN®

Hazelden
Center City, Minnesota 55012-0176
1-800-328-0094
1-612-257-1331 (FAX)
http://www.hazelden.org

Library of Congress Cataloging-in-Publication Data
Perron, Margaret, date.
     Love / by Margaret Perron with Julieanne Carver and Mary
     Kathryn Love.
          p.   cm.
     First work in The Grace trilogy, of which the second work was
     titled Grace and the final work was titled Peace.
     Includes bibliographical references.
     ISBN 1-56838-156-5
     1. Spiritual biography—United States.   2. Perron, Margaret,
     date. 3. Carver, Julieanne, date. 4. Love, Mary Kathryn, date. I.
     Carver, Julieanne, date. II. Love, Mary Kathryn, date. III. Title.
BL72.P47   1997
973.92'092'2—dc21
     [B]   97-23124
                                                                CIP

Cover design by David Spohn
Illustrations by Randy Scholes
Text design by Nora Koch/Gravel Pit Publications

Editor's note
Hazelden offers a variety of information on chemical dependency and
related areas. Our publications do not necessarily represent
Hazelden's programs, nor do they officially speak for any Twelve Step
organization.

     Ten percent of the author proceeds from each sale of *The Grace
Trilogy* will be donated to The Grace Foundation, an organization
established in remembrance of Grace Zuri Love. The Grace
Foundation has as its mission *Creating art and sacredness from the ordinary.*

     For more information on The Grace Foundation, visit its web site
at http://www.gracezurilove.com

This work is dedicated to Ordinary Women and to the children of ordinary women everywhere, especially those we claim as our own:

Grace Zuri Love

and

(listed youngest to oldest)
Peter Carver, Lucia Carver, Amanda Love,
Angela Deeb, Mia Perron, Ian Mulvaney

As you see you share, all of you do, this unfolds.
The story unfolds. You trust, you share, you grow.
This is life. This is what dreams are made of.
This is LOVE.

CONTENTS

In gratitude for *Love* . . .

It is hard for me to imagine that anyone could feel more gratitude than I do. I am grateful to my husband, Donald Deeb, for his recognition of the changes in me and for his telling me about them and naming for me the essence of those changes. Like the night he told me I was more at ease and, because I was more at ease, the whole family was more at ease. Like the night he told my dad he couldn't remember the last time we had a fight. Or the night he simply told me I was good. I am thankful that while I didn't voice what was happening, he recognized it anyway and, in his own way, joined me in making love and grace and peace real in our lives.

For both Julie and me, having our husbands read the *Love* manuscript was a necessary part of sharing our experiences with them. And although both of us feared that sharing, it only proved to us once again that sharing conquers fear. We each extend our gratitude, to both Donny and Kelly, for their acceptance of our story and their willingness to be part of the whole that continued unfolding with the publishing process.

Each family member and friend who read *Love* blessed me with acceptance. Telling this story was like "coming out of the closet" for me. I could not tell anyone what had happened. I had to write it and let them read it. I can't begin to express the relief I felt when each person *Love* was given to gave love in return. Those I most feared judgment from were those whose support was the

IN GRATITUDE

strongest and loveliest, especially that of my mother, Madeline Diprima Perron. Sara Cole and Shirley Koski, Mary's and Julie's mothers, were the other early readers whose acceptance gave us the strength and courage to go on. Then came the encouragement of Deb Bohnen and Jeff Heggem, two people whose words of praise meant more to us than I can convey.

The list of readers went on from there . . . to siblings Susan Lucio, Mike Perron, John Perron, Ray DiPrima, Liz Cole-Degroot, Charlie Cole. To friends . . . Lou Crain, Sally Austin, Deb Kelly. To co-workers Felicia Christy and Sheila Riley. It seemed that each one held our lives in their hands as they read our story. We thank each one for treating them with dignity.

A special thanks, as well, to Vernon Weckwerth for support of another kind but support that was always steadfast.

The Hazelden team became part of the miracle of *The Grace Trilogy*, beginning with Dan Odegard's vision and understanding of the truly real and continuing through each step of the process and with each person involved.

Love's editor, Caryn Pernu, often guided me to where deeper meaning already existed within the text but was hidden between the lines. With a gentleness that was greatly appreciated, she nudged "more" from me even when I didn't think I had more to give.

Although *Love* is almost a prayer of gratitude for my spirit sisters, I note here again how thankful I am for them.

AN ACKNOWLEDGMENT

If every writer doesn't have a faithful "first" reader of her work, she should have. *Faithful* is the operative word. Without the inexhaustible faith that my friend and reader Ann Mulally Reilly has had in me and my writing, I may not have given up, but my progress would have been greatly delayed. A first reader's faith is a miraculous thing—balm for the soul, inspiration for the muse, it buoys the spirit. A writer's faith in her first reader is also amazing. When Ann told me that *Love* was the best writing I ever did, her words were as powerful to me as those of Maxwell Perkins might have been to a writer of a few decades ago. It is not only because Ann likes my writing that I have always found her to be a woman of impeccable character. That is just the way she is. And to have as a first reader a friend whose honesty is never in doubt, who is innocent of judgment, and who loves the written word is the finest combination that could possibly exist. Ann is one of the many blessings in my life for which I am truly grateful.

INTRODUCTION

HOW IT BEGAN

This is a story about the chance encounters that come together and give form to a life, about the impact one life has upon another, about being affected. This is a story, in its most basic form, about friendship. It is about seeing the patterns of chance in the lives of three friends as more than chance. Like the beauty that reveals itself on a slow walk through the woods on a sunny day, the paths, the choices, the obstacles, and the adventures of our journey stood out, clear and simple and lovely and rare. It is a story of observance. As if life stood still while we captured it, saw what it was, and eventually came to write it down.

It was on December 19, 1995, that we decided to tell this story. It wasn't chance that this decision was made at my kitchen table over a conversation with my friend Mary Love. It was simply the culmination of events that had made up our year, made up our friendship.

We began not necessarily as friends but as co-workers. I had worked with another woman, Julieanne Carver, for an off-site adult-study program at the University of Minnesota for several years before we hired Mary. Julie and I thought of our positions as high-stress because we worked for a biostatistician considered to be an eccentric genius, because our program did not "fit" the university's usual mode of operation (making our day-to-day functioning more difficult than was necessary), and because we had adult students on campus throughout the summer. We had just lost a beloved co-worker who was bright and funny and, more important, mischievous and irreverent to job burnout, and we needed to replace a person we considered irreplaceable.

We wanted someone we would get along with, someone whose skills would complement ours, but we wanted more than that too. Julie thought we should hire someone with university experience; she sought the security of known skills—someone familiar with the bureaucracy and forms of the university, familiar with computers and budgets. I thought we should hire someone who had been in a professional career, someone with the less definable skills of knowing how to maneuver in any environment in a professional manner. I sought someone who would possess qualities that were important to me, qualities that I was trying to develop in myself. So did Julie. But skills and professionalism were only a small part of what we were hoping to develop. The larger part fit in the "something more" category and those qualities were like seedlings ready to sprout. They hadn't quite broken the surface yet so that we could identify them. But they were there.

Despite not knowing what it was I truly sought, I realized almost immediately that I knew someone who would be perfect for the job and who also would provide the "more" that Julie and I were looking for. That someone was Mary Love. How I knew Mary Love would be the perfect complement to me and Julie I do not know. But I knew.

I had met Mary only once before she came to interview with Julie and me. She was the daughter of my mother's best friend, Sara, and she had invited my mother, sister, and me to lunch one Christmas. It was one of those polite social gatherings one attends during the holiday season without much enthusiasm. Everyone is busy. Another luncheon on the calendar at Christmas had about as much appeal as a trip to the dentist. I had things to do!

3

But I also had a "thing" about my mother. After years of being in conflict we had made our peace, and I was eager not only to keep it but to build upon it. Her friend Sara seemed a bit of a bridge in that regard, as Sara genuinely liked me in a way I had never really thought my mother had. For years Sara had been reeling off a list of the things we have in common—a fondness for poppy seeds, being Aquarians, and a love of reading—in that way people have of associating themselves with those they admire. If there was any appeal to the luncheon for me, it was the thought of basking in the glow of that admiration.

To my surprise, Sara's admiration seemed to have passed to her daughter Mary as well. She had heard about me, she said, and thought how interesting I sounded. What attracted Mary, in addition to the similarities I shared with her mother, was that I was a writer, a title I was just beginning to feel I had the right to claim, as I had recently completed my first book.

The luncheon was a success, something I've come to believe could happen on Mary's charm alone. She is a warm, sweet-faced, soft-looking person with an animated way of talking that includes much laughter and hand gestures. We are about the same age, height, and weight, neither of us overly pretty or separated by any of those things that tend to separate women: a disproportion of intelligence, education, money, looks. Although she had no children of her own and I had three, she was recently married and had a stepdaughter. Our husbands were of a similar type, obvious from the beginning as we laughed over the reason Mary had almost called off her wedding: her husband's collection of empty plastic yogurt containers he hadn't wanted to part with when they set up residence together. Two men who were savers were something that two women who were not could immediately identify with. But there were other things, about our husbands and about our careers, both of which had veered in the direction of health care for no particular reason. The "liking each other" bond was sealed, however, when Mary produced a seventy-year-old scrapbook she and her husband had purchased at an estate sale. It was the keepsake of a woman named Claire, simple mementos of an ordinary life, tenderly kept, and on that pre-Christmas afternoon four years ago, tenderly shared.

Thus began the connection that brought Mary to my kitchen table and before that to my place of employment. At the time of the luncheon, Mary had taken a six-month leave from her job and was looking for a change. When the job opening presented itself at my office, I sent her the relevant information and she began the tedious process of applying for a university job.

Luckily, she had the right background, the right talents. She was available and I knew she would work hard. But I would have expected anyone we considered for the job to have certain talents, to work hard. It wasn't what I wanted in a co-worker. What I wanted was something more. Something more, even, than professional competence.

When pushed to define it further, I labeled it a warm and outgoing personality that would balance the quieter, more introverted personalities of Julie and myself. But it was more than that too.

At the holiday luncheon, Mary had revealed not a professional self, but a very human self. The part of Mary that had touched me as we laughed over yogurt containers and almost cried over Claire was what I was really looking for. This part of Mary that was a treasure. The Mary who could share her humanness in such a simple yet profound manner. Yet I wasn't ready—then—to admit to that longing to be touched, to connect.

Julie had not had the benefit of seeing Mary's humanness exposed at a holiday lunch, but Mary's humanness was as easily recognized during an interview as at a social event. If I had any doubts they were erased when Vernon, our director, was introduced to Mary. He asked Mary not about her skills, but about her birth order. Mary announced, raising her right hand as if to take an oath, that she was a firstborn, identifying proudly with the firstborn qualities of perfectionism and leadership. He grunted. Seeing that this answer had not been accepted with favor, Mary quickly launched into how she was really like a secondborn because her brother, who had been born just a year behind her, had been sickly. "Charlie got all the attention," Mary said. "I learned to fend for myself." If Vernon didn't want perfectionism and leadership, she'd give him independence.

Yes, I knew it. Mary was the one. Julie knew it too. We offered Mary the job and she accepted.

Mary's joining us was the beginning of the story, the beginning of seeing those chance encounters of life as something more than chance. And from the beginning, there was a feeling that Mary belonged. But it was more than that. It was more that the three of us belonged together in that time and in that place and that Mary Love was to be the tie that bound us, the loop that completed our circle.

Almost from day one we realized that we were together for a reason. But that reason did not reveal itself immediately. For a while we simply worked. Mary had a job to learn; we had programs to run.

We worked in a rather schizoid department where we did everything from the most tedious clerical duties to traveling around the country promoting the program at professional conferences. I, in an effort to get Mary to accept the job, had emphasized its professional nature. It was almost with embarrassment that I listened during Mary's interview while Julie asked how Mary felt about doing mailings.

Mary's job was a twin, or perhaps I should say a triplet, of my own. Mary, Julie, and I each ran separate portions of one program. We each separately admitted students, but jointly prepared their curricula. We each separately scheduled faculty, but jointly prepared a master schedule. We each were in charge of separate events, but all would attend them and assist each other in making sure they ran smoothly. The three positions had to work in concert with one another. We were a team on which having the right skills and personalities was paramount.

I was told once that I could administer a small Third World country. Being a good administrator is a dubious skill, something akin to being seen as an excellent bureaucrat. But still, it was the main attribute I brought to the group. Good at planning and meetings and seeing the big picture, I filled a role that needed to be filled. I was also seen as the communicator, which was equally true, at least in writing. I had less confidence in my ability to promote the program through person-to-person encounters. I did not see myself as warm or outgoing.

I did not see Julie that way either. Julie's unique skill was an ability with numbers and an orientation to detail that had often kept other office workers from making costly or embarrassing mistakes. She often said the important thing was to get things done right, not just to get them done. In the two years we had worked together before Mary's arrival, Julie and I had not developed a personal relationship. She was younger by a decade, tiny in stature, one of those women who, although not from money, looked as if she were. Quiet and dignified, she was a person you could count on to get to work on time, leave on time, and not produce any creative breakthroughs or dreadful mistakes while she was there. In short, she was also one of those people you need to have on a team, and we had been good teammates; we just had too little in common and were both too quiet and reserved to become friends.

We needed Mary.

Almost immediately, Mary did what I somehow knew she would do. She began to transcend the label of "co-worker" and become "friend." And what's more, what she began transcended our individual boundaries. Everyone in the office became better friends.

With the blossoming of these friendships came an appreciation for Mary, the change agent. Mary stories became legend. We retold the story of her interview and meeting with Vernon time and time again. Mary would say, as we sat down to a 2,000-person mailing, "I didn't know what you meant when you asked how I felt about mailings," and we would laugh and talk again, for the tenth, the fifteenth time, about how Mary came to work with us. Even my teaching her to use the computer became story material. As she learned, she would wield the mouse with the sweeping strokes of an orchestra conductor, often traveling off the mouse pad and to the edge of the desk and then exclaiming, "Oopsie! Oopsie!"

Because of its humanness, this story became part of the fabric of our lives. Before Mary, we had not told stories. Our day-to-day existence had not inspired the immediate remembrance, the oral tradition, that working with Mary inspired. It was almost as if from the beginning we were continually recognizing and reinforcing the rightness of our decision, the pleasure that had come from it, the joy Mary was adding to our lives, the feeling that Mary was meant to be with us.

And yet our work lives were still ordinary. We went through six months together before any major changes occurred. And it was a good six months. Julie and Mary got along better than I had ever thought they would and there arose, at times, the difficulties inherent in the number three. The rules every mother knows are true—two kids play well together and three are trouble. We were adults, of course, and we weren't playing, but the trouble came and went and the team functioned as well or better than it ever had.

Mary had been hired in April and it was November when the news came. Not a one of us at work would ever forget it. We had a long, narrow office with the receptionist's desk right inside the door. The desk was our gathering place for morning conversation before the workday began. It had before it one of those modules with a shelf on top. In winter, especially, it invited the laying down of purses and gloves while one took off one's coat and deposited it on the other side of the door at the coat rack.

Mary's hair was cut short and it gave her face a pixieish quality. On this morning, the color in her cheeks was particularly high, her hair (which she changed often) was a burnished red, her look one of pure radiance. I must have just come in myself because I was there to see the entrance. It seems to me in retrospect that everyone was appropriately gathered around. Mary hadn't even taken her coat off when she swept her eyes through the group, slammed her purse down on the shelf, and announced, "I'm pregnant." We would tease her about this later because she had planned to wait three months to tell us and had been unable to wait three minutes.

Julie immediately got tears in her eyes. "Congratulations," she said. Mary could see that the tears were not only tears of joy but tears that reflected Julie's own disappointment. For she had been trying, thus far unsuccessfully, for a second child. As is apt to happen in an office of women, all of our menstrual cycles had grown to be close together and Mary asked, "Have you gotten your period yet this month?"

Julie shook her head and Mary announced that she had the second half of her two-try home pregnancy kit with her. The two scurried off to the bathroom. The remaining nonpregnant among us quickly toted up the months. One baby, possibly two, would be due in July, at our busiest time of the year.

Within a week we had two confirmed pregnancies with due dates three days apart. The bond between Mary and Julie was sealed. While I was happy for them both, I also knew that they would share something I could not. I felt as if I was doomed to be odd woman out in the threesome, the one who would be left to get us through our busy season with no experienced team members. I felt a little jealous of the closeness they would share. That closeness began immediately.

From the first days of being joyous and beaming, through the months of being tired and squeamish, and on to the early days of wearing maternity clothes and feeling the first faint movements of life, they relied on each other for comfort, support, and encouragement. Julie, having already had a child, could say, "Oh, it's normal to feel that way," or, "I feel that way too." Once a month we took Polaroid snapshots of their ever-increasing shapes and mounted them side-by-side on office walls. We guessed at who would have a boy and who would have a girl. We discussed the merits of one name and another. They talked of doctor visits, the thrill of hearing their babies' heartbeats, the coming labor and delivery. They dreamed of how their children would be friends and teased that they would grow up and marry.

As summer approached I planned the shower. With Mary's mother and my mother being best friends, I decided to give a shower with a mother-daughter theme. Mary's mother-in-law drove up from Madison, Wisconsin; her mother and mine had an excuse to celebrate together; all of us co-workers had the chance to meet the other mothers we had heard so much about. I made a game of "momisms" in which the shower guests had to guess which of the moms regularly said things like, "That makes me so nervous," or "a lick and a polish." I threw in a few from the new mothers as well: Mary's

"I'm going to el baño," Julie's "I'm so tired." No one knew it would be one of the last joyous days of the pregnancies.

By early June we had been moved to smaller office quarters. Julie, Mary, and I were in one room and the remainder of the office staff was in another. No longer in private offices, our desks were separated by cubicle walls and we were so close together that if one of us sneezed the other two would immediately say, "God bless you."

So it was that when I received the call from a frantic Mary, Julie was at my desk within seconds. Mary was at her doctor's office, alone and in shock. She had been told that her baby had a malformation, later diagnosed as an arterial ventricle malformation, and that the prospects were not good.

It is hard to describe shock, or a sharing of a misery so deep and primal, but it was all there in Mary's voice, Julie's face as she heard the news. I worried for a time that we would have two babies affected, so deep and immediate was Julie's pain and heartsickness. She alone could imagine what Mary was feeling. All the fears of mothers everywhere converged in Mary's voice, in Julie's face. All the shared joys became reasons for doubt, suspicion, terror. "What if?" replaced happiness in that instant for both of them. For both it continued, sapping their energy. All things were in question.

For Mary, of course, it was reality. For the remaining few weeks of her pregnancy, the tests and the questions continued. *How bad would it be? Was there reason for hope?* The loss of control was complete. The body was no longer the trusted companion of life but the enemy, concealing secrets so devastating that it was obvious life would never be the same again. It was a great rift, a chasm that split life at its core. Mary plunged into it. Julie and I tumbled after her.

Julie gave birth to Peter on July 13, and he was robust and healthy. Little Grace was born on July 22 and lived five weeks. The paradox was complete. The fear, the questions, the "what ifs?" continued. What meaning is there in a hoax of such magnitude? All that was to be joy had become pain for one. The joy of another tempered by fear, by what if?

I wondered about the long-term effect. How, I wondered, could Mary come back—to life and to the team. I felt certain she would never be the same warm, outgoing person; certain she would never work with us again; certain that the pain of the happy memories of the shared pregnancies, and the pain of little Peter's reality, would be too much. I wondered how she would cope. How Julie would cope.

I had come close to losing a child myself during a difficult pregnancy, and the result of that almost-losing was a bond so strong it still gripped my heart, made it difficult for me ever to criticize or punish this child of my almost loss. This child who in her near loss became more precious than anything—than life itself. I felt I knew somewhat the bond Mary had developed with her daughter, Grace, as she struggled through the final days of her pregnancy, wondering how it would all turn out. My daughter had not been the longed-for child that Mary's daughter, Grace, had been, but when I almost lost her, she became my angel, later named Angela. She became the reason for my existence in the final weeks of my pregnancy. I felt as if I willed her to survive with the force of a love that grew more intense each day. I tried to imagine the pain Mary would experience in not being able to bring the bond of love she had developed with Grace into the future.

But I was wrong in thinking that the bond would not continue. The love, the bond, that had grown between Mary and Grace grabbed and held all of us. It followed us through our days. It changed our lives. There was a reason we were together, just as we had known from the very beginning. Only now we knew what that reason was. That reason was Grace.

I believe Grace happened at the right time—as Grace can only happen when the time is right. In other years, under other stars, the effects of Grace might not have been so apparent, so intense, so profound, so compelling. But I came to believe that Grace coming at the right time was all that was possible—that there was a divine plan at work in the universe.

I

ORDINARY WOMEN

P art of our reason for bringing this work to light was
our belief, stated over and over again, that we are
"ordinary" women. We would often say, If this can
happen to three ordinary women, it can happen to anyone. What we, perhaps, meant by *ordinary,* was *familiar.* We
are your neighbors, the women down the street, the ladies
in the next office, the mothers at school conferences, the
wives out for dinner with their husbands, the girlfriends
out shopping, the devout of your church, the nameless

women pushing shopping carts at the grocery store.

We are not, any of us, above average. We are average incarnate. We make less than $30,000 a year. We struggle with bills, with prioritizing, with children and husbands and in-laws. Two of us have been divorced. One has a husband with a disability. One has two children of mixed race. One's child died.

We are ordinary, average, and yet we are different. As each of you are different. We bring different hopes and fears and pains and joys to our friendship and to this collaboration. We have different failings and different gifts. We are three and we are one.

If we could tell you the limited range of our vision before this began. How little we saw of each other: We saw only the ordinary. Only the familiar. We saw what we chose to see, what the habits of a lifetime had led us to see. If only we could make you see that no one is ordinary, that in our ordinariness we are so much more.

It is hard now, even, to go back there, to that place where we were barely distinguishable from one another, and yet so different that we might never have met.

Mary eats so fast, she is done with lunch before Julie sits down. Julie brings a lunch of cheese sandwiches and animal crackers and a piece of fruit for weeks on end. I thought I was lazy. I was surprised when I found a message written at the bottom of my monthly vacation/sick-leave report that I had to start using my vacation time or I would lose it. I smoke and drink coffee and don't worry

LOVE

about either. Mary has occasionally smoked, doesn't any longer, drinks coffee with cream. Julie partakes of neither and never has. Mary and I love to entertain. Julie would rather not. None of us has exercised this past year. We spend too much time talking at work and still get our work done. Mary and I have switched from drinking diet soda to regular and to drinking more juice and water. Julie never drank diet soda or ingested any NutraSweet. My children are almost grown, Julie's just beginning, Mary's stepdaughter in between. Our husbands guardedly like each other but are not friends. One works in heating and air-conditioning, one in alarm systems, and one is the owner of a guest residence. We are all college educated. We are all home owners. I have multiple vehicles (the teenagers), all American made; Mary two, Julie one, all foreign. I am the only one with a functioning garage. All of our husbands cook. Mary is Danish and English, Julie Norwegian, I a blend of Italian, Irish, and French-Canadian. We live in different cities on either side of the campus at which we work. Mary and I would be considered late baby boomers, Julie at the early end of Generation X. Mary is a firstborn, Julie a third, me a fourth. Mary is Sagittarian, Julie and I Aquarians. We all have eclectic tastes in music, but Mary has more jazz, Julie more U2, I more Jimmy Buffett. Julie and I were both born in the state in which we continue to live, Mary was not and spent her early years overseas. None of us is a hobbyist. Two of us have cats (two each). Julie was a cheerleader,

Mary a homecoming queen candidate. I graduated from an alternative high school.

Although this barely scratches the surface of our differences and similarities, it is much of what we initially knew of one another. Much of what most people ever know about one another. It was nothing.

We came from a world in which work was important. Work was our bond and our goal. Work was where the drama of life played itself out. Who would lead and who would follow? Who would do this job and who that? Who would take vacation when? Who would supervise? Which of us would attract the most students to our program? Which of us would be better liked? How would we relate to our boss? How would we split, divide, distribute the workload into fair and manageable portions? How could we each contribute?

We came to work each day ready to do battle with the world. I can still remember Julie's face—she continues to wear it at times—when she would come in late. She had been the most dependable of employees: punctual, reliable, steady. Now, her two young children necessitated a woman who could be flexible. Who could do only what she could do within the confines of changing dirty pants, and finding shoes, and getting children strapped into car seats. This flexibility remains hard on her still, but not like it was then. It was all visible in her face, the defenses she had built to ward off the attack she was sure was coming: Why are you late?

I, too, was late. Sometimes I would arrive apologetic. Other times not. I thought, Julie at least has a good excuse. But she, because of day care, could not stay late to make it up. I could. I was one up on her.

Mary arrived, almost always pleasant. Warm. "I left my pain behind," her face, her voice, her posture all said. Before the baby as well as after, she came with her work persona: "I am fine. I am here to do my job. My personal problems are not here with me, thank you very much."

We all arrived hurried, breathless almost, from the effort of arriving. From the effort of leaving one world behind and entering another. From the transformation from one being to the next. Within the first half hour we were relieved. We had made it. We had arrived. The job would now occupy us. We would flow into its rhythm. We would chat, exchange information, interact. We would adjust our moods to the mood of the workplace. If it was busy, we rushed from one thing to the next, our rhythm staccato, our pace rapid. If it was slow, we would putter. Doing a little of this, a little of that. If the boss was visiting, we would stand up straighter, look busier, feel busier. If a co-worker watched the clock, we became slaves to time. If the secretary was not efficient enough, we wondered what to do. If all was going as dictated by our time line (an actual written document), we congratulated one another. If one person was busier than the next we made adjustments or held resentments. If two people seemed closer than the others, we closed ranks with those remaining. We drank our coffee, ate our bagels, went to lunch, had staff meetings and retreats. We prided ourselves on functioning well. We each fulfilled our duties. There is a reason such a place is referred to as a well-oiled machine.

What we had going for us was a boss who considered our work not a job but a mission, and one who hated bureaucracy. Thus, we were not rule bound, and, although the job was the bond and the goal, it was at least a worthy goal: education. Also, the nature of the programs we worked on, in which students came once a year to campus and became our charges, required teamwork and a social connectedness that went beyond the ordinary and usual.

The summer that the babies were born, at an after-work party in celebration of the end of our busy season, I shocked a student worker by having a few drinks and a good time. He said (after a few drinks himself), "But you're so rigid!" And I thought, *Me? Rigid?* How could this young man possibly have gotten this idea? Where? How? But there was no mystery to it at all. To him, I had become my work. I was only the person who demanded he be on time and responsible, and demanded more of myself: rigid. There I had been each day in my business suit, my work the most important thing in the world. Rigid. Part of me took it as a compliment.

But that was the summer I realized I had worked hard enough to take vacation. That was the summer of the pregnancies. The summer it all began to break open. The summer Mary's baby died. The summer that work was suddenly not the most important thing in the world anymore.

It took a while to catch on. This breaking down of rigidity was like the dismantling of a wall, a fence, a brick building. The wall of rigidity came down slowly. My rigidity, I thought, was still my work. And my work was my identity. It represented all I had "worked" so hard to attain: a place in life, a title, a badge, a business suit, respectability, a good reputation. It was my anchor. Because the job was more than a job. It was also an escape.

My full-time work life had begun when I was the single mother of three young children. I now had a good husband, I owned my own home, and I had paid off every bill that had accumulated over those years of trying to raise children on my own. Yet this had not sunk in. Work was still survival. Vacation was still something to be saved for an emergency. A part of me still believed that work was what kept me sane. There was a hidden undercurrent that said as much as work was my life, it was also shielding me from a life that was even less controllable than the one in the office.

For Mary, the rigidity was now pain. And work was as much an anesthetic from that pain as television can be from life. For a while, for those hours between eight and five, the real could be replaced with the unreal. The pain

22

could be muted, if not forgotten. She could close the door on the home her child had never entered and drive away from the neighborhood in which her child would never run and play and in some way be held together by the rigidity of the workplace and the tasks to accomplish within the office walls.

For Julie, the rigidity was being the lucky one whose child had lived, whose child was perfect. But it was not always easy to be the lucky one who had to stay up all night with a sick child, change another dirty diaper just as she was ready to head out the door, the lucky one who had to pay someone else an exorbitant sum to take care of the children she would rather have taken care of herself. It was difficult to complain when you were the lucky one. For her, too, work was both a prison and an escape.

Identity, suffering, luck. For a while we tried to keep them all stuffed together, lumped into the overriding rigidity of work. The importance, the bond, the goal, of work. It gave us something to do. Something to hang our lives on. Something to fill our time. In a very real sense, it was our survival, monetarily and otherwise. How could it not be the most important thing in the world—at least for the eight to ten hours a day, five days a week we were involved in it?

And yet, how could it be? How simply silly, when seen in black and white, in the written form: Our goal, our bond, our importance, coming from our work. Our jobs. Simple jobs. Jobs that were not the stuff of brilliant careers. Jobs that were not our passions. Just jobs. Adequate, ordinary jobs. The jobs most people have. The earning-a-paycheck jobs. Jobs we were content with. Jobs we didn't want to lose. But still jobs.

Beneath the surface of our work lives ran the stream of our secret lives. Our secret selves. Out of one-dimensional life sprang dimensional life. We've spent the last year learning not to see just the surface but to delve beneath it. We have found treasures there.

We have found happiness in this pursuit. Out of the ashes life. Out of the darkness light. If it could happen to us it could happen to anyone. This is our message.

I I

MOVEMENT

As ordinary women, Mary, Julie, and I were used to our lives proceeding in an orderly fashion, to having the kind of years difficult to discern from any other year. The unusual years were just that: unusual. We might remember the year we got married, be able to place our state of mind by remembering the years in which our children were born or some other major event took place. "Oh, yes, that was the year . . ."

We were, in other words, ordinary women expecting to

have ordinary lives. Some of us, more than others, thought we knew the direction our lives would take.

One of the reasons I had begun to get notices about my vacation building up was that I had been at the university for ten years. Ten years! Where had the time gone? I had not meant to be at the university that long but now that I had been I was thinking of retiring from the university. The first ten years had gone pretty fast, why not the next ten or twenty? As if years were something to be gotten through. And to be gotten through quickly.

Julie, as the youngest, was perhaps most open to possibilities. She thought of graduate school while her husband thought of expanding his business. Ten years into the future could very well mean incredible changes, life-altering changes. Just being the mother of young children made this so.

Mary had thought her life would go a certain way. That she would be raising a child for many years to come. That her life would be full of those child-rearing milestones, from yearly birthday parties to kindergarten and graduation. Her eight-year-old stepdaughter, Amanda, would still anchor her in these events for a little while. But the future loomed, undefinable.

I could dream of having books published and maybe not having to work for another ten or twenty years, but I had that ten or twenty years firmly planted in my mind. It was the most logical course of events. It comprised the most likely direction for my next two decades.

Encased in these various scenarios of the future, our ordinary lives went on. And they were full of not only scenes of the future but scenes from the past. The past seemed to abide in us, in our subconscious minds, keeping us company, a part of us.

There were childhood traumas from which we had not healed. Young-adult rebellions, that while necessary, had caused more harm than good. Grown-up mistakes that filled the mind with guilt.

We lived, as most people do, in part to build uncertain futures, in part to make up for unsatisfactory pasts, in part to survive the present. We were not only our work selves and our private selves, but also our selves of the past, present, and future. And these selves were seldom in accord. More often than not they were battling. The self of my past asked the self of my future by what audacity I could possibly believe I had anything to say that might be worthy of publication. I had made too many mistakes—too many wrong choices, from men, to education, to when to have children—to consider myself worthy. The self of Julie's past crippled her present with fears of abandonment and rejection. Her father's manic depression and parents' subsequent divorce had wounded something in her that had never healed. Mary's past called her to be a perfectionist, to not give anyone reason to criticize or ridicule her ever again. Having grown up wearing her heart and her ideas on her sleeve, she had suffered too much from that revelation to ever want to be revelatory again.

So we brought both our visions of the future and our beliefs from the past into the present with us. Both contributed to our unhappiness, to our ordinariness, to the surface images we projected and fought to be sure no one saw beneath.

We were basically stuck, though we did not know it . . . until Grace.

It is not, sometimes, until you stand back and review, that you see the rhythm and flow, the movement that has taken you where you have gotten. It wasn't until we began to look back, that the wonder of our journey filled us.

When we began to review, to think about telling our story, we thought it was essential to portray the fact that what happened to us was not something we went looking for. We did not join a movement or "get" religion. And yet, what our journey revealed was movement. The movement itself was the wonder of the journey. We were moving on . . . letting go of the past . . . moving forward. We had become our own movement. We had lived an unusual year.

And just as clearly, we realized that it was still going on. That it was not about to be *over*. That there was no over. For the story was still unfolding, as we were. As we are.

The story we tell here unfolded over the course of a year. But as you begin it, it is important for you to know that it continues. Important for you to know that it is not about getting "the answers," that it is not about winning the lottery, that it is not about reaching a static place of wealth or success in which you feel you have made it and it is over. It is more about realizing that it is never over. That we are never anything but ordinary. That it is in our ordinariness that we are so much more.

The unfolding of the story took place over the course of a year. It began four months after Grace had died. It began, appropriately, in January.

III

WHAT WAS NORMAL?

By January of the year following Grace's death, life in our workplace had returned to a semblance of normality. The new calendar year arrived with all the attendant fanfare and resolutions. And, in our department, it was also the beginning of planning for a new academic year. There was a sense of the extraordinary wrapping up. Of the ordinary returning. We had experienced a crisis of both personal and professional proportions. We had survived it. It was time to get back to normal.

Mary, in keeping with the mood of the new year, planned a vacation. There was probably a collective sigh of relief at the news. Mary was putting things behind her, moving on.

Whether Mary felt this way or not, I did not know. It would have been intrusive to ask. But the vacation seemed to be a good sign—getting away, as it were.

Mary and her husband had planned a trip to Florida to visit his parents, to relax, to spend time sunning on the beach, to do whatever needed to be done to complete the healing. To get over it, some might have thought but never would have said.

But if it was to be a journey of forgetfulness, a New Year's journey of leaving the past and the pain behind, it did not work out that way. Instead it became the first time that Mary realized the pain would follow her wherever she went. The first time she realized she could not leave it at home, could not take a vacation from it. She could not drown it out in the wake of all the waves of the ocean. It was hers. It was her. It was.

Back at the office, the sound of Mary's tears reached across the miles to her friend Julie. What Julie heard was that it was not over. That it had only just begun. She stood in the office listening to a cry of loneliness she recognized. For she was lonely too. She stood outside my cubicle and said, "I think Mary is having a bad day."

Mary returned, leaving nothing behind. Returned with all she had brought with her. Julie asked, "Did you have a bad day last Wednesday?" Something had pierced the loneliness. For both of them.

"Yes," Mary said. "I did."

Mary had been on the beach crying. She cried as she looked out the car window while her husband, John, drove them to the beach. Sitting in the sand with John holding her, the wind blowing everywhere, she cried. Grief, as a friend of ours once said, is not compartmentalized like a jewelry box. It is a pool you get pushed into. And it includes all the grief you have ever experienced. It is all there waiting for you. All that was ever wounded is once again tender. You either heal it all or you don't heal at all. It is the archetypal choice between life and death. Mary hovered.

Her daughter, her Grace, had been born with an arterial ventricle malformation. What was God punishing her for? Her daughter, her Grace, had needed one surgery after another. What was God punishing her for? The surgeries permanently damaged the child who had been born with a hope, a chance of perfection. What was God punishing her for? She had watched her daughter, her Grace, suffer. What was God punishing her for? Her daughter, her Grace, slipped from life to death in the arms of her father while Mary was down the hall resting, absent. What was God punishing her for?

Life was not going to get back to normal. For what was normal about what had happened to Mary? What was normal about the death of a child only five weeks old?

What was normal? The grieving was clearly going to continue until this question was answered. Once asked, the question wasn't going to go away. What was normal?

And where could Mary bring this question? To the men in her life? To her husband and her father who, while well meaning, were telling her it was time to move on? To her mother who grieved so with her, that to talk about the baby at all was to invite more suffering? To friends she saw infrequently? How fortunate, how truly heaven sent, was the friend who knew before she saw. "Did you have a bad day?" How fortunate to have someone who had shared all the delight of the pregnancy to remember not only the pain, but the joy as well. How fortunate to have someone connected.

It wasn't a miraculous thing, this sensing, this feeling Julie had experienced that told her Mary was having a bad day while on vacation. No one made it into something it was not. But it was a sensitivity. One young mother realizing that another might, on this "getting away" vacation, mourn once again the child who had died. It was a sensitivity perhaps based on the shared pregnancies or the reality of Julie's own five-month-old. It was a sensitivity of time and space, of the good worker in Julie seeing beyond the work that needed to get done and extending the time of sensitivity to the wounded among us. And to extending that sensitivity beyond work as well. To bringing it home with her, where, on a day in February, she gave it room to bring Mary something more.

33

IV

HOPE

On that cold February day, Julie was home trying to take a rare nap. Yet she was thinking about Mary, her mind wrestling with the pain Mary had faced, tossing to and fro, as one does before sleep, with the sadness of the tragedy Mary had suffered. The conclusion of this fitful reverie was that she heard a Voice say, "God Bless Mary."

Julie told me she began to sob when she heard the Voice. I knew right away that she wasn't talking about a biblical pronouncement from on high. She wasn't having a Moses type of experience when she heard the Voice. She was reaping the benefits of having turned within. She was hearing the quiet Voice of wisdom. She was letting a knowing Voice rise out of her subconscious and speak to her. And she brought the message of that Voice to Mary.

And Mary, who had taken what had happened to her daughter and tortured herself with it, making herself "bad" because of imagined things she might not have done right, imagined things she could have done to prevent the unpreventable, took the words "God Bless Mary" and hung on to them. They were a gift, a prized possession. All she had to hang on to. All she had to tell her, "Maybe God wasn't punishing you, after all."

Mary took the words and believed in them. She didn't question from where they came. She didn't ask by what right or power Julie brought them to her. She *received* them. From her turning within she had learned how to receive.

I often wondered, after that, how quickly things would have moved forward had Julie had more time to herself. We are talking about a woman with two young children. A woman who worked full time. A woman whose husband worked long hours in his own business. A woman who still tried to do it all and do it all well. Because it seemed as if every time this small and seemingly delicate woman found time to be alone, she experienced another connection to Mary. It became apparent that this woman whose life was so full that she barely had time to think of her own needs had somehow made herself accessible, even in her sleep, to the connection with her friend.

Later in the month, her husband out of town at a conference, Julie was home in bed alone, this time in a sound sleep. She was lying face up, an unusual sleeping position for her, when she felt a hand moving from the right top of her abdomen to the lower left, as if someone were underneath her. It was so real to her that it woke her up. It was like a hand caressing her abdomen.

When she talked about the sensation at work the next morning, Mary couldn't believe it. She was so stunned that she took Julie away from the office and down the hall to the women's room.

She said, "I had the same thing."

It was such an unusual experience. They compared the movement. It was exactly the same. "Right over the womb," Julie said. When she said this, Mary told her, "That's exactly what I thought. Over the womb." What had frightened Julie, alone in her house, her husband out of town, had comforted Mary. Because Mary saw it as a sign of connection to someone else: a connection to Grace.

But as Mary freely admitted, she was at that time crediting Grace with any unusual occurrence. Since December, she had been having the sensation of something hopping on her bed as she was drifting off to sleep. She was comforted by the thought that it might be Grace's spirit. She also experienced the sensation of being tucked in. She felt as if someone tucked her comforter around her sides as she was trying to fall asleep at night.

Being awakened by a hand running across the lower part of her abdomen followed these events. She thought it was unusual but she thought it was Grace. She didn't say anything about it, however. Her musings about Grace visiting from the spirit world were personal, private. She thought, perhaps, that they were the sensations of her grief, that pool she could not pull herself out of. Now she wondered. Had the bond she and Julie shared during their pregnancies somehow transcended the pregnancies, transcended the death of her daughter, her Grace? Could it be that what she felt was more than grief? Was there some connection, some bond, between her and Grace, as there seemed to be between her and Julie? Just the possibility gave her hope. And hope is an extraordinary thing, a healing thing. Mary turned within, and through her connection to Julie, a connection that seemed to come more from within than without, she found hope.

It was all about hope, really—this quest for something more, something beyond the ordinary, something larger than ourselves. Mary, Julie, and I were each searching for this "something more," even though we may have hoped for different results from its discovery. While Mary hoped for relief from pain and for some reassurance that her daughter had passed from this life to something better,

Julie and I simply sought the reassurance that fulfillment could be found within our ordinary lives.

We hoped to see and to connect to some larger purpose. To make sense of our ordinary lives. To make sense of the directions our lives had taken. Why had this tragedy happened to Mary? If the tragedy could be made to fit some larger picture, some higher goal, it might become something Mary could live with and that we all could learn from. This became the beauty of the *spirit sisters,* as we eventually began to call ourselves. As the spiritual quest and the connections continued, it seemed possible that they were connected to what had seemed like the senseless death of Mary's daughter, her Grace. That perhaps Grace had come to lead us all on this journey.

How *holy* the journey became once this thought occurred to us. How important! How hopeful! We did not know. We were only ordinary women going about the living of our lives. But if, *if,* we could somehow give a purpose to something we saw as so senseless and sad, *if* we could be changed, improved, made better by this tragedy, then wasn't that a comfort in itself? Wasn't that a reason to hope?

Mary had been writing to her daughter almost from the moment she knew she had conceived. She kept a journal of her pregnancy and of Grace's life. After Grace's death, Mary began to write on her computer instead of in the journal. One night, after writing to Grace on the computer, she realized the computer screen was still glowing after she had turned it off. She spoke of it at work, sharing another thing with her friend, Julie. Julie, once again, did not let her down. She did not say, "Computers don't glow in the dark." She simply went home, observed her own computer, and reported back: "My computer screen does not glow in the dark."

On February 22, Mary wrote this letter to her daughter:

> I feel as if you have left me somehow. I don't know why. It is as if you have crossed to the other side. That makes me sad. Have you? I look at the computer screen and it is dark, not glowing like it used to be. Remember? Were you trying to communicate with me and I was not ready for it? Well, I am now. I love you, darling, and I cry for you. Don't you see my tears? Don't you know what is in my heart, or do you just see my actions and what is not in my heart? Don't leave me, sweetheart. Are you fading into a place I do not know? Or will you reveal yourself to me? Let me know.
>
> I am your mother, always.

If hope was a healer, so was writing. If there was anywhere Mary could be more open about her feelings than she could with Julie, it was in front of the computer screen. She could write with tears streaming down her face. She could write in the middle of the night when she couldn't sleep. She could write about the problems that came and went between her and her husband. About the joys and pains of the mothering still available to her—the stepmothering. She could disclose her deepest fears, her deepest regrets. She could let sorrow overcome her there as she couldn't at work or even during the daily life of her family.

But soon after Mary had noticed the computer screen glowing in the dark, soon after she had asked her daughter, her Grace, to reveal herself, the computer did reveal something! She had just finished a page of particularly intense writing when the cursor started moving backwards, scrolling up, reviewing all that she had written. When the cursor stopped, it was at a sentence she had written to Grace: "The computer has been our only way of communicating." The screen then gave off a silvery light and the letters turned to sparklers before her eyes. The computer, and Grace, were acknowledging that the communication was real!

And Mary did not have to worry that she had no one to share this amazing occurrence with. She did not have to feel as if she were losing her mind, because she knew there was someone who understood connections. That someone was Julie. And Julie was once again accepting, believing. Why couldn't Grace be reaching out to Mary?

The computer was never the same again. It began to malfunction. It was as if a great energy surge had passed through it and scrambled its circuits. Mary could access only certain files and she began to have a difficult time using the computer for typing. It had been a source of comfort to her and now it was a frustration. What was wrong with it? Should she take it in for repair?

One file that Mary could access contained a note she had written to me. A few months earlier, I had asked her to read my first novel and offer any comments. She had typed her observations and saved them in her computer. One evening, when it was the only file the computer seemed willing to let her enter, she opened it in frustration and watched in alarm as the cursor began to move of its own volition. The note listed two typos she had found in my manuscript along with the page numbers they were on. One of the typos was *christmas,* which I had not capitalized. The cursor simply found the word *Christmas* and would not stray from it. At the bottom of the note Mary had written the words, "Thank you for letting me into your writing world." On another evening, the cursor moved until it reached them: "Thank you for letting me into your writing world."

In another file, another day, the highlighted words, from a message Mary had written to her daughter, were, "Love you, Mama."

And so it began.

V

DREAMS, SYMBOLS, AND PRAYERS

J ulie entered Mary's cubicle one morning and announced, "I think I had an out-of-body experience." Mary said, "Julie, I think I had one four days ago." Mary had been afraid to mention it until it happened to Julie.

Julie's experience:

> Before I went to sleep, I started thinking about
> Grace, wishing I had seen her, gone to the hos-
> pital, been at the funeral. Really wishing I could

see her, feel her. As I was going into sleep—I was still conscious—I started to float above my body about two or three feet. I started to get afraid and suddenly was in a dream.

It seemed as if I was in a hospital room with windows on one end. Everything was white. Mary was sitting on the bed. There was a female presence between us. I felt the presence. I went up to Mary, put my arm around her, put my right hand on her chest, over her heart, and started to say all these endearments: "I just want to run outside and tell everyone how wonderful you are, how much I care about you, how much you mean to me," and on and on.

Then we walked to the other side of the room and in my hands appeared several pictures, ten-by-fourteen-inch pictures, and Mary said she had drawn them. They were incredibly detailed pictures of doves. In the background of each was brilliant yellow, royal blue, white—brilliant, pure color. I kept thinking that I could never duplicate them. I kept flipping through them. All doves. All these beautiful pictures. And then this little voice said, "It's time to go back now." I was back in my body. There was a whoosh of sound. I woke up.

43

By this time, Mary was crying.

In Mary's out-of-body experience, she had risen above her bed by about three feet and then went back into her body with a whoosh after getting scared. They compared the sounds. Both were exactly the same. It seemed significant that the two events had happened within days of each other. Even more startling was that Mary had a dream in which someone touched her heart:

> I had had a baby and I was calling the hospital to see how the baby was. For some reason, the hospital would not let me take this child home. They had to check on things first. I spoke to a nurse who was somewhat curt with me. I asked her how my baby was and she said the baby was "blind and confused." I thought to myself, "How can I deal with this again? I don't know if I am strong enough. Why can't I have a healthy child? A perfect child like every-one else had?" But that was not what had hap-pened. I knew that the nurse was waiting for some type of answer, that she was hanging on the phone. It was then that I felt a finger by my heart, either in my dream or otherwise. And I knew then that I had to remember to love, that love would be the answer.

Julie showed Mary how she had placed her arms around

her in the dream. It was just how it had felt to Mary in her dream. Someone touching her heart.

Not long after Julie's dream with the dove pictures, a dove swooped in front of Mary's windshield when she was on her way to work. No bird had ever flown so close to her, especially not on the freeway. All of a sudden it was just there. Mary said the dove just "swooped, boom," in front of her. As she was peering over the steering wheel and the dove was flying away, its head cocked and its wings bent at an unusual angle.

Mary was telling Julie about the dove one morning when I came in. Mary asked me if I knew anything about the symbolism of doves. As it happened, I knew that I had just read something significant but couldn't remember exactly what it was. The next day I brought in the passage from Joseph Campbell and Bill Moyers's *The Power of Myth.*

> Campbell: Well, the dove, the bird in flight, is a pretty nearly universal symbol of the spirit, as in Christianity, of the Holy Ghost—
>
> Moyers: —associated with the sacred mother?
>
> Campbell: With the mother as conceiving of the spirit, yes.[1]

First Julie had dreamt about the doves that Mary had drawn, then Mary had the dove swoop in front of her car, and then Mary asked me what it might mean and I brought in the information. It began a pattern. From that point on, I was the researcher.

Some connections just continued to reveal themselves with little effort. Mary's husband, John, purchased a T-shirt at a sale associated with Minnesota Public Radio. The T-shirt had a phoenix on it and Mary recognized, in the shape of the phoenix, the same configuration that the dove had been in when it flew away from her car. Then, the same night, she read an article in the paper about a new restaurant that my husband, Donny, had worked on. It was named The Phoenix because on July 22 (the date of Grace's birth) the building had blown up in a gas explosion. The article was about how the owners had rebuilt the restaurant from the ashes. Mary knew that her attention had been drawn to the phoenix for a reason. She found a book on mythology and read that, according to Egyptian myth, the phoenix was a beautiful lone bird that lived for five or six hundred years and then set itself on fire, rising renewed from the ashes to start another long life. It was a symbol of immortality.

At the very same public radio sale, I bought Mary a

necklace with the figure of a woman sitting in a lotus position. In her lap was a purple stone. I bought it for Mary because it reminded me of a pregnant woman—of the eternal mother. Mary found that the figure on the necklace was the exact same figure that was on the cover of the book she was reading.

Then the second dream came.

Mary came to work one day and said, "I've got this dream to talk about at lunch." Julie told her she had a dream to talk about too.

Mary was already eating at the round conference table we used for meetings and lunches while Julie was writing out a check. Julie was going to finish that and then get out her lunch. Later she would say, "All I remember hearing was Mary saying she had a dream about an African American man and that in the second half of the dream he was in a wheelchair. As soon as I heard that, I couldn't write; I couldn't finish my check. I kept thinking, 'Oh my God, oh my God.' I couldn't sit still. I think I began to pace. The whole rest of the day, Mary and I couldn't stop talking about it. To the last detail, the two men had been alike. We kept asking each other about it, 'Was he old? Was he young? What had it felt like?'"

Both dreams had started with the man standing up—

walking. In both dreams he communicated telepathically. Both women had felt the same unconditional love from him. It seemed as if he had the same mannerisms. Neither Mary nor Julie had talked about their dreams before that day. They hadn't told anyone. They couldn't get over it. I can still recall Julie visibly shaking as they made their comparisons, wondered at the significance. I could understand that it was unusual and significant to share a dream figure. But for the two of them, it went beyond understanding, beyond something they could intellectualize. It was that bond again.

In Julie's dream, the older African American man helped her when she had to stop her car because a gang of young boys was crossing the street in front of her. As soon as the man extended his hand and said, "Don't be afraid. Give me your hand and I'll show you the way," all fear ceased to be for her. She trusted him completely. Every thought that entered her mind, every "if," every "should," was immediately countered telepathically by this man. He did not speak but nodded as he sent thoughts her way, his lips curling a little as he communicated.

In the next scene, they were in the conference room of a nursing home. They were holding hands and the man was communicating messages like, "I want you to come with me." Julie kept thinking, "But I'm married." Then she looked down and saw he was in a wheelchair. She was surprised. He had not been in the wheelchair earlier. But he just kept nodding and holding her hand, as if it didn't matter. As if nothing mattered but the love he was sending her way. He absorbed every thought that was negative and communicated only comforting thoughts to her.

"The feelings of faith, trust, love, and peace of mind I had from that man in my dream have never been repeated." Julie said. "But the words seemed most important: 'Don't be afraid. I will show you the way.'"

In Mary's dream the scene was totally different but the man was the same. Again, he was older, slender in build, and continuously smiled. He communicated telepathically and nodded as he did so. He wore an expression that was always pleasant. In both Julie's and Mary's dreams ". . . the thoughts and the feeling communicated by this man were of constant love."

In Mary's dream she, too, knew that the man wanted her to be with him. She, too, knew that she was married and, although she wanted to give her whole heart to the man, she feared that she couldn't because of her marriage. But in Mary's dream the man had a baby girl who was motherless and Mary nursed the baby. This made the man very happy. He told people, "Look at what she did for my daughter!"

In the next scene, Mary realized that the man was in a wheelchair. He hadn't been earlier. She worried about the responsibility of loving such a man but realized then that she had fallen in love with him. She wanted to tell him, "Don't you know that I am married to someone else? Don't you know that this is asking a lot of me? Why are you so sure this will work?" But she couldn't, because he kept looking at her with such love and gentleness, so much gentleness.

Both Julie and Mary had been most impressed by the love they felt coming from this man, and the understanding. It was as if he was saying, "Others don't understand but I do. I'm old and wise and I know." And he did. Months later Julie was still commenting on the dream. "I never felt so safe in my life," she would say.

Yet they wondered, What did it mean to share a dream figure? To have dream symbolism and the symbolism of ordinary life collide as they had with the dove? To have someone touch your heart in a dream and to find out that that person dreamt of touching your heart?

They realized that the dreams were, quite simply, experiences that were beyond their control, just as Mary's experiences with her computer had been beyond her control—just as their out-of-body experiences had been beyond their control. And experiences that are beyond our control relate to the very core of the way we look at ourselves and our lives.

We may not actually *be* in control, but we spend most of our lives *believing* that we are. So when something happens to us, either externally—such as Grace's death or the near miscarriage of my daughter—or internally—such as in profound dreams or visions—they become transformative events. They transform the way we live.

Mary and Julie's sharing of uncontrollable events seemed no less miraculous to us than their becoming pregnant within days of one another. We did not need to calculate the statistical probability of such events occurring to know they were unlikely. We did not need to add up all the events that had occurred since those shared pregnancies—from Julie knowing Mary was having a bad day, to her hearing "God Bless Mary," to them sharing out-of-body experiences or a dream figure—to know something unusual was happening. It was as if a neon sign was flashing: You are connected. You are connected.

But why? Why was this happening? What was its purpose?

The simplest answer we could come up with was that the uncontrollable events were occurring to do just exactly what uncontrollable events do: to transform their lives.

It was at about this time that I began to envy the connections Mary and Julie were experiencing. Because accepting that Julie and Mary were connected and accepting that a connection remained between Grace and Mary demanded that I attribute these connections to someone or something. And the only source I could attribute these uncontrollable connections to was God. God was becoming visible in my friends' lives. Where was God in my life?

I, like Mary, had begun to use my computer to advance my spiritual life. But nothing exciting had happened. I had started a file, labeled it simply, Prayer, and was using it as a place to draw connections between a spirituality of soul, such as I had been reading about, a spirituality of connectedness, such as that which I was witnessing with Julie and Mary, and religion, which had been with me all my life. The envy I felt over the visible experiences Mary had on her computer and the connectedness that Mary and Julie shared came and went as I searched for my own path and my own way to connect. In the last days of March, I made this journal entry in my Prayer file—an entry which illustrates the feelings I experienced during this period:

> I am stupidly envious of my friend Mary's spiritual experiences which have grown out of great sadness and pain. There is no great sadness and pain in my life right now—not even any great conflict. There is busyness, ambition, creativity, but nothing exceptionally good or bad. And in some ways, it is difficult. It is so new, perhaps.
>
> It is difficult on some psychological level not to be in the midst of something that is so personally moving. I, too, have turned to spirituality in my quest to fill the role that pain and strife so often filled. I am not fool enough to want pain and strife back in my life. And my life is very full, but all in a normal sort of way.

So, the spiritual journey. I don't mean to portray it as second best, as "I don't have anything else going on in my life, so I am going on this spiritual journey." It has called me. It has captured my mind and my imagination. It has led the direction of my thoughts and my writing. And I guess I can only envy Mary if I don't see this as miracle enough for me. I have been envious because her journey is filled with a different kind of miracle.

Mary, Julie, and I were all realizing that God had a hand in the events that were taking place and we all began to try to open the lines of communication by, in one way or another, talking to God. And once we accepted that we *could* talk to God, we opened ourselves to the possibility of being answered. As my Prayer file often answered me. My writing on March 29 concluded thus:

I guess I had to write this to learn that this is the journey appropriate to me. A journey in words. A journey of reading and writing and slow revelations.

We were clearly traveling different roads, each in a way appropriate to us, to what we were going through, to what we hoped to find. But our travels continued to intersect. While the way in which Mary and Julie intersected continued to be more visible and dramatic, the way they intersected with me continued to be more in tune with what was appropriate to me: slow revelations, often received only after I had taken the events I had witnessed or shared and let them have their way with me as I wrote about them. As their journeys were illuminated by the symbolism of dreams, mine was a journey that, from the very beginning, was illuminated by the symbolism of words.

V I

ILLUMINATION

I write fiction and prior to 1994 I read mostly fiction. But around the time of Grace's birth I became intrigued by the books that were showing up on *The New York Times* best-seller list, titles such as *Care of the Soul* and *The Celestine Prophecy* and *Crossing the Threshold of Hope*. I wondered what was going on in the world that people were suddenly reading books by an ex-monk and the Pope. My curiosity led me to purchase and read *Care of the Soul*, by Thomas Moore. I took it to a friend's cabin with me and did something I never do. I used a highlighter. I, the cherisher of books, guardian of bindings, collector of signed first editions, used this book like a manual, a text, a guide. Every page, every paragraph, seemed to speak to me, to soothe me. Soon after the experience, another startling thing happened. I could not go back to reading fiction. I would buy one novel and then another, by authors who had always appealed to me before. But they no longer held my interest.

Instead, *Care of the Soul* led me, over the next year, to other writers such as Joseph Campbell and James Hillman and Carl Jung who discussed various aspects of psychology and spirituality. And the surprising thing was that each book I read validated the experiences that were taking place in my life and in those of my spirit sisters. Each of these respected thinkers accepted a place in life for the extraordinary. Each saw the importance of symbols, of dreams, of examining the unexamined life. They did not debunk anything that was happening, but rather validated everything! Because of my belief in words, my belief in the intellect, beliefs still older and stronger than my belief in spirituality, the final barriers preventing me from fully believing in the extraordinary came down just a bit further with each book I read.

I purchased a copy of *Care of the Soul* for Mary when Grace was in the hospital. Perhaps I bought it because I did not know how to soothe Mary myself. She was being strong. After the first few weeks, she would come into work and stay most of the day, visiting Grace before, after, or on a lunch break, or all three. Having already used a lot of sick leave and vacation time at the end of her pregnancy and in the early days of Grace's life, Mary had wanted to save what she had left. For she had no way of knowing how long Grace would be in the hospital or even that she wouldn't be bringing home a baby who would need round-the-clock care. She wanted to have time available when Grace might need her most and so was willing to sacrifice her present needs for her daughter's future.

Had Mary spent all of her time at the hospital, few of her friends would have seen her. Only family were allowed to visit Grace in the intensive-care unit. The rest of us waited for improvement, hoping a time would come when the visitor restrictions would be lifted. Eventually it became apparent that this wasn't going to happen. So we did what we could, offering books, or meals, or prayers, or all three.

There were days, of course, when Mary would break down, would need comfort, would be comforted. But most of the time she seemed to prefer to lose herself in work. To come to work to be away from the trauma of the hospital for a little while. It was difficult to know how much solicitousness to show, how much to ask. Julie was on maternity leave. Our busy season was over. People were on vacation. It was quiet in the office. Mary came and went. I tried to take my cue for how to act from Mary herself, hoping I could tell what she needed or didn't need from me on any particular day. The weeks went quickly—for me.

Then it was over; Grace was dead. Most of us from the office attended the memorial service along with Mary's family and other friends. A few days afterward Mary was back with us. Julie also returned. Work took on its natural rhythm, with one exception: We talked more. There was an openness about the office. One of our own was wounded. Whatever unspoken rules there were, they were suspended. It was as if by silent yet mutual agreement we had decided that whatever Mary needed was all right with us.

I had been diagnosed, about this time, with fibromyalgia—a malady considered to be a sleeping disorder that affects the muscles—and was finding it hard to get up in the morning. I was often the last one in to work and, upon my arrival, I would often find Mary and Julie huddled together, in one cubicle or another, talking, something that in the days before Grace would have been unusual.

In October, only two months after Grace's death, Mary accompanied me on a business trip to Boston. It would not be the usual business trip any more than the workdays were now usual. We spent a small amount of our spare time sightseeing, but we spent far more time talking. She was reading a new kind of book too. I didn't know what to call them, exactly: psychology, spirituality, personal growth, New Age. We spent a lot of time talking about our various readings. We spent a lot of time talking about Grace. Somehow Grace made the concepts more than concepts. Grace had opened us to hear the messages of the readings in a new way. To make the concepts more relevant to our lives.

Mary and I had grown very close in our own way, an intellectual way, a way that was not untouched by the personal or the emotional. But despite the laughter and tears we shared, and despite our meaningful conversations, I still did not feel the kind of bond the shared pregnancies had brought about for Mary and Julie.

And so, in a very concrete way, it had taken my reading, and my ability to contribute to both Mary and Julie through my reading, to allow me to see myself as a participant rather than as an observer. And it had taken that reading, writing, and observing time for me to realize that I had always had my own role and connection to events even if I hadn't always shared the *miraculous* connections. My observer role was important, as was my presence at work, the discussions Mary and I shared about books, the talks we had about Grace. We all have our own role and each is important. Our connections don't have to be miraculous to be connections.

We *all are connected*. It is only our own inability to *see* our connections that keeps us from experiencing those connections. Whatever it is that keeps us from seeing, be it fear or guilt or lack of desire, is what constitutes the barriers we must overcome.

My reading, but particularly my sharing of that reading, opened my mind enough to see the simple truth of the connections that had been there all along, and as soon as this realization occurred, I began to experience those connections in a new way. I began to dream, and by the end of the month, I had made my first appearance in Mary's dreams as well:

> Julie, Margaret, and I were in a foreign country. Different time. Different place. We had long hair and shawls on our shoulders. We were speaking fluent French.

> Julie, Margaret, and I were in a boat in a cool, shady area with lush foliage. It was beautiful. Julie was in her own world looking at the essence of things—molecules and such. Margaret and I were talking, trying to describe this place. Our feeling was one of serenity. Margaret trailed her fingers in the water. I knew then that these were the Holy Waters.

And finally, Mary and I shared a dream experience.

> Mary: I tried to get into the light. It was coming up from my feet. It was brilliant. Someone was coaching me. I kept trying—so hard—to go into the light but I couldn't.
>
> Margaret: There was a light beneath my feet: a flat bright light with jagged edges, resembling a cartoon depiction of light. I was descending into it.

Now that I was realizing my connections, I could look up information on symbols from my own shared dream image. One of the many definitions of *light*, for instance, was "spiritual illumination." And this was what we sought!

For Mary and Julie the connections began with the shared pregnancies. For me the turning point was the shared reading, the shared learning. Mary asking a simple question, "Did I know . . . ?" "Had I read about . . . ?"

These were the particulars of our different beginnings. And because we were ordinary women, it had taken both the ordinary and the extraordinary to launch them. The ordinary, as with me, was the following of a trend: the best-seller list. The extraordinary were the births, the death.

But as with everything ordinary and everything extraordinary, each contained parts of the other.

In the ordinariness of the trend was the extraordinary:

ordinary people were turning to something besides Prozac to heal maladies ranging from fibromyalgia to sickness of the soul. No huge external events, no world-wide crisis, seemed to launch this trend. It was as if it came leaping out of ordinary life, talking about ordinary life, reaching out to ordinary people. Saying, as it did to me, "It is okay to bring spirituality into your life. It is what ordinary people like you are doing. It is okay."

And from the extraordinary: ordinary. What is more simple, really, than two friends comforting each other? Or more extraordinary than that comfort extending into the world of dreams?

How could there be a phrase simpler than "God Bless Mary"? Yet how extraordinary that it came as a gift from one friend to another.

How natural that a grieving mother would write to her daughter. How miraculous that her daughter would respond.

How natural that we came to see our connections to one another before we could come to see the miraculous force that was behind those connections.

VII

RELIGION AND SPIRITUALITY

Knowing that our connectedness came from a source greater than ourselves caused us each to look at religion in a new way.

Having found that the Lutheran religion of her youth didn't speak to her, Julie attended several churches in her community hoping one would attract her, or at least not discourage her with talk of sin and judgment. Mary, although confirmed in the Presbyterian faith, was, of all of us, the one who had made the most conscious choice to exclude "organized" religion from her life. Yet she, too, sought something now from formal religious practice. Neither found what she was looking for.

In fact, after searching for a religion in which to belong, they were unsure whether they *wanted* to be religious. They felt more of a distinction than I did between spirituality and religion. But there were no meaningful distinctions between us when we talked about God. And we were beginning to talk about God.

We had never talked about God before. And this wasn't peculiar to our relationships with each other. God just hadn't been a subject that came up in our lives or our conversations with anyone. We, like most people, had discussions of right and wrong, morals and ethics, that occasionally, at least in my household, touched on the subject of God in an obscure way, but this was different. Now God entered through the door of speculation. Through the journey itself. What was life supposed to be about? What did it all mean? God was suddenly part of a larger context. He was no longer, even to me, about going to church. He had become part of a search for meaning.

Into this ripe field of readiness, Julie had brought Mary the message "God Bless Mary" and began to turn her thinking about God from punishment to redemption. Into this field of readiness, our reading had begun to deliver messages that said crazy things like God wanted us to be happy and that we were entitled to a world of abundance. Messages that said suffering and strife were not the preferred state for God's children. We had met the paradox of God being both a God of love and a God of punishment. Up until now we had heard too many messages about wickedness and punishment and hell.

Now we were hearing the messages of love. Was it because that one message, "God Bless Mary," delivered from one friend to another, had opened an unseen door? A door that allowed us each to find what we were looking for no matter how different the ways in which we looked were?

As my reading and talks with Mary and Julie seemed, in one sense, to be leading me away from religion as I had always known it—the religion of my youth, the religion of the parents and grandparents with whom I had prayed the Rosary and listened to Bishop Sheen, the religion of my small parish church—in another sense, they brought me back to it.

I attended a Maronite Catholic church, the parish of my Lebanese husband's family and the Lebanese community that still flourished in my area of St. Paul. It was a rather old-fashioned church and this was part of its charm. I adopted the parish when I married because of its strong sense of community. When I was in fifth grade, I was switched from a small, close-knit parish and small parochial school to a large one that seemed impersonal in contrast. My mother said I almost had a nervous breakdown when this change occurred. My husband's church was like returning to that church and school of my youth, the parish where I had so felt that I "belonged."

But while I loved how all the members of my husband's church knew one another and treated one another as family, I had felt a bit like an outsider. While I loved this parish's ethnicity, seeing it as honoring my husband's culture, I had felt I could never really be a part of the Lebanese culture so evident there. And while I loved this church's traditional atmosphere, the richness of its rituals, the prayers said in Aramaic (so reminiscent of the Latin of my youth), I had not expected to find, in the difficult-to-understand English of its Lebanese priests, priests who seemed of an earlier era, the kind of sermons or discussion of spirituality I was looking for.

But now a change occurred. I began to feel as if I belonged. Because I was beginning to understand what it meant to belong—to be part of something, to feel connected to something. I heard the messages within the Mass differently and I took them to heart. The gospels and sermons no longer seemed to be so full of wickedness and punishment. They were the same gospels, the priest was the same priest, but I was different, and so what I heard was different. The ritual I had always loved was now more than ritual. It had meaning.

As Lent moved slowly toward the holy season of Easter, I knew that I approached a season of rebirth. The externals of my life were the same as the year before almost without exception. I had the same job, the same husband, the same children, but I had not seen the connectedness of them all until I learned connectedness with Mary and Julie. As long as I believed I couldn't be fully accepted in my husband's church, I couldn't be. As long as any of us hold ourselves back from anything, we cannot fully connect with it.

Julie, Mary, and I still held ourselves back from life on many levels, but we each did it in different ways. We were fine people, close to our families and friends. We did good deeds, we did our jobs, we took care—*took care*—of everything but ourselves. But it was in not caring for ourselves that we had suffered the feelings of isolation, deprivation, and unworthiness that had kept us separate. The good people of my church did not *not* accept me, the wife of one of their own, the woman who had become part of their family and their culture when I joined, through marriage, the family of my husband. Yet how could I see this when I hadn't even seen that I had joined my husband when I married him? I had seen the ceremony and the ritual of the marriage but I had not felt it inside. It had not changed me. Because I was still holding back. Holding back all those parts of myself I had deemed unworthy.

It didn't matter that I went to church on Sunday and that Mary and Julie didn't. It didn't matter that Mary was technically Presbyterian and Julie Lutheran and I Catholic. What mattered was our attitudes. When we learned to connect with one another, we had come as close as any of us had ever come to true religion or true spirituality. Our attitudes had become prayerful and God had answered our prayers by giving us each other to learn with. We were beginning to sense that our relationships with each other might just be the chosen method by which God would show us how to connect with Him. Now all that was holding us back were our ideas about ourselves, our pride in our individuality, our continuing belief in our separateness.

VIII
CONNECTIONS

If there was one thing that Mary, Julie, and I had in common as a personality trait, it was being individualists. Fierce individualists. We were not dependent women. All three of us, to the casual observer as well as to those who knew us well, were seen as capable, hardworking, independent women.

We did not see being independent, yet, as solitary or separate. We saw being independent as a goal we had achieved. Something to be clung to and defended at all costs. We saw independence as the ability to stand on our own two feet, make our own choices, be in control of our own destinies. It didn't matter that we had no idea where our destinies might lead, only that we felt in control of the choices we made as we stood on our own two feet to get there.

Think, for a moment, of all the people of the world standing thus, alone. Think for a moment of one person close to you: a parent, spouse, friend. As close as you are to this person, what really connects you? Often it is a shared past. At other times shared interests. And yet, even with the closest of friends, lovers, family, there is no doubt that you are separate individuals. Being a separate individual is the primary principle of life, begun at the moment of birth when we separate from our mothers. Never again are we anything but separate. Never again are we anything but alone.

While we might spend our lives seeking closeness with others, we know there is a boundary past which that closeness cannot cross. No matter how close we might become, our lives are still our lives. Theirs are theirs.

We shared these beliefs in the individual, guarding and at times flaunting our individualism, our separateness. We did not want anyone to tell us what to do. We did not want to be followers. We did not want even to be too closely identified with any particular group. Our individuality was what we had fought to gain from our parents, fought to retain in our marriages, and cherished as that which separated us from the crowd.

We took pleasure in our distinctive characteristics: Mary had a flair with jewelry and accessories; I presented a classic, tailored (rigid!) look; Julie was proud of procuring the best names in clothing designers at the lowest used-clothing-store prices. Our tiny cubicles had our distinct marks on them: Mary's had a little lamp on the desk for proper lighting, artistic prints on the wall, a framed photo of her husband taken on the day he had proposed, one of her stepdaughter, Amanda, at the piano. Mine had a vase of silk flowers in the window and the most copious display of photographs: my husband and me on our wedding day, my son's formal photograph in his Navy uniform, my girls as first-graders and my girls in high school, my mom and dad, all my siblings, and even nieces and nephews, former employees and students. These photographs hung about, some in frames, others tacked with stickpins to my cubicle walls. Julie, like Mary, had only a select few photographs of her husband and children framed on her window ledge. But she also displayed there a small and cherished gift from her husband, Kelly, a delicate box made of fine basket weaving with a hinged lid that tied closed. We liked these outward symbols of our uniqueness.

Often our greatest vices were held up as badges of our individuality: "That's just the way I am." And there was great opposition to change in this stance of individuality, in the declarative statements of "That's just the way I am." Not because we necessarily thought we were so great, but because we thought we *were* those things we had identified as unique to ourselves, and without them, who would we be? Who would we *be*?

Even when some of those things that marked us as individuals kept us in seemingly eternal cycles of self-sacrifice and strife, we clung to them. When challenged, we only pulled them about ourselves more closely, making of them a cloak and a shield. They were the known of a great unknown world. They were security.

Our idiosyncracies were built upon survival—whatever had gotten us through the many ages of our lives, the many phases, troubles, challenges, successes. If being controlling worked, then controlling was what we would stay with. If "doing it all" had kept the family functioning, then that was what we had to do. If being silent when we wanted to speak out had created less conflict than it had caused, we remained silent.

We were imprisoned by the ordinary and the familiar selves we had become.

So, what happened? What shook up the status quo? What broke the familiar patterns of a lifetime? What created an unusual year?

Birth . . . and death . . . and most important, the realization that what comes in between is not meant to be suffered through alone and lonely. The realization that there were things that connected us to one another, things that kept us from being separate and singular. That no matter how hard we might try to maintain our individualism, we still could not escape the bonds of love. The realization that what was unseen about us and others was just as real as the seen.

Where was the bond between Mary and Grace once the umbilical cord was cut? Between any of us and our parents and our children? Because these bonds are unseen does it mean they are not there? As soon as the unseen was given a little bit of room to express itself, as soon as we began to recognize it, the rest had to follow. Had to.

If I was not my business suit, who was I? If I cut my long hair, would I change any more than Mary did when she changed her hair color? Yet having long hair was, to me, part of who I was. Part of my individuality. Being able to control things and always make them right somehow was part of Mary's identity. Faced with a world she could not control and could not make right, what choices were left? Julie had been used to being able to do it all and do it all well. If a second baby made that impossible, what were her options?

There was not one thing going on but many, just like in any ordinary life. The difference was that we had started to experience connections. Connections that revealed that we were not as alone as we had once thought. Connections that asked us to look at the unseen instead of the seen for answers. So Julie, instead of looking for a babysitter or a housekeeper, instead of looking for externals, turned to look within. So Mary, instead of giving up on a world she could not control, turned within. So I, the silent observer observing them both, began to believe, and in my belief, had said, "Take me there too."

For this turning within was not the turning within of isolation. It was not the kind of self-involved soul searching of the usual, normal, ordinary identity crisis. It was not self-improvement. It was different and at first indefinable. It was a connectedness that went beyond the normal and the ordinary. Connectedness that came from within rather than from without. That came from the real self rather than the surface self. A connectedness that revealed choices we had not known we had. A connectedness that brought us each to the point of wondering: If there is really a choice between being separate and alone or being connected, why can't I opt for the second choice? There seemed to be only one thing stopping us.

IX

JUDGMENT

While we continued to judge ourselves and find ourselves lacking, while we continued to withhold parts of ourselves we didn't deem worthy, we couldn't fully experience our connections. Because we couldn't fully be. The concept of "suspending judgment" related directly to our inability to be our true selves because it related directly to how we thought about ourselves and the world we lived in.

The first day Mary brought the phrase "suspend judgment" into work to share with us, she had us laughing until we cried as she described walking from the parking lot and trying, as she walked, to suspend judgment. Every time she talked about it, she would pantomime the act of suspension. She jerked as she showed us literally what had accompanied her mentally on her walk. Every other step was one in which she had to suspend movement because her mind had issued another judgment. She would walk, halt, walk, halt, all with her own dramatic refinements added. The phrase became a catchphrase that we uttered a dozen times a day. "Suspend judgment."

What Mary had us laughing about was the senseless series of thoughts that ran through her mind in a matter of minutes—the few minutes it had taken her to walk into work. We could laugh because they were the same kinds of thoughts that ran through our own minds:

"I shouldn't have worn this outfit today. It makes me look fat. I wouldn't look so fat if I hadn't been eating so much. Boy am I stupid. I have no self-control. Hey, there's someone even fatter than me. She must really not have any self-discipline. I wonder if anybody else is at work yet. I'm always late. Why can't I get it together? Why does everybody else seem to be more together than me? Of course, I can't help it if no one else in the house does what they're supposed to do. How can I get ready on time when they're not organized? I wish they'd help with the laundry. If I'd had the laundry done everything would have gone smoother this morning. I would have had time to make breakfast. I'm a terrible person for not giving my family breakfast."

Each of these thoughts could produce whole tangents of other thoughts, all of them judgments. The laundry might conjure up all the stains we hadn't removed that our mothers could have, or the idea that if we were really good mothers, we would have used cloth diapers. The expensive wool sweater we had accidentally washed and ruined could lead to worry over the dry cleaning bill that was too high and on to all the bills that were overwhelming and to how much money each member of the family spent. Comparison, resentments, anxiety would grow. These were the things that would produce those attitudes we walked into work with and that would find us feeling relieved to fall into work's rhythm.

Recognizing the way we thought, as with any other realization, was the first step toward being able to do something about it. Just as an alcoholic first has to recognize and admit to being an alcoholic, our recognition of the content of our thoughts led us to admit that we were obsessive judgers.

We really felt we had come a long way toward advancing our spirituality, to being kinder, gentler people, and now this! Had we made any progress at all? But we did not ask this question with hopelessness. We just laughed and saw how much further we had to go. We just laughed because we could laugh—because we weren't alone, because we were no different from one another.

Mary's pantomime of suspending judgment with her body, "My house isn't neat enough"—halt—"I'm late again"—halt—"Everyone else is more together than I am"—halt—besides being funny, was a wonderful learning tool because we realized judgment was not of the body. Judgment was of our minds, of our thoughts. And our thoughts were something we could learn to control!

Like Mary, Julie and I tried. We had no more luck controlling our thoughts than Mary had. We walked haltingly in our suspended state. But we walked with the knowledge that we were not alone. And we walked with new confidence. We had identified a problem that we could actually do something about. We might not be able to do it yet, but we could learn to.

It was a bit like problem solving. Thoughts that made us feel bad had not done us any good, had not served any purpose. Even if at first we could not accept feelings of worthiness, of goodness, we could accept that we had been involved in a thought process that had not worked. It was time to approach the problem from a different angle. It was time to suspend judgment, if we could, and see where it might take us.

Nothing about the spiritual journey was fast. It was not a quick plane ride but a slow ocean voyage. So it was with "suspend judgment." We "got it" right away. We understood it. It was a concept that was supported by our various readings, that took up residence with us and stayed with us throughout the year. Yet we never *achieved* it. It was not an act, like saving a thousand dollars, that had a beginning, middle, and end. It was with us in the beginning of the year and with us at the end and it will stay with us for life.

I tried to tell one of my other friends about what I was learning through my new kind of readings, how excited I was about them and about how they were making me feel better about myself and helping me grow. He said he had gone through a similar phase, but it hadn't lasted.

The thought appalled me. That this might be a phase I would grow out of. I told him so. And he said, "So what if it is a phase? I went through a phase of learning how to cook too. I'm not in that phase anymore but I'll always know how to make croissants."

I shared this conversation with my spirit sisters, as it seemed quite profound. What we learned would be forever! It would be nice to think of reaching a place where we judged no one, not even ourselves, but if we were reminding ourselves at seventy to suspend judgment, we would still be suspending judgment.

Suspending judgment had another side to it, of course: suspending judgment on other people. At first it seemed the far easier task. It was, after all, a more familiar concept. We were raised with the notions of "Judge not your fellow man," "Cast not the first stone," "Walk in her shoes." All those notions from every major religion asked us not to judge others. Just ourselves. And we had learned that lesson well.

If only we had learned to *not* judge others as well as we had learned *to* judge ourselves! It reminded me of a conversation I had with Mary one day about the ego. I viewed the ego as the part of me that said, *You're better than so and so.* It was the part of me I had to only occasionally fight down because most of the time I was thinking, *So and so is better than me.* Mary viewed her ego in exactly the opposite way. What we hadn't realized was that either way, what came from our egos was judgment. This helped us to realize that our judgments were always reflective of how we felt about ourselves!

If Julie felt as if she were somehow lacking as a mother, even though she could not point her finger at anything she was doing wrong, she made her husband see her as lacking. When he walked in the door, she put thoughts in his head—her thoughts! While he was much more likely thinking about a hot shower and a good meal, she had him thinking, *What have you been doing all day? Why should you be tired when all you have had to do is care for this one little baby—a baby you love, a baby you wanted more than anything in the world, the baby you are so lucky to have.*

When my twenty-one-year-old son had problems, I heard everyone blaming me. "If you had been a better mother when he was two, this wouldn't be happening."

Mary actually thought she heard people wondering what she had done wrong to cause her tragedy.

We truly believed people thought this way! Because we had never questioned our own judgment before. Once we suspended our judgment, even for a moment, a step, for one small situation, we began to automatically suspend the judgments we placed on others for us.

We learned this even with each other. When one of us would come in and be having a quiet day, another would invariably wonder, *Are you mad at me?* It took a long time, even among ourselves, even as far as we had come, before we started asking the question. "Are you mad at me?" Asking the question was a suspension in judgment. It was being willing to give the other her own thoughts and release her from ours. And never did the one having a quiet day come back with, "Yes. I am mad at you." It was almost always something totally separate from us.

Mary's discovery of "suspend judgment" was mine and Julie's as well. We would each read, find something that moved us, and bring it in to share. Each of us had a continual feeling of bringing forth ideas of value.

"Suspend judgment" was of great value. We continued to relearn its lesson, under different names, for many months, but its initial lesson was perhaps the most important: There was one thing in the world over which we did have some control—our own thoughts.

While we realized that we could make fairly easy progress in turning off our thoughts about laundry and housekeeping, we also realized concerns about laundry and housekeeping were the result of larger issues that needed to be dealt with. We had to learn what those larger issues were before we could control the thoughts they produced.

It didn't take us long to see that the almost unequivocal answer to where our judgmental thoughts came from was guilt. And that, unfortunately, nothing in our lives was more guilt producing than our mothering and issues concerning mothering.

X

GUILT

What was so easy to see and define and understand in Mary's case, no matter how unjust, was that she could not escape going through a period of guilt, of judging herself, concerning her daughter's death.

My guilt, for having been a bad mother when I was first a mother, was hidden, secret, a constant judgment that had endured twenty years. I had been too young, too ignorant, too selfish, too lazy. I had not changed diapers often enough, not been sanitary enough, left my children too often with baby-sitters. I had slept too late, stayed up too late, not read enough books, not brushed enough teeth, not given enough baths, not prepared enough nutritious meals. I had not provided the best father.

I could look, now, at my daughter's girlfriends and recognize the ones who were like me, whose very presence announced that they were "trouble waiting to happen." Their lives were already set on a path of misery. They were going to fall, not choose. Fall from one thing to the next as if in a dream, accepting no control.

I would see these sensitive girls whose sensitivity was so beyond reach, so wounded, so withdrawn, begging to be touched and screaming *don't touch me,* and I would see myself at their age, so raw, so alone, so wanting. I was one of those girls who thought a baby would fill the void. Who so wanted someone to love me unconditionally that I was willing to produce that someone out of my own flesh and bone. My desire had nothing to do with taking care of another human being. It was just sheer desire, sheer longing.

I carried that desire and longing with me from early adolescence through my mid-twenties, through three children, and through marriage and divorce. I let it incapacitate me. I let it keep me from living a life that made any sense. I continued to fall from one thing to the next until I could fall no further. By my early twenties, I had fallen into the rock-bottom pit and thus was forced to begin my upward climb. I never quite defined where all that longing and all that misery had come from, I just started building a life that worked because I had to.

My girls were still babies, but my son, by this time, was almost seven years old. Where had his childhood gone? And what had I given this child in all that time? How had I damaged him?

Julie's guilt was the most ordinary, the guilt of every new mother trying to do her best and certain her best was not good enough. But added to it was the guilt she felt, again no matter how unjust, of having had a healthy baby when Mary had not, of not having been there for Mary during Mary's tragedy.

For Julie had been a new mother in the weeks of Grace's short life. She had been at home with her new son, unable to visit the hospital, to offer Mary comfort. Unable, because of a prior commitment, to attend the memorial service. Unsure, perhaps, that Mary wanted her, the mother of a healthy newborn.

And what was worse was that she hadn't even felt grateful for those weeks of being home with Peter. Her husband, Kelly, was preparing for the opening of their business, a guest residence for university faculty. They had purchased a run-down fraternity house and, with little assistance from anyone other than his brother, Kelly was turning it into an elegant, antique-filled sanctuary, a cross between a European pension and an American bed and breakfast. That Peter's birth had coincided with the final stages of remodeling—the business was due to open in September—was something no one could do anything about. Kelly had to put in sixteen-hour days. Often he even spent the night. Julie had never felt so alone. Because she was alone. She could not turn to her good friend, Mary; she could not turn to her husband; and she could not even find the joy in her new baby that she knew Mary would have given anything to feel. The combination of events had left her feeling vulnerable and afraid—and guilty.

Julie's guilt, over Mary alone, weighed heavily on her for a year. Until she could share it and let it go. Until she could learn to suspend judgment.

I read, "Guilt takes up all the room love would fill," and realized that I could not fully love my children when I remained guilty, accused, condemned, judged, because of past actions.

And the most illuminating realization was that the only ones who condemned us, who could condemn us, were ourselves. We were continuing to reevaluate the thought processes we had recognized when we learned the concept of suspending judgment and were now taking the concept one step further. We were recognizing that what we projected outward—thinking God or our children or our parents had judged us and found us lacking—was literally contained within us, just as our thoughts were.

We realized we were doing it to ourselves! Once we understood this, we could then ask, "Did we want to do it anymore? Was there some value in it?" Had feeling guilty for twenty years over my first seven years of parenting done anything to make me a better mother? Had Julie's guilt that she hadn't been there for Mary helped Mary or herself? Could Mary's blaming herself for what was clearly out of her hands improve her life in any way?

And if the answer to all these questions was no, then what purpose did any of it serve, other than to make us feel bad? The thought process finally came full circle. That was what guilt was for. To make us feel bad. To make us bad. As if we did not deserve to feel good. As if we were not worthy to be called good.

But I could see that Mary and Julie were good. Mary and Julie could see that I was good. Mary and I that Julie was good. What we could not see about ourselves we could see about the others.

Ironically, the one who had the hardest road to travel was the one whose guiltlessness was clearest. Julie and I could see how absurd it was for Mary to blame herself for what was beyond her control. But Mary? Even we did not yet know the extent to which Mary tortured herself with "what ifs?"

Each of us was stuck in the "what ifs?" of the past. How would things be different if we had done things differently? Each of us felt as if we had missed some golden opportunity to do things just right, to do things perfectly. Each of us was certain we hadn't always made the right choices, but that we should have. We knew we had made some mistakes, and that we shouldn't have. We should have been perfect, but we hadn't been.

It wasn't out of our hands, our control. Or was it?

We encountered teachings that tried to tell us that there could be no mistakes because everything happened according to a grand plan. We found these particularly in the Emmanuel books, books that were supposedly messages from an angel told through a woman named Pat Rodegast. Each of us found the messages in these books extremely comforting. One such passage from *Emmanuel's Book III* illustrates this:

> Please remember,
> as you walk through your lives,
> that although your breath of creation
> and intent of perfection
> may become grotesquely distorted,
> everything you have ever done
> has always been, at its inception,
> an act of Love.[2]

Although we found such messages comforting, we did not necessarily believe either their source or what they said. We were not about to let ourselves off so easily. Even so, we knew the mistakes of the past *were* out of our hands. We couldn't go back and do things differently. We could only go on. The choice was in how we went on. Did we go on with judgment? Or did we suspend judgment?

I had always viewed the mistakes I made as a young mother as something I could never quit feeling "bad" about because they had produced effects. Undoubtedly, Angela, the baby of the family who had been read to less than her older siblings, was the poorest reader. Surely Ian, the eldest, who had given up a large part of his childhood to fill in as the "man of the house," would never have run away from home as a young adolescent if I hadn't screwed up his childhood.

While the notion that results or outcomes were what produced my guilt remained in me, I could never give it up. I had to see that guilt was only correctable at its source—within myself.

And what better example could I have than Mary. If she viewed guilt as outcome, she would always be guilty—for the rest of her life—for the death of her daughter! What greater insanity could there be than that? But I saw it all around me. In other mothers who had lost children. I saw it in my mother-in-law, who said to Mary one day, "You never get over it."

Would never getting over my guilt be any less insane than Mary never getting over hers?

I knew there were differences, of course. I knew that Mary had done nothing to cause her daughter's death and that I *had* done things that caused my children's problems. Yes, there were differences. Differences in my guilt and Julie's guilt and Mary's guilt. But guilt was still guilt. The effects of guilt were still the same. Only by looking past what was different in us to what was the same in us were we ready to learn our next lesson: forgiveness.

XI

FORGIVENESS

In a publication prepared for an F. Scott Fitzgerald celebration, Garrison Keillor wrote about F. Scott's life. In one paragraph he talked about how Fitzgerald had drunk too much and smoked too much and spent too much money and generally made a mess of his life. And yet, that one paragraph made me want to do it all with him. It made me want to do it all with him because Keillor had captured the innocence of a young man trying to bring forth something from within himself that was bigger than himself. Because Keillor had talked about it all with such gentleness.

Julie, Mary, and I shared a relationship punctuated by a similar gentleness. We couldn't make it unnecessary for each other to experience what we had to experience in order to learn the lessons we needed to learn, but we could make it easier. The gentleness with which we were treating each other made us want to be where we were even though it was often painful. No one would want to experience the loss of a child as Mary had. No one would choose to struggle with the issues Julie and I struggled with. Just as no one would choose to share in Fitzgerald's problems with addiction. But our problems, like the problems of the addict, called to us to overcome them.

Someone once observed that the relationship Mary, Julie, and I shared had begun almost as a traditional women's group would, with a tight circle forming around a particular issue or need. This comparison implied, however, that Mary was a one-woman issue or the single woman in need—the victim whom our circle formed around. But this was not the case. Mary was never the victim. Mary was never a broken person who needed fixing. Even during the periods of Mary's most intense grief, there was a mutuality, an awareness that we were all in need of healing. Mary never drained energy from Julie and me as a victim might have done. Instead there always seemed to be an energy flow, an exchange that strengthened and never weakened. The only reason I can think of for this occurring was that we were all in the process of bringing forth something bigger than ourselves, just as F. Scott Fitzgerald was. And just like Keillor did, we looked on the process, the bringing forth, with gentleness.

Not overtly, maybe. I never went into work with the thought in mind of being gentle with Mary, Julie, or myself. But as I look back, *gentleness* is the word that occurs to me. Gentleness was the attitude that permeated our friendship and our journey. Because even from in the midst of the work, and the grief, and the puzzles, and the trying to figure things out, we felt a deep respect for the process we were involved in. We were respectful of each other and the journey we were on.

I could no longer look on Mary as ordinary. I could not help, when looking at Julie, being seized with a feeling of anticipation and excitement for what she was becoming. We knew that we were there to assist each other in the transformation. We knew we were there to assist each other in bringing forth all that we needed to bring forth. We were together to hear the dreams, discuss the books, ponder the thoughts. We were together to accept whatever needed to be accepted on a given day. The three of us together created a gentle place where the lessons could unfold and where forgiveness came naturally, as if invited.

Our forgiveness of one another seemed to lead directly to a need to share confessions—revelations that were expressions of our hidden pain and fears. There came a day, for each of us, when we knew we were together to give confessions or to hear them. And on that day a confession was brought forth from within one of us to the gentle place we had created, and there the confession was accepted with the gentleness, the forgiveness, with which the one giving it had known it would be. We had each known that our confessions would be received with gentleness because we each knew that forgiveness had already occurred.

When had it occurred? Perhaps when we stopped judging ourselves and each other. We weren't done yet, with judgment, but forgiveness may have occurred within any one of those singular moments in which we had suspended judgment. Or it may have occurred in one act of gentleness that was recognized in the moment it was taking place as gentleness. It didn't really matter when it had occurred. Only that it had.

The forgiveness we felt for one another seemed to extend across time. A sort of blanket forgiveness that said, "There is nothing you have done or could ever do that would change the love I feel for you." We said the same things to ourselves but the feeling was different. The way we felt about ourselves was almost the reverse. It was as if there was nothing we could ever do that would change our minds about what horrible people we really were deep down inside. It was as if we believed we had done a really good job of fooling people and we hoped we could keep it up even if we couldn't fool ourselves.

Our confessions were about not wanting to fool any-one anymore. Not each other. And not ourselves.

Our confessions happened as a natural outcome of the process of ridding ourselves of things that caused us to feel bad. Our confessions happened because we had grown so close, come so far together that the secrets that remained between us became burdens. But our confes-sions happened mainly so that we could forgive our-selves.

I don't know why it is that we can look at almost any-one else and say easily, "It does not matter," and then look at ourselves and say, "It matters very much." Or why we can treat others with gentleness and remain hard on ourselves. But this seems to be the way it is. We feel bad about something we have done, bad if we cover it up, bad if it is revealed. We can even feel bad about the thoughts we have toward someone we believe has done something to hurt us.

It was as if we were made up of extremes. One day hat-ing ourselves and one day loving ourselves and accepting neither. It didn't make any sense to accept either because what we hated wasn't ourselves and what we loved wasn't ourselves. We hated our failures and loved our successes. Hated our mistakes and loved our choices that had turned out right. Hated ourselves on the days we had arguments with our husbands, loved ourselves on the days we got along. Hated ourselves on the days we blew up at our children, loved ourselves on the days we treated them with kindness. And even on our best days, we still had the little secrets we hid away, the things we loved ourselves in spite of. It was as if we were too close to ourselves to ever stand back the way we did with each other and say, "You're okay just the way you are." But we were getting closer.

Our confessions were about hope. Hope that one day we could look at ourselves as we did each other and give ourselves that same blanket forgiveness. Our confessions brought forth those things that might make that forgiveness possible someday. They brought forth that which we most needed to heal. They were brought forth so we could see that it wasn't the confessions themselves that mattered but the forgiveness. So we could see that forgiveness was a prerequisite to bringing out something bigger than ourselves. So we could see that lack of forgiveness would forever keep us small. So we could see that bringing forth anything from within was a liberation. Our confessions happened so that we could see that forgiveness would set us free.

Like our guilt, the mistakes that we needed to confess were different from one another's. But the need to confess was the same. And the need for forgiveness was the same.

And just as our guilt was concentrated around our issues of mothering, our confessions, too, had a common theme. Even though we made small confessions here and there concerning imagined slights or situations we saw as competitive and consequently divisive, our major confessions were about our distant pasts. They were about the things we thought could change the way people felt about us. They were the things we had been too ashamed to speak of. They were like sins of omission. The things we hadn't told.

Forgiveness was looking back not with judgment but with gentleness, as Keillor had looked back on Fitzgerald's life. It was taking the pain out of the looking back—not glorifying it, not oversimplifying it, not condoning it, but also not condemning it. Accepting it as what was.

Both the confessions and the forgiveness were acts of sharing.

Both the confessions and the forgiveness released us from the limits we had placed on ourselves and on our friendship. And with that release we were freed. Free to connect in the way we had each seen we wanted to. Free to share without limits.

XII

SHARING

Without the sharing that was going on each day there would have been no movement, no hope, no connections, no forgiveness.

Think of all the moments in your life that might have ' been breakthrough moments if you had only had someone to share them with, someone who believed in you and in whatever inspiration had come to you!

That was what we had. Every day, every week. Someone listening. Someone caring. Someone who was also looking at the bigger picture. Someone who believed there was a bigger picture at which to gaze. Someone who we knew would not make us feel foolish. People to whom we could tell, quite literally, anything. We trusted each other long before we trusted ourselves.

Although our story here is the journey of the three, and the events written about have emphasized that journey, there were also three individual journeys going on. Three journeys to the center of the self. And each self was supported by two other selves! That support, that sharing, brought the three journeys together and made them one.

Imagine, if you will, how different Mary's story might have been without the shared experiences. Mary at times called me the "fearless" one, but it was often Julie who led the way. Julie who opened the doors by asking, "Did you have a bad day?" by saying, "God Bless Mary," by admitting, "I think I had an out-of-body experience."

Without the support that came from that act of sharing, what might Mary have done with her grief? Or, perhaps, more accurately, what might grief have done with Mary?

It came to us clearly now—that the bonds, the connections, the sharing were what was important. They, more than the internal life, the turning within, were the essence of it all. As important as our individual discoveries were, the sharing was what taught us the most.

In the schoolroom of three, all the lessons were available to learn, because beyond the teamwork, beyond the friendship, beneath the bonds remained the stuff of

LOVE

humanness, of day-to-day life to sort through. Could we really trust? Really love? Could we learn from each other how to believe in ourselves?

Mary and I were both old enough to be having what society might call an "early midlife crisis." As defined in the dictionary, *midlife crisis* is "the sense of uncertainty or anxiety about one's identity, values, relationships, etc., that some people experience in midlife." Having a midlife crisis would be seen as a fairly ordinary thing for women of forty to be going through.

But we did not call it midlife crisis. We did not call it searching for God, either. If we called it anything, we called it a spiritual quest. And although the stirrings of the quest could be traced in each of us to a time before Grace, it had been Grace who brought them into the present, the *now*, Grace who made the journey *holy*, and Grace who made continuing a necessity for each of us.

For a necessity was what it had become. Not in a dutiful sense, but in the sense of inspired, excited learning. We gathered each day, grateful students in a classroom of our own making. And the more we learned, the more we wanted to know. Our readings now encompassed subjects we had once thought of as disparate and, more than that, totally uninteresting! It was as if someone, could it be Grace? was leading the way for us and we had to follow— *had to.*

Without the act of sharing with Julie and Mary, I would never have read about angels, read the inspiring words of the spirit Emmanuel, would never have gone beyond the intellectual, the safety of the trends in my pursuit, would likely never have created a computer file called Prayer and used it for prayer, would probably never have talked about my spiritual experiences at all—and never have received the benefits of the second kind of sharing: sharing outside of the group.

While I was content to leave my spirituality behind closed doors, both that of my work and home offices, Mary and Julie, to my continual surprise, were willing to speak of what was happening to them within a larger realm. When Mary told me, one day, that she had shared her computer malfunctions both with her mother and mine during an afternoon at her mother's home, I was truly shocked. "You did what?" I asked. "What did my mother say?"

That my mother had listened and seemed to accept Mary's story with her usual grace made me wonder. *Could I talk to my mother too?* But I did not. I assumed my mother's acceptance of Mary's story was the acceptance of politeness, the acceptance of Mary's grief, the acceptance of another woman's daughter. I assumed she would judge my journey, my revelations. I assumed she would find me unworthy of them.

But still, I gloried, hanging on to the stories of every encounter Julie or Mary had in which they reported, "I heard this voice say . . . ," "I felt a hand over my womb . . . ," "Someone touched my heart . . . ," and for their bravery brought back treasures. Simple acceptance. Wonder. Awe. Envy. And information. Someone would suggest, "It reminds me of something I read about . . ." in this book or that . . . and we would have a new source to turn to. Someone would compare a dream to a myth . . . and we would have a new source to turn to. Another would say, "I remember when something similar happened to me . . ." and we would feel still more accepting of our own experiences.

To my surprise, each time Julie or Mary spoke of the Grace miracles, of their feelings of being on a journey, of the signs they were beginning to see to lighten the way, other people shared similar stories and offered new avenues we could explore. Each of these encounters was legitimizing. The part of me that was squeamish about angels and the spirit world was beginning to give way.

When I said, earlier, that I kept my emerging spirituality behind closed doors, I meant it literally. I had been acting as if what I was involved with were some kind of perversion. If my husband walked into the room while I was typing in my Prayer file, I immediately scrolled up so that my computer showed a blank screen. While I would read books on science or psychology openly, I had kept books such as the Emmanuel books concealed, hidden under my side of the bed or in a bathroom cupboard. While I talked to Julie and Mary freely and openly about God and every other subject that concerned me, and spoke to a few people about the "intellectual" reading I was doing, I had talked about what was happening to us to no one else. Not one person.

Part of the reason was that despite my religious upbringing and beliefs, all the images I had in my mind of overly religious people were unappealing. I did not want to be a religious zealot. I had other plans for my life. I wanted to write mystery novels and smoke cigarettes and be an intellectual. I had no desire to lead a "pure" life. But there was no doubt that, as I had written in my Prayer file back in March, I was being called, and whether I always liked it or not, I was answering the call.

The sharing that Mary and Julie were doing, sharing with professors and health care professionals, secretaries and musicians, people of both sexes and from all walks of life was helping me to see that all kinds of ordinary people who were not religious zealots had experiences or were accepting of experiences of the divine. I was beginning to see that I might be able to be a spiritual person and still be "normal."

But this still wasn't the end of my fear. I also feared the spiritual life because, while I had begun to accept that I was worthy enough to have one, being openly spiritual would give others the opportunity to judge my worthiness. Because I thought they would judge against me, I kept it to myself.

It was only when Mary's and Julie's examples showed me that I had no more cause to fear other people's judgments than I had to fear becoming a religious zealot that

I finally uncovered what my real fear was about.

Like a person not wanting to admit he or she needed to see a therapist or doctor, a part of me did not want to admit I had something wrong that needed fixing. A part of me didn't want to admit that if there was something wrong that needed fixing, I couldn't do it myself.

This was the feeling that had me scrolling up my computer screen when my husband entered the room. I feared he would wonder "what was wrong" that I was turning to prayer. Because a part of me recognized something *was* wrong.

Having arrived at a place of nonjudgment with Mary and Julie was not enough. Having achieved the ability to share with Mary and Julie was not enough. And all of Mary's and Julie's faith in me was not enough. They could take me only so far along the path.

There had been a great exchange of books going on. I bought the intellectual books and borrowed from Mary and Julie the books with the embarrassing covers that I hid under my bed or in the cupboard. But on one spring afternoon when I had taken a walk over to the university bookstore, I purchased my first angel book. I bought about five other books as well and when I got back to the office, I displayed the five "other" books boldly and only shyly brought forth the angel book, saying something like I thought it was a "pretty little book."

It was a pretty little book and that was about all it had

going for it. It was called *Ask Your Angels* and was supposed to be a "practical guide to working with the messengers of heaven to empower and enrich your life." I considered it poorly written and corny. It only took one chapter for me to make this judgment. I spent about another half hour flipping through the rest of the book—I had, after all, spent twelve dollars on it—but then I put it aside. I had five other books to choose from. I went on without giving *Ask Your Angels* another thought.

But a seed had been planted. Mary's and Julie's faith in me could take me only so far. My faith in myself could only take me so far. The divine help that I was so afraid to admit I needed was about to be given to me. All I needed to do was "ask my angel."

XIII

FAITH

On May 1, 1995, I sat down at my computer, as I had sat down at my computer on many other days. I pulled up the file I had labeled Prayer, the same file I had written on many other days. And because I had read that it was possible to contact my angel, I decided to try. I did not expect an answer. One might ask, "If you did not expect an answer, why did you ask?" It is a legitimate question, the answer to which is, simply, that I was ready to ask. I wrote:

Dearest Angel,

I think I have felt you with me since my earliest child-hood, certainly in my most tormented times when you would tell me I was special and a part of me believed you. Thank you. That voice that said I was special kept me living as much as I could live. Feeling as much as I could feel. There has always been a wonder in me, something that embraced mystery. It is this part of me that is willing to believe I can talk to you. It is this part of me that says it makes sense. Will you talk to me?

The answer came immediately, my fingers responding and typing the words almost before the thoughts had entered my mind. Like Julie's Voice that had delivered the words "God Bless Mary," mine was also an interior voice. I did not hear a voice distinct from my own. But I knew the words were not my own.

Smell the sweetness. You are sweet. Don't try to force it, to will it, just let it come. It is there in the in between, between thought and feeling. Breathe. Feel your heart.

Why does it feel so heavy? As if it will break?

It's trying to open. To let joy in.

Is that my next lesson?

Yes.

Thank you. What shall I call you?

Peace.

Thank you. You are there in the in between?

Yes. Like white. Like space.

Space between the letters and words?

Like space. Like smoke.

Is it okay that I smoke?

Everything you do is okay.

Really?

If you give thanks for it.

Count my blessings?

No. You are blessed. What you do is blessed. No counting. Look in between.

In between the numbers there are no numbers?

Something like that. You're getting it.

Will you help me with my writing?

I am always helping you.

I want to know if my writing will be recognized. I'm sorry it seems so important to me but it is.

Look in between. This time is in between. Time is in between. Don't worry about time.

Will you help me do that?

Of course I will.

Do you mean that in time I will be recognized, but that there is not time? That's hard to understand.

Everything is. Don't worry about time. This is a very important message. Relax. Smell the sweetness.

I never realized how often time comes up. I was just going to ask, Do you mean smell the sweetness of this time?

Forget time. When it is important that you not be disturbed, you won't be.

Thank you. I like your name.

You gave it to me. It has always been my name. Dearest. Remember to rest.

One of the ways I knew this message had not come from me were those first words from Peace: "Smell the sweetness." I was in the middle of preparing to put my house on the market. I sat at a desk in an unfinished basement surrounded by boxes. The walls and floors were cement. Not ten feet away was the cat litter box. Anyone who has ever been in such a basement would know that "smell the sweetness" would not occur to anyone sitting in it. This is a simple, almost silly explanation of how I knew, but it illustrates the point. From nowhere in my own mind would the words "smell the sweetness" have naturally arisen.

I have come to believe that one of the reasons the words

were so accessible to me was that I am a writer. I am used to going to my computer and turning off the thoughts of the everyday in order to create thoughts about characters or places that live only in my imagination. This may seem like perfect evidence that my imagination created my conversations with Peace. On the contrary: my imagination created the space through which Peace's words were able to enter my consciousness.

Yet, I cannot tell you that I did not question the source of the messages. That there were not moments, from the very beginning, when I wondered, questioned, doubted. But I have chosen to have faith, as I chose to have faith on that first day, as I wouldn't have chosen without everything that led up to the moment.

To have faith or to have doubt. It is the same choice I still face every day. It is not a static choice. I have chosen to have faith again and again. And I know I will need to choose again and again, because doubt has been my companion of a lifetime and we are having a hard time saying good-bye to each other. I continue to choose faith simply because I know that of the two choices, faith or doubt, it is faith that I want to carry with me into the rest of my life. Just as when faced with the choice of solitude or connection, I came to see that connection was what I wanted.

I was afraid, terribly afraid, of what people might think of me when they heard I was talking to an angel. My spirit sisters came to my rescue. First by hearing my story, and later by finding their own angels, Trinity and Water.

After having a second conversation with Peace the following day, I was unafraid enough, I had faith enough, to tell the only two people I could tell, the only two people I felt connected with on a spiritual level. I phoned Julie and Mary at the office (I was taking a few days off to do some work on my house before we put it up for sale). Mary and I spent a few minutes catching up and then I told her: "I talked to my angel." I don't remember having to explain it at all. I remember Mary yelling to Julie so that they could both hear the few details I offered at the time. Within moments they decided this was something we could not share over the phone. They were so believing, so trusting, so intent on hearing a firsthand report of the event that they took the morning off the next day to come and hear my story.

I remember the day vividly. I had just finished stripping the old wax from my kitchen floor and cleaning the room thoroughly. It sparkled. It was spring. The sun was shining and I had big windows that let in the light. I went out and picked some wildflowers from across the alley and placed them in a small vase. They looked delicate and appropriate to the early spring day. And there is something about a gathering of women around a kitchen table, coffee cups in saucers, the windows open to the breeze, the sound of quiet conversation, and the mutuality of laughter. I looked forward to it. I appreciated it as it happened. And I remember it. There is something about things coming in threes.

As soon as they arrived, I explained what had happened as clearly as I could. That I had been painting and that when I took a break, I went to my computer and asked for an angelic communication. I asked because I had read in *Ask Your Angels* that it was possible. But I had been asking for months, as Mary and Julie had. I had been praying, in one form or another, daily. I had been seeking answers. I had been seeking comfort. I had been striving to become a better person, to live a better life, to know how to do that. Literally asking was just the next step in that process.

I did not have a printer at that time. I gave an oral report, but in order to show Mary and Julie the words that had come to me from Peace I led them down into my messy basement to show them the words on the computer screen. I sat in the red wooden chair before the white Formica-topped desk that held my old Mac Classic computer. We read the words together. I told them of how I began to cry immediately as the words came to me. Of how emotional I felt. How I had felt comforted and scared and honored all at the same time.

The day became an important one for me, and I don't think it was an accident that it began with a visit from my spirit sisters and with the love and acceptance that visit entailed. It became the day I opened my heart. The following is an excerpt from the file in which this occurred:

May 5, 1995

Julie and Mary just left. Thank you so much, Lord, for

giving me friends to share this experience of Peace with. Peace, I am sure you were there with us as we talked about you. As Julie said at one point, the whole group of you—all of our angels—were probably getting a laugh out of us. I liked that image.

So do I. It was quite accurate. . . .

My friends were so sweet today. Yet I feel slightly removed from them, from everyone. Why is that?

It is because of your closed heart. Your heart has been closed a long time. Your family has been trying to open it. Listen to them. Let them in. They will not hurt you. . . .

I want to open my heart. What must I do to make it so?

Open it. Imagine a door that keeps feelings in and keeps love out. Here is the key. I am handing it to you. [I see, with my eyes closed, a door that looks more like a window, square and paned, with light only at the edges.] You see, the light was just seeping out the cracks before. Now it is brilliant. [It is.] You didn't need to be afraid to open it.

Now what?

Now prop it open. Here is a brick, as heavy as your heart used to be. That's right. You can keep the brick for a while until you learn to keep it open on your own. It's done. There's no going back. I'll be the keeper of the brick. You aren't to worry about it. When you're ready, I'll remove it. Meanwhile your heart is open. Everything happens for a reason. Remember that. Dearest. And remember to rest.

113

To have faith or to have doubt. My heart was now open or it wasn't. It all depended on what I chose to believe.

If someone had asked me a week before whether my heart was opened or closed, I would have said, "What kind of question is that?" But now I knew, with no doubt whatsoever, that my heart had been closed and had been closed for a long time. I had known something was wrong that I couldn't fix. I just hadn't known what it was.

Closing our hearts is what we do when we can withstand no more, whether it be pain or disappointment or grief or abuse. It is what we do when life gets to be too much for us and the only way to get through it is to put ourselves on automatic pilot and move through our days without feeling.

Opening our hearts again is another story. Once we have survived on automatic pilot long enough, we don't remember that there is anything to open. We don't realize that when we closed that door to pain, we closed the door to joy and love as well. And when our lives start functioning again and we're ready to feel again, we may realize we don't feel with the intensity of our youth, with the intensity of our "pre-closed" heart selves, but we think it's okay. This is the more mature love of an older and wiser person, we might think. This is a good place, a safe place. It's just enough but not too much.

We don't realize we have lost anything until we begin to seek.

Was my angelic communication real? It was real

enough to bring forth from me the realization that there was something lost that I needed to find. It was real enough to bring forth the question, Why do I feel slightly removed? It was real enough to fix what was wrong.

It was real enough to open my heart.

When I read Emmanuel's books, I decided it didn't matter whether I believed the messages were coming from an angel—all that mattered was that I found the messages comforting, that they spoke to me, that they made me feel better. I felt the same way about the messages contained within the Peace writing. It didn't matter how I was receiving messages, only that I was receiving them.

But I did consider Peace an angel. I considered Peace an angel because it was an angel I had requested communication with and it was Peace who responded. And I considered Peace an angel because I had no other idea of where else communication such as this would be coming from. I might not know what my church would think about an ordinary woman conversing with an angel, but angels were supposed to be a part of the beliefs of my church. Guardian angels had a feast day just as saints did. I had been told as a little girl that I had a guardian angel. I had felt, in some of the worst moments of my life, that I would have despaired of any hope if not for a formless belief I had that someone/something was with me—that there was a reason for hope even when I couldn't define what that reason was. So my history, my beliefs, my recent experiences, and my readings had all converged into the moment that I wrote: Dearest Angel.

I look back now and think how simple this communication was. How childlike. How innocent. How it and all the readings I had so responded to were simply telling me that I was okay. That fragile human longing for someone/something to let us know, to let us believe, that for all our humanness, we are still okay the way we are, with all our imperfections. For how else can we start but from the simple premise of okay-ness? One cannot build on a foundation that is seen as inherently flawed. I was being given permission to begin to build—as, eventually, we all were.

The permission was given through a simple act, an act simpler than believing, an act simpler than having faith. It was given through the same act that gave me communication with my angel. It was given through the act of asking.

Once again, it was Julie who opened the gates, who dared to open herself to the possibilities that asking offered. Julie asked me if I would try to contact her angel.

Just as we had quickly become accepting of Grace communicating with Mary through the computer, within a week some of the awe concerning my conversations with

Peace had turned into acceptance too. I had been sharing the Peace messages that I thought might interest my spirit sisters. While Peace and I talked about personal issues most of the time, his answers had what seemed to be a universal significance. They were the kinds of answers anyone could benefit from.

Julie looked at this new source of information with excitement. While Julie and I did consider ourselves spirit sisters, we both recognized that without the connecting force of Mary, we would never have gotten to know one another. Perhaps we were just two closed-hearted people doing the best we could. Perhaps we were just two quiet people, given to shyness when we were alone together. There was no animosity between us, just a quiet acceptance that we needed Mary's more outgoing personality to draw us out and facilitate our communication. Julie's request, then, was the first tentative step in establishing a more one-on-one bond, and I took it as an honor, a responsibility, and a sign of faith.

On the afternoon she asked me to contact her angel, Julie stood outside my cubicle, talking to me about it. Mary flitted back and forth as was her way and Julie asked, "You want Margaret to ask for you too, don't you Mary?" I took Mary's response, a rather vague "whatever" or "I don't know," as a desire to know but a fear of knowing.

I wanted to ask for both my spirit sisters because I wanted to share the wisdom I had found in the writing in a way that would be more meaningful to them. But I was nervous. My nervousness about asking led me to spend a lot of time just writing before I requested this special favor from Peace:

May 10, 1995

Since beginning to talk to my angel I have not talked to myself much here. As I read over the writing I did before talking with Peace, I realize that I still need this talking-to-myself space too. I have to smile here, because, in Peace's theory of oneness, he and I are one. The physical and the divine are one. So, I suppose, I am talking for both of us here, and Peace, I hope you are with me because my doingness tonight is to be a real message-bearer for the first time. Julie has asked me to talk to her angel and the responsibility of that humbles me.

I am glad I shared with Julie and Mary as I have no idea, still, how to share with anyone else. And it is not just about the angel stuff. It's about me. Is it me who puts the restrictions on myself when I am gathered with other friends? Me who says their stuff is more important to talk about? I suppose it is. Restrictions. Another interesting way to think about what I do to myself. Restricting rather than letting go.

I've learned a lot from listening. I've gotten a lot of good strokes for being compassionate—for suffering with others. But not letting others suffer with me—not letting them be compassionate for me—is robbing them of something.

As James Hillman says in his book *Insearch:Psychology and Religion,* we cannot meet all of our own needs. If we could, there would be no human interaction, no "society." But I can meet the needs of another and another can meet some of my needs; and that is the way of the world. And here I have been all my life, trying so hard not to be needy, trying so hard not to let anyone else see my needs—as if it would make me weak. Hillman also says the needs we deny become demands. I wonder—on whom? I feel as if I have been demanding of myself more than of anyone else. I have been hard on myself.

It's funny walking around with an open heart. One of the strangest physical sensations I've had is of feeling smaller, almost as if I am a child masquerading in adult clothing. Perhaps I am a teen again—back in that time period in which I first closed my heart, like an alcoholic whose development is arrested at the point at which she becomes an alcoholic. Lord, I don't want to be a teen again.

I am avoiding talking to you, Peace, because of this responsibility weighing on me, and I am going to quit avoiding it in a minute. But first I want to reflect a little on what sharing has shown me in the past few days.

There has been some uncomfortableness, some pride, some humbleness, but mostly a feeling of bringing forth something of value. I suppose now that this is because of you, Peace, but not as a substitution for being of me, not in a bad way. Peace, you are helping me learn to share by giving me the opportunity to witness the gift that it can be. Perhaps you are a little like the authors Thomas Moore and James Hillman to me, a way of validating my own knowingness that makes it easier for me to talk about. I have no doubt that you are a good thing, but this is a sort of worldly proof of it for me. Thank you for answering my literal request—for literal messages. I suppose that the act of sharing is a literal, literate way for me to gauge the experience by bringing it outside of myself. And maybe this would be a good way to view all my writing—as a gift I bring literally, literately to the world. Another way to help me let go of the fear of it. A way to legitimize myself. I can hear you saying I don't need to do that and that thinking I do is fear talking, and I'm sure it is, but bear with me for a while on this one. I can also hear you saying that anything that makes it easier and better for me is okay. That all I do is okay. Thank you for that. Thank you for being with me.

I feel your presence often—in the heavy beating of my heart, in the voice that says *stay* in the *now,* in the bird that responds to my being in the now with birdsong. And I know for sure that something happened between us today at the little round table in the office after Julie had said I could ask her angel (although she didn't say what I should ask). I know it was you that brought me the word *tenderness* in regard to her. I know it was you because I got tears in my eyes, as I am getting them now, and because Julie got tears in her eyes. You know what Julie needs to know, or her angel does. And if the image we had at my kitchen table the other day was accurate, as you said, and the three of you angels were laughing along with the three of us women, then I imagine you all know about all three of us.

I can only ask humbly, respectfully, Peace, that you who are so wonderfully and thankfully accessible to me, help me to bring a message from Julie's angel to her, about how she can find that same accessibility.

I had some feelings, some images, earlier that I will start things off with and perhaps the two of you can guide me from there. The images, the feelings I got, were that Julie's insight will come more from the inside out than from the outside in. I say this in relation to myself, feeling as if my communication with you, Peace, is coming into me from you and you being outside of me. I know this inside-outside stuff doesn't make as much sense to you as it does to me, but it is the best way I can describe what I felt about Julie. The other feelings, images, were just this: that it, whatever it is, is close to the surface in Julie, and I had a sense of it coming out her pores, almost like sweat. Can you clarify any of these things, either of you? Julie gave me her permission to ask for her. I believe she truly wants to know her angel. I know she has been looking for something for a long time—a meaning, a purpose, guidance. She has moments of physical sensations when she senses she is close to *it*, but she is becoming frustrated—although that is perhaps too strong a word. You, after all, know her better than I. I am just procrastinating because I don't want to get this wrong and I know if I ask in fear rather than in love, I may get it wrong. So I am going to calm myself now, rid myself of that fear, and ask in love that you give me a message that will comfort and guide her.

Peace, I feel you reminding me that nothing that is said here will be wrong. Thank you.

I am there for her. She is already hearing me. She feels me. I regard her with great tenderness. I guard her, more in the way a mother guards a child than with you and Peace. I look out for her with tenderness, great tenderness and great love. She is very special to me. She is the only one for me. There is no other who could take her place. We are meant to be together. We have been together before. I am almost too attached to her if an angel can be too attached. I cannot keep her from learning painful lessons but I would like to. I very much want to make things easier for her.

I keep getting the word *image* in my mind.

There is a great need in her to do the right thing. Ever since she was a little girl. There was such great sadness in her as a little girl. It is why I regard her so tenderly. If she will let herself feel how much I love her, she will be more open to my beingness. I want to help but I cannot help unless she asks. I am happy she asked you. Tell her to ask me and I will be there where she has access to me. I overflow into her with love. Like a cup running over.

You have made me feel such incredibly strong emotions. I can't keep from crying.

That is how she is overflowing with emotions that can't get out. This image you see is solid with holding in, holding on tight, holding on for all she's worth. Clinging to what she has in great fear, so afraid, so alone. It is why you see images of water and pores and sweat coming from her, she is so overflowing with painful things she hangs on to as if they were her lifeline. There is not something she needs to release, she just needs to release. To quit holding herself together so tightly her skin is taut with it. Her very image will change when she releases.

What must she do?

She must want to be. She must let go. Not in the way you need to let go but to let go of the very lifeline she hangs on to. It is a great leap of faith I ask of her. She and I are one; this asking is not in the way you see it—it is not a demand, it must come from within, from our oneness. I cannot ask. She can. Tell her to ask.

Literally?

Literally.

How will she know you are answering her?

She will know the great relief she feels.

Anything else? Will you talk to her?

If she will listen. I have always been with her. Tell her to release what she holds on to so tightly and I will be there.

Julie related to me later that at the very time I was asking for her, a great feeling of relief spread over her. Her breathing became easier, she felt lighter, she felt a sense of release.

I didn't stop with the response from Julie's angel but went on:

While I am feeling so receptive, I must ask for Mary. Dear Mary. She is unsure she should ask, but I think I have her permission. The images I felt of Mary were that she has so much at stake in opening up. It reminded me of how I felt about my mother. I had told a friend once how judgmental I thought my mother was, and my friend had responded that my mother was more judgmental (than my father) because she had more at stake; she had put so much more effort into raising me, had so much invested in me. And that is the way I feel about Mary—that she has so much invested. And I also had a feeling of her doingness—that she needs to do something. Something with the earth. Something grounding. Can you help with these images? Any of you? Can you give me a message for Mary?

Mary is. Mary is in a state like suspended animation, between the depths of despair and the wholeness of joy. She fears she could go either way, so she stays where she is. This is okay. Where she is is where she is. When she has confidence that she can turn her back on despair, she will turn to joy. When she turns to joy, she will recognize me.

Is there a way you can help her or I can help her or she can help herself turn to joy?

She will when she believes she will. She will turn to joy.

And how then, will she recognize you?

In the birds of the air and the seeds of the ground and the smile of a child.

Is there some way she must ground herself before she can turn to joy?

There is nothing she must do. Mary is. Mary is finishing up a long, long journey. She can take her time. I am patient. I have been patient a long time, an eternity. But I am waiting for her with love. Tell her I miss her.

The next day I pulled Mary and Julie out to cigarette break with me to share the writing and to try to explain the feelings that had accompanied the messages. I had been unprepared for the onslaught of emotion that asking for Julie produced. I did not know where it had come from and thought, perhaps, that it was coming from her angel. This led me to speculate that her angel might be a female, even though, I said, I had a sense that the angels were androgynous.

I told Mary that her angel, in contrast, had seemed rather stern—more toward me than toward her. As if he were telling me, "Mary is what she is. Don't mess with Mary." After it became apparent that Mary had not really meant for me to ask for her, the source of this sternness seemed justified—as if I were being rebuked: "Don't mess with Mary." I wrote later about my concerns:

May 11, 1995

Today, after I shared my angelic experience of the night before with Mary and Julie, Mary had to leave work. She had to think. To be alone. Her mind took what I had said and interpreted it in her way, a way that at first was painful and then, I think, I hope, healing. I did not like feeling I was in any way responsible for her pain and a part of me wanted to go into that feeling and dwell there and refuse to ever again take on the responsibility of asking for messages for others.

I really was stunned. It was one thing to get messages for myself. To get messages for another and to have them affect that person was different. Both Julie and Mary had been affected—one positively and one negatively. It threatened to overwhelm me.

But once begun, the messages of Peace became more important to me than anything else in my life. Our nightly conversations had grown to several pages in length and each covered a major issue affecting my life. The relevance of the Peace messages went beyond anything I had felt throughout the year from books that answered my questions or comforted me or supported my emerging beliefs. This was communication geared specifically to me and to my needs. And this was communication that seemed to come in words designed to get through to *me*. It was personal. I had a personal guide. I felt lucky beyond belief. How could I not be willing to share that guidance?

I concluded that the important lesson I had needed to learn from this experience was to be sure that I had permission, to always wait until I was specifically asked.

The concept of asking and being answered was still new to all of us, however. The angels seemed to suggest an ease to the process that none of us quite bought. If it were so easy, why had we not discovered it before? Why wasn't everyone doing it? And yet the things that are difficult in life tend to be the same things that are difficult in regards to spirituality. How many times do we want a hug from a spouse or sibling and not ask for it? How often do we need help and not request it, even of someone we know would be willing to give it? So not asking, then, appears to be a habitual human malady. Asking and being surprised at being granted a request also seems to be a typical state of affairs. So it was, in the beginning, with me and Peace. And so it was with each of us.

Mary was having a hard time asking. Not because Mary lacked faith but because Mary was afraid. Because there was only one thing she could ask. There was only one question.

Mary wanted what we all wanted. But she knew that first she had to get an answer to her question. And in order to get that answer, she had to lay her fear aside and ask. Her asking was an act of tremendous courage. That she asked her question of me and Peace, a tremendous honor.

127

She gave me a card the morning she asked. In it, she thanked me for sharing my spiritual journey with her and she thanked Peace. She thanked Peace before she even asked anything of him. And I knew she asked only what she had to know because she was desperate to know. She asked, "Is Grace all right?" On June 1, exactly one month after we had begun talking, Peace answered:

Mary has only asked because she has reached a point of being where she is ready to know, where she needs to know, where she must know. And I tell you, what Mary needs to know is this: she did everything right. She could not have loved more. She could not have felt more. She could not have withstood more than she did. She had the courage to trust in herself, in her intuition, and she was so right to do so. She was more than right in that there is no right and wrong in following our destiny. She did the only thing she could. And Grace did the only thing she could. Destiny is linked. Not only did Mary live her destiny and Grace live her destiny, but everyone else who was touched by Grace had Grace as part of their destiny, their road to travel, their bridge between the human and the divine. John, Amanda, Sara, the doctors, the nurses, people Mary doesn't even know. Wives, husbands, friends, daughters who heard of Grace's valiant struggle had their destinies touched by Grace.

And Grace, who Mary worried over so, was a being of pure love and pure light. She was all angel. We all have our angelness with us when we are born. We all have a wisdom unrecognizable in the human world. It is the wisdom of remembering. And Grace never forgot! She never forgot for a moment that she was a being of love, a being of oneness. She knew exactly what she came back to the human form to learn:

128

Love. And she learned it. She learned it so fast and gave it back to the world so fast, there was no need for her to remain in human form. She never spent a moment on this planet when she was not sure, absolutely sure that she was a being of love. Why? Because she lived such a short life? That is part of the reason. The other reason was that she lived her entire life surrounded by love. She did not see tubes or surgical instruments as anything but what they were—instruments of love. She did not see nurses and doctors, she saw beings of love. And because she was wise with the wisdom of remembering, she saw her parents with perfect love. She saw them as the angels they are. She did not see one single imperfection because there was none to see.

Tell Mary that Grace remembered! She left this world a being of light just as she entered it. She had everything you seek! Everything Mary seeks! Why do you suppose she affected people so? They were in the presence of an angel, an angel who never forgot. One who could have turned around and left for home immediately, but who stayed to feel the love around her and to fill those around her with her divine love. Is Grace all right? No one could be better than Grace. Grace Is in divine oneness and love.

Thank you, Peace. I think I can rest assured that you have given Mary what she had to have—understanding and Peace. Thank you. Can I ask one thing more? As you know, ever since Grace, through Grace, because of Grace, Mary has been on a journey of her own. Similar to mine but unique to her. Her own spiritual quest. There have been times on this path when she has been certain Grace spoke with her through her computer. Sometimes the messages have been clear and sometimes they have not been. Sometimes it simply seems as if everything is a frustrating puzzle, as if the computer has gone haywire. She wants to write, she wants to communicate, but she is not only confronted with puzzles, but with an inability to go into her computer and write to her daughter. Can you tell her anything that will help her understand what is happening? Can you give her any assurance about how to know when Grace is reaching out to her? Can you help to solve the riddle?

What Mary has received is a reflection of herself. Of her state of being in the Now. Mary has lived through the greatest challenge that humans can face. And she has turned from that challenge, not with bitterness or anger, although these feelings at times fly across her Now, but with hope. What is her hope about? Finding the love she had with Grace. She was so full of Gracie's love that Gracie's loss felt like a great and awful emptiness, an emptiness so great and vast she wasn't sure she was alive. Wasn't sure she could live. How could Grace not return to comfort her and give her hope? How could Grace not return to help her on her journey? Grace is with her every step of the way. Grace leads her to the books, the birds, the signs, the flowers. Grace in her infinite, loving oneness knows the quickest route to welcoming Mary to be with her again.

Why does that way seem full of puzzles and frustrations? Because Mary is full of puzzles and frustrations. This is not something negative I am saying here. I am saying Mary lived through the greatest challenge a human can face and came out of it not with overwhelming anger and bitterness and despair, but with puzzles and riddles. Hurrah for Mary. Because Grace helped her back to remembering more than she has any concept of, she is in a state of puzzles and frustrations. She knows, Knows, more than she ever knew before. She is closer to oneness, closer to her angelhood, closer to the divine all-that-is than in any life-time. Yet that Knowing is hidden from her, much like a name you say is on the "tip of your tongue." It is not Grace, or Mary's angel, or anyone but Mary who keeps her in the state of frustration.

Again, this is not negative. For most humans, enlightenment is a lifelong occupation. There is a reason for that. There is a reason I only answer the questions you are ready to ask. There is a reason Mary is accessing all that she Knows in a slow and seemingly frustrating way. That reason Is. Like Mary Is. In the Now of life on this planet, Mary must function day to day: Mary works, Mary interacts with her family, Mary sleeps and dreams and walks and gardens. Perhaps Mary knows that knowing all that Is would make this impossible for her. For the here and now, Mary is wise enough to ask for only that which she can live with in the Now. But it is all there—on the tip of her tongue!

Why does it seem as if she is asking and searching and not being answered?

Because Mary is in a state of profound forgetting—something she needed to do in order to live with the truth of Gracie's life and death. In your human experience of time, it has been an eternity for Mary since Gracie's death—and an instant. But Mary is not alone. She will never be alone. Ask Mary what she loved about Gracie. Was it her infant face? Her body? Her fingers and toes? Her hair, her eyes? It was everything. And everything Gracie was was love. Pure love. And Mary will never be without it again. No amount of forgetting will rid her of it. There is nothing she can do and nothing she can be that will not carry Grace's love. At this time, it seems a small substitute for the child Mary longed to hold and bring home, but let me tell you, there is nothing greater than this love. Mary is blessed with this love. Mary has touched the divine.

I know these are not the answers in the form you would seek them to be. You want to know if Grace has communicated through the computer? Grace has communicated through love. You want to know what puzzles the computer represents. I tell you the computer represents Mary's puzzlement. You want to know how Mary can communicate. Through love.

All I can tell you is that Gracie is showing Mary the way. How does Mary know that Grace has not just taught her the lesson of asking for help? How does Mary know that This is not more important in the Now than something Grace might have communicated through the computer? If Mary will trust Grace to lead her to the keys, she will eventually be able to unlock all the doors.

Thank you, Peace. Is there anything else Mary should know now?

Tell Mary that she is all right. Tell Mary that everything she does is all right. Tell Mary that Grace and I are smiling.

XIV

DOUBT

The writing I did for Mary brought on a bout of physical, emotional, and psychic illness.

When I handed Mary the Grace message, I knew it became hers. I could not say, "Here it is, but don't show it to anyone. You can have it, but don't tell anyone where it came from. Don't tell them it came from an angel or that it was me who received the message." I couldn't say those things but I wanted to. Mary shared Peace's message with her husband, John, and I thought, *How will I ever show my face around him again? He will think I'm nuts.* She showed it to her mother, this woman whom I admired and who admired me, and I thought, *There goes that relationship.*

I felt horrendously exposed. I hadn't yet told anyone I was on a spiritual quest. And here were people who did not, could not, understand being told about the culmination of that quest. How could they understand without knowing what had led up to it? How could they take it, and me, seriously? And how evil would they think I was if they thought I was trying to deceive someone in a state of grief?

Before my journey with the spirit sisters began, I had been feeling a profound sense of isolation. Things were going well for me for perhaps the first time in my life. Because of this, I had begun to turn inward. I had a lot of internal things going on that I wanted to talk about, but all of my friends had needs that far exceeded my own. My sister was going through a divorce. Mary had lost a child. Another friend had taken her grandchildren into her home. Everyone had concerns that I could not compete with. By the time I began sharing with the spirit sisters, I was ready to bust. Months and months of thoughts and feelings were bottled up inside with nowhere to go. Once I began sharing with the spirit sisters, however, I realized I had not just been withholding for months—I had been withholding all my life.

After giving Mary the Grace message, I returned to that feeling of isolation. And I became terrified. I wanted connection with other people—not something that would isolate me further, not something else that would separate me, make me different. I was overwhelmed with a feeling of vulnerability. It was similar to the feeling I had experienced when I first opened my heart, but extremely magnified.

I realized that if I had spent my whole life holding myself in, withholding, and if now I was all right out there, visible, even if only to myself, I would naturally feel anxiety and imbalance. I knew it would have helped if I could have talked about it. But once again, I couldn't. Once again I was bottled up. Because the only people I could talk to were Mary and Julie, and I didn't want to say or do anything that would taint Mary's joy in Peace's message.

I even wondered for a day if I could talk to Peace. Because I had begun to doubt.

Finally, I wrote about my dilemma:

June 3, 1995

Yesterday was Donny's forty-first birthday and the day Uncle Nino died. And, just possibly, it was a day of rebirth for Mary and Grace. All three events (three again) were disturbing to me. Donny's birthday because he is at odds with his family. Uncle Nino because I mourn his passing and rejoice in it at the same time. And finally, there is Mary, and having shared my experience with her, felt her pain, felt her thanks, felt, too, her uncertainty and my own, I doubted myself, doubted Peace, felt right out there, tender and vulnerable with my feelings.

135

Wondering, *What if it came from me?* Wondering if I'm a fraud. Wondering if this whole business is suspect. Fearful, fearful in a loving world.

Help me, Peace. I have had a crisis of confidence. How can this be so after the gift you gave me? How can I be strong enough to own up to what is happening—to face the scorn of nonbelievers. And why have I opened myself for this? I have felt ill and shaken, as if my balance is off. If I cannot come to you with my doubts, whom can I come to? Can you tell me what is happening to me? I am sick and I'm afraid it is all one—this sickness and my doubt. If I have doubts, how can others not? And if they have doubts about my credibility, it takes from me everything I have worked for, attained. Because it means doubting me at some basic, soulful level. And I know others doubt. I'm only talking about a few people here, Peace. I'm hearing the word *trust* in my head.

How did Mary feel when she said Grace talked to her through the computer? She was sure and then she wasn't sure. You were sure and had your doubts. Yet by talking about it, it became acceptable truth. TRUTH. See how closely truth and trust are linked as symbols for you. It is no wonder that when you doubt you are being truthful, you doubt you can trust. Did your doubt in Mary's beliefs cause you to doubt her as a person? To doubt her integrity? No. But you are saying to yourself that it is different with you because you presumed to speak the truth about another to another. This is true. Truth. You got what you asked for, Margaret. So you immediately think, be careful what you ask

136

for. In a way, yes. As I am careful what I answer. But don't set your-self up with another set of rules. Follow your instincts. If asking for others makes you more fearful than helping others gives you joy, then do not ask for others. Trust your instinct to be your guide.

It's not that I don't want to share your guidance. It's that once I let what you give me out into the world it is not mine anymore.

Like all your writing and it is your primal fear. Can you not honor it and let it go?

Maybe not. I'm not sure. This is different.

Is it? Dear Margaret, it is not different to me. In oneness all things come from the same source.

It might be different if everyone realized that, Peace, but it feels to me like telling people apples are carrots.

Does it really? Or are you merely fearful people will take your apples and turn them into carrots?

Peace, I wanted so much what you have given me—to help me help myself, to go new to the new home, to go new into life. I didn't bargain for this other.

Bargain is a word of commerce. One of those words you want to leave out of your feelings, remember. Remember me? I'm not here to hurt you or to frighten you. You are frightening yourself by predicting horrible things for your future. You said yourself, the knowledge has only been shared with a few. I am not asking you to share it more widely than feels appropriate for you. Give yourself permission to be imperfect.

137

Jesus' apostles denied him. You do not have to rush out into the world and proclaim me. You do not have to give permission for the others you trust sharing with to share with others.

But I can't give something like I gave to Mary and say, "Keep it a secret."

Why can't you?

Because it wouldn't be right?

Right for whom? You cannot judge Mary's right nor she yours. You can only be what you are. If this is part of what you are, it is part of what you are. The choice for public or private is up to you.

But I already made a choice to share, albeit a limited choice. Now I feel powerless to control it.

You cannot control it. You can control very little in your world. I tell you, this is part of the same fear you had about your other writing, the fear of being known. And where does the fear of being known come from? The fear that what you are is not lovable. What in anything you have done makes you unlovable?

What if it makes me a lovable freak? a fool?

Fear of humiliation. Know your fears and practice releasing them.

Why am I adding fears at a time when I want to subtract them?

You have asked to be in the forefront of a movement that is sweeping the world. Those in the forefront are always conscious of those trailing behind. Will they scorn and snicker? If they do, they do so out of fear.

Love them and their fear will fall away. Their scorn and snickers will be just another part of the costume they wear.

I might know all of this, Peace, but I don't think it makes things any easier.

Easy is part of a concept that is essentially false. You are on a journey. You have been on journeys before. You take a trip and the obstacles along the way become the fond memories of tomorrow. Why? Simply because they were. Can you control what will be? No. So you must try to be in the now with love. I know you have heard it many times now and you think, that is Peace's answer for everything. You're right. It IS.

Peace, this has all been acceptable with Mary and Julie because they have been part of the process. Then we hear about others who are going through similar processes and we get excited because we are not alone, and so the whole thing has more validity and we read things that validate even more. But people like Donny, people in my family, I cannot imagine them understanding.

You give them little choice. You give them so little of yourself. I am only a small part of what you withhold.

I know. But suddenly you have become a huge part.

It is so for others too. And as long as they are afraid, the darkness will continue. Fear is the greatest obstacle to overcome. You are expecting a lot of yourself to expect you can turn away fear so quickly. You turn it away for moments at a time, for moments when you are in the now with love. Let those moments grow.

If you were visited by your Uncle Nino tonight, wouldn't that be a gift? Wouldn't you want to share it—to tell people? Haven't you listened to others tell of meetings with the deceased and thought them lucky? And yet there would be part of you that would doubt your visit from your uncle and that would doubt another's experience as well. But only a part. Another part would see luck, would see divineness. That is the duality you are a part of.

Know what you seek, Margaret. Knowing the duality will not necessarily make life easier and it will quite likely make life more complex. But the duality exists and you know it exists, have known it for a long time. Will saying you are afraid of it make it go away like monsters under the bed? Being afraid of it will only allow the shadow side to grow. Loving it will bring out the light. You have felt this. You have felt the lightness of being. Give yourself space to integrate what you have learned. Accept what IS. Love yourself. Trust yourself. Easy for me to say, I know. But what is the alternative?

Okay, Peace. Help me rest well? Help me sleep on it tonight and feel better in the morning?

I will always help, dear one. With whatever you ask of me.

What helped me through this time more than anything was the flow of daily life. My daughter graduated from high school a few days later. I was busy at work. Busy at home. I tried to just ignore my fear for a while longer and go on the way I had been.

Yet even while I continued to talk to Peace, I knew I needed, somehow, to place the messages in a larger context, a context from which I could learn to better understand them, to admit to them, and finally to share them. Help in doing this came from an unexpected source.

A Sunday-morning conversation between my husband and my son caused me to begin to look at Peace as a more natural part of my religious and spiritual life.

On that morning, my son had announced that he did not want to go to church because he did not believe in God. My husband told him that whether he believed in God or not was irrelevant; he still needed to go to church. Donny went on to talk about how he would often be consumed with a problem or worried about some situation when he went to church and how, after that quiet hour of contemplation, he would have a solution or just feel more peaceful about whatever was bothering him. He told my son, "I don't know if it's God or having a quiet hour, but I know that going to church is beneficial."

What Donny's comment did was help me change my perspective. It helped me look at conversing with Peace as a quiet hour, as just another form of prayer, as a tool that was beneficial in helping me solve my problems and feel more peaceful.

Over the coming months, I thought of all the people in the world going to church, going to the quiet, turning to prayer. It made me think of the Rosary and the repetition of those prayers said as one fingered beads, the whole process, it seemed to me now, one of turning off the conscious mind so that a still, quiet voice could be heard. It didn't matter whether it was called prayer in one culture—one religion—meditation in another. It didn't matter whether people called that still, quiet voice that would come and make them feel better their own higher wisdom, or God, or an angel. It didn't matter whether they heard a voice at all.

But I imagined that if, after people prayed, after they went to church, after they meditated, they wrote down their thoughts, their feelings, their questions and the answers that had come to them, that it would be a lot like what I was doing. Saying the Rosary was a means of getting to that still, quiet voice in us just as my talking to Peace was.

Everyone thought the power was in the tool. Some would believe the power of one tool, such as the Rosary, to be more legitimate than that of another tool, such as the computer. But the power was in *us,* not the tool, as Peace would tell me when I was ready for a more philosophical look at the matter:

You worried, when you asked for Mary and Julie about the power of being a channel and about the responsibility. Think instead of the beauty, the symmetry, the flow of it. Honor it. Be grateful for it. Pray. It is a flow. From you to me, from me to you, but both at the same time. Like a river flows, always there and always moving, a place, an idea, a movement. Like thoughts that can't be grasped or proven but surely are. The channel is always open, dearest. You can block the flow but you cannot stop it. Moving with it is the safest, surest way to navigate it. You are always there. It is always part of your actions from the simplest to the most complex. Transmissions. Transforming the mission as you move to fulfill your destiny.

Mary and Julie, too, would find their means of communication and would find that at times it led to doubt. But we had become part of the flow and we each found that moving with it was the surest way to navigate it.

XV

COMMUNICATION

B y mid-June, both Mary and Julie had made contact with their angels. Mary, at first, just wrote
down her thoughts, not crediting them to anyone
but herself. But soon she was reaching out, addressing
others as well. Her journal entry of June 15, 1995, was
addressed to Dearest Angels and Gracie, my daughter.
Her entry a few days later: Dearest Angels and Gracie, my
angel. And it only continued from there:

June 20: Dearest Angels and Gracie and all that is,

July 16: Dearest Angels, Gracie my love, God—all the universe!

August 16: Dearest God, my Angels, and my wonderful Gracie!

September 22: Dearest Angels, Gracie, and the Wonderful, Beautiful Universe!

October 1: Dearest Angels, Trinity, my Gracie, dearest God, and the Wonderful Universe,

October 17: Dearest Trinity, Gracie my love, my dearest Angels, dearest God, and all the Wonderful Universe…

Obviously, Mary's faith, trust, belief, and ability to communicate were expanding over time.

Julie made her first attempt in May and heard her angel's name as Water. Her second entry came on June 19. She made two requests to Water in July and one each for August, September, November, and December. On two occasions she received no response. She despaired a bit at not having the access that Mary and I had. She continued to ask me to ask Peace for words when she really felt she needed them. But what we all began to learn was that words were not our only means of communication.

In one of my earliest conversations with Peace I brought up the music of the Moody Blues and how all of their music seemed to contain divine messages. He assured me that music was a means of delivering and receiving messages.

So when Julie heard the same song, such as U2's "I Still Haven't Found What I'm Looking For" or R.E.M.'s "Losing My Religion," every time she turned on the car radio for days at a time and lyrics corresponded to angel messages, she began to see that there were other ways in which her angel, Water, was attempting to reach her.

By the time of her second journal entry, she knew music was one of those ways and that it was going to be significant to her. She asked Water about it.

How does music fit with me? What does it mean for me to play music?

It means for you to release your soul. Music is like water through your veins, pulsing.

In her entry of November 21, 1995, she asked about a moving experience she had while in a museum in Milan, gazing at a picture of a woman playing a mandolin. Water responded:

It was about what you know and have always known. You are a musician. It is there, bubbling, flowing, waiting for you to say okay, let's go. Believe it.

Julie had two means of communicating in addition to her scanty written communication with Water. Neither were as easily understandable as the written word, but both were extremely powerful and often were combined. Those means of communication were music and dreams. Their messages, when examined, were just as insightful and instructive as those Mary and I received through writing, and on occasion, they coincided with our written messages. It was almost as if while Mary and I were addressing the angels, the angels were addressing Julie, initiating contact in whatever way they could, using every means available to communicate their messages to her.

In July, for instance, Julie awoke in a dream to the sound of the k. d. lang song "Constant Craving." It was so loud that she needed to get up, even though she didn't want to, to go turn it off. The lyrics, which are about knowing that there is something "more" to life, spoke of the exact concerns Julie was dealing with at the time.

Julie's messages were not received only through music and dreams however. One message was delivered by a young Asian man who knocked at our office door seeking directions. When he peered through one of the door's windows, Julie saw his face and knew immediately he was another poor soul looking for directions. We got them all the time. It was a big university and our building a complex combination of A, B, C, and D corridors. Julie had gone to the door reluctantly, but her reluctance changed the minute she looked at the young man. It was like doing a double take, that sensation you get when you might know someone but you're not sure. But it wasn't about whether she knew him. She didn't know him. Yet she trusted him. "There were no barriers between the two of us," Julie said. "And I couldn't understand how that could happen with a complete stranger."

Shortly afterward, she had a dream in which both water and music played a part. It began with Julie dancing the flamenco and then becoming self-conscious about it and worrying about making too much noise. It continued with sitting at a table with an Asian man she was attracted to and then spilling red wine and overreacting to spilling it. Finally, she went to look out through the wall of floor-length windows and noticed that the water level outside was above her head. She put her hands on the glass and could feel the water making the windows bow in and out. She feared that the pressure from the water would break the glass.

She awoke from this dream in the middle of the night and a series of thoughts about the dream's meaning came to her: "You let yourself go and then you start blocking, getting self-conscious. People make mistakes. It's okay to make mistakes." And then she started thinking about the real young man she had seen in the hall and a flurry of realizations washed over her: "Yes," she heard, "he was reflecting your beauty. Your love. You're okay. He was a mirror reflection."

Julie said later that both the dream and the incident with the young man would have seemed insignificant if it weren't for the underlying message, which, not unlike "suspend judgment," followed her throughout the year. That message was about reflection and exchange, a message that also came up several times in our written angel messages.

What the messages seemed to do, in whatever form they took, was to reinforce the life lessons we were learning. The life lesson Julie was trying to learn was that if she could only let go and let her real self be seen, she would find nothing but love reflected back to her. That it would become an exchange. If she gave of herself to others, others would give to her as well.

The messages were like patterns we had to find, puzzles that needed to be put together. An angel message, or a tune that was heard briefly at a significant time, or a dream whose meaning seemed almost within grasp would be the beginning of a theme. The angel would say "release" and the songs would all be about letting go. A dream would reveal a specific fear and then the lesson of dealing with that fear would unfold over the next few weeks.

Unfolding was a theme in more than one way. Several times Peace or Water asked that Julie remove that which was shielding her true nature from being seen. Then she had a dream, a part of which included taking off several bandannas from around her neck and several layers of sweaters.

But unfolding was really just another way of saying let your true self be seen and it will reflect back to you! It was part of the pattern, part of the unfolding lesson.

No matter how the messages were delivered, they were always complementary and never contradictory.

One of Julie's earliest and loveliest messengers was her daughter, Lucia, who asked her why she "did that thing with her face," that clenching of her teeth and tensing of all her muscles that pulled the line of her neck taut. And one morning, after Julie had a dream during which she said, "I want to be a fuzzy white rabbit crunching carrots in the grass and giggling," Lucia gave her a sticker of a white rabbit. She also, with the unerring wisdom of a child, told her mother things like, "You can do anything you want to do" and that she was beautiful. It was clear that one of the lessons Julie was to learn from her children was that she was a lovable person.

Julie wasn't alone in receiving messages in ways other than the written angel communication. Titles of Beatles songs, such as "All You Need Is Love," often came to me out of nowhere. One day it was a John Lennon and Yoko Ono song, "(Just Like) Starting Over," that wouldn't leave my mind at a time when that phrase was particularly appropriate. And I remember clearly how a song came to me one day when I was walking out of work with Mary. Our cars were in different lots, and when we parted ways, the Stevie Wonder song "Isn't She Lovely," immediately entered my mind. One of my favorites occurred on a day on which I was feeling particularly good. I was walking to work with this tune in my head, and it took me several blocks before I could put words to it. The tune was from an old Budweiser commercial, and the words being put with it were, "You have it all, you have it all."

Mary and I also received messages from dreams occasionally; we often dreamed about one another, and Mary and Julie still occasionally shared dream images. Once, within weeks of each other, for instance, they each had a dream about huge angels filling the sky.

Only one further incident had the intensity of those that had come earlier in the year. This time, the event included both a dream and a vision.

It was on a Sunday afternoon in July that Amanda, Mary's stepdaughter, saw Grace. Amanda saw a one-year-old toddler sitting in a chair in the backyard. She wore a pink robe that had heart-shaped lockets on the tie and fur around its bottom. On her feet were moccasins with a moon and star on them. The baby had curly hair and fat cheeks. She was sitting before a pitcher of lemonade, scooping at it with her hands as if she were playing at drinking it. When she saw Amanda, she said, "Bye" in a high, faraway voice, and vanished into a white light Amanda called "brighter than the sun."

On that same Sunday night, Julie was dreaming. It was one of those rainy, dark nights (in the dream), but Julie opened her front door. Right outside, on the porch, was one little moccasin and it was wet around it.

It was obvious by this time that our children, husbands, strangers on the street, all could be messengers now that we were open to receiving their messages.

We knew that, in whatever form and through whatever means, the lessons were all important. Once again, communication itself had a dual meaning: if we hadn't been bringing the "messages" we received forth, talking about them, sharing them, pooling our resources to decipher and understand them, the messages might have just become thoughts that came and went from our minds, as transitory and fleeting as one usually thinks of a dream being. And if they hadn't seemed important, we might have been content to let this be so. But when we shared them, sometimes hesitantly, shyly, saying things like, "I'm sure this doesn't mean anything but . . ." one of us would see the importance behind the image, lyric, dream, thought. Without "suspend judgment," we might not have learned forgiveness. Without the repeated messages concerning revealing herself, Julie might never have come to believe she had qualities within that were worth revealing. Without Julie bringing in the Emmanuel books, I might not have ever attempted to talk to my angel. (Even though *Ask Your Angels* assured me that I could communicate, it was the Emmanuel books that made me want to.) If I had not contacted my angel, Mary has assured me, she never would have tried to contact hers. One communication led to another, led to another. It was an exchange and the exchange seemed to have a ripple effect.

The very goodness of the communications told us that what was happening was worth taking note of. There was never, during the entire course of the year, a dream that said, "Shame on you." Never once did the lyrics that repeated in our minds, or on the radio until we noticed them, speak of anything negative. Was it our state of mind creating the messages or the messages creating our state of mind? We didn't know. But if one could "suspend judgment" long enough to believe in angels, why should the means of the angel messages be judged? And if the messages themselves were repeated in several different formats, wasn't that just calling our attention to their importance?

XVI

FLOW

Our spiritual quest had moved to a higher plane. We had gone beyond the ordinary and yet we were still ordinary women. Perhaps because we had gone beyond the ordinary, perhaps because for a time, everything felt important, significant, we fell back upon the ordinary in the same way one takes comfort from a familiar place, a comfortable pair of slippers. Routine, after this break from the routine, felt good. And rather than asking of us extraordinary things, our spiritual quest returned to the ordinary with us. It joined us in our ordinary lives. It began by asking us to be present in the now.

Mary actually bought a watch that had the word *now* on its face. I quit wearing my watch altogether. We realized we had flexibility, or flow, in our lives. And with this realization, our days took on more depth and time became more fluid.

Mornings that used to be a rush became lovely times to experience the Now. Mary rearranged her daily schedule so she could have her morning coffee on her back steps. I took a new route to work, avoiding the freeway and enjoying instead the trees along one of my city's grand avenues, the view of the river.

Julie came in one morning talking about a pair of new white socks that had been sitting in her drawer for a long time. She talked about them because she saw how they were an allegory for her life. Because she had been *saving* them—as it seemed she had been saving what was best in herself. This saving was the opposite of the phrase "There's no time like the present." For Julie, there was "no time like the future." After talking about it, after seeing what she had been doing, Julie came in proudly wearing the new white socks. She wasn't saving anymore. She was becoming present.

We heard birdsong, saw flowers and clouds, appreciated the feel of the sun on our skin, the breeze in the air. We remembered to breathe. People smiled at us. Had they been doing that all along and we hadn't noticed, or was there something new in our faces, something that invited smiles? Every song on the radio spoke of love to Mary and me, of water to Julie. Where had these songs come from? Old and new, they were new to us. Because we *heard* them.

We worked in what is referred to as the health sciences area of the university. My husband, after visiting once, remarked, "I didn't expect it to be so sterile." But sterile is what it is. The health sciences buildings are on a street lined by dormitories and parking ramps, a street known for its wind-tunnel effect as it snakes between the health sciences towers to the dead-end circle at the front of our building, the former hospital. The area does not have the avant-garde casualness of the university's West Bank campus across the river from us or the grand educational feel of the main East Bank mall lined with its old trees. We imagined that it had more of a corporate-America atmosphere than any of the other areas of the university. Even the people seemed to be different here. There were few of the body-pierced, dyed-hair nonconformists one saw hanging around the art and political science and literature buildings. Health-professions students seemed freshly scrubbed and conservative, their professors freshly scrubbed and conservative and older. There seemed to be a preponderance of civil service women in nylons, high heels, and polyester skirts, a preponderance of white men in suits.

When, in the spring of the year of the births, our

department was moved from offices in the main corridor of the old hospital building to cubes in a far corner on a lower floor, it hadn't been our decision. It was a political decision and our program had little political clout. We moved under protest to the smaller quarters. Only later did we see how the move enhanced our own movement. The private offices of old would not have been conducive to the sharing that went on. The old office with its steady interruptions would not have provided the privacy we came to rely on. The isolated work space became a facilitator of our journey, our haven.

Without knowing how important it would come to be, we established the three members of our team in one room, the remaining office staff, sometimes numbering three, sometimes four, in the other. We positioned our cubicles as best we could around the room's two windows, faced our desks away from each other so that telephone conversations could take place with some hint of privacy, gave our large wooden conference table away and replaced it with a small, round, pink Formica one that would fit the remaining space, and we were back in business: I in the middle cubicle, Mary to my left, and Julie to my right.

We would begin our day joining in the little room we had designed as best we could with our mishmash of office furniture and files and modules. We had too much stuff for too little space. Besides the desks, the files, the computers, the copier, the fax, our office had artifacts. Our students came from around the world and each came bearing gifts, gifts that were on display in every nook and cranny that wasn't filled with office paraphernalia.

Because we had no offices, no doors, we made door-ways out of our modules, and it was in these doorways that we gathered to begin our workday. We called our first-thing-in-the-morning talks our "morning update," which became as habitual as picking up the mail. We had been apart for a dozen hours or a weekend and what we did or felt or read during those hours was now brought to the others for exploration. We would begin by hearing one another's dreams, often pulling out a dictionary to discover the hidden meanings behind a dream image, symbol, or word. Then we would hear about any reading one of the others had done, learn of any angelic messages, signs, or feelings. Learn, too, about what was going on in each other's families. Our morning update complete, we would then wander off three or four feet to our little cubicles and work until my mid-morning cigarette break.

Most mornings, except in winter, Mary and Julie would join me for my break, appropriately, on Church Street. If it was cool, we would stand beneath the entryway arch or sit on the steps. In nice weather we walked across the street to where the sun lit on windowsills large enough for the three of us to sit on together, and there we would continue the conversation of the morning.

Often we would lunch together, either at the little con-ference table in our area or at a nearby restaurant, the Big

Ten. Having read in *A Course in Miracles* that we should ask the Holy Spirit to make all of our relationships holy, we asked in a booth at the Big Ten over turkey sandwiches that He bless the relationship the three of us shared. It was also in the Big Ten that Mary had an epiphany concerning her humanness, and it was here, in the midst of blaring music and lunch crowds, that we often came to new awareness about matters of concern to us.

Mary had begun to carry a "spirit bag," a briefcase in which she toted her dream journal and any books we were discussing. Often the spirit bag came with us to the Big Ten. With a whole lunch hour at our disposal, we could read each other important passages from books or angelic messages, or discuss a dream or message in more depth.

It was a giddy time. A fun time. Everything had meaning: colors, stones, bumper stickers, clothing, jewelry. Everything was a message. A bad day was no longer just a bad day. Having a bad day occasionally may have been normal once, but no longer. Now a bad day was a message. It had something to tell us. An aching back was no longer something to be put up with. It was a message. It had something to tell us.

Our wardrobes were suddenly all wrong. Where were the flowing fabrics? The cotton? The natural fibers that would feel good against the skin, that would move with the breeze? Mary started growing her hair out because she wanted flowy hair. I quit drying and setting and pulling mine off my face with clips, and let it be natural.

We began to tease Julie about the knot in her brow, the tension that pulled the veins and muscles of her neck into taut strings. We could tease her, we could notice, because they were no longer constant. She could be seen, occasionally, to look relaxed. She began to glow with a light that seemed to come from within. I quit taking my medication for my fibromyalgia and I was fine. The muscles that had been tight for more than five years finally relaxed.

People began to remark that we had changed.

Our secretary, Felicia, used to tease me about how little I expressed myself—about anything. I would come in and share some news about something really great, buying a new car, for instance, and she would say, sarcastically, "Gee, I'm glad I can tell you're so happy about it!" Now she was beginning to be able to tell how I felt about things—good and bad. She even remarked about how I touched her arm one day. I had been so standoffish previously that a simple touch on the arm, a touch of understanding, was noteworthy.

Our internal changes were being reflected externally! How could they not? Some things were easily seen, such as my change of clothing, from form-fitting business suits to flowy dresses, my more relaxed way of wearing my hair, my softer makeup. Mary, too, changed her clothing. She no longer needed things to match, but to have meaning. She became a body artist, finding jewelry especially that spoke to her, that proclaimed who she was or who she was becoming. Julie, who had always agonized over spending seven dollars on a skirt at a consignment store, bought and wore daily a forty-dollar necklace that she felt symbolized outwardly the changes that were occurring inwardly.

We stopped reading the newspaper and hardly watched television. It was no longer acceptable to submit ourselves to violence. We just couldn't take it. We realized we didn't have to. We were becoming open and, in our opened states, vulnerable. Vulnerable to good and vulnerable to bad as well. We started experimenting, led by Mary's reading, with energy. We could turn off television violence, but could we turn off another's negative energy? Often the answer was yes!

In large part, people around us seemed to respond to our new personas. We may not have been talking about our dreams and angelic messages with our husbands and families, but we were, nonetheless, different with them.

Mary, who had always had control issues with her husband, John, just gave up trying to win control and reaped huge rewards. She realized that all the "division of labor" fights they used to have, in which she would become angry because she felt John wasn't pulling his weight, had been the result of her feeling *she* had to pull all the weight herself. The fights had been the result of her own feeling that the only way for her to be *good* was to be in control, to maintain what she had. And she had to maintain what she had perfectly. Everything in her home had needed to be in its proper place, perfectly coordinated, matching. It didn't matter that John would gladly have picked up his own clutter when he was done doing whatever he was doing. It mattered that he cluttered at all. It didn't matter that John would do what she had deemed "his chores" when he was ready to do them. If she was ready for them to be done, they had to get done—right then—and so she would do them herself.

She knew the ultimate change had occurred when John asked her, one day, when she was going to get around to doing the dishes and she responded, "When the spirit moves me." Even John laughed. What had ruffled her before—things out of place, things not done, things not perfect—were now signs of living going on, of love going on.

My husband, like Mary's, provides a good example of how my changes affected others. A man of keen wit and gentle wisdom, he is outwardly a gruff, working-class "man's man," a hunter, a fisherman, a man not readily prone to revealing feelings other than those he considers "manly"—like anger. Fiercely loyal, he expected others to be fiercely loyal, and if he felt betrayed, he held grudges. He had, in the past, gone for years without speaking to one family member or another over wrongs he had felt were done to him.

Two major family squabbles occurred during this time, both of which were large enough that in the past, he would have written off those family members with whom he argued. Now the fights were allowed to blow over.

One evening Donny told me about his day and how different it was from days he used to have. How before, if he had been on a ladder and dropped a hammer even once, he would get angry, swear, fume. And now he could drop a hammer, climb down and get it, climb back up, drop it again, and still not be upset. And he said he knew it was because of me. He didn't elaborate on why he thought I had anything to do with this. But I was thrilled! It was as if my new peacefulness was extending to him.

Another night he told me that I was at ease now, and so now he and everyone else in the family could be more at ease. It had been the perfect word choice. I thought about Thomas Moore's definition of *dis-ease,* and concluded, "That is what I used to have. I was so full of dis-ease it might as well have been an illness."

We were becoming unified in our marriage. What had previously been "his" church and "his" family was gradually becoming mine as well. Donny's nephews were no longer "his" nephews and mine, "mine." His nephews were the same little boys they had always been, but now I suddenly loved them like my own, as if they were part of me, because they were. And as subtle as these changes were, they were noticed. I was treated more like one of the family—both by the family of my husband and of my church—because I was.

I felt some of the biggest rewards within my family were those that came from slowing down and, in slowing down, no longer resenting the small demands others made on me. When I slowed down, I was no longer uptight all the time. I made the choice to slow down when the spiritual lessons I had been learning came nose-to-nose with a life lesson one morning.

I had been on my way out to work when I found my daughter Mia's car parked behind mine in the driveway. I was furious. I was in a hurry. I woke Mia from a sound sleep and demanded that she immediately move her car out of my way. I sat impatiently in my car, watching as she came out in her pajamas and shoes, bleary-eyed and stumbling, and then found that the car wouldn't start. I listened to the car whine and whir, watched my daughter's frustration grow as she tried it again and again. But I was in too much of a hurry to have any compassion for her. I hopped out of my car and demanded that she put the car in neutral. With the strength of my impatience, I pushed the car down the driveway and out of my way. As I drove out past her, I saw my husband coming out the door of the house. He would take care of it.

But I hadn't even gone a block before I felt absolutely horrible. What was the matter with me? What did five minutes one way or the other matter? If I had calmly gotten Mia's keys and moved the car myself, the car probably would have started just fine. She had probably flooded it because I had made her so nervous. My impatience had led to a rotten start of the day for me, for Mia, and now probably for Donny as well.

What hit me as I drove on to work was the teaching,

"Act from love and you cannot act wrong." I had been too impatient to remember love, too much in a hurry. I had forgotten to love and now I, and others, would suffer for it the rest of the day. I vowed it wouldn't happen again and it didn't. Because the thing was, it wasn't about minutes, it was about love. And this was clearest, most evident, in the little things. The little things that add up to make life hellish or heavenly. In a hundred little ways each day, we each have the choice of acting from love or not.

Julie's theme of being the lucky one traveled through her marriage as well. Her husband, Kelly, who was affected by retinitis pigmentosa, or RP, a genetic degenerative retinal disease that causes blindness, was slowly losing his vision. What right did she have to complain or to make demands upon him when he was facing something so devastating? Consequently, she had always placed her own needs— from the simplest to the most important—last, if she had let them be known at all. If she wanted to do something on the same night Kelly did, she gave up her activity in favor of his. If Kelly wanted to spend money in one way and she in another, she gave in. When he had wanted a career change and decided to start his own business, she went along even though the change terrified her on many levels, particularly financially. She had gone along even though she realized this change meant that she would always have to keep a job that provided the stable income and medical benefits the family still needed.

Even while Kelly's decisions and the changes they made in her life had been positive, she now felt as if she could have more of a voice in things. And this "coming to voice" was quite literal—as Mary and I saw in our conversations with Julie. Where we had both, in the past, often finished sentences for Julie because she just didn't seem to be able to find the words to do so herself, we were now seeing that she carried on. That she kept going until she got things out. She was coming to voice.

Now she was beginning to realize she could not keep holding all of her dreams and desires within. Now she saw that what she kept from her husband injured him as much as it injured her. Kelly did not want a woman who would sacrifice herself for him, but one who would accept him and accept herself, just as they were, without pretense, without withholding.

We weren't preaching what we were learning; we were living it, and it flowed into every area of our lives. Things went well for us. We were, quite simply, happier, and others were happier to be around us.

My husband and I didn't fight anymore. We sold a house, bought a house, had the usual, normal, ordinary problems with our teenage children, and we just dealt with them. And what was more, we recognized we weren't fighting anymore and were pleased. In a conversation one evening, Donny told me he thought it had become fashionable for people to complain, that people never used to complain about everything like they did now, and how he recognized that we weren't like that. We were happy. And he hoped our happiness would set an example for those around us.

Almost without realizing what we were doing, we had brought some of what we had in the office beyond the office. But the office, and our day-to-day interaction with one another, was still what was most important.

When Julie, Mary, and I were together at work, all of our emotions were given a place to be, and given that place they came. We were happier, but we cried often. We became emotional beings. We cried tears of happiness and tears of sadness. Some days we were drained by noon because we had laughed and cried so hard during the morning. I cried more in those months of discovery than I had in my entire adult life.

It is impossible now to remember what it was all about—all that laughter, all those tears. One thing simply seemed to lead to the next. It seemed as if every feeling we had, every thought, was universal. There was almost nothing we had experienced that one of the others had not experienced also. Everything was acceptable. We were not alone. We were not lonely!

Every day, every hour, someone brought something that another seemed to need. A bit of advice, a bit of humor, a bit of compassion.

There seemed to be an end, for brief periods of time, to

struggle of any sort. We could simply *be* in each other's presence. We could rest. Let down our guards, our defenses. It was a peaceful place. Like a stolen moment in time.

It seemed impossible that what was happening was happening. Not the big stuff so much as the little: the peace, the cessation of struggle, and the work getting done in the midst of it. I look back and wonder how we did it all. We were busy at work by this time. We did just as much as any other year. We scheduled faculty, produced curriculum, admitted students. We got it all done. We had it all! It was exhilarating and exhausting at once. We were aware every day of how lucky we were. And we talked, during this busy time, of what it would be like when we weren't as busy. It was so new. Everything was so new. Our days were so different. What would they be like when the busy season was over? It was almost too much to imagine. We didn't know if we could take anything more. There was a collective feeling of operating at our peak, of getting the most out of everything, of being in a time that would be impossible to top.

And in a way, it was. It was the beginning and had the energy of beginnings, of innocence, of exploration. We met each day with awe. By the end of the year, we were experimenting with saying "I believe it" instead of "I can't believe it" about everything. By the end of the year, the freshness of it had worn off a little bit. We were becoming used to it. We were beginning to believe it. But for now it was new and it didn't seem as if anything could be better.

In our program the end of spring quarter was the peak of the season, the home stretch, the eve of our students' arrival. All of our work during this time was teamwork, no one could take vacation; we had a common goal, deadlines, schedules to keep. In the midst of the increased pace, we began to look forward to routine tasks that had once been monotonous and dull, because they allowed our minds to be free. Mailings became causes of celebration because we could do them together—one labeling, one folding, one stuffing—producing while we talked, while we laughed, while we cried. There was a unity about the work that went beyond teamwork. We began to dream about a world in which we could work together toward a common goal that was our own, even while we were doing it! Even while we were in the midst of it, we voiced our concerns, one or another of us, that it would end someday, that we would go on to other endeavors that might not include each other.

There we were, three civil servants, working in a small office of a large institution where no one would believe, no one could imagine, what was going on. We said often, if someone had told us six months ago we would be happy about sitting down to a mailing so that we could talk about angels and our spiritual life, we would have said they were crazy. We would have said we would be crazy if this came to be. But it had come to be and we were not crazy. We were happy. We felt alive! We were present. We were integrated. We brought to work all that we were in a pure, raw form. We became our true selves when we were at work.

Our days had reversed themselves. Now we could hardly wait to get to work so we could be who we were, and when we left for our homes at the end of the day, we often felt we left our best selves behind. When we left, we took on our other roles. We became wives and mothers and daughters again. We did our ordinary things—went grocery shopping and picked up the dry cleaning and went to the bank. We gassed our cars, washed our clothes, read our mail, and paid our bills. But these activities no longer felt like "real life."

It was nice that I was more at ease in my home environment, that Mary was less controlling, that Julie was coming to voice. But these things were all offshoots of the journey, not the journey itself. We were grateful for these benefits, these by-products, but we knew we still needed each other and the office environment for our journey to continue. We didn't want to let the distractions of our work and our ordinary lives halt our progress toward our real lives and our real selves.

In the office, everything was fuel for our fire. But we *were* the fire. We were finding the something more we had sought all along and it was *us*. It was what we had when we were together.

What went on in the office between the three of us felt like real life. It was as if while we were there, while we were together, we "got it." We knew what it was all about. It was why we started to dream up schemes of working together forever. How could we possibly repeat the string of events that had brought us to where we were? It felt like a once-in-a-lifetime, unrepeatable occurrence. It felt unique to the three of us and to that time and place.

It was a time when we would gladly have brought in cots and set up residence. It was a time that felt too good to be true. It was a time that had to end.

It was the honeymoon, the fairy tale, the dawning of the quest, the start of the adventure. It had to face the test of that other life, that life we no longer thought of as real life. It had to face the reality of our move out of our office to the conference center where we ran our summer program. It had to face the test of "after the students were gone" vacations. It had to move with us or we would lose it. And it had to do more than that. Unless it could become more than a side benefit in our ordinary lives, it would become a fantasy, a fairy tale in which we would not live happily ever after. Because we didn't live in our cubicles in our tiny office in our large institution. Because we couldn't bring in our cots and our toothbrushes. What we had found was meant to go with us into our lives. It was meant to be more than a by-product that made life easier. It was meant to *be* our lives.

XVII
PREPARING

We were still, however, not quite ready. In June, as my daughter Mia was about to graduate from high school, Peace had taught me the lesson, "know for what it is that you prepare." I had been busy with work, busy with my spiritual quest, busy getting ready to sell my home. Planning for Mia's graduation and all the related activities had felt like a burden until Peace reminded me to be aware for what it was that I prepared. I was preparing to send my daughter into the next phase of her life, the life of a young adult. I was about to honor all that she was and all that she hoped to become. I was preparing to honor all that was possible for her. The limitless possibilities of her future. The graduation planning ceased to be a burden. And the thought of "being aware of what it was that I prepared for" stayed with me through my days, as "suspend judgment" did.

Julie, Mary, and I had been preparing to go out into the world new, as my daughter went out into the world new. In July, leaving the office was thrust upon us just as leaving high school was thrust upon my daughter a month earlier. It did not mean that we were ready. We were, in fact, still preparing. As my daughter was still preparing.

What was new was the sense of limitless possibility, the sense of becoming. New, appropriately, for my daughter. New, because of the spiritual quest for us ordinary women well beyond the years of growing up, well beyond thinking our possibilities were limitless. We had a sense of something awaiting us.

And at the same time we sensed we were putting something behind us. It was July again. The month of the births. Peter would have his first birthday.

It became a time to get through so that we could go on. What awaited seemed to be on the other side of July, on the other side of August. Waiting beyond the busy season, my move, the birthday, the anniversary of the death. Waiting for the time we would be together again in the office. Waiting for the three to gather in what had become our holy place. We had become dependent. And we fought that. We reasserted our independence. We became individuals again.

There were times during our "on-campus" sessions when we were able to use what we had learned thus far. We no longer expected crisis. We experienced a new sense that what will be, will be. That what needed to get done would get done. That there was no need to panic. When a problem arose, the point was to solve the problem and go on rather than to dwell in the problem and give it control over us. When things needed to get done, we did them. I remember winding extension cords from audio-visual equipment at the end of a long day and, instead of resenting the task, enjoying the quiet of the moment, enjoying the act of forming it into circles with my hands. There were times when we remembered to be in the now even while waiting for the now to be over.

But there were also times when we forgot. The biggest stresses came when we tried to re-create what we had in the office by taking ourselves away for a long lunch or a short break, when we tried to create artificially what had come naturally in another time and space. We were going to bring what we had learned into the world, but we weren't going to be able to bring the world of the office with us. What we had in the office was going to have to transform.

There was a hint of melancholy, of mourning, about this time, even while we prepared for the limitless possibilities that were coming. I was eager to move into my new home at the same time that I was feeling sentimental about the old. Julie was eager to celebrate Peter's birthday and wistful for a year that had gone by too quickly. Mary was eager to put the year of her daughter's death behind her and yet resentful of the healing properties of time.

We were eager and reluctant both.

And so we struggled once again. We had good days and bad. We weren't always crazy about each other. We would arrive at our conference center by 7 A.M., set up for 8 A.M. classes, break down after classes were over at 5 P.M., and then prepare for social activities or evening sessions, sometimes stretching well into the night. After these long days, there were times when we would be grateful to get away from each other, when other things were more important. We felt ordinary again some days, separate most days. There wasn't time to read or write. There was hardly time to think. And so we concentrated on what would come later . . . after our work in July was over . . . after the vacations we would take in August were over.

For we all had our secret fears. We would get through this busy time, this work that had been our goal and our mission. We would get through the July and August anniversaries. We would come back from the vacations and we would join once again. We wondered if things would be the same. We wondered if things would be different. We knew we would go on to something more. We *knew* this. We knew we were preparing. But what we were preparing for remained a huge unknown.

XVIII

SURRENDER/LETTING GO

With the coming of September, we were back together with time stretching before us once again. We were back in the office. Back in our own little world. We were *back!* We greeted each other with enthusiasm. We had missed each other.

The cycle of a year different than our ordinary years was now complete. Mary had survived a whole year without her daughter. She had watched summer turn to fall, fall to winter, winter to spring, and spring to summer once again. Fall was upon us—again. That Grace had left Mary at the time the sun was waning, the gardens ending their growth cycle, the gloomier skies of fall approaching, had somehow seemed appropriate. That the fall of the following year would begin differently was a measure of the potency of the cycle. The year following the death of her daughter was behind her. She had survived! She had found she could go on living! Mary felt a burst of new energy. Something finally felt completed, and it seemed as if it might be the cycle of pain. It seemed as if it might be time to let go.

For me a different cycle was wrapping itself up. My move from the old house to the new was now complete. The move had long been an allegory to me, an outward representation of the change occurring within. I had known I would go new to the new home. I had prepared myself as I had prepared the old home for its sale. I had worked hard to shed those things I no longer needed. I had sorted and sifted, throwing some things away, putting a fresh perspective on others. I had left the old home with love and fell in love with the new. Peace had said: "Honor the old home. The new home will honor you." Perhaps he meant that home is within, a place of love and contentment, or he may have been speaking literally of the new building, the new structure. Because everything about the new home was a joy and everything went well. It truly seemed as if the new home honored me, blessed me. I, too, was full of a new energy. Released from a time-consuming enterprise, I could settle into other pursuits, including my spiritual quest.

Julie approached the fall with impatience. She was tired, too, of the old self. She strove to define what blocked her from moving forward. She strove to let go. To quit letting those things she could not define hold her back. She strove to come into being.

We were back in the same familiar setting but we were different. More confident. We had survived being away from each other, survived a trip into the world, and we had carried many lessons we had learned there. Even if we could not carry the experience of the office into the rest of our lives, our lives could improve. We could bring with us the enthusiasm of the journey. We had left behind our mourning for what couldn't be and we were anxious to discover what could be. We had come back together and found that we still had much to learn from each other, found that the office still offered us a place to be while we were discovering what we would become.

We came back knowing we were each going to continue on our journey . . . even if it meant that our paths would diverge.

Yet it was more as if we were each in a different place on the same path, or perhaps we were heading in the same direction through different routes. Still sharing the spiritual journey yet living three separate spiritual journeys, learning to blend them with our three ordinary lives. Learning to let go of willfulness and to accept guidance on the journey from sources higher than ourselves.

My surrender/letting go had happened almost accidentally:

August 27, 1995

I am writing from my new office in my new home. It is in a corner of a damp basement (if you can believe it, I let my husband appropriate the sunroom for the TV) and I don't care. It feels so good to be back. I sat down, pulled up the file I now called Peace rather than Prayer, and there it was. It felt almost miraculous to see it here, in this new house. In this new house where everything has come together so beautifully.

But this is the biggest, the grandest, the happiest. Peace is here! I have read the whole Peace file, and I am moved by it, by my own innocence more than my knowledge. I haven't thought of myself as innocent since I was thirteen. There is a sweetness about the Peace file—from the first day when I was told to smell the sweetness. It is the sweetness of innocence, of teacher and pupil. To read it is like learning to read all over again—the knowledge, the excitement, the adventure. The love of words! I cannot begin to say how much it all means to me.

And so, here I am, about to ask Peace to join me once again, putting it off only so that I can wait until I have a quiet hour with no pressure to do other things. Because I know Peace is my still, quiet voice within and I know he has led me and will continue to lead me to breakthrough moments of higher consciousness and greater creativity.

I have begun to say affirmations from a book I just bought, *Higher Creativity: Liberating the Unconscious for Breakthrough Insights,* by Willis Harman and Howard Rheingold. Those affirmations are

> I am not separate.
> I can trust.
> I can know.
> I am responsible.
> I am single-minded. I have no other
> desire than to know and follow the will
> of the deepest part of myself.[3]

And I realize that this is letting go. Turning events over to the higher self, the unconscious, surrendering, if you will, to the will of God.

And this is where I am. This is my beginning in my new home. Happily, contentedly, surrendering, letting go. What a relief!

I cannot wait any longer. Welcome Peace! Welcome back! Welcome home! It's me, calling you home. Will you answer?

I am here and I am happy to be with you. I am smiling. We are not Home, but we are home on earth, home in the physical, home in well-being. Safe, comfortable, surrounded by beauty. Home. Peace on Earth.

Thank you, Peace on Earth, for bringing Peace to my little piece of it. For bringing yourself here. This, too, is a relief. You're here! My eyes fill with tears of joy to have you here, to have what we have here continue. Thank you. Welcome.

You have learned much in our break.

I have tried (for want of a better word). I have been mainly involved in the physical, but as I said before, as it comes together it has risen to a higher level.

Yes! It has living spirit. Like the words that come together to form a beautiful philosophy, a living message. Everything is coming together.

Is it, Peace? Is everything?

Everything has come together for you to the point of trust. Why trust? Because you have decided to let go. No. Not decided. You have let go. With your innermost being you Know, you Trust that you can let go. I could not force it upon you with my words. You were the only one who could make the choice. And you did it now, today, on this time of our rejoining. Hurrah for you, dear one. You are one step, one giant step, one leap closer to Home.

I didn't even realize I was going to surrender until I did, until I had, and the relief flooded me. I think it was an unconscious decision as much as it was a conscious one. I think this is the way it is supposed to be.

That is the goal. To let go and let your highest self, your connection to all that is, do the planning, the deciding, the choosing for you. It is not

not you. It is the best you. It is us. It is from oneness. You and the all that is connected. Linked. Xed. Joined.

This is so new to me. Now what do I ask you, dearest Peace?

If surrendering has lulled your curiosity, it is only so that you can rest in the relief. Rest as you have never rested before. Rest, and in your resting will come the stirring of the still, quiet voice, the voice that asks for more out of a whisper of calmness rather than the raging of necessity, desperation, frustration.

I have no other desire than to know and follow the will of the deepest part of myself.

Look deeply and there I am, reflecting back what you are. . . .

Welcome to my new home, Peace. Thank you.

Rest in relief in your new home. That is all the thanks I ask.

On my first day back at work after the move, Julie very casually said that she had been thinking she just ought to ask me to ask Peace what the heck was wrong with her. She very humorously told of her steps backwards—the tension and gritting of the teeth, the strain she was under. Just as Mary had pantomimed "suspend judgment," she played the two sides of herself that were in conflict, one side constantly saying, "Yes I can," the other, "No I can't." And she asked: How do I get out from under it?

The answer I received, as so often happened, was very

simple. Condensed, it simply said, *Tell Julie to have a dialogue with herself. What is at the center of Julie? Who is she?* She was being asked to get to know herself. *Tell her I am aware that this is not new advice; not the timeless wisdom she seeks. But the timeless wisdom she seeks will be found on the journey inward.*

This message wasn't news. Few of the angel pronouncements were. As Peace told me early on, he wouldn't tell me anything I didn't already know. But, oh, how I wanted him to. How we all did.

We were back and we wanted More, More, More. We wanted answers. How could we proceed without direction? No matter how many times we were told to turn within for that direction, we still hoped for external answers. We looked to each other, we looked to the angels, and finally we looked to a spiritual retreat.

We were lucky enough to have access, through one of the professors with whom we worked, to a wonderful, secluded cabin not far from where we lived. We had used the cabin before for work retreats. Now we sought to use it for a spiritual retreat. We wondered again, What would happen if we had "real" time together. If we could get away from it all. If we didn't have to work while we were together. Our fantasy had changed from one in which we would work together for the rest of our lives to one in which we could just *be* together.

I wrote to Peace about my expectations before the big event, saying: "I want things to grow around me and to become more than what they have been. With the spirit sisters, Peace, I truly feel that anything can happen. That if we go about it right, the possibilities are limitless. With the spirit sisters, Peace, I feel hope for myself."

Our yearning was so poignant, really. We were all expectant, we just did not know of what.

Mary had begun her search because death wasn't good enough; it had no meaning for her. She had not asked for and had not wanted to experience any of the unusual things she had encountered in her grief and her recovery from that grief. She went resistingly, as she had resisted getting an unsolicited message from Peace. Mary asked only for what she had to know. She was on this journey to find Grace, to discover the meaning of death. It was all that mattered to her.

Our searches had been different based on what we sought to find. While I often sought comfort from my reading, much of Mary's reading, such as her reading on energy, was geared toward understanding the physical nature of life and death. What were we while we were here and what did we become when we left?

Mary only told us later about the underlying sense of urgency she had felt about going to the retreat, as if propelled to take this first step into uncharted territory. Propelled because she could take it with people she trusted.

Julie's approach to the retreat was almost clinical. She looked to it as she would a doctor's appointment at which she would hope to discover what was wrong and how to fix it.

Throughout the year, the three of us had been, for each other, almost a place of joining. Whatever happened, happened when we were away from each other and then was brought in, to the place of the three, for sharing, for examining, for understanding. Now, at the cabin, we would attempt to make something happen while we were together and it was new to us, foreign. We did not get together on weekends; we did not go to movies together. We had once or twice entertained each other in our homes. But this was different. It was like going to a church and not finding a priest or minister there. We did not know how to proceed. We were not totally at ease. We only knew that we had this precious, precious time and that we could not waste it.

We were so expectant, in fact, that we made ourselves anxious. Much like on one of our workdays of old (we had worked that day, leaving on a Thursday night), we arrived rushed and breathless: expectant. We had changed our milieu. We weren't in the office. We did not have tasks to structure our time around. We did not have familiarity. It seemed, at first, as if the retreat would be a bust. As if we would go home disappointed. We did not stay up talking all night. We were tired. Our expectations had drained us.

But the new day dawned differently. We had not wanted to waste time preparing food and so had just brought good bread and cheese and fruit. We ate a little and then we adjourned to the living room and sat on the

185

floor with the sun coming through the windows. This was not a rustic cabin. The living room had floor-to-ceiling windows on two sides, floor-to-ceiling mirrors between wood beams on the other. The floor was carpeted in a plush, soft cream. Throw pillows abounded. A stereo played CDs we had brought: Van Morrison, Angela Bofill, U2, k.d. lang. We were sitting in the lap of luxury, surrounded by the green and gold of a dozen varieties of trees just beginning to wear their fall colors. They were right outside our windows and in the room as well— their reflection held in the mirrors—so that any way we turned, we were surrounded by nature and light.

As Mary was preparing to leave home to drive to the cabin, Amanda had given her a little gift she had made. It consisted of two popsicle sticks tied together with pink and white yarn to form a cross. When Amanda gave it to her she said, "Mom, take this with you. It's a God's Eye." Like at one of our workday morning updates, Mary brought out her God's Eye to show us. We sat on the floor, our bodies forming a little circle, and with the introduction of the God's Eye into the center of the circle, the circle became altarlike. When placed in the circle, the candles and incense I had brought to mask the smell of my cigarettes continued the theme. And when Mary brought forth the program from Grace's memorial service, it was very much as if we were in a holy place as she read the Litany of Memory:

At the rising of the sun and its going down
                    We remember her
At the blowing of the wind and in the chill of
     winter
                    We remember her
At the opening of the buds and in the rebirth
     of spring
                    We remember her
At the blueness of the sky and in the warmth
     of summer
                    We remember her
At the rustling of leaves and in the beauty of
     autumn
                    We remember her
At the beginning of the year and when it ends
                    We remember her
As long as we live, she too will live, for she is
     now a part of us
                    We remember her

We bowed our heads in silence.

Then it seemed as if the Litany of Memory and the objects
we had brought were calling us to join hands and
continue to pray. We asked our angels and Gracie to join
us. We said words of prayer. Our hands did not feel natural linked with those of our friends. Our attempt to
organize ourselves to action felt a bit stilted. But we

carried on, sitting on the floor, me in my robe and slippers, Mary in her sweat suit, all of us without our make-up, different to each other, but earnest and trying.

After our prayer, we were able to chat more easily, more companionably than we had since we arrived. We were sharing our dreams of the night before, each of which had included glass in some way, when Mary jerked and stared with an expression on her face akin to what one might wear after having seen a mouse. Her gaze was off to Julie's right and Julie jumped too, as if whatever it was, was contagious. "What? What?" she cried, realizing Mary had seen something—a spider maybe. Julie moved a foot from where she had been sitting, casting her eyes around for what it was Mary had seen.

Then Mary told us. "I saw light."

Mary described what she saw as a fairly large, conical blue light that seemed to surround many smaller bubbles of white light. It had been just to the right of Julie's shoulder. Mary was in awe. She said that while she gazed upon it, she experienced the complete cessation of time. Several days later I asked Peace about it and he said:

The light was Mary's own light and it was her Gracie as well.

Explain this to me, Peace.

The blue light was Mary's own light projected out and filled by Grace. Filled with Grace. You each have your own lights which are more truly you than the bodily forms you are in. The truer you are being to the self, the more visible the light becomes. The more you share and trust and connect, the more they expand to encompass those you share and trust and connect with. The clearest way I can describe it is that Mary's light reached out to Julie—not just at that instant, the room was charged with your lights—and that for a moment the light illuminated the presence of Mary's angel.

What do you mean by Mary's angel? Is Gracie Mary's angel?

Gracie will always be Mary's angel. This does not mean that she is also Mary's guide in all things. The term Guardian Angel *would fairly accurately describe what I am to you and what Trinity and Water are to Mary and Julie. But every being that has affected you in your life is, whether you feel the connection or not, connected to you. Those who have affected you and have passed out of this life to the next remain connected. Remember that when you called upon the angels, you called upon Gracie too. Do you think you could call upon her and not have her respond? This would be impossible. She was there and she was basking in her mother's light.*

Did she mean to become visible? And if so, why did she not become visible in a form Mary could recognize? And if not, was it an accident? Are accidents possible?

It is more an accident that you do not see than that you see. There is a little bit of each one of us in each other. When Mary sees herself, she will see Gracie—the essence of Gracie—as well. Maybe because Mary was not trying at that moment, her vision cleared and she saw in her light—in what might more accurately be called your combined lights—herself in love, and that is what Gracie is in her essence: light and love given form, light with substance, life subtly manifested.

189

Mary's seeing the light should have been enough for one day. Yet when we fell quiet, we once again felt awkward.

I had brought my computer at Julie's request, so that we could talk to Peace if we decided that was what we wanted to do. But it was as if none of us wanted to take charge and say let's do this or let's do that. We didn't quite know how to be but we knew to be respectful of one another. When we fell quiet, I went into the other room where I had set up my computer and opened the Peace file. I knew if the others wanted to join me they would.

Soon Julie came in and then left again to get Mary. Mary said she had been feeling "persnickety," resistant once again, and hadn't wanted to come. She was afraid Peace might say something bad about her. But Julie had said, "You've got to come now," and she came.

I addressed the angels, rather than Peace, and the first question I asked was if Mary's and Julie's angels were with us. Peace responded:

Their angels are where they are as I am where you are.

We're all feeling this energy so strongly. What does it mean?

It means you are connected. What once was one, singular, is now one, joined.

Julie: Thanks for joining us, for letting us feel you, for the release.

Julie is welcomed with open arms to our presence, our being, our reality. She can join us at any time. She can Remember now how to evoke what is within her all the time. She can Feel. She can fill with spirit. It is coming out from within. She is reflecting. You are a prism, Julie. You are your own rainbow to the divine, your own gateway. You only need to open like a flower opens to the sun—an unfolding. Unfold. Release. Let go. Let your light shine.

Julie's skin is like a conduit. With you, words are a conduit; with Julie, her very skin is—like an electrical field, attracting and repulsing depending on her openness or closedness. She will attract or repel what she desires in this way. Her most direct route to her goals is through opening and remaining open. Unfolding. As if there are layers and layers of swaddling wrapping her. Like an infant protected from the elements. Yet it is the elements she needs. She should stay away from all synthetics. She should not wear any unnatural fabrics against her skin for they block her connecting with the elements she needs to feel. She should be aware of the purifying nature of water. Ingesting water will help her to purify her body, her skin, her soul—for it is through her body, her skin, that she reaches her soul. Everyone is different in their access points. This is hers.

Look at her. It is in letting herself be seen that her unfolding will take place. People need to really look at her. To see her skin, her eyes, her hair, even her clothing. The reflection of being seen will show her herself.

For every need you let another fulfill, you fulfill a need. It is the exchange. And the exchange is very important for Julie. For everyone that sees her, she will grow. Every time she is seen, she will grow.

Julie: Meaning seen as in my true self—really letting my true nature be seen?

Yes! In being open to be seen, you remove the veils of illusion. You have been wrapped in the veils from head to toe. Your face is your visible point—your access point. Take off the mask and breathe.

Julie: But what if people don't like me? It's scary. It's scary to let these two know me.

Let go of the fear, sweet one. Open your heart. There is so much love waiting to flow in. You have no idea, you cannot comprehend the boundlessness of the love you have been blocking. When people see you, they will see love, pure love, divine love. You are worthy, unique, completely lovable in every way. When you let people see you, you will see this, because it will be reflected back to you. You may at first be stunned by it, by the strength of it. It is a powerhouse of love awaiting you.

Befriend your fear for now. Pet it. Make a pet of it. A small thing. Something that can fit in a box or beneath a bed. It is small and will get smaller. Only in your mind is it huge. Think of what your daughter, Lucia, sees when she looks at you—of what Peter sees. Then think of giving this gift to the world. That is what you are—a gift to the world. You only need to unwrap yourself.

Mary: Hello to Peace and my Angel and to Gracie. I just want to thank you for coming into our lives. And I want you to know how grateful I am for Margaret's courage and Julie's light and how much it means to me. And I'm afraid to do this but you guys are helping me to do this.

You can ask, Mary. What is it you want to ask?

Mary: Am I just a big fear basket case?

You Know you are not. You Know so much more than you allow yourself to see. Is this fear blocking your path? Blocking you from knowing what you know? Yes. But you still Know. It is there, tappable when you are ready to tap into it. Like dipping a ladle in water. The well is deep. It will never run dry. It is a well of plenty, of abundance. Remember the abundance, drink from the well. Do not go thirsty. It is as if you have a tool—a dipper—and you choose to use a sieve. Choose the dipper. It is always your choice.

Mary: What will give me more clarity to see?

You already see. You Know this in the deepest part of yourself. Your clarity is like a pure, clear tone that you listen for—a whisper, a sigh. It is not the clarity of thunderstorms. It is the clarity of a gentle breeze. Your access is from the everyday, the beauty of the now. The way a curtain blows in through a window tells you more about the divine than many people know in a lifetime. And this is because you already Know. You only need to remember. And the daily reminders that you are beginning to recognize but sometimes think are not important are. They are!

Be gentle with yourself. You cannot be gentle enough. Treat yourself with loving care. It is in how you treat yourself that you will see how to treat others. There is a way in which you are your own guinea pig— your own testing ground. You find how to see self first and then you see the world. You learn how to comfort yourself first and then you comfort the world. The kindness you show yourself is paramount. Without this kindness to self, you cannot bring yourself to the world, and yourself, your Self is what the world needs from You. The world is incomplete without the trueness of you. You are like a link in a chain. Forget about being strong. It is in your weakness, your sweetness, your lovingness that your true strength is. You do not have to carry the burdens of the world on your shoulders. All the world asks from you is your love. Give yourself a break! A literal break! You are weighted down with the burdens you carry. Tell yourself that you deserve a break, a breather, a rest, a retreat. As often as you need. This is a key to the clarity you seek. Lay down your burdens and rest.

Mary: I don't know how very well. Can I get a little help?

Thank you, dear Mary, for asking. I will help you constantly. You do not even have to ask twice. I will show you the way. Let go of trying. You try so hard, dear one. Never has anyone tried so hard. It is as if you try hard even when there is nothing to do. You do not ever stop trying. I will help you remember. Now that you have asked, leave trying to me. I take it from you. You no longer need to try. If you never try again it will be too soon. Every time the word or the feeling of trying comes to you, tell yourself you gave that away. You no longer have trying in your vocabulary. Believe me.

Julie: Do children have a significance in the oneness?

They have a significance, a divine significance for you, Now, in this time, this space. Because you need them to learn to love yourself. When you have learned to love yourself, all people will be equally significant.

Julie: So does this mean you'll help me?

That's what it means. I heard you. You hear me.

Julie: Thanks. And I'll drink lots of water.

You are welcome and welcomed. Don't forget you are welcomed.

This is a condensed version of the afternoon, but even if it had been printed in its entirety, it could not capture the feelings, as I cannot capture the feelings. The closest I can come to describing what we all felt was a sense of being overwhelmed. Tears ran down our faces. I visibly shook as I typed the words. And there is no way in rereading the words to recapture the import that they had. There was wisdom in the words, but it was as if there was a wisdom outside of the words, a wisdom that could be felt, a wisdom that felt almost like a shared emotion.

My heart was beating so hard, I felt as if I had just run a race, as if I were flushed with it, and when I looked at Julie and Mary, their faces were flushed as well. Their hearts, too, they said, were racing, pumping, it seemed, with mine, beating the beat of oneness.

It was also the most peaceful I had ever felt about asking for messages for others. Perhaps because Julie and Mary were with me, feeling what I felt, interactive with the process, it wasn't so individually overwhelming. To be overwhelmed with the emotion when I was alone was completely different than when I was with Mary and Julie. Together we had a strength and a courage I did not have alone. Alone I felt an awesome responsibility; I experienced all those feelings of, *Who am I to be able to do this?* With them I felt only the miracle of it.

There was a peacefulness to it instead of an anxiety. I felt it immediately. And there was also a credibility. If any doubts lingered, they were now gone. We had not only received words, we had received feelings, and we had shared them. We had not only received words, but words that confirmed what we already knew: that we were connected. For Trinity had spoken almost the same words, about drinking from the well, to Mary once before, unbeknownst to me. And it seemed as if the words, given to her again through *my* fingers, were a gift that said, "Yes. You are connected. If you needed further proof, here it is."

And here it is—Trinity's words to Mary on June 17, 1995, which she did not share with me until December, when I began this book.

You are a well of love. Dip into the well and take a drink! Feel the coolness of the water, savor the taste of the water, let your body sing with this delight, this awakening. Put the ladle back. Lower the bucket. Know that the well is there for you always, with the cool, soothing, refreshing liquid of love.

Yet it wasn't only the words but also the tone of the words. Mary said that she could tell, feel, sense the change immediately when Trinity began to speak. She had been writing to Trinity for four months. She knew his voice. She *recognized* his voice. That I could access that voice, that my fingers could type Trinity's messages, was a miracle to her. It was the greatest sign any of us had had that we were connected by something beyond ourselves.

It was much later still before I realized the full impact of the messages. I had always seen or envisioned the messages as coming directly to me from the angels. Even though I was overwhelmed with emotion every time I had spoken to Peace or Water for Julie, I had not known where that emotion came from. I had remarked on it to Julie, to Mary. I was puzzled that I generally felt more emotion when I asked about Julie's concerns than when I asked about my own. It wasn't until the end of the year, when Mary asked Trinity a question for me, that the truth began to reveal itself. Because Trinity told Mary she was feeling my energy. And Mary knew that she was.

Even then I didn't see. I credited Mary's feeling my energy as a unique talent that she had, something produced by her awareness and interest in energy. But eventually I came to see, to know, that the overwhelming emotions I experienced when I asked for Julie were Julie's own overwhelming emotions.

This wasn't a lesson of this retreat, but it was a lesson so huge that not to mention it here would be to dilute the full measure of this story's message. Because the realization that another's feelings, energy, emotion, and spirit were accessible was a truly miraculous realization, more miraculous to me than that of being able to access a divine spirit. Because I had thought of divine spirits as different. Angels, after all, were not human, were not ordinary. Their function, if I could guess on it based on my limited experience, was to be message bearers.

I would have thought, before this realization came to me, that Julie's function was so entirely different, so entirely separate from my own, that communication of this sort between us would have been impossible. Nothing in what I had read had prepared me for this—not even the messages of other spirits such as Emmanuel or Orin. Yet I knew it was true and Julie, when I told her, knew too—in fact, had known at some inner level all along.

I was taken aback by this knowledge, newly amazed at Julie's courage, at her openness. If I had realized Mary would feel my energy when she spoke to Trinity for me, would I have asked it of her? This was the deepest possible knowing. And its implications went beyond anything I felt ready to deal with. It spoke to the very lessons we had been learning all along, but it changed everything. I thought I had realized our connectedness the previous spring. I hadn't.

Mary and Julie were more circumspect about this new dimension. And it was because they *had* realized the connectedness last spring. They knew they shared a bond, that they were connected in a way that I had no concept of until I realized I had felt Julie's emotional energy. I didn't understand how they could have dealt with this concept so easily, this concept that changed everything. But it hadn't necessarily been easy for them either. They had just been dealing with it longer than I. They had known almost from the beginning what I didn't learn until the end of the year. . . .

Those unseen connections we had talked about were

real! And they said something about the nature of the universe itself. They said something about the nature of us ordinary humans. They said just what I had said here, earlier, thinking I understood it when I didn't understand it at all: that we are not meant to be separate and alone. Are not meant to be alone and lonely. For we must be joined. If I am to believe my own experience, I must believe, too, that we are not as ordinary as I once had thought. That something links us. Something that makes us accessible to one another.

XIX
SAFETY

As I left work a few days after the retreat, still trying to define the new feeling of peacefulness that had come over me, the word *safe* came to mind. I realized "safe" was how I had felt since the cabin. The next day I went into work and told Julie how I had defined what I was feeling as safe, and she got that "this is unbelievable" look on her face, and she said safe was exactly how she had felt. Finally, Mary came back to work after having been out sick for two days, happy, glowing, warm, so excited to talk to us she was ready to bust. She had gotten safety out of the weekend too, and she had never expected to feel safe again after her daughter's death.

The power of what had happened at the cabin stayed with us. And it led me to take a class that began in late September, a class titled "Ways of Knowing."

When I saw the title of the class in the university bulletin, it seemed as if it was meant for me. I had discovered, through Julie, the *Noetic Sciences Review,* a journal that explores our "ways of knowing," even before I discovered its president, Willis Harman. And through the journal I had found more readings to accompany me on my journey. Here was science, once again, exploring the same ideas that I was exploring in the context of spirituality. A science that seemed open to the limitless possibilities of the human mind, the human subconscious.

One of the reasons I decided to take the class was my new feeling of being safe in the world. And it seemed that the place of safety was as good a place as any from which to rejoin that world. The inward journey had been going on for nine months: the length of a pregnancy. It seemed time to give birth to this new self I had been becoming. To bring it into the world and see what it would find there and what it would be.

I was not alone in either my feeling of safety or my desire to take advantage of it. We had all found it during our spirit sister retreat and we all found it a luxury we could not afford to waste. At times it felt as if it were a new car or a shiny new sailboat or some space-age vehicle that would know the most expeditious route to where we were going. At other times, it felt like a place from which we could launch ourselves, a place of sure-footing, an even ground from which we could get a running start. It was like being handed a break, like an athlete being seen by a scout. It was a window of opportunity, transparent with possibility. It seemed to call us to venture into the world again.

While in reality we had never left the real world of ordinary life, the feeling of safety seemed to contradict this notion of reality. It seemed to say we had. That we had been somewhere else. We had visited a foreign land and now we were home safe. Safe. We had been in retreat all along and now it was time to forge ahead. It seemed to say we were *ready!* It seemed to say *begin!*

We had a new and different energy level that we yearned to expend on what was important. Work became something to get done in a hurry so that we could go on to other things. And amazingly, it did get done in a hurry. We became extremely efficient. We started talking about completing tasks in terms of minutes rather than days and hours. "Oh, I can have that mailing, that memo, that budget done in seven minutes." Sometimes it was a joke. Sometimes it wasn't. Mary began to have dreams in which I was always on vacation and she was always getting twice as much work done at superhuman speed. I began to have retreat dreams. Over and over, dreams of being at a lodge or cabin with women friends surrounding me, with time and space to *be* surrounding me.

The only problem was that we still weren't sure what, besides the spiritual journey, was important. I was stymied in my writing because I could not tear myself away from the Peace writing long enough to pursue new projects or decide what to do about either the old or the new. So I chose a class. Mary, while trying for a new baby, was looking for ways to turn the ordinary into the beautiful. Julie was on her way to realizing music played some part in her destiny. We all wanted to begin. We could not begin fast enough. But what were we to do?

The quest had subtly changed from one of "Who am I?" to one of "What am I to do with who I am?" The feelings of it were just as primal, just as spiritual. Julie was no longer content to receive a paycheck for a job. She sought a calling!

What was our purpose? What did God have in mind for us? What was our contribution to be? What unique talents did we possess that the world was waiting for? Although the angels seemed to have been telling us that the world was simply waiting for us, the real us, to emerge, we added a spin in one part unique to our culture and our time, in one part universal. This place of safety seemed to call us to not just be, but to be all we could be, the best we could be. It seemed to say, jump in, the water is fine.

I bring up my class again because it was largely a class on philosophy. It looked at the great thinkers of the past and how they determined how we know what we know. Then it looked at present-day thinkers, many of them women, many of them women of color. People who came at our ways of knowing from a completely different place than men of old. It excited me. I inwardly applied all the arguments to spirituality and felt that I kept validating what I knew. It was invigorating. Until I wrote a paper discussing how our ways of knowing are different when we approach them from a place of safety. Until I realized the professor had no idea what I was talking about.

My vocabulary had changed. It was different. The same words had new meaning. This had been happening to Mary, Julie, and me all along, but I had not realized how complete the transformation was until that moment. I realized no one in academia would understand what I knew unless I talked about God. Unless they understood the new meanings everything had. This discouraged me from the class, but it added a new dimension to my reality. I had changed. My world had changed. My *words* had changed. And the only ones who understood the change were my spirit sisters.

Mary perhaps came closest to describing safety when she called it a "way of being." We did not realize we had not felt safe before because we had not realized how safety felt. None of us had ever experienced it, either within ourselves or with anyone else. It was like realizing that we had spent our whole lives waiting for the next bad thing to happen and that this hadn't been a passive waiting. We had waited with anxiety, with the feeling of lurking danger or disaster. Our lives had been, until this point, about trying to keep the next bad thing from happening, trying to stay one step ahead of the game, trying to be prepared for the worst.

But for Mary, when Grace died, the worst had literally happened. And, as much as anyone other than her family could, Julie and I had been through the worst with her.

And now here we were, feeling safe. What had happened?

Waiting for the next bad thing—for the worst to happen—had felt normal before. What we had learned through Grace's life and death was that this was not normal. Now we could see it for what it was: fear. We had all been living in fear. Fear was what we had called normal.

Safety was the absence of fear. Safety was, according to the dictionary, freedom from danger, injury, or damage.

We might not have literally spent every day of our lives feeling as if we were in mortal danger, but we had spent our lives feeling that we were at the mercy of life, at the whim of fate. Fearing that for all our hard work, despite whatever minimal control we could exert, what we had to look forward to was simply the luck of the draw, was life having mercy on us. Life refraining, if we were lucky, from harming or punishing us, its offenders, its enemies, we who were in its power.

The words we used, either for or against ourselves, whether conscious or subconscious, made up our thoughts. Where our words, and thus our thoughts, had previously been full of the danger and fear, the punishment and doom we had been expecting, they now reflected our new feelings. This place of safety seemed to say that if we weren't in control, it wasn't fate or luck that was, but God.

Taking the class showed me that others did not know they were living in fear any more than Mary and Julie and I had before our retreat. This is why they could not understand safety as we understood it: because they did not understand fear. We learned that what we knew and how we knew it were different now that we were not looking at the world through fearful eyes.

The Ways of Knowing class had been about what and whom we trusted. Did we come to feel we knew what we knew by listening to what experts thought? by listening to the media? by studying history and philosophy? What proof did we need to convince us of new knowledge? Whom did we trust? Who was the final authority? Everything was suspect. Especially us. Especially our own ways of knowing. No one even asked if we trusted ourselves. It was as if everything that was knowable was outside of ourselves.

The experiences of our year had taught us to know things on a new level. To know from within, based on our own internal authority rather than on any external authority. What we had learned together had given us more than any class we had ever taken—more than the combined knowledge we had acquired from years of schooling. It was our first inkling that knowing ourselves was what it was all about.

And, as if to prove that now that we were safe we were also ready, real life intervened and pushed us from the nest. We had literal journeys to embark upon in October. Mary and I would go to New Orleans, Julie to San Francisco. We would return and all of us would depart for Europe. It was that time of year on the calendar. It was work once again. Work that couldn't be compressed into seven minutes. It was life and we looked forward to it. A literal journey to correspond with our inward journeys. To bring us back into the world.

XX

CONTEMPLATION

Before our spirit sister retreat, I had discovered the word *contemplation*. In James Hillman's *Insearch: Psychology and Religion,* I read: "Curiosity about fact and detail gives way before the open contemplation of what is, just as it comes."[4]

We had gone to the retreat with contemplation. We went forward on our worldly journeys with a state of contemplation as well, a state not active but open. We were together for a part of our journeys, apart for a longer period. What we each contemplated was totally different. How we each reacted was totally different. But the result was the same.

The part of our literal journeys when the three of us would be together would be spent in Barcelona. Two firsts were occurring. We had never before had our jobs offer us the opportunity to travel as a threesome, and we had never before had the chance to travel overseas. We did not go alone, however. My mother and I had long planned a trip to Italy to visit relatives. Being in Barcelona for work afforded me the opportunity to make the trip to Italy more cost effectively and I asked her to join me. From there sprang the idea of also having Mary's mother accompany us. The two mothers could keep each other company while we worked. And finally, Julie brought her husband, Kelly.

We had talked excitedly for months of the possibilities that awaited us. Because we were contemplating something new, something none of us had done before, we had no expectations except those of pleasure. We would be together. We would be in life and away from our ordinary lives. Anything could happen. And it did.

We had barely entered the lobby of our hotel when the unexpected occurred. Julie, catching up with a woman attending the symposium we were putting on, brought out her pictures of her new baby, the now one-year-old Peter. And Mary plummeted. She had no pictures to share.

Pictures had been shared before. Peter had visited the

office. Mary had felt no pain. Mary looked at Peter and imagined how Grace would be. He was a visual representation of how Grace would have been had she lived. Mary looked on him with awe and wonder. She rejoiced in the love that visibly linked Peter and his mother, knowing that the same love linked her and Grace in a different way.

But now she mourned anew. Now the pictures were a reminder that Grace wasn't with her. There was no explaining why the pain had waited, why the pictures shared in a lobby in Barcelona more than a year after Grace's death had triggered a fresh bout of mourning. But there was also no denying it.

Mary did not want her pain to affect us. She isolated herself. When she wasn't working, she was in bed. Crying. She fought with her mother. We each wondered what had caused Mary's mood. We each asked, "Is something wrong?" But this time Mary could not share her feelings. She could not say, "Julie shared her pictures of Peter and I had none to share." So she said nothing.

Mary grew angry and sought to understand her anger. She grew sad and sought to understand her sadness. She was on vacation, she "should" have been enjoying herself. But the sadness had waited. The anger had waited. They had waited for her to be open to them; then they waited for her to identify them before she could go on.

Julie's experience was similar.

Julie traveled on from Barcelona with her husband on

what should have been a second honeymoon, a time of relaxation and joy. But she could not relax, could not enjoy. She found she did not know how to *be* without her children, without the mother and worker roles she played in her everyday life. She was not happy and she was mad that she was not happy.

For me, having expected to share the pleasure of the journey with my two friends, their discomfort was a source of perplexity and insecurity. What was wrong? Why weren't they sharing what was wrong? In order to enjoy my vacation, I had to let Mary's feelings be Mary's feelings, Julie's be hers. I had to accept that I could not fix things—that some things just had to be allowed to be what they were. I went on from Barcelona with this thought in my mind. I went on seeking added meaning for my spiritual quest. I found it.

How could anyone be luckier than to go to Rome, to Assisi and Florence and Milan in the middle of a spiritual quest? I could not fail to see that the glory of God and the glory of humanity were reflective of one another. I could not fail to see that the "faithful" who flocked to holy places were seekers, just as Julie, Mary, and I were. I felt a connection to God and to the whole.

What we each contemplated was totally different. How we each reacted was totally different. But the result was the same: gratitude.

XXI

GRATITUDE

Appropriately, it was in November, at the time of Thanksgiving, when we reached a place of gratitude. We had gone out into the world and had returned grateful. Each in our own way.

Mary, who had returned from the trip first, found her gratefulness first.

She had finally allowed herself to feel her sadness, to embrace her anger. In all the time since her daughter's death, throughout all we had shared, Mary had withheld her anger, had withheld that deep, wrenching, heart-breaking sadness of grief. She had withheld it from us because she had been holding it all within. Now she had felt it and released it. Now she had allowed herself to move through it and to reach the other side. Having done so allowed her to feel closer to herself, to know all the sides of her humanness and make them one. She had felt the emptiness of what she didn't have and moved past it to gratitude for what she did have.

Julie, the next to return, returned determined. Her photographs of her trip told the whole story. There she was, a person unable to enjoy herself. Now she was home and she was going to be different. She was determined. She was going to enjoy what she had.

I waited two days after I returned from Europe to call anyone. I waited because I did not want anything to disturb me. I had at last found joy! And it was, as Peace had been telling me, right in front of me. It was what I had. It was my ordinary life, my present. It was found in appreciation for what I had just as soon as I quit longing for what I didn't have.

When I began to call people, I would tell them, "These past few days have been the happiest of my life." People expected to hear about Europe. I could hardly quit talking about home.

I knew my contentment with the present, that my joy, was fragile. Part of it centered on my foresight at planning my vacation so that it extended through Thanksgiving week. I could be a hermit for a few days. I could live within my own personal heaven. I could wipe my counters, polish my furniture, hold my husband, kiss my children, putter around my house, listen to my music, look out the window at my yard, the same trees, the same birds, the new beauty of it all.

We were going to host Thanksgiving for my husband's family. Our first holiday in our new home. Yet I did not think about it, in those first days.

Christmas was approaching. I generally had my shopping done by this time. Yet I did not think about it, in those first days.

I avoided the newspaper, especially the advertisements. I avoided television. I avoided thinking about paying my post-trip bills. I just *was* for a few glorious days.

Then I phoned the office. I told Mary, as I had told everyone else, that I was happy, grateful, so appreciative of my home and family. She told me she and Julie had felt the same way on their return. All the spirit sisters were grateful!

When I talked to Mary on the phone, I could tell that whatever place she had been at in Barcelona no longer existed. She had not needed to tell me she was happy. I could hear it in her voice as clearly as, I'm sure, she could hear my happiness in mine.

And I could feel the difference the instant I saw Mary and Julie again when I went back to work after Thanksgiving. I knew that our relationships had proceeded to a higher level, that everything was good between us. I knew it was not just me. We had, at least with each other, transcended our ordinary shortcomings. No pettiness remained. No barriers. We were grateful for each other.

I hadn't often remembered, during my travels, my night-time prayer: "I am not separate; I can trust; I can know; I am responsible; I am single-minded. My greatest desire is to know the desire of my higher will." But now it came to mind and made me realize what was different.

That final line was what it had all been about for each of us in the past few months. *Knowing.* And I came to see that what was new was our understanding that knowing would come when the time was right. Accepting that we would know. Somehow, our return from our travels had ushered in a time of finding the value of patience, of stillness, of waiting, and of doing it with gratitude rather than resentment. We hoped our wanting to know was a desire that sprang from contemplation, a desire to serve. And we realized that, perhaps for now, it was service to ourselves and our families that was required.

We weren't any more sure of anything than we had ever been. We were still just ordinary women. But we accepted that we did not know what was to be and did not have to know.

What we each had found was that gratitude was not possible without a prerequisite. That prerequisite was acceptance.

We became safe. We went out into the world. And we

returned, first, foremost, and finally, accepting. We were so grateful, we leapt right over the act of acceptance to enjoy our gratitude. We almost missed it.

But could Mary ever really feel gratitude without accepting the death of Grace? Could Julie ever really feel gratitude without accepting where she was at the present time and how she had come to be there? Could I feel gratitude while I continued to believe my happiness rested on an external such as being a published writer?

Acceptance. And through acceptance of what *was* we were released from the final barriers to our connectedness. The envy, competition, distrust, hurt feelings that had come and gone throughout our year together were to be no more.

We had finally accepted ourselves—as we were—all of ourselves. We no longer said I accept this but I don't accept that. We would still wonder, we would still question, but we would find that wondering and questioning did not shake our acceptance. We accepted ourselves. And from the acceptance of our *selves,* we finally, completely, totally, accepted one another.

XXII
GIVING

As Christmas approached, we each tried to turn our backs on commercialism, to do Christmas right, and to find ways to be moved by the real message of Christmas. And surprisingly, we each found it for ourselves by beginning to understand the phrase "give and you shall receive."

I had always thought the saying was a little odd—as if the purpose of giving was to receive something in return. But it was not about that at all. What it meant was give and you will receive *through* your giving. My spirit sisters and I had been learning this lesson all along. The biggest lessons were yet to come.

Giving, like sharing, like suspending judgment, had two sides to it.

The first began with giving as we commonly know it. The giving of a gift, a bit of advice, compassion, humor, knowledge. We thought this kind of giving was what our year had been about. Until we saw that our giving had gone beyond this giving as we commonly knew it. The Christmas season showed us how much we received *through* our giving. That true giving was circular in motion.

With one another we were teachers and learners equally. By being so we realized we never lost one thing by giving. That we *had to* give in order to receive. That the more we gave the more we got. The more we gave the more we grew. That in being open to one another as teachers, as learners, we had given of ourselves. Not parts of ourselves. All of ourselves. Because we were no longer divided, because we no longer saw one part of ourselves as good enough to give and another part as unworthy of giving, we truly gave for the first time in our lives and just as truly received.

It was no accident, no coincidence that we had learned each lesson of the year together, simultaneously, that we were in sync. It couldn't be any other way because what we gave we received and what we received we gave. Circular.

We didn't *make* confessions to one another. We *gave* them. And how we benefited through our giving! We rid ourselves of painful burdens we had carried at the same time that we gave a gift that said, I trust you, I want to be *who I am* with you. By *giving* our confessions, we *could* be who we were. We saw that what we had so long held on to in fear and in pain, *could* be given up. That all the energy we had used to suppress what we thought we could not reveal could be freed. That we could reclaim the power we had given those things over us. From the simple act of *giving* our confessions, so much was received in return! From giving confessions, we learned to *give* forgiveness—a giving that, in true circular fashion, returned to us so that we could eventually give forgiveness to ourselves.

We didn't come to know hope and sharing and connectedness through some form of osmosis. We came to know through the act of giving and through the act of receiving. And we found that the gifts we gave kept *on* giving. They stayed with us. Once we began to forgive ourselves, that forgiveness reached into our pasts to forgive all of ourselves, reached into our pasts to forgive others, and came into the present to forgive as we went along. The suspension of judgment, too, was a gift—a gift for life. We would never be done with it, anymore than we would be done with forgiveness. What we gave and what we received, like what we learned, would be forever.

But there was another side to giving that was equally important. The other side of giving was *giving up.*

Trinity had asked Mary to give up trying. To give it to him. Peace often asked me to give things away, things like guilt and worry. Water had urged Julie to make a pet of her fear until the time came when she could give it up for good.

It was about *giving up* control. We didn't have it anyway. But while we thought we did, we struggled. It was about laying down our burdens so that we could quit struggling and rest. So that we could get closer to that still, quiet voice within.

It was another way of saying let go. Let go of those things that did us no good—like judgment and guilt. We just hadn't yet learned that it also applied to our greatest desires and fears.

XXIII

ANSWERS

The end of our year began to reveal itself as being about confronting our greatest desires and our greatest fears. We were all seeing that our jobs were no longer enough, could no longer be our goal and our mission. Our purpose. And we were each seeing that this left a void. Something had to take its place. We turned to our greatest desires to fill the space of goal and mission our jobs no longer filled. We turned to our greatest desires to give us our purpose. The first lesson we learned was that our greatest desires *were* our greatest fears.

Mine was writing. Mary's was mothering. Julie's was expressing herself.

They were all about producing something to fill the void. Something to fill our lives, to give them meaning, to take up our time, to enable us to make a contribution. They were all about externals.

Being asked to confront our greatest desires, our greatest fears, showed us what power they had over us. They had power because we gave it to them. We gave these things the premier position of being our *answers.* Being a published writer was the *answer* for me. Being a mother the *answer* for Mary. Finding a means of expression the *answer* for Julie.

No matter how different our greatest desires and fears were, they were all, in the end, about the same thing— they were about having an answer, a solution to the problem of not seeing where we were as good enough.

As much as we were shaped by our culture, influenced by the best-seller list and other trends, we were also part of a culture in which we had begun to refer to ourselves as things such as consumers and products. We had started to believe that it was our culture, our education, our families that had produced what we were, and if we were not producing in turn, we were doing nothing, were nothing.

So integral was this belief to our culture, to our nation, to our very way of life, that we did not see it as being as insidious as it was. Mary wrote in her journal about her need to produce; about how a good day was a day during which she had been productive. Julie lamented over being unable to produce all she desired because of her young children. When my greatest desire/greatest fear took me over, it no longer mattered to me that I loved to write if the pages I wrote weren't in a form I could turn into a product.

We had not yet separated our thinking from that of a culture that valued producing and consuming above all else. We were, in fact, so entrenched in it that even in the midst of the transforming events of our year, we *stopped* in order to discover what to *do*—in order to be productive.

We had been seeking purpose. Where was it? Somewhere beyond our grasp, outside of the office, outside of the three?

We were all mothers. We were all educated and saw the way our children were educated. Education, like so much else in our culture, was about production. How many worksheets on math, spelling, history did our children do in a week? Our children's productions became their grades, became their success or lack thereof, became who they were. Our jobs were about producing. Education for adults was about getting jobs or keeping them: being productive. The goals were all "out there" somewhere. Waiting. Even education had become about production instead of about understanding. And production was becoming increasingly about information.

It was as if we were being told that when we collected

enough information, we would know what to do. Information was the "in" thing and the wave of the future. It was all there waiting on the Internet, the World Wide Web, the information highway. That call to connect electronically. To see ourselves as machines, the brain being the computer control center. And to see things as animate; the computer with its brain, as susceptible to viruses as the human body.

So it was that I didn't see right away that I had begun to expect the angelic messages to be another source of information. I didn't see that my questing had become one of looking for facts as I would look for an answer in an encyclopedia. My seeking for one answer had blinded me to everything except what I sought to find.

My spirit sisters knew of my desires, as I knew of theirs, and had similarly looked for answers from the angels. Julie had asked more than once for me to talk to Peace about her purpose. His answer invariably had been for her to seek within for her answer, even while offering clues that were tantalizing. Mary had asked if she would have another baby. Her answers seemed to suggest that she would but still she waited.

When our greatest desires/greatest fears took us over, we could not *see* that no answer would be good enough, we were simply driven to seek an answer. Since I had asked about my writing dilemma so many times from Peace without satisfaction, I even turned to Mary. If I couldn't get the information I sought out of Peace, maybe she could get it out of Trinity. I asked her to ask Trinity for advice on my writing. Why was I stuck? In which direction should I go? Mary asked and Trinity answered:

Her writing will unfold as a flower does. You will see. Will be there.

Go to your dreams. You SEE. You know. Margaret looks too hard at what already is in front of her—around her, within her. Look to your dreams. This is not difficult. It unfolds, as a flower does.

Patience is a friend during this time—especially for Margaret. It is there. Trust. BELIEVE.

This trust is paramount. As you see you share, all of you do, this unfolds. The story unfolds. You trust, you share, you grow. This is life. This is what dreams are made of. This is LOVE.

I thanked Mary and Trinity for this response, but because I was looking for *my* answer, an answer I believed I already knew even while I sought for it, I did not *see* Trinity's response for the answer that it was.

I continued my reading, continued my searching, all with an eye to supporting my goal, to defining and clarifying my answer. What I didn't realize, what Mary and Julie didn't realize, was that we had to separate production from purpose or we would never be happier than we were, more content than we were, be more than we were. We would always be seeking. We would never realize what we had found.

XXIV
TRUST

We knew we had been caught up in extraordinary events. We knew these events had been improving our lives. We knew we were kinder, more peaceful, more loving, more accepting. Life felt easier, gentler, more meaningful. But we thought that without an external purpose, something was incomplete, that *we* were incomplete.

Even while we sought what we thought would make us complete, a part of each of us tried not to pin our hopes on those things—because those things might not come to be. I might not ever be published. Mary might not ever conceive. Julie might not ever discover her calling. We tried to be content with where we were and what we had, we *were* more content than we had ever been, and yet our very belief in a more loving God, a more loving universe, made us, at the same time, more hopeful than ever before. It seemed as if we were caught in a double bind: we knew we should be accepting and happy in our present lives, but how did we reconcile present happiness with future longing? If God made us who we were, didn't our desires also come from Him?

We each now had an expectation of happiness. Fulfillment seemed to be a promise that was held out by this new life we had begun to experience. We simply could no longer believe that our ordinary lives and our work at the university were all that were available to us.

We knew there was more to life than what we had earlier expected and had been willing to accept. Where a year previously I had been willing to accept the notion of eventually retiring from the university, this no longer seemed an adequate use of the life God had given me. While Julie had been previously content to make a living, now she expected that she had something unique to offer and that she would not be fulfilled until she could discover what that was and accomplish it. Mary thought the least of her future work life because it seemed her life would go unfulfilled if she could not give the love and nurturing she had found within herself to another child.

Despite the events of our transformative year, we were still living our lives as if what happened in them was up to us. Still living our lives as if we knew what would make us truly happy. Still living as if . . . if we but wished for it, willed it, planned for it . . . we could make it be.

We were still living our lives as if we knew what our answers were.

This is where all the lessons of the previous year had to come together. This is where we had to integrate what we had learned into our lives. The feelings we had experienced earlier concerning going out into the world while still preparing had been accurate. We hadn't been ready yet, because we hadn't put it all together yet. As much as we thought we had been listening, as much as we thought we had been hearing, when it came to our greatest desires/greatest fears, what we had really been doing was saying, "Thanks very much for your answer. Now what about my answer?"

We had recognized a force greater than ourselves at work in the universe, but we hadn't fully realized the impact of that force upon our lives. The totality of our connection to it. Its link with us. Its power.

We hadn't really recognized God. We hadn't yet invited Him in.

For before this point, the learning really had been about ourselves. About our humanness, about living the day-to-day ordinary life.

Now the learning was about something greater than ourselves. About our divinity rather than our humanity, about living the day-to-day life in an extraordinary rather than an ordinary way. While we continued to think in ordinary terms, we would limit ourselves to the ordinary.

While I continued to think finding a publisher for my mystery novel would be the ultimate achievement of my life, while Julie continued to think finding her calling was hers, while Mary continued to think having a baby was hers, we were limiting ourselves. We could see it when we looked at each other. Mary and I could see that Julie would never *be* her career, no matter how fulfilling she found it; Mary and Julie could see that one book or twenty on the bookshelves would not define my life; Julie and I could see that Mary would always be more than a mother whether she had another child or not.

Now was the time for letting go of our ordinary ideas about ourselves. Now was the time for seeing that if we could truly suspend our judgment, Someone else would judge for us and judge us good and innocent; if we could really forgive ourselves, we could be worthy of what He might offer us; if we could really surrender, we could rest.

If we could trust, Someone else who really knew what would make us happy would plan for us.

It wouldn't be up to us anymore. It had never been up to us anyway.

On the day we began our spiritual retreat, I had purchased

the book *A Course in Miracles* and had been reading it daily ever since. On December 18, after failing to find the answer to my greatest desire/greatest fear, after failing to come to peace with my writing, I felt hopeless for the first time. Everything in my life was better. Everything except this. My greatest desire/greatest fear, like the desires and fears of Mary and Julie, had produced nothing but conflict. It seemed that these desires and fears were the only things that could still lead any of us out of peace. We would be moving along just fine and then these desires, these fears, would trip us up. We would become frustrated with not being able to force what we wanted out of our lives. Like a revolving door, we would start with the Why questions again: Why couldn't I publish? Why couldn't Mary conceive? Why didn't Julie know what she wanted to do?

It was something we were all beginning to see clearly but that we were unsure what to do about.

My hopelessness of December 18 led me to pick up *A Course in Miracles* and find within it a passage that told me I could give all of my decisions to the Holy Spirit. That He would solve any problem in the way that was best for everyone that would be affected by it. And in my hopelessness, I said take this from me. I don't want to be conflicted about it anymore. You decide if I should write or not, or if I should write, what I should write. I had realized that if I could not have peace *and* writing, it was the writing I would give up.

What I did that night was give up the illusion that I was

in control of my life. It was totally different than giving up guilt or judgment. Without realizing it, the lessons of the year had finally come together in my mind and heart.

XXV
PURPOSE

On December 19, 1995, I knew this book would be written. The decision was made at my kitchen table over a conversation with my friend Mary Love.

It was a day on which I was going to go Christmas shopping. I had written a list, even though I had been trying to give up making lists in favor of doing. Angela, who had just gotten her driver's license and just as quickly lost her head over the ensuing freedom, was consequently taking the bus that morning. I didn't have to drive her to school. This was the first break in my routine.

I also wasn't scheduled to work; I had taken vacation for the week, and before the shopping day began, I was going to roll out cookie dough that I'd prepared the day before and left chilling in the refrigerator. I didn't know if it was because of these things I had planned to do or if it was for other reasons that I felt anxious, but I did. And I'd come to a place already, by this time, where I expected to be able to control anxiety or at least to determine where the anxiety was coming from.

Because of this anxiety, I sat down to a bowl of cereal and a book. It was before eight and I told myself that at eight I would get up and go about my business. But the anxiety persisted, along with a desire to talk to Mary. I realized, eventually, that I was biding my time, waiting for her to arrive at work so that I could call her. Just as quickly, I realized that if I invited her, she might join me for coffee before she went to work. I phoned her and she said she'd come.

I was still in my robe and the pajama top in which I had slept. I didn't feel a need to dress but I slipped on my pajama bottoms, made a fresh pot of coffee, did up the breakfast dishes, and put Christmas cookies on the table. When Mary still hadn't arrived, I decided I had time to set a mood and put on classical Christmas music and lit some incense. Appropriately, it began to snow. The morning was just growing light and the Christmas tree sparkled in front of my large living room window as Mary came in the door.

As soon as Mary came to my table, I knew why she had come, why I had felt anxious. I needed to tell her of my decision of the night before, of the place I had reached, both with my spiritual quest and my desire and fear of writing. Because what had felt like frustration the night before, in the morning light felt bigger than that. I knew some shift had occurred but I didn't know what it was.

Mary did. Mary not only understood, but said she had awakened to a message for me. That message was, *This is the story.*

Mary said she knew that what was meant by "the story" was *our* story, what was happening to us, the story of the spirit sisters, the story of what could happen to three ordinary women. As if to emphasize the rightness and certainty of the message, Mary's voice took on an otherworldly presence, an echo, a power. *This is the story.* There was no uncertainty. Nothing like it had ever happened to either of us before.

And I realized, right then, right there, that Mary was giving me my answer from the Holy Spirit. I had asked him to make my decision and He sent me an answer the very next morning. He sent me Mary and she knew what I was to *do.*

She, like me, was afraid to have what she *knew* taken for knowledge, taken for *the answer*. She worried, *What if it just came from me?* But I wasn't the only one who knew. Sitting in the morning light at my kitchen table, warming our hands on round little blue coffee cups, we could not deny that we knew. Because we could not deny that a new place had been reached within us. A place of trust. A place not of trusting in *our* answers, but of trusting in God's answer.

On December 19, the writing that had long been my goal was given to me like a gift. Another giving that I received in friendship, as an act of friendship. I thought it was the ultimate gift, given because I had reached the ultimate place, the place of trust. It felt like the ultimate gift because I had asked and had been answered. I felt as if for the first time in my life I knew exactly what to do, I was certain about something, there was no doubt in me. If this was what it was like to have a relationship with God, I knew there was nothing better.

But feeling as if we had reached a place that couldn't get any better was familiar by now. It was a feeling we had experienced before at other places along the path. My spirit sisters and I had thought finding hope was the greatest place until we found "suspend judgment," and that the suspension of judgment was the greatest thing going until we surrendered, and that surrender was the ultimate feeling until we arrived at safety, and gratitude the very best of places to be until we found trust.

As great as I felt to have my answer, that answer still had only been one of knowing what to do. Perhaps part of the reason that I was given such a clear answer was so that we would all learn to separate production from purpose. We all might have a unique contribution to make, a divine "something" to do in our lives, but what we do is still not what we are. The product we would produce, while it might become our goal for a little while, could not sustain us.

We each needed to realize that seeking purpose outside of ourselves was not what it was all about. Seeing our purposes as producing something outside of ourselves was just another error in judgment.

Purpose is innate. Something everyone has. Universal. As unseen as love. It wasn't "out there." It was inside. It wasn't about producing. It was about being.

Purpose doesn't change. Purpose has to go deeper than goals to find stability. Goals change. They aren't always meaningful. They are sometimes accidental. They often involve settling for less—settling for something achievable, producible.

What we came to find was that purpose is, by design, as much a part of us as our vital organs, as our spirit and soul. Something God gave us. Something we were born with.

It was something little Grace had.

It was something three ordinary women found for a while and almost didn't see as they searched for something else.

Purpose is something you cannot lose, so it cannot be a job or money or even a calling or a dream. Purpose is something that cannot fail, so it cannot be a goal one wishes to achieve but may not. Purpose is something that cannot be taken away, so it cannot be another person, or a home, or even the respect of others.

Purpose has to be inside the heart, the soul, the spirit. Because purpose is about *who we are* and how we choose to live—in whatever circumstance. It is about the intentional effect our lives have on others—as little Grace's life affected each of ours. It is about living our lives as God intended them to be lived rather than as we have determined they should be. Purpose is about God's intention, not ours.

To learn the final lesson of purpose, my goal of writing had to be shared with the spirit sisters. It had to be shared so that we would realize we shared a common purpose.

XXVI

LOVE

I t was in collaborating on the writing of *Love* that we learned together that the end and the goal and the purpose was the love itself.

Writing this story was an act of friendship and of love. It wasn't about me and my goal—me in the singular, my goal in the singular. It was bigger than that. It seemed for a while that it was about us. About our learning, our sharing, our combined purpose. Learning that it was bigger than all of us was the final lesson.

As we worked to create *Love* out of the story of three ordinary women, we realized that the attainment of our individual goals could not be the end, the reward, the purpose of our journeys or our lives. Our individual goals—our wanting of only one thing for only one person—as much as we might have thought of them as the most important things to us, were, finally, only goals. And goals were, finally, limits.

There is another error in our judgment much more difficult to see than that of self-criticism. It is the thinking that says that by setting a goal and achieving that goal, all is attained. When the error of this limited thinking was corrected, we saw that limiting ourselves was impossible once a combined purpose—a higher purpose—was realized.

We had needed to see and contemplate the whole story, see it in black and white—in the written form—before we could *see* with fresh eyes, the real message we had been given about purpose:

As you see you share, all of you do, this unfolds. The story unfolds. You trust, you share, you grow. This is life. This is what dreams are made of. This is LOVE.

When Trinity and Mary and the Holy Spirit, and later Peace told me my purpose was about *Love*, they were clearly telling me to write the story, to produce the story, but I was as clearly told I could not do it alone. It had to unfold from the love and the trust and the sharing of *all of us.*

When I was told my purpose was *Love,* it was the love itself that was being spoken of—not the book. It was about the effect the messages of *Love* would have in the world—not the product. It was about the love Mary, Julie, and I shared—not just the story.

Our search for one answer, our quest for information, our desire to produce was what had kept us from seeing. Looking at our goals separately from those of each other, separately from those of the whole, was what had kept us from recognizing the connecting force that had been at work throughout the story, throughout our year. The force that connected us to each other and to the whole. That connecting force was love.

I couldn't believe, when months later I reread Trinity's message, that I had ever missed it. Trinity was right that the story was about love, and Trinity was right when he said, "Margaret looks too hard at what already is in front of her—around her, within her." I looked so hard that I didn't *see* what *was.*

I was so blown away when I reread and finally *saw* Trinity's message, that I immediately called Mary. I read Trinity's words to her over the phone at 9 P.M. on a Friday night. She gasped. We sat in awe on either end of the telephone line, me looking at the message, Mary hearing it from my voice, hearing it freshly once again. I said, "Mary, I can't believe I never saw it. I can't believe I never realized it. Love is what it's all about, isn't it, Mary?"

LOVE

Love was what everything had been about from the very beginning. From Gracie's life and death, to Julie hearing "God Bless Mary," to me opening my heart—it had all been about love. The love we gave and the love we received and the love that was surrounding us. The love that unites. The love that joins. The love that makes whole. The love that makes holy. The love that is our purpose. The love that is our Grace.

XXVII

GRACE

Grace is what happens when love and purpose come together into acceptance of ourselves as God created us and intended us to be. As we were created, we were perfect, as Grace Zuri Love was perfect. And all that is asked of us is that we return to what God created us and intended for us to be: ourselves.

As much as Julie, Mary, and I had spent the last quarter of the year searching for our purpose, we had, in a sense, missed it. For we were living our purpose.

Purpose is really about finding the self-love that allows us to see who we truly are, the self-love that enables us to look beyond ourselves with love, the self-love that allows us to act from love rather than judgment, to act from love instead of lack, to act from love instead of fear. It is about living the day-to-day ordinary life with love and grace and hope and connectedness and gratitude. It is about *trusting and sharing and growing.* It is about friendship and about extending friendship to all we meet in our day-to-day ordinary lives.

Purpose is the realization that the search for self and the search for God and the search for love are one and the same. That they are united as we are united. We had been living our purpose even when we hadn't realized it. And it was this unity of purpose that had brought us our connectedness. Unity of purpose is oneness. Unity of purpose is unity of will, is unity of mind, is unity of thought, is unity. This was the purpose that had sustained us through our beliefs in separate goals, separate journeys, separate selves.

Purpose is the realization that the search for self and the search for God and the search for love are, in their unity, about finding out who we are—in our unity. Not separately, not individually, not singularly, not alone. Our searches couldn't be separate for they had a united end. For there is only one purpose any of us can have and that is to *be who we are.* And none of us are who we are in a vacuum. Who I am is different from who Julie is. Different from who Mary is. We are different. But we are also the same.

We couldn't just concentrate on the different and find ourselves or God. We couldn't concentrate only on what was different and come to find love. We had to see the sameness, the equality, the unity, the oneness. We could each, by turning inward, find our uniqueness, but only by turning to each other, by sharing with each other, could we find our sameness. Both had to be found before we could be whole, before we could be united, before we could be who we truly are.

Being who we truly are is what allows us to meet life as it truly *is* rather than as we would have it be. It is saying "Thy will be done" rather than "I would have it be some other way." Being who we truly are is recognizing one united will. Is knowing that what God wants for us and what we want for ourselves and each other is the same— and that it is all there within our ordinary lives, just waiting for us. Waiting to be found in who we are.

Peace had told us:

Everything Gracie was was love. Pure love....

Grace, a being of love, had come into our lives with her own purpose, a purpose that was the *same* as ours. She came to *be who she was.* She came as love to give us *Love.* When Grace entered our lives, the ordinary and the extraordinary met. The human and the divine came together.

GRACE

Grace can enter your life too.

Out of the ashes life. Out of the darkness light. If it could happen to us, it could happen to anyone. This is our message.

Notes

1. Joseph Campbell with Bill Moyers, *The Power of Myth* (New York: Doubleday, 1991), 222.

2. Pat Rodegast and Judith Stanton, *Emmanuel's Book III: What Is an Angel Doing Here?* (New York: Bantam, 1994), 57.

3. Willis Harman and Howard Rheingold, *Higher Creativity: Liberating the Unconscious for Breakthrough Insights* (New York: Tarcher, 1984), 226.

4. James Hillman, *Insearch: Psychology and Religion* (Woodstock, Conn.: Spring Publications, 1994), 28.

ABOUT THE AUTHORS

Margaret Perron majored in English at the University of Minnesota where she won the Jean Keller-Bouvier Award for literary accomplishment. She has been a public relations director in the nonprofit sector and has worked in administration at the University of Minnesota while pursuing her interest in writing. She grew up in St. Paul, Minnesota, where she continues to find sustenance from her faith, her friends, and her family.

Julieanne Carver lives in Minneapolis with her husband, Kelly, and two children, Lucia and Peter. They own and operate a 10 bedroom Victorian guest residence. She holds a bsb from the Carlson School of Management at the University of Minnesota, enjoys music, quiet time (when she can get it!), and is working on several children's books.

Mary Kathryn Love lives in St. Paul, Minnesota, with her husband, stepdaughter, and four cats. She enjoys gardening and conversation, and has a deep appreciation for the quiet solitude that books and reading offer. She grew up in South America and attended high school and college in Minnesota. Love continues to write, having found this to be one of the aspects of life that contains her joy.

All three authors are currently program associates for the isp Executive Study Program at the University of Minnesota. The authors can be contacted through the web site of The Grace Foundation: http://www.gracezurilovefoundation.com

GRACE

GRACE

MARY KATHRYN LOVE

Shannon,
Grace be with
you always.
Mary Love

HAZELDEN®

Hazelden
Center City, Minnesota 55012-0176
1-800-328-0094
1-612-257-1331 (FAX)
http://www.hazelden.org

Library of Congress Cataloging-in-Publication Data
Love, Mary Kathryn, date.
    Grace / by Mary Kathryn Love.
      p. cm.
    Second work in The Grace trilogy, which the first work was
titled Love and the final work was titled Peace.
    ISBN 1-56838-157-3
    1. Love, Mary Kathryn, date—Diaries. 2. Spiritual biography—
United States. 3. Love, Grace. I. Title.
    BL73.L68A3 1997
    973.92'092—dc21

                                       97-13288
[B]   CIP

Cover design by David Spohn
Illustrations by Randy Scholes
Text design by Nora Koch/Gravel Pit Publications

Editor's note
Hazelden offers a variety of information on chemical dependency and
related areas. Our publications do not necessarily represent
Hazelden's programs, nor do they officially speak for any Twelve Step
organization.

Ten percent of the author proceeds from each sale of *The Grace
Trilogy* will be donated to The Grace Foundation, an organization
established in remembrance of Grace Zuri Love. The Grace
Foundation has as its mission *Creating art and sacredness from the ordinary.*

For more information on The Grace Foundation, visit its web site
at http://www.gracezurilovefoundation.com

This book is dedicated to two angels:

Gracie
My daughter
This is my gift to You . . .
and
Matthew
My brother
who was there to
greet you when you
arrived.

We speak of writing here, Mary. Let us examine this writing. What is it you want the world to know about your love for your daughter?

That all continues. That love transcends time and space. That I learned so much on this journey with Grace. That I am a better person to myself because of my love for her. That having you and Grace and the Holy Spirit in my life had made it worth living. That we maybe cannot understand all, but that there is a reason for everything. We just may not see it at the time. That love is all there is! I feel it! I am living proof of it!

This is what we speak of here. The freedom to choose not pain but joy! To choose joy! This can be done. Others need to understand that this can be done! You can show them and help them with this lesson, this journey—the journey of choice!

CONTENTS

IN GRATEFULNESS

I could never have made it without the love of my husband, John, who shared this experience of Grace being in our lives. I have never been closer to another human being, as I was to my husband, at the time of Grace's life. We shared something beyond intimacy. There is something we have touched as a couple that will forever be a part of our beings. To him I give my heart.

My love knows no bounds for my stepdaughter, Amanda. Somehow I felt I might not be able to love a child again, but Amanda simply would not let me do it. She knew more about living than I did. I thank her for this every day.

Margaret Perron was the first to see these letters. By gently guiding, and literally blowing dust off the pile of papers I gave her, she helped give this book life, because she believed in it. Margaret led me to Grace. I am forever grateful. Forever.

Julieanne Carver walked with me as a friend, both of us sharing our pregnancies and later the tragedy of Grace's death. In her embracing tenderness, she made me her son Peter's godmother. I love both Julieanne and Kelly, her husband, for this generous gesture.

I thank my mother, Sara Cole, who loved me as only she could, with compassion and a heart that kept me afloat when I thought I would sink and surely drown. I thank my father, Charles Cole, who has always stood by me, every minute—always wanting me to "become" who I needed to be. That time finally came.

I thank Nancy Love, my mother-in-law, for caring for me after Grace's birth. Both Jim and Nancy Love showered us with their compassion. I thank my brother-in-law Peter, for his ability to make me smile, even in the midst of deep grief.

My sister, Liz, never stopped being there for me—from Grace's birth, until the last moments of her life. Liz blessed me with her presence. I thank her husband, Dean, who in his kindness, quietly took care of things that needed to be done. I thank my brother, Charlie, who always made time to talk to me, long distance, always supporting me with his words.

I thank Shirley Koski for tenderly reading this story. I thank Mary Jane Madden, who gave me courage to continue writing, and I thank Debra Kelley, who always was with me in spirit. I thank the nurses and doctors who did all they could for Grace. Especially Sandy, Grace's nurse, who became Grace's second mother. They all loved and fought for her as much as we did. For them I am eternally grateful.

I thank the whole wonderful editorial team at Hazelden Publishing—including Dan Odegard, Steve Lehman, and Caryn Pernu, for bringing this vision to fruition, for believing in life. In particular, I thank my editor, Betty Christiansen, who with her own deep wisdom knew what to do every step of the way with this book. Her spirit is reflected in this work.

My gratefulness extends to my workplace—to Felicia who held me as I cried, to Sheila who always knew what to say, to Fonda's sensitivity, and to my boss, Vernon Weckwerth, who became a father figure to us all, allowing us to grow spiritually, even at work.

And ultimately, I give thanks to my best friend, Debra Bohnen, who dropped everything, day and night, to be by my side, who gently guided me through my pain. Though she is only mentioned briefly in this book, her place in friendship will be forever realized.

NOW

The summer heat is beginning to let up, and I know that autumn will soon be here. We live in a work-ing-class neighborhood in St. Paul. There are five homes on our side of the street. We happen to live on the corner. This summer, we have attempted to grow flowers in the backyard, but with the heat, we have seen the grass dry out and the flowers wither. All in all, though, it has been a beautiful summer.

Today I began cleaning our home. I am upstairs, with an old dust rag in my hand. I have made a mental list of all that needs to be done before school begins. For some

1

reason, as fall nears, I want to put the house in order, as if I am getting ready for something. I wonder if this is how people felt in days gone by, as they prepared for the harvest. That is how I feel, as if I am making things ready. I begin to dust.

As I am dusting, I find myself noticing the objects I am picking up. I dust the brass lamps in our bedroom, and I remember how my husband and I had each brought something, each brought a lamp, to our bedroom from our former lives. I thought of how I had bought matching maroon shades for these lamps two years into our marriage, unifying the lamps with color. My lamp is short, my husband's taller with tile work on it. Yet they come together in some type of harmony now. That makes me smile.

From the lamps, I cannot but help notice the prayer hanging above my dresser. This prayer had also hung in my grandmother's bedroom. It had been my grandmother's favorite, according to my mother, and was read at her funeral. It is the prayer by Saint Francis of Assisi. I memorized this prayer recently and noticed, for the first time, how gentle I have become with myself. Every night I would stumble on the words, attempting to remember them. I love the rhythm of these words. This prayer has come to mean so much to me.

But I am not religious.

I have always considered myself to be spiritual in some type of "modern" sense. I have always believed that there is a God. Recently, little by little, my home has begun to reflect this—a deeper side, an inner side of my nature. I see this as I dust. I know when this began. I keep dusting. . . .

I enter my writing room with the dust rag and spray the antique desk with furniture polish. This desk once belonged to my other grandmother, the one who still lives close by. I feel a pang of guilt when I think of how I rushed to get her off the phone earlier, saying I had to clean. This is something I know she can appreciate. Cleaning. I rub the desk with polish. This desk had been with my grandmother ever since I can remember. When I was eight, I told her that someday if she wanted to give it away, I would "take it off her hands." That time came, and now this desk is in my home.

I take all the objects off the desktop. I look at the seashells I once gathered on a Florida beach. I see the picture of my stepdaughter holding her cat, Bob, in an old tarnished silver frame. I dust my favorite photo of our wedding. I then dust my antique perfume bottles. I rub the front of the desk. The wood seems so rich. I have never noticed it in this light before. I put an angel picture in a cubbyhole on one side of the desk. The cutout is in the shape of a crescent moon. My hand moves inside the moon, dusting.

I love the lines of this desk.

I move on to dust a small bookcase. As I did with the desk, I take everything off this bookcase and put it on the daybed we keep for company. I spray the top with polish.

It gleams. I first place a doily back on the top. This doily, I am sure, had also been my grandmother's. It was something she made, in between raising my father and working full time at a department store, in the women's clothing department. She had been a buyer and each year she had come from Austin, Minnesota, to the Twin Cities to buy clothes. My brother and sister and I always looked great after Grandma came to visit. We always got what didn't sell at the store. But it is this handmade gift, this piece of her, that means so much to me now.

Over time this bookcase has evolved into some type of sacred place for that and other objects that have meaning for me. My stepdaughter had given me a postcard of an Indian maiden. On the back, the card read, "She is innocence and all the colors will dance within her." I don't know why it resonated with me but it did. I place it back on the bookcase too. I replace the candlesticks from my old home. Wrapped around the top of one of them is a Rosary that my dear friend Margaret gave me last summer. I am not Catholic, but through a series of events, I have become interested in Rosaries. They seem exotic to me, full of mystery. Those Catholics have such wonderful rituals to fall back on: the incense and the waving of brass containers filled with smoke—all the stuff that makes you wonder. The beads are worn on this Rosary. This was particularly appealing, since a Catholic obviously had held them and used them. They were broken in. I just do not know how to use them.

Next, I place a pair of baby booties back on the doily. These booties belonged to my baby daughter, Grace. As I touch the soft fabric, my mind goes back to the days she was in the hospital, to her short five-week life. She died two years ago this month. I place a crystal on top of the booties, and I wonder if I will keep these booties here forever. Will there ever be a time that I will put them away?

This room had been her nursery, and now it is the room in which I write to her. I call it my writing room. I think of all that has happened in this room, of all the letters I have written to Grace here. I think of how I have cried so frequently in this room. I keep dusting.

I go over everything with my dust rag—my computer, the bedside table with a prayer book, the enameled frame of the daybed. Somehow, in doing this small chore, I am honoring Grace's memory and my life. Somehow, when I work like this, I honor who I was and who I have become. All these objects I touch as I dust are a part of me. They all mean something to me—to my past—and somehow they have propelled me to this moment. To this time, this exact space, of realization.

I realize that we lose something by not touching our things, by not bringing them out to look at. In the mere act of looking, we are taken back in time. All the feelings of that time surface like waves that break on a shoreline, only to flow back to some bigger body of water. Touch brings the glance, the memory, into a more physical reality. When I touch my daughter's baby booties, I can almost imagine touching her for that second. They are so soft, just as her skin had been.

I put my dust rag away.

Now as I sit here writing, I feel the breeze come through the curtain. I have paused here, in honor. By simply dusting, this sacredness has come about. As we rush through our days, speeding faster and faster to keep pace with it all, we lose something of ourselves. I know I have. I remember the pain and then the joy of knowing my daughter—of knowing myself. I think of the love and friendships that have sprung from her short life. I don't know why, but this makes me think of God. Was it the gratefulness of this moment?

Since Grace's life and death, God has kept popping up in the most unusual places for me. . . .

I.

LOSING

BEFORE

Hello Little One, November 27, 1993

I want to let you know that I found out I was pregnant at my dear friend Deb's on November 2. I could not believe it. I was so surprised and happy. I drove home, and your father (for some reason) was out in front of the house waiting to let me in. It was a brisk evening. I ran up the steps, put my arms around him, and said, "We are going to have a baby!" I could tell he was as surprised as I was, and very pleased. He kept saying, "I don't believe it!" We were just beaming all evening and so excited. I called your Aunt Liz, my sister, and she made me tell my mother.

Your father kept trying to call your Grandma and Grandpa Love, but they were not home. Finally, we reached them, and they were as happy as we were. Today is two days past Thanksgiving, and there is beautiful snow on the ground. We put the Christmas tree up early so your sister, Amanda, could enjoy it longer. You are turning into a reality for me. I can feel that I love you already. I am so happy.

Dear One,   December 1993

Well, it's Sunday night. I have some beautiful medieval Christmas music on that your father really wanted me to play. Your sister is upstairs watching the *Flintstone's Christmas.* The house is warm and toasty as I write. The Christmas tree looks beautiful. I have felt a happiness lately that I have never felt before, and a connection to all things. Are you giving and producing those feelings within me?

Today your father and I went to a brunch for his work, and then we went to the Mall of America for Christmas shopping. We held hands and loved each other deeply. You are so lucky to have a father like him.

Let me tell you how I met your father. Twelve years ago I was interviewing for a job. Your father was standing in the office lobby as I walked through the doors for my interview. He offered me a cup of coffee. When I finished with the interview and went to the elevators to leave— there stood your father. I don't know why, but we ended up going out for lunch. And I didn't even know him!

That afternoon, he told me how he had just gotten back from Paris. He taught music there. When he came back to the United States, he found out his grandfather in Minneapolis had been very ill. So John, your father, came to the Twin Cities to care for him. Your great-grandfather eventually passed away, but your father stayed on in Minnesota.

Your father and I went out a couple of times back then. One night he made me this incredible lasagna dinner. It's funny what you remember when you look back, but this meal was perfect. It was the first meal a man had ever made for me. Your daddy played the saxophone for me that night. I could see how talented he was. Shortly after this, your father gave me a gift of a crystal heart to wear around my neck. He told me it was for courage in the future. I'll never forget that. . . .

Back then, your dad was very intense. He still is. He seemed like such an artist. He seemed so strong. As I look back now, I don't think I was ready for that type of intensity, not at first.

I went on to date and later marry another man. This marriage was very short-lived. Your father also had a brief marriage, in which his daughter Amanda was born. The odd thing about all of this was that our paths kept crossing every couple of years.

And then one day he called me at work, out of the blue. He said, "Hi, this is John Love." My heart melted. I have always loved his voice. It is so deep, so protective.

When we began dating in earnest, we were a threesome: your father, Amanda, and me.

I met Amanda before she could talk. She lived with your father part time, and so it became the three of us. When I made candlelight dinners during our courtship, it was always for three. It was when I saw your father with Amanda that I really began to love him. I saw how gentle he could be. I saw how much he loved his daughter, and it touched me deeply.

After dating for a while, your father took me to northern Minnesota under the pretense that we were going on a little getaway weekend. We arrived at this condominium on the shores of Lake Superior and he immediately wanted to take me hiking. I thought, *hiking?* But I went along with the idea reluctantly. What I didn't know was that your father wanted to ask me to marry him from one of the highest peaks in Minnesota.

I was sitting on a log, rubbing my feet in the middle of this forest when your father got down on his knees, right then and there, and proposed. I started crying and clinging to him. Your father said that I really deserved this—a total and complete proposal. . . .

We were married four months after this.

Hello little babe,   December 23, 1993

Last night we had an early Christmas at your Grandmother Sara's. Sara is my mother. We had dinner, opened presents from Liz, her husband, Dean, and Grandpa. Your sister, Amanda, got a new kitten named Bob, whom you will meet in July. She just loves him!

A week ago I was at the doctor's and heard your heartbeat. It was so strong. It made you feel like a true reality. I got tears in my eyes. Daddy and I will be celebrating our first Christmas Eve in this house. We love you.

Dear baby,   December 1993

I am so happy. Christmas is close, and I am in the middle of buying presents. I keep wrapping things and putting them under the tree. Daddy and I are going to be having my friend Julie, whom I work with at the university, and her husband, Kelly, over tonight. The best part of this is that Julie is pregnant too! Although we are nine years apart in age—I'm the older one—it feels wonderful to be able to share this experience with another woman. Julie and I compare notes, about morning sickness and what tastes good. Her baby is due right after you are. Only three days apart! Can you imagine? I tease Julie that if I have a boy—which I think you are—and if she has a girl, we could hook you two up when you're older! I get such a kick out of that—imagining you as some wonderful little boy running around, making your father and me laugh!

Dear Peanut,   January 16, 1994

We call you Peanut because a while ago, I tried to explain to your sister, Amanda, how big you were, and *peanut* was the only word that worked. So, hello little Peanut.

13

Right now, I am sitting in front of the fire, writing and listening to classical music. It is Sunday morning and the snow is falling outside. The weather has been so cold it makes you cry.

Your father is upstairs reading the paper and probably watching TV. I like the calm peacefulness after a long week at work. I saw your Aunt Liz and cousin Sarah yesterday. Sarah is growing so much. She is a sweetheart.

I have felt some movement and flutterings. I could not believe it. You seem to move when I am resting. I wonder what you are doing downstairs! Until the next time I write, dear one. I love you so much.

Dear Baby,   January 17, 1994
(a letter from your sister, Amanda)

Mom said that it was vary hard to have a baby. I'm looking forward to seeing you at age eight. I want to teach you how to talk, and read, and everything like that. I LOVE YOU.   SINSIRELY, ⌒ Amanda Love
P.S. I will help you with your homework.

Dear One,   January 17, 1994

Today, your father and I went to the doctor's and had a picture taken of you. You are so cute. You moved your legs and arms and turned around in my stomach. Your heart was going like mad. We both feel you are so much alive. We love you so much! You are coming around July 9. The nurse thought this was right. I called Grandma Sara and Aunt Liz and told them.

BEFORE

Little Peanut,   February 15, 1994

I was at the doctor's and heard your heartbeat again. I wish I could find out if you are a girl or a boy. It is in your chart, but I promised Dad that I would not really find out. I told them at the clinic not to let me know. Anyway, it is very difficult because the information is there. No problem though; either way, you will be loved. We love you now! I do wish that I could see you and say hello.

Dearest One,   March 28, 1994

Well, it has been a long time since I have written. Much has been going on. Your father and I finished your room last weekend. It took much longer than we had thought. But we got your crib up and moved the TV room downstairs. Dad is now working in the basement, getting the French doors ready for the new TV room. It is all very nice.

You have been kicking and rolling and turning like crazy. You really enjoy being up at night. Almost every night I get up because you like to move or I have to go to the bathroom. I can tell you must be getting bigger because my appetite is getting stronger. I go into the nursery and look at your bed and I think that you will be in it soon. It is such a sweet room. Right close to Dad and me.

Amanda, your sister, is at my mother's now for school break. She is playing with my brother's daughter, your cousin Emily. Emily, Aunt Betsy, and my brother Charlie (your uncle) will be reunited in Washington, DC, where

15

they have moved and bought a house. Uncle Charlie got a new job. Your Aunt Betsy wanted to finish her degree here at the university before joining him, and they did not want to have Emily switch school in the middle of the year. I wish that they did not have to move, but that is life.

Dearest child,   April 1994

I just wanted to let you know, my little baby, that you are precious to me. I feel you inside of me. So active and growing and strong. Already, you have a mind of your own. I play a game with you. I think of you and, to see if you are thinking of me, I wait for you to move and you do! There is a bond between us that even you can feel.

You have taught me so many things in such a short time. I quit smoking because I wanted your lungs to be clean. I am watching my diet so you have the right nutrients. All of this started out just for you, but it has also influenced me as to how I live my life. I want to thank you for your wisdom at such a young age. You are amazing!

You seem to like the evening hours, another trait I understand. I do my best thinking at 3 A.M The house is quiet and we have it all to ourselves as we prowl downstairs to read, to watch TV, or to simply just be who we are. No interruptions, right?

How can I tell you that having you in my life, right now, has made me a better person? That giving to you before you are born is a side of me that I never knew I had. That protecting you from harm and being your champion are things I had heard about from others, but that I felt were depths unreachable to me.

I ask myself, as I scurry through my busy days, how can all of this be happening to me? How can you penetrate through my most controlling habits and let me know that now it is time to rest, and now it is time to be active, and most of all that some things just have to wait?

Somehow you knew. You appeared in my life at just the right time, to teach me just the right things.

Darling baby,   May 1994

Tonight your father and I sat out on the back porch, the little one on the second floor. I guess people used to call them "shaker porches" because they would shake their rugs out on them. Dad and I sit out there after work and watch the clouds go by. The evenings are so beautiful. I wear an old robe and pull my hair back. Dad shows me the clouds. Honey, I think that you are bringing your father and me closer. Tonight Daddy took a picture of me with these funny glasses on. Then he wanted one of my stomach. I let him do it because it makes him happy. It is so funny, but sometimes he watches me take a bath. He sits on the floor and looks at my body. I feel so big, but he loves this miracle as much as I do. I feel this from him. He is so proud of both you and me.

We talk and talk out on that porch. I have never noticed clouds like I have recently. You and Daddy are showing me so much.

GRACE

Dearest child,   June 12, 1994

Today I went to the clinic to have an ultrasound done, because I am gestationally diabetic and the doctors wanted to know your position. I was lying in a dark room while the technician did the procedure. Suddenly she went outside for a moment, and I started feeling scared. She came back with a doctor, who then went over my stomach again with this instrument. There was so much silence in the room, and I felt one tear roll down my cheek in the dark. The doctor went over my stomach again and, again. He said things like, "Did you see the head?" and, "The heart is enlarged." The doctor then turned on the lights and told me that something was very wrong. He wanted me to see a specialist. The doctor put me in a room with Kleenex and a telephone, so I could call family members. I was so alone.

I tried to call your father but could not get through. I called Margaret, another friend I work with at the university, and I could not hold my tears back. I started crying so hard—I don't know what I told her. I remember her saying "Yes, yes, yes," like she understood. I told her how I was alone in a room with Kleenex. I felt her alarm—just like mine—I felt it through the telephone wire.

My dearest child,   June 1994

As I told you, last week I had an ultrasound during a routine checkup, and the doctor performing the ultrasound said your heart and brain looked somewhat

18

enlarged. After I went into a panic, Grandma Sara came to be with me in the waiting room, at a clinic for pediatric specialists. Your father left work to be with me. When Grandma and I saw him come through the clinic doors, we both somehow relaxed. I was so happy to see him. I was so grateful that Grandma could even sit and wait with me. We found out that things were not as bad as first portrayed.

Tonight, Dad and I were talking about you on the back porch, and we know you will be unique and strong and beautiful. I feel you move and I am so happy. Please know how much we love you and how much you have entered our lives and changed them for the better.

Dearest child,   June 1994

Last night I had a dream that scared me. I told your Aunt Liz about it when she called. I think she became upset with me. I have to write this.

I saw the face of a child—it was almost transparent and it had a golden hue to it. The face kept fading and fading until it was gone, like the still pictures of a camera. The baby was fair and its eyes looked at me. In the next scene of the dream, I saw another child's face—this time in full color, not the faded golden color of the first child. This new child's hair was dark like your father's. I knew when I awoke that something was wrong, very wrong, with the first child. That is the feeling I had. The second face was strong and healthy. I feel unnerved by this. I am now thinking maybe I will have a girl and not a boy as I had once thought. Maybe that is what this dream means.

I will write later.

Dear child,   June 1994

It has been hard for me the last two weeks. Dr. Calvin, a pediatric specialist, told me that you could possibly have a heart problem. I have been up night after night wondering what all this means, most of all to you and then to me. It has been one of the most painful experiences that I have ever undergone. Then I feel you move and I know how strong you really are. No one can ever really understand this feeling unless they have gone through the process of fear and hope. You are the sweetest of things, and I am so excited that you will be here soon. I packed our bags for the hospital.

Dear little baby,   July 1994

There has been much that has happened in the last week. Dr. Calvin told us that you may have a heart condition. I have worried so much, but I have faith in the specialists that will be close by to help. We are scheduled to be at a different hospital that specializes in these issues.

I feel you move around, and you seem to be getting ready to be born. You move at the darndest times. Usually at night. I have been up at night thinking many times. It has given me the quiet time I need. I see many beautiful things like the moon and the rising sun, and I hear all the chirping birds. This calms me in so many ways. It will be soon that we meet. I love all that you are.

I am waiting for you to be born. Your father and I have spent the weekend on hold. I could tell that your father wanted to go agate hunting but would not leave me alone in case you decided to come. I have stopped working so I can get the rest I need and also to make sure your heart will be strong enough. I have been sleeping quite a bit recently. This is all different for me because I am used to being more active, but I guess I need the rest.

I had a bad night last night. I could not sleep. I kept getting up and going downstairs. I cried, thinking that I might have done something to have caused you these problems. I keep trying to think what it was. Was I sick, and you got what I had? Maybe I didn't eat enough vegetables. Maybe it was the coffee I drank sometimes. What was it and how has it affected you? I keep worrying and wondering what it could be. I have all these thoughts in my mind. I wonder what you feel and if you can feel what I feel. I keep thinking that if you can, you may not be getting enough strength from me. I worry that, because I am worried, you will have doubts about your place in this life, and I do not mean for you to feel like that at all. I feel so bad when I have feelings of doubt, because you are not getting the positive energy that you should have from me. I have to say these things because they are true. They are a part of me—a part that I am not proud of. But please realize that this is my fear, not yours.

You will soon be independent when you are born, and I will be able to take care of you and see how you respond. It is so difficult when I am just waiting. Your father does not know what to do with me at this point. I know that he has his feelings, but he does not want to worry me. Well, I must go. Bye-bye.

GRACIE'S LIFE

My darling daughter,

You were born on July 22, 1994, at 10:30 A.M. I had been in labor for two and a half days. It was tough going then, but I knew I would see you soon, so that kept me going. I felt so close to you then. With each contraction, we were together. I could not wait to see you. Your father was there every step of the way. He stayed at the hospital with me, sleeping in a chair.

The doctors put me on potosin to go into labor because it was ten days past my due date. Each contraction was like a wave. There was some pain and then it subsided. I basically felt like I was in a different world. The only thing that kept me focused was the thought of you.

My water broke on Thursday sometime, yet my cervix never opened. By Thursday night, the doctor planned on a cesarean and I knew you would come the next day. I was calm. I knew we would be together. Your father was wonderful. He was in the operating room. You will see how soothing he is. He sat by my side and later told me he had looked into the area you came out of. He said that the space was huge. The doctor had to bat my uterus around to get it back in shape before he could put it back in my body.

After I woke up from the surgery, I was rushed to my new room, put on my bed, and then wheeled through a tunnel, which was a city-block long, to see you. I was under morphine for pain by this time. When I laid eyes on you, I thought God had given me the most wonderful, unique angel I had ever seen. You were so beautiful and perfect. You were incredible. I started crying—everyone did. I loved you completely when we met. The nurse asked what your name was. Your name, which your father actually picked out, became Grace Zuri Love. Dad was reading *The New Yorker* one night out on the porch, and he said, "What about Grace?" I loved it immediately. We were then reading in a book of names and came across the name Zuri. It meant "beautiful" in Swahili. I loved the sound phonetically; so did your father. It all came together when we saw your little face. I have to pause and cry at times because so much of this is hard to write.

When I saw you for the first time, I knew that you were my angel. Oh darling girl, I love you so. We all were admiring your beauty, because when I saw you, I knew that for the first time in my life, I knew true love. I have never felt this, ever. There you were, and I was crying with so much happiness—I was overwhelmed. A doctor had been writing in a chart across the room; he raced over and told all of us, your Aunt Liz, Daddy, and me, that this was not a time to be happy. That your condition was very serious. I knew something was wrong because you had a breathing tube in, but I did not know what. . . .

I had been so happy and then my tears turned to fear, Grace. Please forgive me. I want to be strong for you.

Later that day, we were told by a Dr. Meyer that there was an arterial/ventricle malformation in your head. The arterial/ventricle malformation is a malformation of a vein. It can happen anywhere on the body, and surgery can usually correct it. Yet because of the location of this in your head, it is difficult to correct. Although this malformation is simply in the veins near the outside of your head, it has affected the main vein in your neck and is pumping blood rapidly to your heart. This vein has enlarged due to this and, consequently, it has enlarged your heart. It is like a river going into your heart. The surgeons are attempting to stop this blood flow, but the surgeries have to be done in your head. Your veins are so tiny, they keep collapsing.

When I got the news about how bad the malformation was, I started crying. All of this is so hard, and you are so tiny. Otherwise, you are perfect.

Grandma Sara stayed at the hospital with me at night, to keep me company. I kept working on getting stronger to see you. That is all I thought about. By Monday, an emergency surgery had to be performed—your heart would have given out, it was beating so fast.

Gracie,   July 1994

I am still at the hospital. I am trying so hard to regain my strength so I can be there for you. I know I already mentioned that my mother stays at the hospital with me at night. Daddy is watching Amanda at home. I think the hospital is making him nervous. Grandma walked with me tonight around the nurses' station. It is the first time I have walked that much and it was difficult, but I just focus on how much you will need me. I have to be strong for you. I am so grateful for your grandmother, Gracie. I know this is hard for her, but I am optimistic. I showed a nurse your picture tonight. I said, "Do you want to see my daughter?" It was the first time I ever called you my daughter. Grandma turned her head from me. I think she may have started crying. I am so proud of you. I have to keep thinking positively so you can get better, Darling.

Today Daddy took me to see you. He wheeled me in a wheelchair all the way to the intensive care unit. We were at an elevator somewhere in the hospital when Daddy kneeled down by my feet, took my hand, and said that we would always be together, no matter what happened. He just looked at me with such big eyes when he said that. He is so gentle. But I wonder if he knows something I do not. I am going to get strong, Grace. I know that if I think good things, then maybe you will be fine. I know your condition is severe, but I am so strong as a person. I have always been able to get through tough times somehow. We will get through this, Grace. I promise.

I am tired, honey.

Darling Girl,   July 1994

Today Dad and I were in the intensive care unit watching you. We just watch you and are full of wonder. You are to have your second surgery. I get so worried when this happens. Each time, Dad just paces. I am still in the wheelchair. Then a nurse asked us if we wanted a chaplain. *A chaplain?* I thought. *Why?*

And then I realized what she was saying. I can hardly write these words.

A man, the chaplain, came to us soon after this. His name was Okon. He was from Nigeria and is a Presbyterian, which is what I am. He held a shell with water in it and said some words as he baptized you. I was crying so hard I had to hold on to your little bed in order to stand; I could not see you if I sat in that wheelchair. A nurse started crying too. We all were crying. No one had told me you could die.

Gracie,   July 1994

Today I watched your father with you at your bedside.
I watched his face. I watched how he talked to the nurse,
asking about your breathing and heartbeat. I saw him as
so beautiful—his quiet way of expression, his calming
effect on people—especially me. He caught my eye, and
we both looked at you. And never have I seen a more
beautiful child. I know Dad felt it too. We touched your
little toes.

Dearest Grace,   July 1994

Margaret stopped by our home a couple days ago with
a book for me, *Care of the Soul,* by Thomas Moore. We both
love books—we both love words so much. She just
looked so normal.

She asked about you. I wanted to tell her so much
more than I did. Gracie, I know she wants to help. I just
know she does. . . .

But I can't let anyone in now. I think I have used all my
feelings up.

Dear Daughter,   August 1994

I felt so guilty yesterday. Everyone at the hospital has
told both Dad and me that we need to take some time
off—away from the hospital. Dad does this every now
and then, but I have only missed seeing you one day. That
was the day after my cesarean.

Yesterday I went to get a haircut. Judy, who cuts Dad's

hair, asked about you. She gave me a card with the patron saint Jude on it. I am not Catholic, but I will take anything now—everything, if it will help you. Judy told me that miracles happen. I believe that too. You have made it through so many surgeries. I keep hoping. . . .

Grace, I know this is crazy, but I try to look pretty for you. I comb my hair and put on lipstick, in hopes that you see your mother as beautiful, as I see you. I try to be optimistic. But it is getting harder. A fear has come into my life that I have never known. I cry and cry. The other night when Dad and I were out on the porch, he told me that I would have made a good mother. I was furious. I am a mother now! Doesn't he see that? Gracie, I felt so much anger when he said that! He has Amanda. He can watch her grow and run and play! Doesn't he know that is all I want?

When he said that, I wanted to run and leave him and Amanda. I want this pain to leave. I want to be able to have my life the way it was, with you in it. I cannot even tell him how much this pain hurts.

Dad got up and left me on the porch alone after this. I just gripped the railing and wondered, *How will this end? How can I survive?* I went back inside the house. I knew then, I could not leave you alone in this world.

Grace,   August 1994
I am here again writing because I just need to express what is going on. There is so much happening so fast. I

29

feel as if I am mechanical, going through motions. Dad and I never eat during the day. We only eat at night. We drink coffee during the day—all day at the hospital. We have discovered a place outside of the intensive care unit where we can go to get away from things, in the sun. It is there that we talk about all that the doctors have said. We discuss every detail of your condition. But it is the sun that I love, when we sit there with our coffee cups. It is by the children's play area, which is for the siblings of children who are sick in the hospital. Sometimes your Grandma Sara joins us and we talk. My sister, Liz, has left her family so often to be here also.

Deb Kelley, my dear friend, has organized dinners to be brought to us each night. She has called all my friends and everyone has a night to fix us dinner. I can't believe anyone would think of that.

Deb Bohnen, my best friend, has become some type of central station. I call her almost every day to tell her the news. She then passes this on to whoever needs to know. I just cannot be on the phone. I cannot talk to people now. I have gone so far inward. The other night your father was late, and I went into a panic thinking he might have driven off the road or was in some type of car accident. I called Deb and left her a message. She came over at 11 P.M. to be with me. We just sat and talked, and I cried. Oh, Gracie. . . .

I ask myself, *How can there be this much love in the world? How can these people come, almost out of the woodwork, to help us?* It seems as if strangers are extending their love to us somehow. We meet other parents in the intensive care unit, and we are bonded together by the love of our children. Gracie, all the medical staff shows you, and us, so much love. But they do not even know us.

Darling Gracie,   August 16, 1994

I spoke to Sandy, your night nurse, at 6:30 A.M. She said you had slept on your stomach. You need to rest to get your strength up. I will be going into the hospital soon. I am bringing some shirts Grandma Sara got you and booties and a mobile. Your blood pressure is down a little and you are voiding. Yesterday, you had your eyes open and you were trying to focus. When you look at me, you give me the world. I adore you.

I have to keep in mind that those tubes are saving your life. I worry so much that you may be in pain, darling. The thought constantly makes me cry and my throat hurts. You are incredibly brave and strong. You give me strength.

Daddy goes to see you after work, and I am there during the day. We love you so much, sweetheart. Thank you for blessing our lives. I love you, darling.

Dearest child,   August 1994

I am at the hospital now. We did your hair and put a shirt on you. Karen, one of your nurses, said I could hold you. I can't believe it. I only could hold you one other

31

time, and you are nearly a month old. You look so sweet. You are so courageous. Your little eyes are wide open. I brought your mobile in today so you can focus a little bit. The doctor wants you back on your feedings again today. Your little digestive track is slow because of your medication. Your blood pressure is good, in the 70s and 80s. Your heart rate is in the 140s. You are also going to the bathroom on your own. I have your wonderful baby smell on my hands. The weather is turning fall-like. I will be going back to work on Monday. I need to start getting ready for that. I am going back in to see you now, sweetie pie.

Darling Grace,   August 1994

One of the internists, a woman, came to do rounds on you. I was feeling so good to be there, next to you. She checked you while I held you, and she told me that things are not good. I said, "You mean she may not survive?" When she nodded, I sat and held you and tears came down my cheeks. She was so gentle, as gentle as anyone could be. I tried to contain myself, but there is no way that I will ever understand this pain. I have no words left.

Gracie,   August 18, 1994

I am in a coffee shop now, having some coffee. I had a bad day yesterday. I thought I saw a tear in your eye and I thought you were in pain, and my heart tore in half. The thought of you being in any pain makes me crazy. I look at your beautiful eyes and I want to give you the world. I keep thinking that when you look at me, you think, "Why Mom, why?" Yet you are so brave. Those tubes and everything bother me so much sometimes, sweetheart. You mean the world to me. Every day I cry for you. If I could only take your place. If I could only lie beside you and keep you in my arms all night. Gracie, when I write these words, I cry, darling. I am on the way to the hospital now. I paid bills earlier. I must buy stamps. I tried to pick things up a little. The house has been kind of disorganized. I still cannot find my work clothes. I am going from maternity clothes to regular, from summer to fall.

I look at your room and I think maybe I will see you in it! I imagine you in your crib with no tubes. You are a miracle. I love your curly hair, just like Daddy's. Your forehead and eyebrows are Daddy's also. I think you may have my lips and coloring.

Will you forgive me for not being able to stay twenty-four hours a day at the hospital? I stay as long as I can. And next week I have to go back to work.

Sandy, your nurse, will be on nights again soon. She is so good with you. She really knows how to do your hair. Our nickname for you (really it's mine) is Gracie Boo. Daddy calls you the "Eveready Bunny," like the bunny in those battery commercials.

When I write this, it is as if I am talking to you. Even as I carried you, we had a connection, especially at night. You would move like crazy. It always made me feel secure to know you were alive. Your alertness at night is so much like me. I'm always thinking and problem solving at night, and somehow I always have the energy and answers the next day.

Darling girl, hang in there, keep living, and know that Daddy and I love you more than the stars in the sky. You can do this, Gracie Boo. Mama is on her way to the hospital. With love, hopes, and dreams. . . .

Darling Gracie,   August 21, 1994

Tomorrow you will be one month old. I cannot believe it. I love you so.

Today, when I saw you, it seemed as if you could focus a little better. Your eyes have been moving around quite a bit, and you quiver sometimes, possibly due to your drug withdrawal, as the doctors decrease your medication. I spoke to a neurologist today, and they will be giving you some tests this week. They feel you may have some neurological damage. I see you and I see a lovely, courageous child who so would love to live. I see your little face and that circular little mouth you make when you get a little shaky. Oh, darling, I want you to be safe and strong. Daddy and I have tried to save your life through the surgeries seven times. If we hadn't tried all these things, you would not be alive today. I hope you can feel and know this. Please try and be brave and know that God is with you, that the doctors are helping you, and that Daddy and I will never leave you.

Sweetie Pie,   August 22, 1994

I am waiting at the bus stop to ride to my office. I spoke to Sandy, your night nurse, and she said you had a fun night last night. You had a bath. You kicked your legs and also tried to focus more with your eyes. Sandy is so good for you.

It is my first day back to work. I think about how you and I waited at these bus stops when I was pregnant with you. It was you and me. Me and my baby.

You are starting to breathe on your own. There possibly may be a little neurological damage from your surgeries and the malformation. We can cross that bridge when we come to it. Your eyes seem to be able to open a little wider. I believe in you so much. You are one month old today! Happy Birthday!

Darling daughter,   August 23, 1994

I stopped by the hospital before work started today. You were sleeping. You were not up a lot last night. Today you go for a CT scan. They are checking your brain to see how it is working. Your respiratory machine was turned down to twelve breaths per minute, but your CO_2 level went up. I worry about your breathing, your pain, and at times your sleeping. You are my angel, that is why.

Today you looked so peaceful, so beautiful. Your lips are gorgeous. Your hair is light brown, almost blond, and curly. Your skin is so smooth. I look at you and cannot help but be captivated by your beauty. Your hands and fingers are so perfectly shaped. I want to hurry you home, take care of you, protect you, love you with all my heart, darling. I'm at the bus stop again. It looks like rain today.

I have a confession to make. I smoked ten cigarettes after I spoke to a doctor last week. I could not stand the pain any longer, and so I weakened. I have not touched one since then. Your father was furious with me. We fought for two days before we resolved the conflict. It is so hard for both Mom and Dad at times, honey. We love you so much and cannot think of anything else.

Sweetheart,   August 1994

Daddy called at work today and said you have water in the ventricles in your head. The doctors need to perform another surgery at 6 P.M. tonight. I am waiting at the bus stop again to catch a ride to our car. Everyone at work asked about you today. I feel so upset that you have to go through another surgery, honey. It is too much for any-one. When will this end? Why has this happened? You are so innocent. I don't want you to suffer, darling. Please know Mama loves you and that I will be by you no mat-ter what transpires. I am going to the hospital now so I can hold you. You are my angel. I love you so.

Darling child,   August 1994

Daddy and I have been talking about you every night and every moment of the day. Your father and I haven't left each other's sides for days, when we are at the hospital or at home. The doctors said there was nothing more they could do for you. We, in turn, came to the decision that your life is in God's hands. God help us all.

·

Grace Darling,   August 28, 1994

Today we are in a private room with you. It seems as though the end may be near. Dad and I are with you. Okon, the chaplain, came to be with us. He had the day off, but he heard that you may be dying, so he came. People keep appearing out of nowhere. Okon sang "Jesus Loves Me" with his sweet accent. Grace, I have turned to stone. I feel myself hardening against life. How can this be real? Where did God go?

Why can't it be me instead of you?

AFTER

Dearest Daughter,   September 1, 1994

You left this earth on August 29, 1994. I write here at five in the morning. I am sitting outside, waiting for the sun to come up. I hear the birds, and the paper woman just dropped off the paper. I told her you had died. She looked at me silently—not saying anything, probably wondering how this woman could be sitting here, practically in the dark, smoking a cigarette. I have my journal with me—I am going to read a passage of it for your service. Grace, I am in a place where nothing touches me. I feel so wooden. I go through motions, but it is as if I am looking at myself from the outside. I have left who I was.

Gracie, here comes the sun with all its streaks of pink in the sky. Where are you?

Dear Grace,   September 1994

We had your service and it was beautiful. There were so many people there. I kept looking for Julie, my good friend from work, but couldn't see her. Finally, at the lunch at our house, someone told me that she was out of town. I miss her so much. No one had told me she would be gone.

Dearest Child,   September 1994

For some reason, I can't stop thinking about the day you died. Daddy was holding you in his arms—he and Grandpa were sitting with you in the private room. You had your little fingers wrapped around Daddy's thumb. Then you died—you were just gone.

But Gracie, I was not there. I was in another room lying down. Dad made me go lie down, because he thought we would be at the hospital for a long time. And then you were gone. Just gone. I held you and rocked you after you died . . . but I had no idea, not one inkling how much I would miss you. I felt like stone—like I had turned to stone.

You died with Daddy. Grace, you didn't wait for me. Everyone made me lie down. I didn't want to. And then you were gone.

Have I done something wrong? Will you ever forgive me, darling daughter, for not being there? Gracie, my heart is breaking. . . .

Dearest Daughter,   September 1994

I just remembered a day when you were still alive. Daddy and I had come back from the hospital. I was outside sitting on the back steps, waiting for your father to join me. I heard these funny noises coming from the house. I could not place the noise at all, so I went inside. There was your father on the floor of the sunroom. He was all alone; his head was in his hands. It was his sobs that I heard. My heart broke with the sound. I went to put my arms around him, and he looked at me. He promised me we would always be a family, no matter what happened. That's just what he said, Grace, "You, and I, and Gracie will always be a family." I know he meant Amanda too.

Grace,   September 1994

Some time has passed since you left us. I keep reflecting on things. I have to tell you about something that happened the day we were planning your service with Okon. When we got home from the hospital, my eyes flew to the dining-room table, which was covered with pictures of you. Madeline, my friend Margaret's mother, had brought us some flowers and they were way at one end of the table. My favorite picture of you was at the other end,

40

and my eyes went right to it. There were three little stems of baby's breath surrounding your little face in a perfect circle. I knew that these represented you, me, and Daddy. I knew that you were trying to tell me that all was okay. You were fine. Gracie, I told your father and he just stared at me. But I know this is so. I know it is. I keep thinking of those little flowers, on my favorite picture.

Dearest Gracie,   September 1994

Today I saw Julie. She is on maternity leave with her son, Peter, but today she came in to work. I heard someone say, "Julie is here." My heart started beating hard. She came into our office and asked to see me in the hallway. It was the only place we could be alone. I went out with her and we just stood there facing each other. She started saying, "I am sorry. I am so sorry," over and over and over. She gave me a pin, an angel pin. We both started crying and I saw her eyes and I cried harder. I look at her eyes, Grace, and I know she feels my pain. And all I want is just who she is— Julie. That is all I want. I have missed her so much. I don't know why, but I see my heart in her eyes. . . .

Darling Daughter,   October 17, 1994

You are in heaven now. I cannot believe that you are not here. This past weekend we took down your crib. It was so sad. Daddy unscrewed all the bolts and nuts, and I looked at him. We both felt that we would never have to do this. We put up a daybed in your room—which has really turned into my room. Last night I lay in there and just cried. I could not believe you were really not going to come home. I guess that by keeping your things around, I kept you alive on a certain level. You are my angel. I still love you with all my heart. Can you feel it in the clouds above?

My throat aches for you now. As I write this, tears come down my cheeks. Daddy got me a CD player for our new room. I can play music now. It really is quite nice. But it is only an object. It is not you. I think your father feels so bad. He had a rock engraved for you with your name on it for our wildflower garden. I think Dad really wants to make things up to me, as if I can't be happy now that you are gone. He is such a good man. But doesn't he know that no thing can take your place?

Last week, I really wished that I could hold you one more time. I really had a hard time with that, I didn't hold you enough when you were alive. Oh, darling child.

Until we talk again.

Gracie,   October 1994

I felt so low today. Tonight, I am up, wandering around the house. Everyone is asleep but me. It seems as if all the world is quiet, but inside I am torn to pieces. I got out your picture—the one that was in your service, the one with me touching your face. I started crying again. I kissed the glass of the picture, and it was so cold. Gracie, why did you leave me?

Dearest Grace,   October 1994

I am distant from your father now. It is as if we both
have our ways of dealing with your death. I still want to
cry, and your father wants to move on. He told me today
that you were dead. Like I didn't know that! I think he
does not want to hear me talk about you. He wants life to
go on. We try to talk and end up fighting. It is because of
this, Gracie, that I turn to this writing as my solace, that
I sit down at my computer in your old room. It is all that
I have, it seems.

Almost every night I cry. While your dad sleeps, I cry.
Some type of fear has taken hold of me. If death can happen to a baby like you, what does that say about life? I
know that I do not fear for my safety—Gracie, I don't
know what to do.

Dear Grace,   October 1994

The funniest thing has been occurring recently. This
started after you died. At night, it feels as if the down
comforter on our bed is being tucked around me from
the inside out. It is as if there is an exact outline of my
body being made. I keep looking in the dark when this
happens. But it is so consoling. You know that I always
think of you when this happens. I think of you now,
when anything happens—like when my computer
screen glows. I've noticed it seeming to glow at night,
Gracie, after I write to you, but when I get up to turn it
off, I find it was never on. Grace, I think that if you can

connect to me, then maybe this is you or something. And then I fall asleep just thinking of you.

Darling Grace,   October 1994

I have been in Boston for work. Margaret and I go to these conventions every year. We work for a health care program at the university, and we promote the program at these conventions. I talked quite a bit to Margaret about you. She listens so well. The nice thing about her and me is that we are both the same age, we both love to read, and we are both usually in bed with a book by 7 P.M.!

Anyway, when I was getting dressed one morning for the convention, I looked in the mirror and saw my face, and for some reason, I thought of how you looked so much like Daddy. When I looked at my eyes, it seemed as if your eyes were like mine at that moment, and it almost felt as if you were looking through my eyes. This was only momentary, but the feeling was strong.

That night, after Margaret turned off her reading light, I continued to read. Finally, I turned off my light and went to sleep. I was awakened about 1 A.M. by a child's voice saying, "Mommy, Mommy." For a split second, I thought it might have been Amanda, that I was at home. But then I realized I was in Boston. I looked at the window and saw that the drapes were partially open. A little cloud floated by. I fell asleep, once again thinking of you. But that voice, Grace, was such a tiny, tinkly, far-off voice. Was that you?

When I later told Julie about this, she said that clouds don't float that low. I had never thought of that.

Hello little one,   November 2, 1994

Isn't it ironic? This is the exact day a year ago that I found out I was pregnant with you. I was so happy and excited. I was so filled with wonder. At last you were going to be in my life. I had waited so long to have you. I wanted you to have the right daddy. And then there he was, and you were to be in my life, and everything was going to be wonderful.

But Grace, that isn't happening. You died and my dreams crashed like glass around me. Now your father and I are not talking. He thinks he doesn't have any say with me, that I always get my way. When I open my mouth to say anything, he gets mad and walks away. Amanda is acting out in school. What's left? Everything is going haywire. I do not know how I can keep it together. I miss you so much. I drive home every night and cry. Tears come to my eyes on the bus. I find that I have gotten shy and quiet. I have never been at a loss for words, but now I am. I used to see the good in things, but now I feel empty. I thought, the other day, that I do not have a purpose. What am I going to do? What Gracie? What?

Some women are born to sorrow. I read that in a book once. Maybe I am one of those women. All I can think of is, where is my baby? Why can't I see you? I pray that you will show yourself to me somehow. There is all this talk about angels now. I read where people have actually seen angels. I guess that God does not want me to see you. Maybe this is some karmic debt I have to pay off, some lesson I have to learn. Life can be cruel. I know that people have lost loved ones before, but I never believed it could happen to me.

I have cried and cried as I wrote this. Amanda tried to come into the writing room (your nursery), and I told her I was busy. When I left to get toilet paper to wipe my eyes, she called out, "Mom." I dried my eyes quickly and went to see what she wanted. We read stories—some fables—together. She asked if I had been crying. I told her yes, and then she wanted to know if that was why I would not let her in the room. I told her yes, and she said that it was okay.

Somehow I feel more normal after reading those stories. Your father still is not really talking to me except for business matters. What does he want from me? He thinks I do not hear a word he says, but I hear everything. He won't hear me. He does not realize how strong he is. He wants to influence and influence. It really gets my dander up, but you know there is no one whom I respect more. My heart hurts when we are at these impasses. Things should be so much easier than this, but you know that sometimes the simple things are the hardest. Should I go and try to talk to him again? Oh, sweetheart, it feels as if I am talking to you in some way. Like this computer is our connection.

I don't know if you remember this, but after one of

your surgeries, you were so quiet and still and beautiful. I reached out to touch your face, and my hand was shaking really badly. There was such a big lump in my throat. I swallowed my tears and tried to be brave. I kept thinking that if I was strong, somehow you would sense this and get strength from me. But I could not hold you then. You had to lie in that bed all by yourself, so alone. Gracie, will you ever forgive me for not holding you enough? I didn't know that time would run out. And now there is no more time. All I have now to be close to you are these computer keys. Writing is the only action I can take. And the fact of the matter is, I would give anything to touch you again. Just your little hand or your little toes.

I better close now, but I just hate to say good-bye.

Grace,   November 3, 1994

Things have gone from bad to worse. I just spoke to your father. He thinks I control too many things, and that he cannot be different from me. That somehow I force my will on him. He said that he feels humiliated by me when I do this. He feels that everything is on my terms. I stood there and just cried. I have so much to go through now, as I am sure he does, and yet he does not tell me these things as they are happening. I find out this way. He must have built these things up inside. He said he needs space. That things just have to be left to be.

As he told me these things, I felt his pain. I did hear him. I asked him if this had just happened, or was it the

47

way I was? He said he didn't know. I tried to hug him, and I bumped his glasses—another thing that drives him up the wall. I felt like such an idiot. I wanted to tell him about the pain I felt with your death and how hard it has gotten for me recently. But I couldn't. His expression seemed to be more important at the time.

I am worried. I feel that he needs time, and I need to express and make things come forth through communication. I make him nervous and he drives me crazy by not wanting to talk. Then I feel controlled. Then the cycle starts. This is very difficult. It is so painful. We are at such a delicate time in our relationship. We are only two years into our marriage, Amanda is having attention problems at school, and you have died—it has all combined into this boundaryless mass that leaks into all areas. We search and each come up with our own conclusions, so sure that the other will understand as we present our cases, not realizing that the other does not have the patience or the strength to be receptive to new ideas. It is such a luxury, really, to hear someone for what they are, and in a time of crisis, it is almost impossible.

I'm running out of steam. For the first time in our marriage, I am really frightened. It feels as if we could lose this, like our relationship is really threatened right now.

Darling Daughter,   November 4, 1994

How is heaven, sweet angel? It is Friday and things are quieter than they were earlier this week. Amanda is at her mother's house, and your father is downstairs reading. He still does not really want to deal with me, so I am left with all my feelings. You are my only solace. I look forward to talking to you this way. It is as if we have our own special time.

I saw Deb Bohnen this evening, and I talked to her about you. She talked about her life. Somehow, no matter what Deb and I are going through, when we get together, we end up feeling better.

And yet, I feel lonely tonight. Daddy is not ready to open up. He is having problems inside himself. I know he wants to practice his music, I know he would love to record songs, but he has not even played CDs since you died. So now there is no music in his life. It makes me so sad. Maybe he has just not had the time he needs to play. But I too feel as if I am put on hold, with no way for resolution.

Darling Daughter,   November 14, 1994

Tonight things look better than they have in a long time. This past weekend, we started to be a family again. Amanda and I went to a movie. It was the first time in so long that I have been able to enjoy myself. We also each bought some music. I have my new tape on right now.

Dad is opening up more—he is beginning to talk. He said he is lost now. He misses you. He is afraid of doing what he needs to do for his own fulfillment. He seems sad. What can we do for him? I wish you were here for him. I know he would be so happy if you were alive. It is hard to have a broken heart. I somehow feel stronger, but I cannot figure out why. Are you helping me? There is this movement now regarding angels. It seems as if every magazine or book I pick up has some type of article about angels.

The minute I saw you, I said, "There is my angel." I did not know at the time that you would die, but you were my angel from the beginning, and I loved you from the first moment. I have my most favorite picture of you in front of me, one from the first day of your life. You are so beautiful! I could not believe you could be so gorgeous. But you were, and I cried when I saw you. Why did things have to work out this way? I accept things more now, but there are days I would give my eyeteeth to have you with me.

There was a time after we found out how sick you were that I sobbed and cried and cursed God. I played music at the highest volume to try and let something else penetrate. But this pain was swirling inside of me, jabbing me like a knife would. It felt as if the pain took over and I went through a dreamlike state with sleepless nights and tears—so many tears.

Sweetheart,   November 26, 1994

Hello, angel. How are you doing? I have so much to tell you. Dad and I are doing much better. We are actually talking and feeling close. He is off his trip about me. Or himself. He is the old guy we know and love. We both miss you dearly. I talk of you every day. Yesterday I had a hard day. It was my birthday and I felt fine, and then I missed you something fierce. I got so sad. I thought of how we could have been so close. How we could have been together. How beautiful you were and still are.

Lately, some things have weighed on my mind. First of all, the day you died I woke up from a dream with this euphoric feeling of extreme well-being. Although I could not remember the dream, the feeling stayed with me. This feeling was like none that I had ever felt before. I felt as if I could soar. It only lasted for seconds.

I realized then that you were at the hospital, still struggling. I had to take a tranquilizer before I went to see you. When I got to the hospital, I rushed to see you. The minute I walked through the doors, your breathing started getting worse. I went to a private room with you, and Grandma Sara came in to see us. Your breathing was more difficult, and I went to a place inside myself where there was no time, there was nothing but pain. I did not know what to do except hold you. There were no rules, no laws of love to follow. Your dying was so real. A sword had pierced my heart. I hung on and you lay in my arms. Daddy made me go lie down. Forty-five minutes later, he came and told me you had died. I thought he had made it up, that it could not have happened. Grandpa Cole, my father, was holding you when I came into the room and saw you. I must have started sobbing because Grandpa made a weird sound in his throat when he saw my distress. Your color was gone, but you still had this golden hue. I kept holding you and rocking you. Oh, Gracie, as I write this I am sobbing. It's so hard to relive all of this and not have you. Death is so final.

Three months after your death, I went to see this astrologer that everyone at work has gone to see. Her name is Pat. I told her about the feeling I had awoke with the morning you died, this euphoric feeling. I could not understand this at all and I have often thought of it. Why?

Before I go on, I must tell you that I had never told Pat about your death or that I even had had a child. I had barely gotten through the door (I could tell that she was a little nervous), when she said that she had seen, through this formation of the stars, that I had this particular thing resembling the Greek Demeter story where Demeter (a Greek goddess) had lost her daughter, Persephone, to the underworld. I started crying and told her that you had recently died. Pat said she knew I had been through something traumatic. She told me that I had lived an actual archetype. That I had lived my worst fear, that this was a universal fear of all parents. When I asked her about the euphoric feeling the morning of your death, she said that it was the feeling you had when you met God and left the earth. I felt this rush of understanding at that moment. I felt and knew that she was right. That emotion I'd had was unlike any I had ever known. It was so powerful. If only I had known that you would have felt that only hours later . . .

Darling, I must go. This was all so much to write. To actually write of your death is . . .

Darling Angel,   November 29, 1994

Tonight I finished a picture book of your life that Dad had started. It was so interesting to see myself pregnant with you in the spring and summer, and then to see your first days of life. I came across a picture tonight of you looking at me and actually seeing and knowing me. It made me so happy. At the end, it was so hard for you to see, and I worried so much about how you were feeling. Were you in pain? To feel you might suffer was the worst feeling for me. I cried, Gracie, again, so hard. But so much of this was the reality of your life. And it was such a valiant life. So complete. So real. I saw in those photographs how strong you really were and how much personality you had. There was so much life in you. You gave me so much happiness, and now I don't know how my new life will be.

Daddy is not doing well, himself. He does not want to talk about things, like your death, or even his job at times. He keeps things within, but I sense these things. I want to talk, while he is a man of few words. Yet, when he does say something, it is always with so much sensitivity. Daddy has a need to stay what I would term "balanced." He prizes the fact that he can be even-keeled. I, on the other hand, do not mind going into my feelings. I let my feelings become a part of me, but maybe too much. In this way, your father and I do balance each other out—I can take him to the stars by my excitement, and he can make sure my feet stay on the ground by his sense of balance. Right now, though, we are both off center.

He is quiet and he is trying not to smoke. We both, unfortunately, started after the fifth surgery. The pressure was too intense. But more on that later. I do love you, Sweetie.

Well, honey,   December 12, 1994
This will be a Christmas that you will not be with us, and I, personally, will miss you. So much reminds me of you. This is the first time that I have been able to write lately. The pace is picking up.

Amanda just dropped something off at my door. (She says it came from you.) It reads:

> *A Memory Box To Mom*
>
> *From Grace Love*
> *Here's some of Bobs fur*
> *I got & fools gold my sister Amanda got me.*
> *please thank Amanda for letting me watch her*
> *movie Monkes trouble and allso for letting me have*
> *naps with Bob on her coutch!*
> *LOVE,*
> *GRACE LOVE*
>
> *I love you Mom*
> *I love you Dad*
> *I love you Sis*

Wasn't that sweet? Even though it was not from you exactly, it was from you in so many ways. Love comes out when you least expect it.

Your sister is something else. I remember how she wanted to read stories to you at the hospital. Both Amanda and I kept reading and reading to you, hoping you could hear us. My favorite story was *Goodnight Moon,* and Amanda's was *The Runaway Bunny,* both by Margaret Wise Brown. I feel my throat getting tight again.

I am just so grateful for what I have. I love this room, honey. This room is your room, really. It would have been the nursery. It is just so sweet. I have my books close by, in this little wooden bookcase. Everything is in a wonderful neutral cream color—it is such a simple room. There is also the writing desk I got from my grandmother Sylvia. Every piece of furniture in here was chosen with tenderness. I didn't know that was happening when I started redoing the room—but it has. I didn't even know that I would write in here, of all places. But I do.

I just feel love when I come in here. I calm down. And it seems so appropriate that I feel so close to you when I am writing. You are my angel! I love you with all of my heart and I will never stop. Yet each time I write, it is as if all these emotions that I have bottled up come rushing out and the tears start. I think that I am living some way fully in life and then I realize that I really am not, that a part of me will always belong to you. And that this wound will not really be gone. And would I want it to be? Would I want it to be?

Dear Daughter,   December 20, 1994

It is five days before Christmas. I have most of my

shopping done and that feels good. I have been in a funk in some ways. Amanda's other mom had a baby girl last week and I felt so bad that we did not have you. All these emotions came out again, and I have had trouble keeping the tears back. I hate myself for having these feelings, but I do. And it hurts. I am so angry that I can hardly stand it!

It is funny how you can get stuck on one emotion and have it consume your being for that time. I can really understand how people who have been hurt severely in their lives just build up these walls or let hate stop them from life. It is so hard for me to accept my base emotions. I feel ugly for not being able to carry on. Your father has a hard time with me when I really feel. He wants to fix me, and I cannot stand that. He blames himself and wants me to have a happy life; he wants to give me all that is within his power.

Those thoughts are so beautiful. But when you feel, you feel, and I miss you and wish that things were different. I want you to have a life with me! I want you to have Christmas with the family! I want to dress you in little dresses and comb your hair. I want to hold you and not have you leave me. I want you, Grace! I want you so much. I want to smell your baby smell on my hands and know that you are in the next room when I hear you cry. How can a person want something so much and not have it be?

When I finally got the courage to have you, because I loved your father so much, it turned out so tragically. Is God punishing me? Why could I not have the child I wanted? Why? I write and write and that is all that I have. I do not have my child, just computer keys. Please come to me, Grace. Somehow, please. Let me wrap my love around you. Let me hold you once again. Let me be the mother I could not be when you were on this earth. I was so stressed out when you were alive. It wasn't who I really am. I was just a shell of someone who was trying to hang on. I'm sorry, darling. I'm so sorry.

Grace,   December 21, 1994

I miss you, honey. I dare not even think of how old you would be now. Let's see—I guess I will go into this feeling, you know how I get. You would have been five months old, almost to the day. Five months! Oh, if I let myself dream, to think of you on this earth, I kind of torture myself. You know that I have to pause for long moments as I write this. Sometimes I just find myself looking out the window of this room, but I do not even see what I am looking at. I've got to start leaving a Kleenex box in here. I never know when the tears will start.

Across the room, I see the tear-shaped antique bottles that I am collecting. The story goes that in the Middle East, when a man left his love, she would collect her tears in a bottle. When he would come home to rejoin his love, he would see how many tears she had cried in the bottle. Well, I did not know the story behind this when I began collecting these bottles. I just saw how beautiful they were and I knew they would be perfect for your room.

And then I read the insert that told their meaning. They were made to collect tears. It seemed so appropriate for my love for you.

Dear Gracie,   December 22, 1994

Well, I am having a bad evening. I went to get Amanda at her day care and everyone thought I was her other mother. They wished me "happy new motherhood." It seemed like a cruel joke. It is so hard for me at times because Amanda has her feelings and I have mine. Amanda has her feelings of excitement for her new sister and I have feelings of envy. I want excitement and happiness too.

I wanted to have a sister for her. You were her sister and now you are gone. And she has a new sister. And I think she has forgotten you, even though it is so hard for a child. I have so many base, ugly feelings about this whole thing. What can I do?

Dear Grace,   December 31, 1994

It is New Year's Eve, and Dad and I are home. We decided not to go out tonight, but that is okay. We need some quiet time. Last year we went to a little French restaurant in the Cathedral Hill area in St. Paul. Little did I know that the dress I wore that night was the one that I would wear at your funeral.

You know that I think of you every day. It has been hard for me at times. Very hard. I look at your picture, and I ask why. It is almost as if I still cannot believe this has happened. Sometimes your memory is not quite as clear as at other times. Sometimes the pain of your loss gets fainter, and I feel as if I am losing you. I know, if I have the pain, that things are so real then. Oh, Grace, Dad and I talked about having another baby last night. But no one could replace you. No one. I am not ready yet. And I am scared, but maybe someday it would be possible. We love you so much. So much. Is it the right thing to do?

I love you, darling girl. I love you. With all my heart,

Hello sweetheart,   January 8, 1995

How are you? Mom has been thinking of you in the best of ways. Guess what? I had Sandy over. She was your night nurse. She is the most wonderful of people, and we had such a nice visit. She knew how special you were. I thought that most new mothers had this feeling about their child, but when I talk to her, I know that you really were different. You had the power to move people, honey. Sandy told me that all the nurses had said how wonderful you were and what a good little girl you were to take care of. Oh, sweetheart, I can't believe that you could be that good after so many surgeries. But you were, and I was so proud of you. And I bet that you are flying around right now just being the most precious angel. There was nothing but goodness about your life. You were pure.

The day of your funeral, I was facing the audience—it was right at the end when things were wrapping up—and I looked up and saw an angel hovering by the far corner of the chapel. I knew that it had to be you. The robes this angel wore looked too big for it, and everything was fuzzy for me because I had tears in my eyes. But I did see that this angel had wings and that the wings had light blue along the edges. The robes were of an antique fabric, like old silk. Well, I blinked a few times and I kept seeing the angel, but on the third blink it went away. Was that you? I told people about this right away, and they must have thought I was crazy, but I did not care. Especially on the day of your funeral. But I thought that maybe God had let you just take a look at us when you were whole and could see and understand. If this is what happened, then I know that you saw how much Dad and I loved you and how much everyone loved you.

Honey, that chapel was so packed. There was standing room only. The medical staff came, the nurses, friends of the family, and work friends. It was amazing. Love came out of every corner of the room. The music was beautiful. Daddy sang "Amazing Grace" a cappella. I do believe that you wanted me to see you, and that at that moment, you did show yourself to me! But I don't know why those robes were so big for you. It's like you had to grow into them or something.

This brings to mind my friend Julie, from the university. We had grown very close, and even before we shared our pregnancies, I had this connection with Julie—this unspoken bond. I knew it and I knew that she knew it. She has been my pillar of strength, and we don't even need words to understand what the other one is feeling. I told her about your death the other day. We were at a conference for work, and I just started talking at lunch. It is so hard for me to speak of the painful parts of this. I cried again, another trait I have picked up. But Julie, she sat and listened and was so present. I can't put words on the feeling I get from sharing time with her. It is truly so special.

Darling girl, I must go now. I may write again today, but there are things I have to get to. You can see that I have not talked to you in a while and that I have had a lot of things to say. I feel so much better, Grace! It is as if I am healing, and I cannot believe it! Thank you, little one. . . .

Dearest Gracie,   January 23, 1995

I have not written to you in so long. Dad, Amanda, and I got back from a Florida vacation. Dad thought it would really be nice to get away for a while. I want you to know that we had such a nice time. Amanda stayed with your grandparents, Jim and Nancy, so that Dad and I had time for ourselves, at least at night. The beaches went on for miles. The water was an emerald green and the waves would hit the shore and make beautiful white sea froth. It was lovely. Dad and I both felt our cares melting away. We laughed and loved and became very close again. When I can make your father laugh, it makes me so happy. We were so silly. On the last day, we were at the beach by ourselves and I tried to do a rap song for Dad (to make him laugh) and I totally screwed it up. My rhythm is not the best in music.

It just got me to thinking that maybe you would have been like me. Amanda is like your father, and when I am who I am, I am probably quite impish and funny, and serious at times and very searching and focused inward toward bigger things. Evolving is important to me. I wondered, would you have had my temperament?

These things all came to my mind and then I thought that I will never know the answer. I thought of how brave you had been during your lifetime—how incredibly strong—and I knew that you did have some of me in you. You had my strength to live. I started crying, and the tears would not stop. Dad was sitting by me, and we were looking out at the ocean, and these tears were streaming down my face, and the wind was blowing hard. I could not stop crying. Dad always feels so bad when I get like that. I kept thinking, *I can't believe you died when I didn't even get to know you.* But somehow I knew you in my own fashion. I knew when you looked at me that you knew me, that you recognized my voice, and that we had shared something rare. We knew. We shared life and death. But honey, I wish it could have been different. I really miss you. With you, I came in touch with that lost side of me, that side that you will always have.

I wonder how women and men who have lost their children survive? I was getting ready for work recently when I heard a news report about the anniversary of the space shuttle that had blown up nine years ago, the Challenger. The mother of the teacher on board was talking about all the good things that had come about because of her daughter's death, and I could not imagine this, that a person could be that healed.

I realize that I have to look at the fact that you have died. Everyone but me has accepted this. People say move on, but it is so hard for me. Last night I was driving home in my car and the tears started, and I began to moan and cry just like I used to do when you were alive. It is such a pitiful sound when you hear yourself make those noises. I realized that we as humans are so close to animals, really. Pain is pain. And the sounds of pain are universal and cannot be claimed by one species or another as only their own.

I must go, honey. I am so tired, and I have to work tomorrow.

Dear Gracie,   January 27, 1995

Another one of those days . . . work and going home. I wonder what I am to do with my life? What will I do? Where am I left? What is left for me? What? "How can I forget you?"—that is what Betty Carter is singing just at the moment. I feel kind of listless and mad, and I have a hard time thinking of what I have lost. If all matter is energy, then where is your energy? When I feel good about things, I feel as if you are so close to me, and when I am discouraged, you seem so far away. Why is this? When will this feeling of melancholy leave me? Right now, I have some incense burning and I have lit a candle; I am trying to create a loving environment for myself, but

I really do not have a lot of energy. Grief is such a strange thing. Does it ever pass?

Dear Daughter,   January 30, 1995

I am feeling better than the last time I wrote. I was feeling so low. I really do not know what it was, except that it probably had something to do with you. Dad and I kind of had it out because I felt that he was not really helping out around the house. I would ask him to do something, and he would say he would, and then he'd just blow it off and never do it. At times, he is very threatened by who I am. This was one of those times. I think it's because I have been carrying on and organizing things, and he cannot stand it.

He has a problem in that he hears so much criticism when there is a request made of him. I, on the other hand, have it totally together—wrong! I have my issues too, which you would have seen, had you lived. My big issues are that I am somewhat of a perfectionist and have control issues. I do think that I have good ideas and that I often see solutions quite easily. Your father has wonderful qualities also. He can say he is sorry, he can be as gentle and as soothing as anyone I know, and he is incredibly bright and insightful. But I do not know how much of a worker he really is. Oh well . . .

Dear Grace,   February 1995

I have been having so many unusual dreams lately. Recently I had a dream in which I was taking care of a black man's child. In fact, I even nursed this child. He was the most caring man I had ever met. We did not talk with our mouths; everything was understood through our minds. I kept feeling nothing but love from him. He told people, "Look how she has loved my daughter." He had the most loving of eyes. The next scene, I was in a doorway with this man, and he was holding my hand. He was in a wheelchair. He looked up at me, again with such incredible tenderness, it made me want to weep. I had never felt this kind of love before. I knew if I loved him, I would never be the same again.

Well, because so much is happening on this level, I had to tell someone. So at work, I started relating this dream. Julie almost dropped what she was carrying. She said that she had a dream the week before with a black man in it too, and in the second half he was in a wheelchair! None of us could believe this! She and this man also communicated through their minds. The nature of each dream was different, but Julie also felt love from the man. I know this is because of you, Gracie. But what does it mean?

Darling,   February 22, 1995

You would have been seven months old, today. Seven months! Julie brought in Peter today, and he was so sweet. An angel, just like you. His energy is wonderful. It gives me so much solace to see where he is in life and to know there is so much love.

I am filled with love tonight. We had a school problem with Amanda, and we worked it out. She is so close to me and we both know it. We have this unspoken bond that I treasure. How could I have made it without her? Or is it you working your magic? I feel as if you have left me somehow. I don't know why. It is as if you have crossed to the other side. That makes me sad. Have you? I look at the computer screen and it is dark, not glowing like it used to be. Remember? Were you trying to communicate with me and I was not ready for it? Well, I am now. I love you, darling, and I cry for you. Don't you see my tears? Don't you know what is in my heart, or do you just see my actions and what is not in my heart? Don't leave me, Sweetheart. Are you fading into a place I do not know? Or will you reveal yourself to me? Let me know.

I am your mother, always.

Darling Grace,   March 4, 1995

I love your name so much. I have been ill this past week and haven't felt like doing anything, even reading. Then I started reading this angel book that I got for Christmas. I wonder if you are an angel. . . . They say angels are a different species from humans, "messengers of God," not on the physical plane as we humans are but on the spiritual plane. We are all energy. I know that your energy is somewhere, and I know that if I were more evolved, I could accept that you are gone. I understand that the energy is what is important and that it is love. Grace, I can grasp this intellectually at times, but there are other times when I would give anything to have you on the physical plane.

I wonder if I am being punished for something that happened that I am unaware of. They say in this book that there are no accidents, that everything is for a bigger reason, and that to get it, you have to go through it. But in my usual, questioning way, I wonder why. I read all this stuff, and it sounds so good, but then it comes right down to the fact that I simply miss you. And I long for you—to hold you. There will always be a hole in my heart.

One good thing came out of this reading. You know that I can be quite unbending if I think I might be right. Well, I have spent two and a half years trying to convince your father to "see things my way," and then all of a sudden, I realized that he will never change; he is who he is. And I am who I am. Acceptance is the only way. It was really a breakthrough for me. It is so simple, yet so hard. What I love about your father is also what I have the hardest time with. And so it is. So it is.

I guess the key is to let go. Like a cool summer breeze, let the airflow take you there, and you cannot fight it.

Gracie,   March 1995

The strangest thing happened on my way in to work, on the freeway. A white bird flew right in front of my windshield. It was right smack dab in front of me. I worried for a moment that I might hit it, but it started ascending with its head cocked to the side, just like pictures of the American eagle or the phoenix. It was so close that if I could have put my hand through the window, I could have touched it. I have driven this route hundreds of times, and a bird like this, let alone a white bird, has never come this close. I was so rattled by the time I got to work that I had to tell Julie about this. I think it might have been a dove. But why a dove?

Dearest Daughter,   March 1995

Gracie, I have to let you know what is going on at work. All of us—Julie, Margaret, and I—have been reading books. I got a book from your Grandma Love about angels, by Sophy Burnham. I had read her book *Revelations* recently, and then all of a sudden, this book was mailed to me from your grandmother. I brought it in to work one day to show everyone. When I was done with it, Julie read it, then Margaret. We have started passing books around. We each kind of have our own bent, but sometimes our tastes intersect. It is so much fun discussing things and sharing ideas. We have even begun comparing notes about our dreams. Julie has always been the avid dreamer in the group, but Margaret and I are beginning to notice our dreams more. There is this feeling of shared events going on now. I am beginning to trust and open up a little more. I have to do something, Grace, otherwise this pain would somehow take over.

I have to go, Honey.

Darling Grace,   March 14, 1995

So much has been going on since I last wrote, a lot of

emotional and spiritual activity, with dreams and sharing with Margaret and Julie. First off, I should tell you that Daddy and I are very much in love. Something short of a miracle has taken place in love with your father and me—a deeper understanding of sorts. Although I always knew how much Daddy loved me, I have never felt or seen it more than now. I knew it intellectually, but not from the heart. I changed my approach with him, and I have been getting all this love back. You know how defensive I can be. You know how defensive he can be. We both wanted to defend our place in our lives together, and now I have let it go. He is who he is. And I am who I am. In certain ways, he can grow through my knowledge, and in certain ways, I can grow through his. So much of this revolves around acceptance. But I had to let him in.

When I speak of letting him in, I realize there is another spirit that is entering me. . . . I have been reading these angel books, and I guess I am so open or receptive after your birth and death that, through a series of situations, I have started thinking a lot about God and angels and you and your spirit. I have mentioned before that when I have been in tremendous emotional pain, this computer has glowed at night. I went to turn it off the first time and discovered it was not on. There was only a glowing computer screen. This has happened at least six times. Was that you? When I realized that this had happened, I just went to bed, until it happened the next time. I had prayed that you would reveal yourself to me as an angel or something, and then this started happening. The computer has been our only way of communicating. I know this. I have gotten frightened by this, and I have not known how to react. But I am working on my fear.

I have been having dreams; some of them seem to have spiritual symbolism in them. I also read this book about a woman who had a near-death experience. I know, dear daughter, that you are in the most loving of hands and that you are pure and chose to come here for a reason. Your purpose touched so many people around you. Oh, please, know how much I loved you and still love you. You may have awakened a love in me for God and myself that was in hiding for so long. It is as if I am seeing love in the smallest and simplest of places. I always thought that I was pretty spiritual in a modern sense, but ever since your birth, when I have heard love songs, I think only of my love for you, not the typical love. Now I hear songs about being blinded by the light and love, and I think of God. I wonder if I ever was truly spiritual in the right sense—if I have ever truly loved myself and God. It is as if I am being awakened.

I have read that there is free will, and that on this earth we can choose to use it as we see fit. This is God's promise to us. But if we do need anything, all we have to do is ask. When was the last time that I prayed other than when I was pregnant? At the first sign of problems, I started to pray. But I didn't when I thought everything was fine.

Did I thank God for anything before all this? I think maybe twice a year, if that. I was so out of touch with everything. I thought that I was a decent person, but maybe I was mean and horrible. Was I missing something? Was I too selfish and did I only think of myself, ultimately? (I just took time out to look at your pictures and I had to cry again. You were so wonderful.) I am ashamed that I worried about how we would care for you. I worried that we might not have the money or we would become so tired that things would fall apart, and yet, that too was simply selfish on my part. I am ashamed as I write this. I have learned so much since we were together, but was it because of your death? And did I cause you to suffer?

If I only knew then what I know now—that love can cure anything, that all of life is about love and hope and faith. But darling, know one thing: I will always feel this love and loss for you. No one has affected my life as you do and have. And if I caused any of this to happen to you and you died because you did not feel enough love from me, then I do not know how I can bear that thought. Oh, Darling, I love you with all of my heart, and if you were here I would show you, but please know this. I love you.

Darling,   March 26, 1995

I have not written to you in a while. It is not because I haven't been thinking of you, though. Almost every minute is taken up with thoughts of you—while working, driving, looking at the trees, feeling the spring winds.

All these things bring back memories of when we were together while I was carrying you. Remember when I carried all those boards from under the bushes in the backyard? They had been left by the former owners of our house. The yard had looked so bad after the winter, until we started picking it up. Just you and me. Dad kept looking from the window in the house, holding his coffee cup. I would look up, and there he would be, looking at me. I must have been seven months pregnant. It was then, in the spring, that I really started loving you. I felt good. Strong. The sun would warm my skin and I would feel my muscles working and you moving. I knew you felt strong then. We worked as one. We were quite a team. I felt nothing could have been sweeter. You inside me, the love I felt for your father, the spring sunshine, and the dirt on my hands. I felt so alive! Was that what you did for me? Open me up to life? Make me feel more alive? What, Gracie, what? You live inside me even now! And in my stubbornness, I don't want to let you go.

Spring is coming again and you are not here. I have only the trees and the grass. I keep raking because it reminds me of a time when I was so happy—waiting for you to arrive into this world. When I look up to the window that would have been yours, I feel empty, and sometimes tears sting my eyes. When I hear the same birds that sang to me as I worked last year sing to me now, I realize this is how it is. That you won't be coming. That I cannot turn back time. That I must carry you in my heart. But I know that you were my deepest love and my deepest pain. The wind carries you to me, softly. As your spirit swirls around me, I am filled with the wonder that every mother has for her child. Although I cannot hold you in my arms, you fill me with your purity. And I thank God for that.

Dearest Grace,   March 28, 1995

I have to tell you that things are happening so quickly to me now. I'll try to explain.

Ever since the day that you died, the day I had that dream feeling of euphoria before I realized you were still so ill and suffering, I have had dreams, had thoughts, been filled with love, watched my life change . . . and now I have had the experience of leaving my body. One night I was sleeping and I felt myself leaving my body. About halfway up from the bed to the ceiling, I got scared and went back into my body with a *whoosh*. I still felt as if I had the same personality, but I was not in my body. Well, I just told Dad about this and he said that it was not a bad thing, just to let these experiences happen naturally. But I am one for naming things, and I have to put words on some things. It gives me strength and comfort. But. . . .

(The cursor begins to scroll through all I have written.)

II.

SEARCHING

QUESTIONS

Gracie,   April 1995

I don't know quite how to put this, but I will do the best I can. The last time I wrote to you, on March 28, something occurred. In fact, I have to write this by hand because the computer is on the fritz. I hesitate because I am searching for words at the moment. . . .

Let me start at the beginning of the night. I had told Dad about these out-of-body experiences I had been having. The time was right, and I was feeling so safe and close to your father. We were both sharing on this wonderful level. You know what a good listener he can be. I remember we were making spaghetti, and I was just putting the noodles in the boiling water, when your father told me he had a gift for me. He pulled this tape out of his briefcase—it was called *Calling All Angels.* He knows how much angels mean to me now, because of you.

After dinner, Daddy and Amanda were watching television, and I ran upstairs to write to you. I put the tape in and began writing. Your father then came upstairs, during a commercial, to give me a kiss. Grace, it was a wonderful kiss.

As your father left the room, I resumed typing. As I did, the cursor on the computer screen began going through my writing on its own. I became alarmed and tried to gain control of the cursor, when your father's words rang in my ears. He had just told me that the out-of-body experiences were nothing bad and that I should be "natural" about them. I kept trying to control the cursor, but then I stopped to see what would happen if I didn't. My heart, by this time, was in my throat. I could hear the blood pounding in my ears. The cursor disappeared, and the letters of my writing began to glisten, as if they had some sort of diamond quality. Then I watched as the computer scrolled upward, through all I had written. The cursor stopped at a point in my writing where I had told you that I knew we could communicate like this, through the computer.

Gracie, at that moment, the cursor began flashing normally again, I had an intense desire to sob. I was filled with an awe of some sort. I began to cry, but I couldn't define what I was feeling. Because I could not understand what had just happened, I got down on my knees and said a prayer. I then ran and told your father. He said that there was probably some type of energy surge or something. The whole evening I felt somewhat dazed. I kept thinking, *How can this be?* I knew in my heart it wasn't a power surge. It had something to do with you.

Darling Grace,   April 1995

I have to tell you that I had a dream in which I saw five huge angels in the sky, flying around in robes. In the next scene of the dream, I saw myself landing on the ground. My skin was flesh colored, and I had wings that were also of a flesh tone. I saw my feet touch the ground, as if I were landing lightly.

Gracie, I have also had a dream in which I saw the Star of David, and another in which I saw a multipetaled white flower over my head. I found out later that this was the lotus flower, which in Hinduism means divine energy and divine grace. What is going on?

Grace, it seems as though I am coached by someone in my recent dreams. I hear a voice, but I do not see anyone. Yet, it feels as if I am learning something. I keep wondering why I am getting these religious symbols. And are all the religions connected somehow?

Julie has also had the Star of David in a dream, so it is not just me. Is it because we were pregnant together?

Dearest Daughter,   April 1995

I have some concerns again. I went into my computer after this last episode I told you about. I wanted to write to you, and when I opened the program, a file was highlighted and the warning bell sound on my computer was chiming again and again. I opened the file, and saw that it was a note I had written to Margaret in January, after I read the mystery novel that she is working on. The whole time, the signal bell was chiming every second!

It got me all rattled again. I tried to write something, and the letters kept going to the beginning of whatever I typed. Finally, I turned the computer off. I told your father again, and he said that the computer was malfunctioning. I know this is not so. But I am wondering if you are trying to tell me something and I cannot understand. I am concerned about this, Grace. Why can't I understand? This bothers me so much.

Dearest Grace,   April 1995

When I was eight years old, exactly the age of Amanda, my mother lost a child, my brother Matthew. He had something totally unrelated to your condition and he only lived four days. At that time, people did not deal with death in the way they do now. Mothers could not see their newborns if they were really sick in the hospitals. So Grandma never saw her child—ever. She lived with that loss for years. When you came into her life, Grace, you were a child—a grandchild—whom she *could* hold and comfort, as she couldn't hold and comfort Matthew.

Grace, Grandma has been so affected by your life and death. She cries every time I bring up your name. Yet, ironically, with all that emotion, she has a very logical way of looking at a problem. I have always felt comforted by this. So I knew I could confide in her. I knew I had to talk to her about what has happened to me recently. I drove to her house last night.

I told the computer story—how I had been writing to you still, how the computer screen had been glowing at night, how the cursor moved by itself. I related the out-of-body experiences; I even mentioned the similar dreams that Julie and I have had. My mother just listened. I also told her about the dove flying in front of my windshield.

Grandma started crying. There was no judgment coming from her, only support. She told me that her best friend also had seen a white bird outside her window after her mother had died. Grandma said that it was a sign. I kept wondering, *Why is it that people never talk about these signs?* And yet it seems that everyone who has lost a loved one believes in some type of connection. Some sign that will keep them connected. Is this based on trust?

Gracie Darling,   April 1995

I am sinking. I keep trying to get into my computer, but I cannot get it to work. I know that this is connected to you. Your father still thinks the computer is just on the fritz. He told me to get it looked at, so that I won't get hurt if it is not you. Gracie, I keep trying to understand what you may be trying to tell me. I am worried that maybe I have done something wrong in my life, and God is mad at me or something. I am even thinking that my reputation, along some line, has rubbed off on you in the heavenly realm. I am so frustrated that I can't get the computer to write. What if you need my help? You are pure, Grace—I know this has to do with me. If I have done anything to tarnish your reputation in heaven, I'll die. Grace, I have so many questions. And no answers.

Dear Gracie,   May 1995

I look at my life now and I wonder, *How can all of this be happening?* As you know, I have begun sharing things with Julie, but after the dove incident, Margaret was brought into these discussions. She is Catholic and is more familiar with religious symbols, or at least she knows where to look for information on them.

When I asked her about the meaning of the dove, she came back the next day and said that it represented the Holy Spirit or the Eternal Mother! I almost fell off my chair. Margaret continually strikes me as so steadfast and gentle; Julie, as full of such tenderness. Both of them are so different from myself. I have had to open up to them, Gracie, because I cannot hold these events inside.

Well, the other day Margaret called me up at work, from her home, and told me she thinks she has spoken to an angel—her angel! This really came out of nowhere. I had no idea she was even thinking of doing something like this.

I was somewhat shocked; I even felt jealous. But with everything that has happened lately, I am beginning to feel that anything may be possible. When I told Julie about this angelic communication, she wanted to go over to Margaret's the next day. Margaret has been home from work lately, getting her home ready to sell. Although I responded willingly, I only halfheartedly went.

Gracie, we sat at Margaret's kitchen table on this beautiful spring day, and Margaret told us what her angel had said. Julie and I were all full of questions. "How could this happen?" "How do you do it?" Things of that sort. When I read the words on Margaret's computer, I was overwhelmed. There was so much truth in the words, however they may have come. I started getting quiet.

Grace, I have fear in me. This is bordering on things I do not understand. Margaret has been able to connect to this angelic realm, but I cannot write to you, and you *are* an angel. I feel this verifies the fact that something is very wrong with me.

Several days later, Julie asked Margaret to talk to the angel (now named Peace) for her. I felt myself withdrawing. Although I had shared the aspect of physical events with these women, I had not shared my growing fear. I kept feeling so flawed. But this was my secret.

I know that I am rambling now, but I must get this out. The next day, Margaret came in with news for Julie, from her angel. Margaret then turned to me and said that she had felt that I had also given her permission to speak to *my* angel. This was my worst nightmare! Margaret's first words with her angel, Peace, had rung with such truth that I knew the angels would spill the beans about me and let everyone know what a horrible person I am. Why else could you have died?

Margaret then went on to tell me what my angel had said. He said he missed me or something like that. I took this to be a sure sign that I was somehow out of circulation in this angelic realm. Gracie, I am just sinking here. I had to leave work.

I tell you, first you die, then all this starts happening, and I am supposed to make sense out of it. Isn't your dying enough? I just cried in the backyard. Margaret even said that my angel seemed "stern." They had to put the tough one with me! Gracie, I am convinced that I am a tough case for anyone—even your father. It's probably better you are with God than with a mother like me.

I know this sounds fierce, but it is how I feel. And I am stuck with this churning in my insides. Gracie, I am sinking.

Dear Grace,   May 1995

We are a couple of weeks into this angel writing of Margaret's. Remember how I told you that I had to leave work after Margaret talked to my angel? Well, the next day, on my way in to work, I got behind a car that was

filled with balloons, and one read "To Cheer You Up!"
The whole back window was covered with these balloons,
but the only balloon with writing on it was directly in
front of me. I thought that the car would go on to the
university hospital, but it didn't. It turned where I usually turn into the parking lot. I couldn't miss it.

Dear Grace,   May 24, 1995

I had another dream last night. In this dream I saw a
woman, the mother of a friend who had died. The dead
woman was laid out on a sidewalk, and everyone was
walking around her. I kept asking people when this
woman would be buried. No one would answer me.
Then, I was looking from behind this scene at an incredibly magnificent dog—a German shepherd—sitting
beside a mound of dirt. The dog was so beautiful. It was as
if he were watching over this pile of dirt.

Well, I told your father about the dream, and I said, "We
have to bury Grace." You see, Gracie, we have your ashes
at home. I wanted to bring you home somehow, to be
with me. But I think that now is the time that we have to
do this. Daddy doesn't even question these dreams. He
just said, "Okay."

I called your Grandma Sara and there is a plot in
Austin, Minnesota, where the rest of the family is buried.
I think that is the best place. Julie told me that when we
buried you, she wanted to be there, because she felt so bad
about not coming to your funeral.

I spoke to your father, and we both agreed that we would all say a few words by the burial site. I just want to keep this simple.

Dear Daughter,   May 1995

I could not believe it, but I got so nervous about the burial. It rained cats and dogs that day. I had written something to read to you, and I brought that little teddy bear from Amanda to put in the grave with you. You were buried by my brother Matthew. My parents, Deb Bohnen, and Julie and her husband, Kelly, were all there. Margaret has had all this stuff going on with selling her house and her daughter's graduation, so it was just this small group. My sister, Liz, and brother, Charlie, also could not be there.

We stood in the rain, under umbrellas. The wind kept whipping the pages I had written to you, and the ink ran down them as I read the words. It was Memorial Day weekend. Everyone said something from their hearts. Dear Julie, who always is so tender, said her words. I know how important that was to her. Then Grandpa interrupted Julie to say his piece—I think to speed things along because of the rain. Even Kelly said something. Deb's words were also so touching. She is the only one of my friends who ever saw you. Time ran out for the others. I kept thinking that time would not run out.

I got so uptight with all of this, just like I did on the day of your funeral service. I felt so wooden inside. I got so cold in the rain. The back of my dress was so wet.

But you know, Grace, I felt then that I had done the right thing. That I had listened to my heart. That it was time to put your body to rest. And for this, Grace, I am grateful.

Gracie,   May 1995

I cry nightly for you. I cry into this space, this nothingness, in hopes that I can somehow find you. I have so much fear in me. I am so worried that I might have mucked things up somehow. Honey, if I have, I didn't mean to. You see, I only have love for you. I cannot express in words how much in love with you I am. And if God can see me, He must know I have done something wrong. I tried to do everything so right. But maybe He thinks that I am too controlling or maybe that I holler too much. But because of how I feel about you, I have to take a chance and have Margaret ask this Peace angel for any word of you. I am scared that he will say I am just somehow no good. You see, Gracie, in my family we are such self-sufficient people. You just don't ask for help unless you are really desperate. But who could I ask for help with this angel stuff anyway? My only hope is Margaret.

Dearest Grace,   June 1995

I finally got the courage to ask Margaret if she could ask this Peace angel about you. I did it today when we were outside talking. I remember Margaret bending her head down, listening to me, letting me say my words. Could she tell how nervous I was? I tried to make the request seem somewhat light but inside, this fear still has a hold on me. In fact, as I write this tonight, I am in more despair than ever. I know Margaret is probably writing right now. I keep thinking of everything that this angel might say. I think of my childhood and how rebellious I was as a teenager. I think of how selfish I have always been and how headstrong. How I try so hard to be good, and then I screw everything up. I think of how many surgeries you had. Were they too many? I think of how Dad and I said "no more" to medical science. Was that right? I think of when I was carrying you . . . what if I walked by a microwave oven and got some type of radiation that hurt you? I am examining everything in my life, Grace, and I keep coming up short. But I have to know. This is an unusual situation, in that I have a friend who is able to do this. And if I have done anything to harm you, or if God is mad at me for some reason, or because of who I am, and I can make it right, then I have to risk everything to find out. Even if the news is bad—which I am almost positive it will be, because of who I am—somehow, Darling, I will help you. I promise to make this right.

I can't write anymore . . .

The next day:

Gracie,

Today at work Margaret brought the news in from her angel about you. We sat out on a veranda by a beautiful fountain. Flowers were everywhere. The sun was so hot. It was Margaret, Julie, and me. Everyone was quiet as I began to read. And Grace, I cried so hard. Tears just ran down my face. I didn't care. This is the first news I have had of you since you died. The first news! Somehow a weight was lifted from me. It was as if I felt the same joy as the first time that I saw you. Peace, the angel, said you are fine! There was a glimmer of light in my heart today. All I needed to know was whether you were okay.

I don't know if Margaret knows what she has done for me today. I don't know if she knows that she has thrown me a life raft. There has never ever been a time in my life where I have ever known such profound gratitude. I kept crying into a napkin. Gracie, I have never received a gift like this. I felt as if Margaret had carried my heart and brought word of you to me. She carried my heart as if it were her own. That is how I felt. That is how much I trusted her.

Gracie, even as I write, I cry, because when a mother loses her child, all she does is look for the reasons why it could have happened. Oh, Gracie! You are an angel! Relief swept over me. I cannot even begin to tell you. It was as if floodgates opened in my heart.

Here is what Margaret's angel, Peace, said:

Mary has only asked because she has reached a point of being where she is ready to know, where she needs to know, where she must know. And I tell you, what Mary needs to know is this: she did everything right. She could not have loved more. She could not have felt more. She could not have withstood more than she did. She had the courage to trust in herself, in her intuition, and she was so right to do so. She was more than right in that there is no right and wrong in following our destiny. She did the only thing she could. And Grace did the only thing she could. Destiny is linked. Not only did Mary live her destiny and Grace live her destiny, but everyone else who was touched by Grace had Grace as part of their destiny, their road to travel, their bridge between the human and the divine. John, Amanda, Sara, the doctors, the nurses, people Mary doesn't even know. Wives, husbands, friends, daughters who heard of Grace's valiant struggle had their destinies touched by Grace.

And Grace, who Mary worried over so, was a being of pure love and pure light. She was all angel. We all have our angelness with us when we are born. We all have a wisdom unrecognizable in the human world. It is the wisdom of remembering. And Grace never forgot! She never forgot for a moment that she was a being of love, a being of one-ness. She knew exactly what she came back to the human form to learn: Love. And she learned it. She learned it so fast and gave it back to the world so fast, there was no need for her to remain in human form. She never spent a moment on this planet when she was not sure, absolutely sure that she was a being of love. Why? Because she lived such a short life? That is part of the reason. The other reason was that she lived her entire life surrounded by love. She did not see tubes or surgical instru-ments as anything but what they were—instruments of love. She did not see nurses and doctors, she saw beings of love. And because she was wise with the wisdom of remembering, she saw her parents with perfect love. She saw them as the angels they are. She did not see one single imperfection because there was none to see.

Tell Mary that Grace remembered! She left this world a being of light just as she entered it. She had everything you seek! Everything Mary seeks! Why do you suppose she affected people so? They were in the presence of an angel, an angel who never forgot. One who could have turned around and left for home immediately, but who stayed to feel the love around her and to fill those around her with her divine love. Is Grace all right? No one could be better than Grace. Grace Is in divine oneness and love.

And Margaret replied:

Thank you, Peace. I think I can rest assured that you have given Mary what she had to have—understanding and Peace. Thank you. Can I ask one thing more? As you know, ever since Grace, through Grace, because of Grace, Mary has been on a journey of her own. Similar to mine but unique to her. Her own spiritual quest. There have been times on this path when she has been certain Grace spoke with her through her computer. Sometimes the messages have been clear and sometimes they have not been. Sometimes it simply seems as if everything is a frustrating puzzle, as if the computer has gone haywire. She wants to write, she wants to communicate, but she is not only confronted with puzzles, but with an inability to go into her computer and write to her daughter. Can you tell her anything that will help her understand what is happening? Can you give her any assurance about how to know when Grace is reaching out to her? Can you help to solve the riddle?

What Mary has received is a reflection of herself. Of her state of being in the Now. Mary has lived through the greatest challenge that humans can face. And she has turned from that challenge, not with bitterness or anger, although these feelings at times fly across her Now, but with hope. What is her hope about? Finding the love she had with Grace. She was so full of Gracie's love that Gracie's loss felt like a great and awful empti-ness, an emptiness so great and vast she wasn't sure she was alive. Wasn't sure she could live. How could Grace not return to comfort her and give her hope? How could Grace not return to help her on her journey? Grace is with her every step of the way. Grace leads her to the books, the birds, the signs, the flowers. Grace in her infinite, loving oneness knows the quickest route to welcoming Mary to be with her again.

Why does that way seem full of puzzles and frustrations? Because Mary is full of puzzles and frustrations. This is not something negative I am saying here. I am saying Mary lived through the greatest challenge a human can face and came out of it not with overwhelming anger and bitterness and despair, but with puzzles and riddles. Hurrah for Mary. Because Grace helped her back to remembering more than she has any concept of, she is in a state of puzzles and frustrations. She knows, Knows, more than she ever knew before. She is closer to oneness, closer to her angelhood, closer to the divine all that is than in any life-time. Yet that Knowing is hidden from her, much like a name you say is on the "tip of your tongue." It is not Grace or Mary's angel, or anyone but Mary who keeps her in the state of frustration.

Again, this is not negative. For most humans, enlightenment is a lifelong occupation. There is a reason for that. There is a reason I only answer the questions you are ready to ask. There is a reason Mary is accessing all that she Knows in a slow and seemingly frustrating way. That reason IS. Like Mary Is. In the Now of life on this planet, Mary must function day to day: Mary works, Mary interacts with her family, Mary sleeps and dreams and walks and gardens. Perhaps Mary knows that knowing all that Is would make this impossible for her. For the here and now, Mary is wise enough to ask for only that which she can live with in the Now. But it is all there—on the tip of her tongue!

Why does it seem as if she is asking and searching and not being answered?

Because Mary is in a state of profound forgetting—something she needed to do in order to live with the truth of Gracie's life and death. In your human experience of time, it has been an eternity for Mary since Gracie's death—and an instant. But Mary is not alone. She will never be alone. Ask Mary what she loved about Gracie. Was it her infant face? Her body? Her fingers and toes? Her hair, her eyes? It was everything. And everything Gracie was was love. Pure love. And Mary will never be without it again. No amount of forgetting will rid her of it. There is nothing she can do and nothing she can be that will not carry Grace's love. At this time, it seems a small substitute for the child Mary longed to hold and bring home, but let me tell you, there is nothing greater than this love. Mary is blessed with this love. Mary has touched the divine.

I know these are not the answers in the form you would seek them to be. You want to know if Grace has communicated through the computer. Grace has communicated through love. You want to know what puzzles the computer represents. I tell you the computer represents Mary's puzzlement. You want to know how Mary can communicate. Through love.

All I can tell you is that Gracie is showing Mary the way. How does Mary know that Grace has not just taught her the lesson of asking for help? How does Mary know that This is not more important in the Now than something Grace might have communicated through the computer? If Mary will trust Grace to lead her to the keys, she will eventually be able to unlock all the doors.

Thank you, Peace. Is there anything else Mary should know now?

Tell Mary that she is all right. Tell Mary that everything she does is all right. Tell Mary that Grace and I are smiling.

Dearest Grace,   June 1995

I carry the Peace writing everywhere with me. I keep taking it out of my purse to read it. I showed your father, Grace, I read it to him on the back porch. He said the words were beautiful.

I showed this writing to my sister, Liz, in the powder room of the St. Paul Hotel during my father's retirement party. She started crying too. We both cried. Liz kept saying, "That little angel." I started to tell Liz of all the happenings, of all these connections, one thing after another with Margaret, Julie, and me. It felt so good to talk about them.

TRUSTING

Dearest Grace,   June 1995

As I think more about you and wonder where you are,
I find myself thinking a lot about religion. I mean, what
does religion mean to me? I have never been a church-
goer, but I have always had this kind of strain in me to
embrace certain things, certain beliefs. Does this mean
that I am spiritual? I am wondering what that even means
now. Everything I had once believed seems to be in question. I somehow could never buy into the belief that so
much of religious doctrine surrounded the concept of sin
and punishment—the wrath of God. And how much

fear has been used to motivate in religion. When you are good, you know that you can't keep it up forever, and so you wait for the other shoe to drop. Then there it is—staring you right in the face—sin. It makes me squeamish. And for some reason, it has never added up for me.

I have done so much reading, Grace, on all levels—from mythology to energy to consciousness—trying to make some sense of your death and attempting to figure out where you are. I am probably the only mother in the universe who cannot accept death.

All of this has gotten me to thinking. Margaret is writing like a maniac with this angel, Peace. Each bit of writing holds so much wisdom. A blind man could see that. And this writing is so beautiful; it almost stuns me, it is so much so. I have been thinking, if Margaret can do this, maybe I can too. I have talked to her about how it is done. She simply asks to talk to her angel, and then thoughts come into her mind. I have read enough about energy and consciousness to know that we are all connected through consciousness, through spirit.

Gracie, you see, I still cannot write in the computer, and I just have to express myself. I have always been a word person, a communicator. And so, if somehow you hear me, can you let me know when the time will be right to try this for myself? And if my angel, my guardian can also hear me, I just want you to know that I am thinking of somehow talking to you. I will have to do this by hand, because of the computer. But I figure, thoughts are thoughts. And if somehow you can put your thoughts in my head, then maybe I can write them. I figure it cannot be any different, Grace, than when your father says what I am thinking right at the same moment. He does that all the time. I do believe that these things can happen, and that maybe my angel will help me.

Dearest Angels and Gracie, my daughter,   June 15, 1995

I have thoughts in my mind, and at 12:05 A.M. I felt I had to put them down. I have so many questions. I ask that you help me, my guardian angel or angels, with under-standing, if this is possible. I give thanks to all for these thoughts and perceptions. I am feeling words come into me now. I will begin writing. . . .

You live too much on the outside, the external. When you have a bad day, you think you have not done enough. When you have a good day, you have produced. You have worked. But all this lies on the outside of self. Not who you truly are. You feel as if you are dead now, almost wooden. So you tell yourself that this is who I am. But it is not who you really are. You have so much goodness inside. Locked inside.

Today you saw a window in your mind's eye; you even read about the window. This is not a coincidence. This window is open. There is a rea-son that this thought has come to you. Think of this as a window to the soul, think of transparency, where everything is revealed. Know you are loved. Trust and believe in this love. This pain you cling to will also reveal itself. It will also show you the way, as in any dark room, there is safety. You would reach for the light or let your eyes grow accustomed to the dark. Trust that you can be in the dark room and your eyes can see in this darkness. Trust can lead the way. Trust can lead you to safety. There is nothing in the darkness to hurt you, to scare you. We are here, close to you. Trust that you can trust, that you have permission. This is not punishment for you to realize the darkness, it is only to reveal the light that is there, the safety that is there.

You are so much more than work, than production, but you view yourself in such narrow terms. Stop and Remember, tonight, that if you give to yourself, giving to others will not seem so great, that you will have energy. Remember to simply be. Always be. Do not worry.

These are my thoughts—I want to say angel thoughts. I feel as if I became calm with this writing. Oh, angels and Gracie darling, I love you. Thank you for getting me to write again.

Gracie,   June 1995

I tried it! I did it! I tried speaking to my angel. Oh, Gracie, I don't know if what I heard was from my angel, but it was powerful. I could hardly wait to show Julie and Margaret at work the next day. Margaret just beamed when I told her I had done this.

I just sat outside with the journal from Sandy. She gave me this journal the last time I saw her, and there it was in my bookcase, waiting for me to write. So I just began writing, and things started flowing—just flowing. I lost all track of time, and then I read it and felt so connected. I am somewhat hesitant to claim this as angel writing, but I think it might be. This voice seems to have a different tone than that of the Peace angel. I guess when you look at how different Margaret and I are, there's no reason the angels can't have their own way of expressing themselves. I'll include the letters to my angel from now on. . . .

Gracie, I want you to know that I am doing this not to move away from you, but to somehow try and understand things. You will always be a part of these angel letters. I want you to know this. You will always be my special angel. . . .

Dearest Angels and Grace,   June 1995

I have been talking to Margaret about speaking to angels. It appears that when I do this, I do not remember what I have written. I have some vague idea, but nothing in detail. I simply write what comes to me. At times I remember nothing. I have noticed that my handwriting changes when my angel speaks. It still feels as if I should name you, angel. It feels awkward, not knowing what to call you. Margaret had the thought that your name was Trinity when she spoke to you the first time. I keep sensing Bridge. I don't know what to do. More later.

Dearest Angels and Gracie, my angel,   June 17, 1995

Thank you for this breeze, the flowers, the bird singing, the sun. As I sit here this morning, I try to enter a calm.

The word *trust* has been going through my mind all day. What does this mean? Can you help me with trust? My trust in life seems to have been broken now that Grace has died. Everything appears to be in question. Everything. Is it life I do not trust? Is it myself I do not trust? Can I trust what I hear from you? When I woke up today, I looked *trust* up in the dictionary. It meant faith, hope, confidence. Am I on the right track? Can you guide me?

Faith is something that Is. It is there. You search for proof. Yet, many things in life will never be proven. They simply are. What is meaning-ful to you? Trust? Hope? They are all a part of you that you have denied. You see these qualities in others and believe, but in yourself you doubt that this is possible. You really doubt love of self, of your own worthiness. You have protected self so long because you felt you had to. Self says, I cannot do this any longer. Mind says, I need proof.

But the road is bending, turning for you. The light is there, yet you stumble, you have fear, you do not want to walk, you want to turn back. Realize that you are turning toward life. Do you not see that you are believing? That proof can be disproved? Some things ARE. Proof can be hollow and lead to emptiness. Love is all that is. Love will take you and comfort you when proof stands by you. Your mind fights also to be believed. Take it by the hand. Welcome it. Your mind will believe. You are turning, Mary. You know this.

With knowing, there is hope, faith, and love. Your goodness, which has been denied to you, is bountiful. You have never been able to truly allow this to be revealed. You need this goodness for yourself now. Past hurts and pains have made this so. Believe in this goodness, for it will guide you.

I love you, my dearest angels and Gracie. Thank you. Thank you. Thank you.

What is needed is chosen by you. You choose this to learn. You are

100

communicating. Believe this, Mary. You are seeing. Believe this. You worry about angels' names. They will come in time. Feeling, which is an important realm for you to be in, is here. Know and trust these feelings to guide you to truth. Trust even the pain to be your friend. Because it is. You then can let it be.

The hardest part for you is the "ISness." ISness is simply being. You feel that this is difficult to handle. You fear, and then you doubt. Give yourself credit! You are a well of love. Dip into the well and take a drink! Feel the coolness of the water, savor the taste of the water, let your body sing with this delight, this awakening. Put the ladle back. Lower the bucket. Know that the well is there for you always, with the cool, soothing, refreshing liquid of love.

Suffering for you feels difficult, but it just IS. Once again, proving it is unnecessary. You ask "why" with suffering, "why" it cannot be proven. It IS. Love cannot be proven. It IS. You say, "But I am this or that." You ARE. You feel with each emotion. Look at this, Mary. Examine what I am really saying here: You feel you are with an emotion. You feel you ARE this emotion.

If you feel bad, then you think you are bad. You are this emotion. If you feel good, then you are good. Do you not see how you become your feelings? You wear feelings as if they were clothes. You adopt the total stance of that feeling as if it were you! Do you see that feelings are not trust as it IS? You have been told that you were bad. So you have thought, I AM bad. Don't you see this is NOT who you ARE? You adopted feelings as truth, because you were told so. And you believed. You thought that something was so wrong with you. That you were wrong! Wrong to BE!

The truth was there, and once you fought to believe it. You had to

101

fight to be believed. But when you are so young, you cannot defend yourself in such a big world. You adopted beliefs. You stopped fighting for self. You became the feeling.

This is a lot to digest now. I have to think this over. But I thank you, dearest angels and Gracie, for these jewels of thoughts.

I love you, my darlings.

Dearest Angels and Gracie and all that is,   June 20, 1995

Thank you for this day and for my family, for the music and for the cigarettes. Can you please guide me with Amanda and my feelings? I feel all this love for her and then I get scared. When I get scared, I know I appear more rigid than I feel inside. I lost Grace, and I ask myself, *Can I love again? Can I open up to a child?*

Turn toward the light. You have already found what is needed. It is time to clear your mind. You know what is needed. Love who you are and your higher self will be seen. Love will always help you. Clear your mind, Mary.

How can I love myself more?

Go within, and you will be guided. Go inward with a clear mind. You search and want signs. They are all around. Amanda needs to love self. You can teach her this love of self. She struggles as you struggle. Her pain is your pain. But you take this pain on. You become her pain. You blame yourself for her pain. This is her pain. You take on pain that is not yours. Realize this pain is a teacher to indicate what is needed. Remember, what is needed is chosen.

Look at pain, for it is only an indication that will point to love. Love self and go within for these answers. Dip into the well. Take a drink. Your frustrations stem from nonlove. Emptiness. Love yourself and allow this love to guide you. Ask what you can do for self. You use work to get away, to hide from who you are. If you are busy, you do not need to go within. I say to go within. Do not fear. Your strength is great. You know love.

There are those around you who want to show you love. There is healing all around. There are ways. What gives you pleasure, Mary? Examine this closely. Does this also give you love? Do not be afraid to ponder. As you ponder, you will Be. You are wonderful. Celebrate this.

Dearest Angels and Gracie, my love, and all that is, thank you for these insights. I feel calmer. Once again, you are working your magic and LOVE.

My dearest Angels and daughter Gracie,   June 1995

I am sitting here in the morning, feeling the sun, listening to birds, and sipping coffee. My mornings used to be spent running around and feeling stress. Thank you for helping me to create time where I thought there was none. Thank you for helping me notice my love, my goodness. Thank you for opening my eyes simply to notice.

I sit here and I think and I wonder. Could you guide me with the issue of having another baby? Some days I desire one, and then I think, *Oh, no, I am fine.* What is going on inside me?

Mary, go inward. You have your answers. Give yourself space. You are creating it now. You are changing your LIFE. SELF is becoming blessed. Your desires are your desires. There is no right and wrong. There Is only being. You want to figure it all out. There is no figuring. Simply Be and trust. You worry constantly. You have spent so much time involved in the future. Just Be in the now.

Think of strength. You are seeing how this carried you through your worst fear. You felt you would crack, not be able to go on, but you did. You believed.

I realize now that I believed in love. Didn't I? I had to hang on to this love, because the pain would only lead to a black hole. This love was like some type of boat in a sea of huge crashing waves. I just clung to the boat in hopes of something.

Yes! In your darkest hour you believed in love. Only love. You ask yourself now, "Would I be patient and responsible with a baby?" Think of what you have just asked. You are patient and responsible now. You work, you listen, you are there for people, you are a true friend. Would it be different with a child? You fear you do not have qualities. That you lack something, somehow, because your daughter died. This is thinking with scarcity. This is thinking that you have some type of drastic deficit. Realize all you do have and are. Say, "I am wonderful."

Know what a good mother you already are. A child can be a reflection of love, of All that Is. Celebrate all that is, all that you are! Take time to love self. We love you also, dear one. Your preciousness is there and we are with you in this awakening.

Dearest Gracie and my angels,   July 8, 1995
I am back on the back porch writing this by hand, and once again I am struck by the beauty of the yard, the

flowers, the robins. Thank you for this appreciation, for the ability to notice things that surround me. I keep feeling as if I need to be working on something. Can you guide me? I had another thought of thanks, and that is for Amanda. She was so dear to me today—serving me food and bringing my books to me here on the porch. I feel as if Gracie is working through Amanda.

Amanda's love is Gracie's love. It is all love. There is a connection here—love flows through children. They are pure in so many ways until there is forgetting. Keep these memories alive. Remember love is all there IS. Learn from this love. All is as it should be. Feel. Do not be afraid. Past hurts may come rearing up. You cannot redo, undo, for they are in the past. To cling is not to live in the present. Feel and know silence. All you are reading reflects the pause. This is the place in which you can be. It is between all moments. It is in the timelessness of being. This is needed for good reason. Busyness keeps one away from self.

Working to escape can be difficult for the soul. You tremble at the thought of quiet and knowing. What could you discover that you do not already know? Trust, which is so crucial in life, is there. Remember to Be. The need to control feels troublesome to you. But why? What can you control? Yourself? Others? Reflect on this. You are changing. You are seeing. Dear Mary, you have all the love inside. It is there. Do not be afraid to bring it forth. Love is in the air. Breathe in love. Exhale worry. We are here in your heart. Trust that we will guide you always, should you ask. It is in asking that the knowing is revealed.

I say this often, but love who you are, as you are, now! Know we are there inside this love. To be busy is not always what one needs. Please rest. Feel us within your love.

You tend to work at everything. You continually are working at an improvement for some future goal. What of now? Do you feel as if you are nothing until you get there? Base your thoughts on the internal. Like in between—that is the now. That is The Moment. Let things be. There is no other way to love self than in the now. When you love self, all will fall in place. You will be able to recognize the flow and the integration of self to higher self. You are seeing how one can divide one's self into compartments—integration will come. All this you sense because it will help you. Practice in the moment. Take time for yourself. Know we love you!

Thank you dear angels—Gracie. Mama loves you! I know you are with me.

Dearest Angels and dearest Gracie,   July 1995
    I woke up today with questions. Once again I am on the back porch, feeling the sun on my skin. I feel love in my heart for my husband, for Amanda. I feel so blessed. Thank you.

It is true you are at the right place at the right time. Questions are a beginning point, a knowing. To ask questions means the answers are there. Let us speak of perfectionism. Your thoughts recently reflect that you are knowing and seeing that the imperfect is perfect. That one does not have to be perfect as you have been taught to think. Perfection is not joy. Joy is in knowing that imperfection, as you term it, is perfection. This was revealed to you—through Gracie, your daughter. Through physical imperfection of the body, you saw only love.

    Yet you struggle. You say, "But I felt I could not care for her." This is your own prison. You create this thought. It has been revealed to you, through Grace's physical problem, that this is not so. Gracie was much more than a body with physical ailments. And you know this to be truth. Gracie came to you, in one sense, to reveal this. Yet you blamed yourself, saying, "But I did not love her enough." That was fear. Do you not see how much you did love her at this time? The angel was there and you felt her presence. Your fear stems from taking care of things—that you do not do it perfectly. It is in the imperfection that there is perfection! Are you worried about your own imperfection? Do you not spend hours needlessly worrying that you have done something wrong? This is a long tradition in your family—one shivers to think of making mistakes, saying something wrong, doing an action differently. That is fear. Believe that you Are. That all you do is perfect in its imperfection.

Gracie blessed you with this. Make mistakes. Celebrate! The goal is to be with all one is, with imperfections. Celebrate your seeing this wonderful condition of humanness. It is through this that joy can be attained and seen.

Notice all around you. This will lead to ultimate forgiveness of self, to integration, to love. I say that in the loving forgiveness, we become whole. It is in the splitting of self—this self is okay, this self is not— that things take on lower vibrations. Vibrate with the knowing. All is well, my dear.

Thank you so much—this is what I need to hear. Yet it scares me, this letting go.

What would happen if you let go? Would you disappear? Lose your mind? Fear again—it is familiar for you. Ask if you fear happiness. Turn inward. Go deep, Mary. Think of Love. The ultimate chuckle is that all is as it should be. Know that! Love will come!

Thank you once again, my dears, and precious Gracie.

Dearest Grace and my Dear Angels,   July 1995

I want to thank you for dear Amanda. So often when I go into this shell, she is there to pull me out. One of the things that touches me so deeply is this dance we do. Grace, we have done this ever since you were alive. . . .

When you were still living, Amanda and I just had to get away. I had hardly spent any time with her, so one day, on the way home from the hospital, we went to listen to CDs at a music store. I remember feeling so lost. I found an old CD from a woman named Angela Bofill. I bought it because it brought back a part of my past, so many years ago. There was a song about an angel on the CD, which we listened to when we got home. We joined hands and began twirling around. We kept going faster and faster. I remember hearing my laugh and thinking it sounded so far away. Grace, it felt so good. What would I do without your dear sister?

Dear Angels,   July 1995

Tonight I feel so tired. I made a mistake at work. I had these booklets printed up with the wrong title. I thought they were proofed, and I was wrong. I feel "bad" now. Please help me! I need to be able to live in the moment and I feel I am always somehow taken out of it.

The now is a strange and wonderful thing. This is not a contest. You are learning. You expect so much so soon. Be, dear one. Be. The more you are able to Be, you will Be. You know, through your mind, that you need to quiet down. Yet you ask yourself why? how?

You feel the warm caress of the breeze. That IS. You see the colors. They Are. Quiet brings internal focus. You are not stuck on the outside of self. Go inward and love. You are so important. Yet, in so many ways, you put yourself last. When I say rest, Rest. Gather. Stroll. Be quiet. What would your life be if you just rested and loved and did not work one weekend? Savor life! Feel it! Be with love. The rest will follow!

Thank you so much my dears! I am so tired I must sleep.

Dearest Gracie,   July 1995

I don't know where to begin with yesterday. I was on the sunporch reading. Your father was out running errands. We have a rule in the family that each of us can ask for "private time" to be alone and uninterrupted. I had told Amanda that I would be taking some private time, but right after I started reading, Amanda knocked at the French doors. I told her again that I was reading, but she said that she had to talk to me. I could tell by the look on her face that something had happened.

She sat on the futon beside me and said that she had gone outside to get some lemonade, when she saw a toddler on the chair I had left outside. At first, Amanda thought it was a neighbor kid, but then she saw white light surrounding the child. I grabbed Amanda's arm; I had goose bumps. I said, "Amanda, who was the child?" Maybe I said it too loud, but Amanda said that it was you,

Grace! I asked her how she knew—she said by your curly hair and your eyes. The child then went into this light.

I told Amanda to show me outside. We went outside and Amanda showed me how she had looked under the cushion of the chair after the child disappeared. She said the child had dissolved "into light." Amanda did not know the word for *dissolve*—she just made fluttery motions with her hands. She went on to say that the light was "brighter than the sun."

Gracie, you would have been a year old next week! Amanda said that you had a pink robe on, with stars and moons on your moccasins. Moccasins? She said that there was fur around your robe, and that there was some type of sash that had hearts on the end of it. Gracie, this is almost more than I can bear.

That evening, Amanda wanted to go to the park, so we went. Instead of playing like she usually does, on the monkey bars, she took my hand and told me that Daddy and I should have another child! Gracie, is this from you?

But things don't end there. When I told Julie today at work about what Amanda saw, she told me she had a dream last night in which one moccasin was left at her front door in the rain! Julie has never dreamed about a moccasin before in her life. Gracie, I know you are trying to reach out. I just want to thank you for all of this—but I have to try and figure what it all means. . . .

BELIEVING

July 16, 1995

Dearest Angels, Gracie my love, God—all the universe!

I am sitting on the back steps listening to church bells. I just reread the passages of this journal. It is so wonderful, a blessing, and it helps quiet me. I think of angels and miracles *all* the time. I think of Gracie appearing for Amanda. I ponder the mystery and beauty of life. I realize the pain of Grace's death is turning into a beautiful awareness—a gift of eternity. A revealing of love—a love that knows no bounds. A sense that love is always there. Thank you so for showing me.

I am here and I know instinctively that I might be pregnant. I have felt that I have to take care of my body, that my life is changing. This thought of a new baby makes me feel so hopeful, alive, grateful. Thank you again, my angels.

Yet, there are times when fear crosses my path with this happiness. Can you guide me through this thought?

Dearest Mary,

Fear is fear. It is nothing. Believe in all— All that Is! You saw how fear can control you, yet this is illusion. Illusion appears as fact. Yet there are no facts. Life simply Is.

This is the time for strength and joy! Your strength is in your decision to have another child in spite of fear! You lived your worst fear and came out with more love in your heart. Dear Mary, celebrate life. Know that joy is with you. Feel it. Allow yourself permission to rejoice—welcome love with your family. Know that the time for love is here. Your heart is open. Love yourself and all else follows. Go inward and see. You will be a wonderful mother.

Thank you, Angel, but how can I work with this fear?

To deny anything gives power to what is denied. Accept that this happened. That was then. You are in the now. It is a new experience with all the differences and pleasures of the new. Be gentle. You have already seen that you can turn an argument—whatever it may be—around through love. All of life may be turned around through love. If fear crosses your path, say: "My lesson is learned. I am in a different place, a different time. I am different!" You have nothing to fear. It is only a thought that you choose to think. You can choose to think many things. CHOOSE dear Mary. It is your right! Choose to say, "I am happy."

You have looked fear square in the face and you have found love! Ponder this! You felt fear and grew to love! An immense thing has occurred! You turned something around through love!

Dearest Angels! You wonderful, wonderful beings! You are so helpful. Thank you. And my dearest spirit daughter—you are my precious angel. Thank you!

Dearest Angels, Gracie my darling,   July 23, 1995

Thank you for leading me to the book for parents that have lost their children. It could not have come at a better time than on the eve of Gracie's first birthday. There are so many universal feelings that parents have during this time. I felt as if I were not alone! Thank you.

Yet, I am struck by going back to my grief, anger, bewilderment over Grace's death. I realize I may always have a hole in my heart. I was so upset yesterday, crying and lost. I feel angry. I looked at the outfit Grace would have worn home and the outfit just lay there on the bed—empty.

I sometimes feel as if this was punishment for me—that I did something wrong in this life or a past life. I know death happens to us all. But this seems so hard to deal with and to make sense of—that it happened to a little baby. Can you guide me in making any sense of this? I feel so lost right now. Even as I write, I am somewhere else—jumping up to tell Amanda what to do, talking to John.

There is something in this. Look deeply at these distractions. What is hardest for you to bear? That you have gone back to the place of

113

Grace's death? What are your feelings? Shame, anger, envy? Look inward. Bring the light. You feel doubt right now as to how far you have come. You want things to be happy, not uncomfortable. You want to move on, yet an emotion says wait. Examine why this emotion has made you pause.

Your humanness keeps you back in this place. Yet you realize there is also a place where spirit rests. Dear one, you are only resting for a moment here, in this place of discomfort. You know the depth of your love for Gracie. You judge so harshly. Do not judge. Gracie feels only love for you. Why do you punish yourself for her death? She had a malformation.

Gracie wants you to know she felt all your love, every moment. And what a love it was and still is! You think back and say, "But there were times I wanted her to die—I was not strong enough." Instead, know that you did not want her to suffer—this is love. Your humanness also had concern about her care in the future. This is all right! Gracie felt only your love! Do you not think she sees beyond doubt and despair? These choices that you rivet yourself around were all about love.

This was an extremely difficult, unbearable situation on your physical plane. Know that Gracie knows. She wants you to forgive self. When doubt springs into mind, know Gracie will guide you. She knows how difficult these thoughts and feelings are. Know that they will be replaced with love. Deep, true love.

Dear Grace and my Angel,   August 1995

Your sister, Amanda, and I were at the Bruegger's Bagels restaurant on Grand Avenue last Sunday, when we noticed this older man, kind of a fatherly type, kept looking at us. When Amanda got up to get something, he told me what a beautiful daughter I had. I thanked him and didn't go into the stepdaughter thing, but then he looked me square in the eyes and said that I should have another child! I was somewhat stunned, because I know that I don't look like I'm in my twenties. Amanda just told me to have a child—now a total stranger! Gracie, you know that your father and I have been trying to have another child. But nothing has happened. Maybe I am afraid or something. Yet I found this comment so disarming.

Dearest Angel and Gracie,   August 1995

I am seeing connections everywhere! I have to talk to Margaret and Julie about this tomorrow at work.

Today your father and Amanda and I went to the Minnesota Landscape Arboretum. I thought it would be a good family thing to do. Well, your father and I each had our own agenda of the afternoon. Your dad got a map and I hardly ever read maps, so he was mad at me about this. I thought that we could hike and just be out, and maybe sit in the woods, or a field, or something. But your father wanted to drive everywhere! It was so hot and sticky that everyone started getting crabby. To make a long story short, we ended up in the Japanese garden, then we moved into the shade gardens. I took my little notebook out to write down the names of flowers and plants. While I was doing this, Amanda said that one of her favorite girl's names was Persephone. I tried to ignore this, but I got goose bumps when she said it. Persephone was the daughter of Demeter in Greek mythology, the one that the astrologer had said was in my chart! Well the day went on, and it kept getting hotter. I had to find a place to sit down. Your father and Amanda went out on their own. After I rested, I went to look for them, but I got the directions mixed up.

All of a sudden, I saw this statue by these bushes, so I went over to read the plaque. It was a life-size statue of a man in a loose-fitting garment, with a bird on his hand. It said it was St. Francis of Assisi, the patron saint of small animals and nature, or something like that. Well, I looked over to the side of the statue, and I saw a statue of a German shepherd. Gracie, it was the same one that was in my dream about the burial! It was this magnificent animal. The statue was in the exact position that it had been in my dream, except in my dream, the dog was alive.

I have to ask Margaret about St. Francis. I may even have to stop at a bookstore to get a book on him. Gracie, when I saw that dog statue I almost collapsed. Maybe it was the heat. And the funny thing about this is that no one else was around. It was just me, St. Francis, and his dog.

That night . . .

Dearest Angel and Grace,

This is almost more than I can handle! Tonight Amanda and I were working together, cutting some fabric for a dressing table for her room. As we were doing this, Amanda said again, "It's just like Persephone." I couldn't stand it anymore! I asked Amanda how she knew that name. She said that she had heard it in her "dream of favorite names," and then she added that she'd had that dream last April. She wanted to know why I wanted to know. I told her it was an old Greek name and not many people knew it (let alone a nine-year-old child). That was all that was said. But Grace, it was about last April, actually March 28 to be exact, that all of this started happening, with the computer and all. Have these connections spread to Amanda?

Hello again my Angel and Gracie,   August 1995

Well, this St. Francis story continues. I told Margaret and Julie all about my dream and what I found in the arboretum. They have been having dreams as profound as I feel mine to be. The wonderful thing is that we can share. No one is alone.

After that, Margaret brought in this picture of St. Francis she "happened" to find. I have it by my desk at work. Then, when I was out at my mother's the other day, I was relating the story about the dog in my dream, and the statue at the arboretum. My mother told me that the prayer of St. Francis of Assisi had been my grandmother's favorite prayer! It had been read at her funeral, at which I had given the eulogy. My mother then ran and got the prayer that had hung in my grandmother's bedroom. She gave it to me, as a gift from Grandma.

The interesting aspect of my grandmother is that she was an incredible animal lover. When we were kids, she could not even watch a cowboy movie if horses fell down or were shot. A few days after my grandmother died, two years ago, I had a dream in which I saw her in a white car. I remember she was trying to tell me something, but I could not understand her through the car window. I also remember finding a kitten at a gas station, after planning my grandmother's funeral. I ran to the car with the kitten and showed my mother. My mother ended up keeping this kitten. It was right before John and I were married. It's funny, I never put any of this together before. I'm even beginning to see how animals may be connected to healing . . . and St. Francis is the patron saint of this . . . it's really got me thinking. Thank you, Angels.

August 16, 1995

Dearest God, my Angels, and my wonderful Gracie!

John came home the other day and said, "We have to get another kitten." I was in total agreement with this. I had been thinking how lonely Bob, Amanda's cat, must get when we are at work. Your father does this all the time. It is as if he can read my mind.

We got in the car and headed for Taylors Falls, along the St. Croix River. The animal humane society there is located in a renovated Victorian mansion. I immediately fell in love with the woman who was running it. She took us upstairs and showed us a small orange kitty with golden eyes. The woman gave me the kitten to hold and then said, "She was found on July 22." My heart started pounding. That was your birthday, Grace.

"What?" I said when she told me this. "July 22," she said again. I would not put the kitten down. I told John, "This is the one!" When we were downstairs and John was filling out the papers, I happened to glance at a table and I saw a card that read:

> "Cats are angels with fur,
> Welcome to the tunnel of Love"

Gracie, I knew this to be a sign. First the kitten was found on your birthday. I found it so odd that this woman would even tell us the day that she was found. And then the card. It was all too much. I cried all the way home. Your dad kept looking at me and holding my hand. I kept my fingers in the cat carrier, touching this new kitten. You see, I never took you home, Grace. This was the first thing I could hold in my arms. I just knew that you wanted me to have something to hold. This kitten became christened as Carli. I think she opens up my heart.

Thank you, darling.

August 29, 1995

Dear God, my precious Angels, Gracie my darling,

As you know, I am on the North Shore, sitting on some huge rocks overlooking Lake Superior, hearing the waves crash against the shore. It is a mysterious day, a little dark, almost as if it might rain. John and I have taken some

119

time off to come up here. This was the starting point of our love, years ago, and it continues on, each visit here to these cabins contains a new depth, a new layer to our lives. It is also the perfect place to be on the anniversary of Gracie's death. Even as I write these words it is hard for me.

Mary, look at the water. What does it contain—the beginning of life? The depth you are feeling? The mystery? Reflect. Everything comes forth as it should. Your destiny, your love, your life. You are in the void. What do you see there? What do you feel? It is from this point that answers may be formed. The mystery of life is that it IS! It will always be! Acceptance is crucial now. To love All includes love of self. Savor the furry spiders of your dreams. For they are only furry pets! They are nothing to fear! Your fear has controlled you—almost stopped you, deadened you from movement. But in the void, you can walk and touch this fear. Hold it near love. It is only by love that life will be transformed. You are in exactly the right place on this trip. To add a new layer of love! To visit the void, to gain strength! You had strength for Gracie. Now it is time to have it for yourself. Everything that you were for your daughter still lies within you. This time, this day that you have been waiting for, is here, and it is from this time that the new beginning can occur.

Thank you, my angels and Gracie. I love you, too.

Dearest Angels, Gracie, and God,　　　　　September 1995

I am sitting outside. The summer is almost over. The breeze is blowing. I keep sensing something about "illusion." I know I should look it up.

Illusion is set up to teach, to break through to the light and love. When illusions are cast aside, one can see.

Do you think I need to let go of my illusions? Do I have illusions in my life?

You thought today of illusions; therefore, you questioned. But you also heard. You cannot see illusions, yet one knows the difference when one is on the other side of illusion. There is no illusion. There is only fear set up to deceive. Yet what is fear but what one thinks is so? Nothing is meant to harm you. Nothing. The illusion is a trick, a sleight of hand in perception. Nothing more. Go to the quiet. Love is there! You worry so about this and that, about tricks, about mistrust. Be still. Be quiet. The answers are there.

I feel as if I have trusted and I have been tricked in love. I have believed and then I have been hurt! What does this mean? Was this not done to me? Against me? What do I need to learn?

Mary, you have made your heart like armor for protection—in many ways with good cause. It is difficult to convey on your terms what choice means, that you have chosen certain paths to learn from. Reflect on your life. Have you chosen pain?

Does anyone choose pain?

The picture of life is much bigger than how you are examining it. The stage for your life was set a long time ago. You chose, yet your journey is what you are remembering—the pain of the journey. My dear one, has not this journey taught you, deepened your perceptions of life, stretched your imagination to the wonders? Do you not see that with

121

each painful lesson, you have reaped benefits far greater than what you cried over at the time of pain? Your divorce propelled you to know what true love meant and is. Hence, John. Your marriage to John is a symbol of your happiness, your choice even through pain! The life and death of Gracie have brought you toward spiritual transformation. This pain that humans try so hard to understand is merely a lesson of choice. But this choice is hard to fathom.

Yes, you are on the brink of letting go of illusions, but part of you clings to the familiar. What awaits is true happiness. Joy! Trust in this movement toward joy! There is never too much. When perplexed, when filled with insecurities, go to the quiet. Know your answers are there. Do not be afraid of what you try so hard to deny. You are on the road to Joy and Joy awaits you with open arms.

You want to do it all so right, so correctly. Just be! Have you not thought that by acceptance a major lesson has been accomplished? Listen to your inner voice, the voice that IS. If something is nonsupportive, hard, difficult, berating, it is fear! Do not worry about outcomes. Just be. Take time and enjoy.

Oh, my angels, with all of your help, I will learn to simply be and accept. Thank you. I love you all.

Dearest Angel and Grace,   September 1995

I have to come to you once again. I feel as if I do not understand. I have tried to get into my computer—I can't count the times, and all I get are those bells. I can't write with it. Once again I am not complaining, but this is unnerving. As much as I see all these wonderful things, all these connections, I still have this fear. And I still cry at night so much. Not as much as when you first died, Grace, but every time I think of your being gone, I start crying privately in my pillow. I just stare out into this dark room and wonder about everything. *How could this have happened to me?* How come I still wonder and have fear? And why won't the computer work?

BEING

September 2, 1995

Dearest Angels, my God, darling Gracie,

Today, Amanda came back home from her other house, and I was a mother again. It feels so good when she and I set up our rhythm—our way of being. I really love her. I love being a mother. It means so much to me. Thank you for this in my life.

You have come to this point in your life because you have chosen it. What Amanda reveals to you is a reflection of yourself, the self you need to love. As you see and admire parts of her, are intrigued by parts

124

of her, and are repelled by other parts, know that you do this with self.
You are who you are. You are Mary, as Amanda is Amanda.

And now you question. You are seeing connections for the first time!
You are being. You look at the measure of your thoughts. You are ques-
tioning: Is this thought right for me? You are solving the riddle of love,
of acceptance, of knowing.

Mary, dear, you are trusting. As you have thought, you are treating
this writing, this journal, as valid. You come here to know. You realize
that by holding this journal, it is real, concrete. These are so much more
than words. You see the truth within the words.

Do you not feel your joy? Open your arms, my dear! You believe
these words, and in so doing love yourself! The miracles are soon to be.
We love you. We shall always be close.

September 22, 1995

Dearest Angels, Gracie, and the Wonderful,
Beautiful Universe!

Today I am sitting at a cabin with Julie and Margaret.
We are here on a retreat. We have wanted to spend time
together, away from homes and families. These women
are so special and giving. We each have struggled, and
may continue to struggle, but the support and love we
feel for each other is wonderfully loyal and poignant at
the same time. Yet, as I drove here, I felt anxious or
excited or something. Can you shed some light on this?
Can you help me?

There is a connection here, a knowing. Where does this lead? Anxiety

*and excitement. It is a discovery, a new road, the point at which you all
come together. This love is so revealing. Let go at this moment and blow
the past away as dust on your fingers. For it is done. This moment, this
time, is the beginning of the new, and from this—through this—love
springs forward like a babbling brook catching the sun. Imagine the
life! The vitality! The love! As you turn from pain, you can feel the
transformation. This will replace the pain. Your love is like a jewel to
be examined on all sides.*

Thank you so much for this space and time, for this
insight, for this love, my angels. Thank you.

Later that day . . .

Dear angels,

Today the most incredible event happened to me. Next
to seeing the scrolling computer, this has to be the
strongest visual thing I have ever witnessed. . . .

Because Margaret and Julie and I did not know what we
were going to be doing at the cabin, we just let things go
on their own. We talked and ate bread and cheese. We
played music. We said the prayer from Grace's funeral
service. We burned candles and laughed and cried. We
were just women together.

At one point, the three of us were sitting on the living-
room floor. I happened to look over at Julie. As I did, I saw
a shaft of light come through the living-room ceiling. It
was light blue and had white iridescent bubbles in it. The
aspect of the light that was so very striking was that it was

moving. As if it were alive! The bubbles moved within the light. At this moment I knew and felt that time had totally stopped. It was the most beautiful light I have ever seen. I can only attribute this to you, Grace. This light was completely without fear. It was simply beautiful.

Dearest Angels and Gracie, September 26, 1995

I dreamed last night that I was running down a hallway at work. My job had moved. I entered what I knew to be the "Zeus Room," because I saw this picture of Zeus on the wall. I saw a table with a puzzle on it. The puzzle had intricate and tiny pieces. I started to pick up one of the pieces, but decided it would upset the whole puzzle, so I left it alone. Angels, when I think of this, I see how perplexed I am with my life, how the pieces don't seem to fit. Is it better left alone, or do I need to figure something out? Yet, I cannot help but be comforted by these dreams.

I sit here now, on a warm autumn day. I hear the birds, feel the sun, see the bumble bee on a flower, and I want this moment to last. This beauty that surrounds me, this way of nature seems so perfect. It all fits. One season blending into another. Change and harmony. Can we talk of my destiny? My purpose? Does it have anything to do with beauty?

You sense and you know. All of your life has been about beauty. But what is beauty but a reflection, a reflection of who you are? You have worked so hard at making things beautiful on the outside that you have hungered for beauty on the inside. But you knew. You see so much. And

127

with this seeing is the need to transform, to touch something and bring out its beauty. This all springs from your inner beauty. You see, you touch, you transform—all because of your inner beauty. Everything in your life has centered on beauty—your clothing, your home, your food, your life.

But it is only now that you know this. Beauty, like all else, can hold a duality, a lesson. Beauty for the sake of externals can lead to emptiness, hollowness—just as love can be hollow if there is no self-love. You have passed through these gates in search of beauty. You pushed beauty to the limits, to mold a perfectionist attitude that imprisoned. But this is not inner beauty. This is what you have always sensed—always known.

This perfectionism became evident in Grace with her malformation. Your biggest fear was that your child would not be "perfect." That you were not perfect! Yet, you truly saw that Grace was perfect just as she was in physical form. Your heart held the truth through LOVE. And nothing matters now but love. Your "imperfection" is your perfection.

Beauty has taken you down many roads, from the physical to the celestial. And yes, this knowing of beauty is magical, transformational. When you understand this beauty, you will be free!

How can I use this beauty for the highest good?

You have knowledge. You know that human perfection on your plane is impossible. To strive for this leads to emptiness, to loss. What do you give away to reach this goal? Your heart! This is what spirituality all points to. It is accessing What Is! What will always Be!

You have known the brittleness of beauty with no heart. Yet you sense this knowing, this teaching to reach beauty—inner beauty. Feel the feeling of looking at a beautiful flower or seeing a curtain blow in the breeze. What happens to you? This is what we speak of.

As you reflect on beauty totally in the moment, you are present. You know perfection. You know that everything contains beauty—even pain. Dear one, this road you have traveled has held its arms open to you. And you have embraced it! Do you not feel a lightening of spirit?

I keep sensing that I have seen this beauty in others but not in myself. That I know beauty, although it seems distant. . . .

You know! You know beauty in others—you bring out the beauty in others because you see their beauty! You reflect this back to others. When others have walked the road of pain, you have seen their beauty! You have reflected this back to others. Do you not see that the beauty you saw in others was your own beauty reflected back? And what beauty! What love! Through pain you saw beauty in others! Celebrate this awakening! Your beauty is bountiful!

I feel my spirit is lighter, happier, knowing the beauty has always been in me! And I never knew until now. I didn't realize how beautiful I was. Oh, thank you, dear angels! My God! I love you so! Gracie darling! What an angel you are. I will celebrate my beauty.

September 30, 1995

Dearest Angels, my daughter Gracie, God,
and the Wonderful Universe,

I am in bed now on a Saturday night. All is quiet in the house. I have reflected on the name Bridge for my Guardian Angel. This sense has been with me since I first wrote. Am I on to something?

You are Mary, and it Is. Bridge. A connection from one side to the next. A means of traveling, communicating.

Is it okay that I call you that?

What stops you?

I am afraid.

Why?

Afraid that I named you. That you already have a name—that Margaret said you were Trinity. I know you are with me but I have not felt any communication coming through—as if there were silence. I wonder if you are mad.

Are you sure you are not angry? At yourself? You worry about being who you truly are. So you seek approval from outside, even when you have answers. Why do you do this? Why do you torture self and set self up for defeat? You know. Act on this. You don't need my approval to be who you are and to feel how you feel. Be, dear one! We speak now of responsibility to self. This is essential to trust. One must trust self, and to do so, one must be responsible to self.

Thank you for this insight. I am still in a quandary about your name. I feel somewhat insecure in this regard. The act of naming anything just seems so important. I guess if Margaret heard "Trinity," I'll go with that. I hope this will be okay with you. Perhaps bridge was the symbol for you, my angel.

October 1, 1995

Dearest Angels, Trinity, my Gracie, dearest God,
and the Wonderful Universe,

I just want to thank all of you for the love and kindness you are sending me—the insights and illuminations. I feel as if I am growing and understanding more each day. I just want to be! Yet as I pause here, I think of my frustration today. My needing to get things done, my not being pregnant. I felt edgy. Then I get snappy and controlling.

You want to control what you cannot. This has been evident to you. Think of the pause and what it contains. There is a reason for the pause—a most important function. The richness and depth are within. Be ever so gentle with self. All will get done! Sort—see what can be discarded and what contains your true essence. Realize your beauty! Be gentle.

The pause is the most important moment you will experience. It is in the unexpected poignant moments with your child, petting an animal, allowing life to unfold within. Control defeats the purpose of this. The riches come from within, from noticing, from being present. Don't "do" anything. Try being, giving your all to the moment! Then you will see. You will treasure being Mary!

Think of your happiest times. Were they not the sunset? the music? the fire? the unexpected pleasures of love? the realness of spoken truth? Be real! This concept of being genuine Is. This will help you touch what you search for. The more you love yourself, the more we are able to help you.

Thank you my beings of light and love, my darling Grace. I love you all. Thank you so.

October 5, 1995

Dearest Angels, Gracie my Light,
the Wonderful Universe,

I guess I didn't get too angry with Amanda this morning—she was running late for school again. Yet, I am still left with a residue of feelings, of feeling unsettled—bad somehow.

Look at this word—bad. What does it signify to you?

I feel as if I am bad because I have these feelings.

Feelings are not bad or good. They simply are. In the transparent state they can enter and leave. Send yourself love on these occasions. Work from the internal out. Go to the quiet when you feel these feelings that are not favorable. As you go inward, you will understand. Love is there. But it starts with self. You are thinking of authenticity. Start with your emotions. Do you accept them or do you push them away when they arise?

You want the feeling of love in these situations, yet you show no love to self! If you are sad or angry, shake hands with this emotion, send it love. It is at this point that you turn on self. You punish self for being human, and therefore you punish others. This love of self is paramount. Start here.

Do you always have to wait until you feel positive emotions before you love self? Integration takes time. Start by loving you! Celebrate by loving you. You looked fear in the face. How about anger? Hold its hand and by doing so learn to love.

132

Thank you, Dear Angels and Gracie and the Universe.

October 17, 1995

Dearest Trinity, Gracie my love, my dearest Angels,
dearest God, and all the Wonderful Universe,

It has been so long since I last wrote. As you know, I
have been to New Orleans for a work convention. I will
soon be off to Spain for the International Symposium.

I did feel more personal power in New Orleans. I know
that I am able to connect with people effectively. I know
that I do a good job. I feel so happy at times and then
angry. I feel I have so much in so many ways. Why do I
feel so upset now? Is it because I am not pregnant?

*Mary, listen to your heart. It will guide you. Go to the quiet. You won-
der about answers. They are there. What bothers you is a reflection of
self. Pause in this moment. Call on us. We are there for you.*

*Remember, when you are troubled to go to the quiet. What are you
afraid of? What you will see? What you are? Your beauty? Your love?
All are there. Yet you hide—as if this were not your right. Know love
is there. We are there. You search for all outside of self. Yet it is all
within you. Do not let the externals fool you! Give yourself time daily
to be, Mary.*

Why am I so sad?

*You are sad because you have chosen this. Is it sadness for what is or
what could have been? Certainly, when you look at what Is, there is no
sadness. You look at the past. Look at the now, the present. Within the
present is a present—you! Unwrap this gift.*

133

When you love something, what do you love most? What is perfect? Or is it the crooked smile, a little shuffle in the gait of someone you love? Is it not the moment of imperfection that cements—endears you to that person for life? Is it not slipping and falling and being picked up by someone you love that cements the trust within for that person? Is it not the tears and fears that you share with someone that open your heart and bridge you to that person? Is it not the flaws, the very flaws you condemn yourself for, that promote love for others in your eyes?

Give that to yourself. This sadness is yours to hold for the moment. So be it and it will pass. Do you not see that when you are—fully— sadness has no need to stay. You have denied your emotion. It was only waving its hand and stating, "I am here!" Now that you have said hello, it can go!

Mary, when you allow yourself to feel, the feeling passes. When you do not allow the feeling, it stays until you do see it! Treasure this humanness.

Thank you dearest Trinity, Gracie, Angels—thank you—

Dearest Trinity,   October 1995

Trinity, this really is for you, dear Angel. It is you that I want to address. I have been speaking to you, well, since last June. And I have to tell you that it means the world to me. At first, I wasn't aware of the impact of it all. But then I began to reread all our conversations and I began to learn from what had been written. It is as if there is a tailor-made way of looking at my life—of being able to see my life and see it with some type of balance and harmony. You give me that, dear Angel. It is almost as if you are

correcting my thinking, getting me to see through different eyes. And even more than that, I have come to believe
that the words you use have power within them, some
type of healing agent that enters me. Otherwise, how
could I feel this calm—even in the midst of this chaos I
sometimes find myself in? How could that be? I think of
the phrase "just BE." How many times have you told me
that? But maybe if I hear it enough, its power will affect
me and affect my perception. I know this—because even
during periods of fear, I can feel some release when I
speak with you.

Trinity, I will take anything. I want you to know the
gratefulness of my heart for even one minute of your
soothing voice.

November 7, 1995

Hello there, you Wonderful Angels, Dear God,
and the Universe!

Guess what? I am feeling better! I voiced my emotions
to John and my mother, saw my role in things—how my
upcoming birthday and not having a baby and my getting
older all were getting to me. I started feeling closer to
myself, as if there was a place, a time, to forgive and to
love my anger, my emptiness. And love truly does bind
and heal. I know in the big picture, I am learning, but at
the moment it can get difficult. Yet, I wonder, how I can
live with this duality and strive for oneness. I realize meditation, just being, is part of all this. But sometimes I work

so hard at trying to get closer to God, to oneness, that I get frustrated. I know I should not try, but I do.

You do try. Let it be. You quickly jump to conclusions, to specifics. This is all part of it! These are your lessons. Let it be! Do not force things. Already you have learned much about self. Integration takes time. You sense that you have to "put this together." This is integration. It will happen. Trust, dear one.

Watch as the tide turns. As you see. Marvel at this stage. Treasure who you are. Time is put on the physical plane to promote sequence. Things do not happen all at once as in thought (inspiration). Time heals and cures. Marvel at this lesson of patience. Patience is your friend. Patience has come to say hello, to slow you down. Savor this.

Thank you for helping me see, to look with gratitude at what I do have. I know you know what is right for me. I will learn (notice I took *try* out of *will learn*). I think it is being in the pause that I must *savor,* for I am here for a reason. Even if I pause with anger, I can hold this emotion and send it love. We can become one together. I can do this with all the dear sides of my being human.

Thank you dearest ones, my Dearest God, and, as always, my Sunshine Daughter, my light beam, *my* wonder—Gracie Darling—thank you!

III.
CONNECTING

BALANCE

November 19, 1995

Dearest Angels, Trinity, Gracie, Dearest God,
and the Universe,

It is Sunday and John is in bed already. It is only 6 P.M.! I had time yesterday to rest and read. Thank you, Gracie darling, for leading me to the books. Thank you for the curtains I got for the house. The light streaming in the windows is so beautiful. Every time I see beauty, I feel love. I love this house so very much. I love John and Amanda so, so much. My life was empty without them. Thank you for bringing them into my life.

Yet John and I had a fight (I should say *I* had a fight with John) about doing the laundry—twice he rewashed clothes that had already been washed. I became so upset. What is it with me? Why do I do that? Why do I react so strongly over something so insignificant? Can you help me?

Yes, Mary—I am here to help. You ask why? Why do you think? You are restless. You question work and, more important, what to do with work. What to do with time. What to do with balance.

You want balance and harmony. Yet an outbreak such as this upsets the balance. Why is this? What is to be learned? Think of the process. You have time, therefore, how shall you fill it? By doing, by being, by fighting, you choose. Remember, you choose. But why choose a fight? You choose because it is known from long ago. Yet, the concept here stems from doing, working. Are you angry at self for working or not working? This loss of control makes you wonder what is happening. Your productive, working self is confused by the new rules—the rules of being. It feels lost. Embrace this side of yourself. All is not lost—just be!

Love all sides. This argument was a reflection of your inside. Love who you are at the moment. John can take care of himself.

Thank you my dear ones. I love you all so much.

November 20, 1995

Dearest Trinity, Gracie, and all the Angels,

I started feeling better today toward the end of work. A calm came over me. I felt I had all this time. Thank you. It's as if my days have opened up with time. I don't know why, but I am getting my work done quicker. I'm trying to be authentic, true to myself. Thank you for this insight.

You know I had that fight with John tonight. I wanted to pay bills and he didn't know where they were. It escalated until, well, you know. I felt awful after this fight. My energy was so sapped. Another outburst. I feel I really need help with this part of my integration. If you think this is for the higher good, and that help is what would be for the best, could you help?

Love is there, Mary. In your heart. Think of how you feel during an "outburst," as you put it. Confused, angry, threatened? These are triggers, clues for you. To protect yourself in the past you have fought. As you reflect on your life, know that the justice you have sought has only been the justice you wanted internally.

What is it that you really want at those moments? Love? Give love and you will receive love. It is difficult when things appear unfair. Leave if you must—go to the quiet.

This is a misunderstanding, this conflict. Treat it as such—you misunderstand, you miss understanding the situation. You keep wanting to know if this is a reflection of your inner sides. Yes! Something is misunderstood. That creates conflict. Look into your heart. These interludes are there for a very good reason. You pause and see the lesson! Do you not see that you are seeing? Caress the part of you that needs understanding. The conflicts with John will cease. I promise! Dear Mary, realize that this way of being has been known for a long time. It is a protection. You tremble at change. Yet, on the other side is Joy waiting with open arms. Please be gentle first with your sides, all the aspects of you. It is from this point of gentleness that you will know how to treat others! Breathe in gentleness. Exhale pain! We love you!

I will practice being gentle with myself—I mean my selves, all my dear sides. That poor threatened side needs my love. I think it may be my heart.

You are right! Love your heart. The rest will take care of itself!

November 29, 1995

Dearest Angels, my Trinity, my loving daughter,
the Wonderful Universe,

I had my birthday and it was very special. Amanda, John, and I sang together that night. John recorded our singing. It was wonderful. Yes, there is music coming back into our lives. We also put up our tree and it feels like Christmas. Amanda and I have been wrapping gifts.

I'm having a hard time loving myself. I'm comparing, angry, sad, tired, sick. My emotions seem to fluctuate. I am happy one moment, sad the next. I guess I'm upset because I am not more whole or together. What does this mean? Only if you feel I should know—if you think it is for the higher good.

You have reflected on your shoulders recently. How bowed and droopy they have become. This is weight, the weight of worry, the not knowing, the burdens of life. You have carried so much extra weight. And now it is time to discard your burdens! You fluctuate between two worlds. Make your burdens lighter. Give them up! Just say, "I give you up!" Up to the heavens! I will take your troubles. Now! I will take your sad-

ness. Now! I will take your fear. Now!

Replace these burdens with love, light, and joy! Know this surrender-
ing will last forever. There is no need to carry more. Enjoy your family.
Enjoy! As of this moment, you are done with pain. Know this, dear one.
Feel this within. Your pain has flown on wings to the highest peak. Love
remains. Love shadowed this pain you chose. Believe this is gone—this
pain. It has taken wings and flown away. Love remains. Feel lighter!

Thank you DEAR ONES! Thank you.

Look at yourself as convalescing. Healing. Give yourself time to heal!

Dearest Angels, Gracie, and Trinity,   December 1995

Work has felt so fragmented lately—we have all been
traveling. My world just has not been right until recently,
when Margaret got home from Italy. Julie had gotten back
from Europe shortly after I did, and we could catch up on
things, but I kept watching the days on the calendar. Julie,
too, kept asking, "When is Margaret getting back?"

Now she is here, and we can all be together. All three
of us have felt such gratitude, just in being with our families. Margaret called me today and wanted me to stop by
before work, for coffee. We live only five minutes from
each other. Her house was decorated for Christmas. It
looked so beautiful.

We sat at her kitchen table, both of us had our dream
journals, and we read from them. We both kept smiling.
I couldn't help it, I just blurted out how much I had
missed her.

I watched her move around the kitchen, getting me coffee, sitting down, and looking at me, and I did not want to leave. I knew how special this moment was.

I just feel so complete with her. It is as if where there are gaps in me, Margaret fills them. I come home when I am with her. That is how it feels. Just like being home.

December 4, 1995

Good morning my dearest Angels and Gracie my love,

Well, I am taking the day off from work. It is a gray day. It looks as if it may snow more. I do like the winter. I like the change of seasons. Is there anything you would like to tell me?

You are pensive regarding change, and it is so—change is on the horizon. Let it be, for it will come. You have asked for this change, and so it shall be. Dear one, you have come far. Please relax! Let us handle the details. You are not used to allowing others to do for you. If I can hold your hand gently and lead you, this will be so. You do not have to work for anything. Your fear has gone—flown!

You move within this new realm as if you were a stranger in a foreign land. The land of allowing. For you have worked hard for this. Yet all one must do is believe. We are in your thoughts. We are part of you. Savor our love for you.

I do feel a shift, a major shift in my perceptions. I'm not waking up angry. I feel as if I do believe and everything is possible!

Yes! Yes! Yes! You are treating your dream life with equal importance to your waking life. You see! You are moved by beauty! Celebrate the beauty of the soul! Love has called and you have heeded it.

Thank you my angels and Gracie darling.

ASKING

December 10, 1995

Dearest Angels, Trinity, my darling Gracie,

We arrived home from Madison tonight. Every year we go to John's parents around Christmas. John's family is so warm. Nancy, his mother, always makes sure that there are activities planned for all of us. I've always admired that she takes such good care of herself. She even told me that I could take a nap if I wanted. It was the middle of the day!

Gracie, I know you are with us in spirit. But as you know, sometimes I long for you so . . . thank you for your love. Amanda is such a great kid. Thank you for helping and guiding her.

Trinity, you know I have been thinking of Margaret, for Margaret. We have grown so close. I feel as if we are traveling together now. She asked for guidance of any type. Can you help? She wonders about her writing and what to do next with it. Please shed light on this if you can, but only for the higher good.

Do not force this; let this flow, for this is an honor. You have crossed this bridge through love. Only love. Feel lighter! You close your eyes and see green, the color of healing, of love. Breathe in and know Love is there. Your heart beats and you feel Margaret's energy. For you are both now connected in this realm.

This connection is of value, you both have traveled far, very far, together and now you are bound by love. As Margaret has lit your path, you too shall light hers. You show one another the way. If one falls, the other is there to console. You are bound by love. Your hearts beat together. You travel together. Your dreams are significant. Let the unfolding take place, for this can only happen with trust. This trust has developed through love.

You speak of unfolding. Does this mean with her writing?

Yes. Her writing will unfold as a flower does. You will see. You will be there. Go to your dreams. You SEE. You know. Margaret looks too hard at what already is in front of her—around her, within her. Look to your dreams. This is not difficult. It unfolds, as a flower does.

Patience is a friend during this time, especially for Margaret. It is there. Trust in this. BELIEVE. This trust is paramount. As you see you

147

share, all of you do, this unfolds. The story unfolds. You trust, you share, you grow. This is life. This is what dreams are made of. This is LOVE!

Thank you my dear ones. Thank you. I will show this to Margaret tomorrow.

December 14, 1995

Dear Angels, dearest Trinity, and Gracie,

I am worried, if I might say, about talking to you, Trinity, for Margaret. Is what I tell her accurate? What if I got something mixed up in the message?

You worry and therefore it is. Do not worry! Do not do this to yourself! Be! Strengthen this tie, this bond. Allow this to happen. What holds you back?

I think of my back—it has been aching this morning. Aching from worry!

Do not do this to self. It is wasted energy. Second guessing. It puts you in a place of never knowing, never being right. Always deficient— scarcity once again. When you make a decision, realize you can change your mind, and then that is it. That becomes your decision. If you change your mind again—then that becomes your decision. You divide self with worry. Go deep within. Let the waves of love surround you. Nurture yourself. Let things be. Love for love's sake only. Caress those parts of you that tend to wander off—just as they are now. Know this is all of you. Don't make yourself right or wrong. Just be! We love you and are with you always.   *Lovingly ⌒The Angels*

Thank you my dear ones.

December 18, 1995

Dear Universe, Trinity, my Angels, Gracie, my love,

My car was acting up before work today. I ended up walking home because it stalled a couple blocks away. I am grateful for this time. I tried to meditate but I could not silence my mind. I am feeling bad, somehow, again. I am so tired of this feeling, of waking up and feeling bad. Please help me to understand. I feel as if I am trying to make myself wrong. If you think this is for the higher good. . . .

Do not feel there is somewhere you have to be. You are fine just as you are now. You want knowledge, to be at a certain point by a certain time. When I say go deep, go deep! Know this is where your answers lie. Do not fear, Mary. Just be! The present is a present you give yourself. In the stillness, you will find what you are seeking.

Why is it that last week I was so full of the Christmas spirit and now I feel so sad? Why have these feelings come over me? Where does all sadness spring from? Not caring, not having, not being?

Mary, all these sides are a part of you. Do not alienate them and push them asunder. They are gifts of humanness. Treasures. One does not cut one's arm off over a mere splinter. You work with the splinter, soften it, clean the area, ease it out. Or it will work its way out. Love your presence. Cherish these moments.

Your sadness is an ally. It brings you peace and comfort even in distressing times. It says, "I am." Do not judge this emotion. Do you not feel your sense of lightness with no judgment? It is! As with all emotion. Do not rate these feelings and thoughts. They are. Yes, Mary, gentleness is needed! With all emotion!

Thank you dearest Angels, Trinity, and Gracie. I love you.

December 25, 1995

Dearest Trinity, Gracie, my sweet Angels, dearest Universe, dearest God, and Jesus,

Happy birthday, dear Jesus! I never thought that I would ever write a letter to the Son of God, but here goes. And I'm not even religious!

I sit here in the quiet of the morning. Your day, Christmas Day, and I feel love and happiness.

I love John, Amanda, Carli, Bob, my house, my life. I have so very much. As I contemplate the mystery of life, I see how my dearest friends bless my life with their love. Margaret is working on a new book, the story of what the three of us—herself, Julie, and I—have been through as friends. Thank you for all the insights and love; the trust is strong and good and such a wonderful flow.

It is nearing a year since I started writing in this journal. It has been a year of grief, shakiness, learning to live, but, most of all, of love. Trinity, as you speak to me, through me, are with me, you have opened up worlds, depths, layers. You have shown me how I can open up. You stand by me no matter what I experience, and I love you for that, that your love spans over time, without judgment, always pointing the way. You have influenced my life in such positive ways. A kiss and hug for you!

Darling Gracie, you know what you have done for me. You came into my life, a jewel of love. I cry as I write this.

You were so brave, every step of the way. Without you, dearest, I would not be at this point. I will love you for eternity; I will do anything for you. You are my Angel, my highest star, darling! When we meet again, it will be so joyous. I hold you in my thoughts always. . . .

My other Angels, I know you are with me—guiding me, beside me, in my thoughts, my dreams. Although sometimes I don't understand or get the message, know that I want to. I get a little scared or confused if I don't understand. Please bear with me, dearest Beings of Light. I may be a tough case but no one wants to understand more than I. With your Love, I can do it! I love all of you! MERRY CHRISTMAS!

Dearest God, dearest Jesus, I know there is an eternal plan. The vastness of all of this overwhelms me at times. You and only You bring light into my life. Your angels have been wonderful this year (or I have noticed them more!). Thank you for loving me always. Please help me to evolve and move toward you, keeping you in my heart always. May I learn what I can give to humanity in love. Dear God, thank you from the bottom of my heart! I love you!   In Peace and Joy, ∾ Your loving Mary

Dearest Trinity, my Angels, Gracie,   December 27, 1995
I write today because my heart is troubled. Amanda told everyone at work that her mother, John's ex-wife, has written a story about Grace. I felt so bad—it seems so unfair. She was my daughter. Please help me! This troubles me so. . . .

This story must be told, should be told. This story of humanness, of love. You say "my daughter," and yet you care for another woman's daughter. This is a story, and you are Grace's mother. No one can take that away from you. Know this! What Amanda's mother does, she does. You are Gracie's mother and always will be! You feel robbed, but what you cry over is that Grace is not with you in human form. This is the feeling you are picking up, that this was yours and it was taken from you.

Yet, dear Mary, this is every mother's fear—there is no greater pain than the loss of a child. You are all mothers, your friends, your spirit sisters. You walk together on the same path—with love, only love, for your children.

Do not fault yourself for these feelings, dear one. They are. But know that Gracie was born to you, only you, and this love is every woman's story. The bond between you and Gracie knows no place or time. You know this. You have lived this. You could not be writing books as you grieved the loss of Grace—you grieved, and through this your story grew. Know this is your story, your life, but that it belongs to all who touch it. Thank you for turning to me in times of need. May your heart be filled with peace.

Lovingly, ⌁ The Angels

Thank you again for your tenderness.

December 27, 1995

Dearest Trinity, my dearest Angels, and as always, darling Gracie,

Margaret just called. I think she is worried about me. She said some pretty amazing things, loving things, at a time when I really needed to hear them. Her dear Angel, Peace, told her to tell me. Thank you for this. She told me her heart was peaceful, or that she was in a peaceful place, and could share it. These are your words to me today, "May your heart be filled with Peace." Yes! I do want peace in my heart, and love! Wonderful love! It is so simple, yet so hard. But it doesn't have to be, does it? I can choose love. I will choose love, only love! Her kindness touched my heart.

Please, dearest Angels, help me to let go and open up to love, if you feel it is for the higher good. I believe in you all so much. And I really, really need you all! Thank you for your love and guidance.

January 4, 1996

Dearest Grace, Trinity, and the Angels
and the Holy Spirit,

Gracie, as you know, I have been writing to you and Trinity for almost ten months by hand. Yet, as much as this has been working, I cannot help but wonder why this computer still will not operate. I have tried and tried to write with it. It has unnerved me more than you know. This has been since it first scrolled that one night. I hear the bells when I turn it on, and I get so rattled. I keep blaming myself for not understanding something. But how can a person understand this?

I ask you Grace, if you could do anything to help. I don't know if you know or anyone knows how upsetting this is to me. I pray that you can help me . . . please help me. I will ask you again in my prayers tonight.

Dearest Gracie,   January 5, 1996

I had to write as soon as I got up this morning. Gracie, I am going to trust in this dream of last night. My heart is just pounding again.

When I woke up, I had the feeling that all was well with the computer. I had a very simple dream last night, but one which I will never forget. I was above a map, an old antique scrolled map. I was looking down at the map when I saw a clipper ship. I knew this to be my ship. It was at a halfway point, heading for some land. I kept squinting from above, trying to see what this land was called. Finally I saw the name. It was called Grace. I knew this to be Graceland. The dream scene switched immediately, from that point. I saw a computer cable, and I knew instinctively that this was my connection to you, Grace.

Grace, I am beginning to look so deeply at my dreams, so very deeply. If you heard me, and this dream really means what I think it does, this alone seems prophetic.

Darling Grace,   January 7, 1996

Two days ago I turned the computer on and wrote my first words. I cannot tell you how relieved I was. I guess I was afraid to trust the dream at first. The signal bells go off when I type certain words, but I can write! I thank you so very, very much, Gracie! I cannot put words to how I feel. I told Margaret and Julie that I had been able to go in and write on the computer. It is the first time in ten months! Julie got tears in her eyes.

I thank you also, dear Trinity. Thank you so very much.

Dearest Grace and Trinity,   January 1996
  When I went into the computer just recently to write
to you, Grace, I wrote, "Can I †ell you how proud I am of
you," because of my being able to write again in the computer. The *t* in *tell* printed as a cross. Now for three weeks,
I have been seeing these crosses pop up every now and
then in the writing. The bells still go off, but not as much.
It appears that the bells emphasize certain words. This is
comforting to me, because it makes me think that this
connection to you is very right.

Dearest Gracie,   January 1996
  I was in my cubicle, working on something this morning, when I turned around to see Margaret. We were the
only ones in the office. She had these papers in her hand
and her eyes seemed all watery. I still did not know what
was going on. She then told me that she had read these
letters to you, Grace.
  I had given her the letters to look at, because we are
working on this book of our experiences together, the
three of us—Julie, Margaret, and me. No one has ever
seen these letters, because I have been afraid to show
them to anyone. Margaret put her arms around me, and
I heard her say, "I never knew, I never knew." I felt her
compassion for me, and I let it wash over me, Grace.

I felt, Gracie, that a dam of tears was inside of me, waiting for this moment of safety. All the shame I felt just broke when Margaret touched me. It was the first moment that anyone really knew me, for what I was.

It was the first time that anyone ever saw inside my heart.

RECEIVING

Dearest Trinity, Gracie, My Angels,   January 18, 1996

I have come here to understand what is happening to me. I feel sad, as if I have to let go of having a baby. I know I sound like a broken record. John and I are distant. What is happening?

You have a need now to be quiet. So be quiet. This is perfectly fine. Go to the quiet. You can mourn there and touch All that Is. In this place is the splendor of Being. Your heart is leading you. Listen. Know the motions you go through are not in vain.

You think of a baby now, Mary. But what does this really mean to

157

you? Sadness? Are you over the pain of Grace's death? By moving on, you move on. Are you sad thinking that you will leave Grace behind? You sense that you must look to the future, turn your face to the sun, that change is on the horizon for you. It Is! Dear, dear Mary.

Hold on, for we are so very near. This writing is monumental for you and it takes courage. Hope. There is nothing wrong with hope. You despair—replace this with hope. Be true to the place that you are in. Embrace the very fact that you are human. Turn softly, move gently. Love is all around. You hear music—move into the music. You feel the sun on your cheek—move gently into the sun. You smile—feel the smile stay on your lips. You pray—feel the words of the prayer.

Know love by knowing yourself. Softness enters your being in real-ization, just as a doe moves into the mist on a summer's morning. Let the light shine on you. This new side has been hidden. Give it light. Savor this new friendship with an old friend. Your sadness has been keenly linked to your gentleness. Gentleness will remain for self when sadness leaves. The softness that you have sought for self is finally here, Mary dearest. Say Hello! You are finally reunited!

Thank you, Dear Ones.

Dearest Gracie,   January 26, 1996

Two weeks ago, Daddy and I were in Florida, on vaca-tion again. It was a beautiful sunny day. I was on the beach; your grandparents and father were looking for seashells further up the shore. I watched the ocean. It was at that moment that I knew. I knew I might always cry for the child I lost. But I, as your mother, knew the spirit you have become.

I knew in those moments that I had given you all the

love I could possibly give. That I had been the best mother I knew how to be. I accepted that. My doubt had been just that. *My* doubt. Not God's. Not the doctors'. Not my family's. Not your father's. Mine.

I knew also in those moments that I had chosen to love. That as I turned my face to the wind, I would always choose love, from that day on. And if I lost my way again, I would know that I was never alone.

Grace, I turned a corner that day. That moment. Forgiveness had slipped in quietly one night and said, "I will lie with you, I am in your heart." I forgave myself. It was then that I knew I loved myself honestly and with truth. It was only then that I knew that God had been in my heart, always. I just had not been able to see.

Gracie, you gave me that. This love. This ability to see. This ability to embrace, put my arms around my humanity with love. The ripples of love are just beginning, aren't they?

February 3, 1996

Dear Trinity, Gracie, and the Holy Spirit,

I have thought so much about my dreams lately. It seems incredible to me that this part of my life has opened up, as it has. Each morning at work, Julie, Margaret, and I have what we call a "dream update." Each of us has been blessed somehow with this ability to dream.

I think of myself and how much is revealed to me in my dreams, how you are guiding me to these dreams and through these dreams. It is as if I have been given clues that help to unlock the mysteries of my life. I want to thank you for this.

In my dream last night, John went to watch television in another room. Without my knowing how it happened, there was a piano in front of me. I started playing (even though I do not play in real life). I remember touching the keys and having beautiful music come out. It was as if I felt the notes. Each touch was wonderful—the tones were fantastic. I remember thinking, *But I can't even play the piano!* I then saw Margaret's piano right beside mine, also appearing miraculously. Her piano was different from mine, but equally beautiful. I then felt waves of ecstasy go through my body. Wave upon wave. I remember thinking, *No wonder Margaret likes to play the piano so much!* She, in reality, does not play piano, either.

Does this have anything to do with writing?

Always in love, ∽ Mary

Trinity,   February, 1995

Can we talk? Can we speak of my feelings? I need guidance with these feelings of sharing Grace with the world in the book that Margaret is writing about our friendships. . . . Please?

You are robbed of nothing. Let your emotions reign. Know that these feelings guide you. Your love is within—believe and treasure this. Allow this to unfold. Your search is over now. I mean over! There is nothing left to do. Allow yourself to feel the luxury of your gentleness, without pain or sadness. Your emotions are the way. Not blocking them releases them for you. It has been the stuffing of them through your past that has built up momentum and lowered your energy. All the emotions that have controlled you in the past will cease to be a burden.

The world of emotion now, as you pass through the gates of acceptance, allows you to see! Your sadness was only saying, FEEL YOUR GENTLENESS—FOR SELF. This is one of the reasons you have chosen sadness frequently—to allow yourself this gentleness. It was at these times you allowed yourself your humanness. Dishes piled up during these times. You took time off work to be. I am not speaking of the times you may have escaped, I am speaking of the times you were sad and did not mask it. You were gentle.

Now in this time, you can proceed with gentleness as your friend— without the need to choose sadness or pain. As you allow this for self, you allow this with others. You have lived with a shell of protection for so long. A scared little girl was hiding. You have been hidden so long, mostly from yourself.

Caress who you are and all will fall into place—including the book. What a special book this will be. You have lost nothing, my sweetheart. You have only gained. The shell is gone. You have taken it off. You have found the key!

Thank you, my beings of light. I will be sweet and gentle—to me.

March 5, 1996

Dearest Trinity, Gracie and the Angels
and the Holy Spirit,

I want to start by thanking you for today—the laughter,

the happiness at work, all of it. Julie, Margaret, and I just keep enjoying things more and more. Even our jobs! The most mundane parts of our jobs have somehow become filled with pleasure, in that we are sharing so much more.

I have recently thought of how little I sometimes thank you for things—how I just take things for granted, like I am out of touch or something. I want to thank you now. As a matter of fact, I did not thank you for the great dinner we had tonight. I am always so grateful that we can put food on the table. Please do not think I am not grateful. I am. But I thought of this, this not thanking, and how long I had been doing it. I also do not thank people when they help me at times. I want to practice being more thankful.

This file of Amanda's was highlighted just now. Is there something †hat I should do for her? I just saw the cross. Is that a yes? Can you shed light on this?

Know that what you do is all right, Mary. Know this. What are you thinking?

That I should be with her tonight. That you want me or are guiding me to do this tonight. And I struggle with this, this taking care of myself and taking care of her. I struggle with my wanting to write and having a child that may need me.

All is well. Love is there. You might ask yourself what is inside. Why would one think this?

Because of shoulds. Because that is how I have been raised.

It is. And simply that is it. It just Is. You ponder these things, these situations. Let them be. There is nothing that you need to worry about. Think of self and where these feelings lie. What do you want?

I want to write and rest and just be. That is all. But I feel guilty leaving Amanda. What should I do?

Just be, Mary. Allow these feelings to surface. This is fine. You are fine. Amanda is fine! Why do you question this guilt? What makes you feel guilty?

I think of things that I should be doing and am not doing, and I feel guilty. Whenever I want to be who I am, I feel guilty. Mostly, now, with people.

If you do what makes you happy, there is no room for guilt.

Now my neck is all wacky. I wonder if I am communicating †he right way. Oops, there is the cross again. You are with me, I know. Please guide me so that the decisions I make are for the highest good. You know, the more that I write, the more I am getting into this. It is almost interactive, isn't it?

I want to really let you know that my dreams are so fulfilling to me. Thank you! Especially the one with the interview. I really got a lot out of that one. In this dream, I see this man I know. He is well groomed, impeccably so. The perfect businessman. Not a hair out of place. A tough cookie. I was interviewing for a job with him. I saw this man as so gentle, not tough, as he appeared on the surface. I told him, "You have a big heart, you know." He hung his head, almost crumpling in his chair, and said, "I know." I asked him, "When did this happen?" He told me that this had happened with his last marriages. I then told him, "I have to be able to trust that this is a two-way street." He said he knew. There was such relief for him when he said this, when he heard the word *trust.* I was so happy that I did not want to wake up!

My sense is that I somehow play different roles in my dreams. I am all the characters of my dreams. This man was a side of me. The exact, precise, getting-the-job-done side. The perfectionist. The action side of my being that was so prevalent in my past. I saw this man saying his heart had been hurt by his past marriages, just as this part of me, my past marriage, or my other unions had been hurtful to me. I saw this man needing to have everything done perfectly. Always having to work, just like me. It was the productive side of who I had been for years.

You know, I just felt my anxiety lifting. I see now that I was carrying some guilt around—maybe because I felt I should have seen my grandmother tonight but didn't. I will do that tomorrow. But tonight I will do what pleases me. That makes me happy. I feel as if I can give more. Thank you for this insight.

I look at the angel wing card that I got from Nancy, my mother-in-law, and I think, *Wow, angel wings!* She sent me this just about the time I started feeling self-love. Thank you again. I finally understood that message today! It takes me some time. I love you all. Till next time.

March 1996

Dearest Angels, my Angel Grace, the Holy Spirit,

One of the reasons I have begun to include the Holy Spirit in these letters is because of another dream. In this dream, I am talking to someone. I hear a voice in response, but I do not see this person. Yet I know we are having a conversation. I know that this conversation has been going on for some time. It dawns on me during this talk that I am talking to the Holy Spirit! I say in the dream, "Oh, so *you* are the Holy Spirit." And that was the end of this dream.

This all seems so incredible to me. When I was talking to this voice, I felt as if I were talking to some friend or someone very familiar. I could not believe that I could be that relaxed with the *Holy Spirit*. And I am not even religious!

I really feel as if you have opened up my dream life— all of you. Thank you for all the help that you have given me.

March 6, 1996

Dearest Angels, my Gracie, Trinity, and the Holy Spirit,

I want to thank you again for my day and for the wonderful way Amanda and I are able to talk. It means so much to me and, I know, to her. This is what being a mother is all about to me. The best part is that I can use some of the lessons I have learned through all of you and through my dreams. These lessons are giving my life meaning now. Thank you.

At work, everything is more than I could have hoped for. Things are just flowing, and I feel freer. I see my goodness now. I see it in the eyes of others, and I want to give more and more. It helps so much to give to myself. I think of how many times I never gave to me. I always made sure someone else was taken care of first when what I have really craved was giving to myself. I never realized that I had to give to myself in order to truly give to others. That would have appeared too selfish in my eyes. I just kept trying to be better and better—until I was just a shell of who I was. No wonder I would wake up angry so frequently. No wonder I struggled internally. There was a side of me that needed attention so desperately. Thank you. Is there anything else that I should be aware of?

Listen, Mary. Listen to your heart and follow your heart. Do you hear? These are the things that we speak of.

I guess that I cannot hear.

You can hear. Listen. Pay attention to what you hear.

"To be born again." These are the words of a Van Morrison song. I can only hear the words and not what is inside of me. Is this what you mean?

We speak of distractions at this moment. Do you have distractions in your life? Listen to your heart. What does it say?

I guess that I am not quite hearing.

Relax. This will come. You have great wisdom inside. You know so much that you can share with the world. You are at the point at which you can share this with the world. Do you not feel this?

Yes, I feel something. Some deep connection. Something that is so right. What does this mean?

Listen, you will be guided. You can do this, Mary. Listen to your heart. We are here with you at this moment. You can count on us being with you at this time. Do not think for a moment that you will be left alone. We will guide you.

Okay. I will listen to my heart. I hope that I heard everything right here. Please stay with me. I need you all so much at this time. I must go. I'll see you in my dreams.

March 9, 1996

Dearest Angels, Gracie, Trinity, the Holy Spirit,

Please watch over me, if you feel that it is for the highest good. I would like this writing to be what it should be—what it is. Something for the world. Please guide my fingers and thoughts. I really need you. You guide me so much throughout the day.

You know that the more I write, the more I love writing and that, in and of itself, is so wonderful. Thank you for John and my friends and Amanda. I want to write my feelings for her soon, so she can see how much I love her. I learn so much from her.

Mary, you are guided. Say no more. We are here with you and always will be. Forever and ever. Let yourself feel the words, let yourself be. There is nowhere that you have to get to. And the story is still unfolding, as it always will be. These thoughts that you reflect on are there for a reason. Follow that reason and you will be there. This is the natural part of your writing—the heart. You have recognized that you are so much from the heart. This was hidden from you in the past. It has now revealed itself for you because you have chosen love. Yes! Your writing is different because you are different in love. But all of this is necessary for the story to unfold. The rest of the story contains the light that others seek. Allow this to show through. You are in a different place and time now. This is fine! It is to be celebrated. Rejoice in love!

Thank you dearest Angels, my Trinity, and Gracie, and the Holy Spirit. I love you all. Here I go with the writing. Wish me luck!

March 12, 1996

Dearest Trinity, Gracie, my dear Angels,
and the Holy Spirit,

I want to thank you. I had my friends over today. It has been so long since this has happened—since Grace's death. Margaret sent off her book, about our friendships (Julie's, hers, and mine) and the connections we have shared, to the publisher today. She is very excited about this and wants so much for it to be published. I wish this for her also. Thank you for all the help.

I am sitting here wondering what is going to be happening with me and this purpose stuff. Did my dream of the porpoises have anything to do with any of this? Swimming with my "purposes," side by side?

Mary, all dreams have to do with the reflection of purpose. The mirror. The being. YOU ARE SO RIGH† WHEN YOU EXAMINE THESE MEANINGS.

I just lost my thoughts. I saw the cross again. Is this my purpose? The cross? God? I mean in the literal sense? I have been seeing crosses everywhere. It may mean God is in my life, sacredness, all of you. . . . Am I on the right track?

You are on the right track. God is in your life. In your heart. This is so. Relax, Mary. You are thinking too hard. This is not something difficult, dear one. You are right when you know that it is something close to you, in front of you.

Are you saying "in front of me" meaning the computer? Is it something with the computer? Is it writing? Is it my thoughts?

You have so much to share at this point. Think of how you can share. This is what you will endeavor to do. Share. Now, sharing comes in many different forms.

Will I be sharing my ideas?

You already are. You are sharing with Julie and Margaret now. This

169

will increase. This sharing will increase. This sharing is so much a part of you. You will see. Doors will open for you in this realm. You will share. You will share so much.

Will I speak?

Yes. You will speak.

Is this about what we have seen? been through?

You will see!

Should I prepare in any way for this to occur?

You need not do anything. Just be open. Things are coming to you rapidly. You sense this.

I cannot figure this out. I have to let this go. I have a sense of drifting, of things almost being on hold, as if this is all right. I am getting tired now. I feel as if I really need to go to sleep and yet it is so early.

Thank you so much. Thank you! And thank you for helping me get out into the world. I think I am ready. I love you all so much. You make my life so worth living. Thank you. I love you all.

March 14, 1996

Dearest Angels, Trinity, Gracie, and the Holy Spirit,

I give thanks because of what is happening to my friends at work. Margaret is so happy with the book she has completed and I am happy for her. She is so ready to be an author, if this is for the highest good. And Julie is getting new energy and feeling so content. It really is good to see them like this.

Yet, I see this, and I wish it for myself at times. Not to take anything away from their happiness. I wish that I could know what my purpose is. I am getting into doubt at times. Do I have a talent? I mean something that I can do? I feel as if I could cry now. Why is this? Can you help me? Am I selfish? I feel as if I do not have anything to offer. I am stumped.

Mary, be. You are not alone and never will be. Allow things to come forth and they will. Time is here as a teacher for you. You are not selfish. You only feel this. You are. You want what all want. To understand what life holds and is about. Think of how far you have come in such a short time. Is this not a miracle?

Miracles come in all shapes and sizes. You experience these daily. Yet you want verification. It Is. So let these feelings arise within you. Give them air. You are ready to breathe. Ready to be ready. This is fine. You search and search and think and think. Where does this take you? To more searching and thinking. This is fine, but it can wear one out. Be and It will be. Dearest, all the answers are within you. Everything you search for is already there! Clear your vision.

I am unhappy because I do not have Grace and it appears to me that everyone I know has children and I don't. I guess I have been angry. I know that I can't make things happen that are not in the divine plan. Yet I feel so sad. I also know that a child is not the one and only answer for me. Is there something I am missing? Please help me. My throat just aches now. Have I been so awful that this is happening to me?

Your sadness has been with you since Margaret told you of her daughter's car accident and how she got the phone call that nothing had come of this accident. You wanted this to be how your life went. That with one phone call, you were told that all was well, even though something had occurred. This is fine, dearest Mary. To have these feelings indicates you're being human. This is your beauty—your humanness. People relate to you on such a human level. Yes, you can hide your emotions, but when you choose to reveal them, they ring with such humanness.

It is amazing that when one gives something voice, it can then leave. You have given your sadness voice. It can leave and it will. This I can guarantee you. Never forget that one of your greatest gifts is the ability to connect to people. This is your beauty! Your love! Mary, when you are who you are, you will not want. You have traveled this road. You know what it involves. Be who you are. Know this is the most comforting of decisions for you.

When something comes to mind, ask, "How can I be me? Who am I now?" And it will be. You will be. It is as if you have a list of what you should be, and if a part of you is not on the list, you panic. You punish yourself. Relax. Sadness and happiness and joy and wonder are all on the list. There is only one list.

Truth lies in who you are. Let this be known.

Thank you for all of this. I will practice being who I am at all times. And I will attempt being true. Thank you for this insight. I love you.

March 20, 1996

Dearest Angels, Trinity, Gracie, and the Holy Spirit,

I must tell you why I have come today. I have had a major breakthrough of sorts. I need your assistance, Trinity. I would like to discuss my dream of last night.

In this dream, I am in an elevator going up. In the elevator are my mother and Margaret's mother, Madeline. We are on the way to a college party. I remember feeling very emotionally wounded and hurt. I felt so empty, as if I were some type of pinball being bumped around. The man I was seeing wanted only a physical relationship from me. He didn't want *me*—who I really was. This hurt me deeply. This felt like such a random period in my life.

I press the button and then all of a sudden the elevator goes sideways. I grab on to Madeline's wrist. She looks upset with me when I do this.

The wrist is a connecting point. A point that connects the hand with the body. To hold on to the connecting point is significant, Mary. To hold on to Madeline's wrist is significant. Comfort is significant. To hold on to the wrist of a mother is significant. Madeline is also your mother's friend. To hold on to a friend is highly significant. The fact that she is female is significant. Examine this now.

Could it be that I was holding on to a friend, the female part of me? And then Madeline got a little miffed for my doing that—that in itself seems significant. The female mother, friend, old friend that is not used to me wanting comfort from her. My female side needing comfort. The

173

fact that it was not my mother that I held on to was important, I feel. Is this so?

YES! YES! YES! You chose to hold on to an old friend in need. An older woman, mother, friend—all are significant. You are reclaiming the part of you that was ignored—the female side. The side that needs to give you much. From this point, you will see how to view and treat yourself by just being. By just receiving. You need not worry about action, as in the male side. You have not been in the female side. You have rejected that in the past to survive. This was necessary at one time but is no longer. This is hugely significant! You need to be able to receive! By that act of reaching, and reaching only, you are reclaiming. You reached out for someone else to receive comfort.

And the party with people from my past?

You were revisiting your past and a painful part of your life. This may have been one of the most painful times you experienced, the most lost you have ever felt. This was necessary to revisit. And in the revisiting you reached out for comfort from Madeline. You hung on to someone, an older, wiser woman, a female. These are symbols for you.

You are reviewing your past and going back to these moments to give them new meaning. Congratulations! You have rewritten a part of your life! This will help you in your view of self. Your interpretations are excellent. This will benefit you greatly in the future! Now write and we will be with you.

Thank you, my dear angels.

Trinity,   March 1996
    I had another dream, I need help—once again. In this

dream, I see a rat in the garage of the home from my first marriage. The rat was called Bluebeard. This old rat had long whiskers and blue-gray fur. He even looked almost friendly. The whole dream seemed so odd.

I knew nothing of this Bluebeard, until I asked John about it last night. It appears this is a legend about a man who was rumored to have killed his ex-wives. Bluebeard then married a young woman and forbade her to go into many rooms in the castle where he kept his former wives as part of his past. The hidden part of his life. Well, as the legend goes, the new wife went into the forbidden rooms one by one, bringing each wife out to the light. Yet, in knowing her husband's secret, she still loved him. And consequently, she lived. But she too became part of the past. . . .

Could this have anything to do with my female side being "put down" or suppressed symbolically? Somewhere in my past life—my past marriage? I feel this, too, was done for protection. I grieve the fact that I have done this to myself. I feel now that I want balance. That this is what has been out of whack for me. The yin-yang of it all. Am I on to something?

Mary, this is why you grieve. Your heart cries out for this balance. You know this balance, and these dreams are lessons for you to rewrite what has occurred. It is time to give up what you knew, what you thought was real, to proceed into the future with integration. With oneness. Have you not had recent dreams in which you reached out to the female for help? You know this is important, that this is so! This is all to assist you in this transformation. This change of being. You know! Therefore, you are. Do not be afraid to ask for this to be so.

Will you assist me in this transformation of self? with this integration of being? with this knowing? this move toward oneness? I feel that the barriers I once had are coming down. This makes me so happy, and I am able to trust myself so much more with this! Thank you!

Of course, Mary, we will help! We know that you are at this point. Believe me when I say your life will become infinitely better, easier, loving, embracing, wondrous! Dearest, cherish this point in time. Know how significant this is! Ask and it shall be. Do you not already feel some of the tension is gone? What you held on to is gone? It can happen that quickly! Move into this realm. We are there for you. We love you so!

Thank you, dearest Ones. My heart is with you. I am with you. Love surrounds us all in oneness. Thank you for all this wisdom. I will ponder. I love you all.

Dearest Grace and Trinity,   March 22, 1996
    Every time that I see the number twenty-two, I think of you, Grace. It is the number of your birthdate, and today is March 22. Last night, in my dream, I got a new white bathing suit. It was beautiful and I felt great in it. I put it on and then John appeared. Each time I took a step, your father would give me a kiss. With each step I took. He kept kissing me all the way.
    When I awoke it struck me that John represents the male side of my nature—once again. With this dream, it

appears that the male side of me is loving the other side of me (the female) and with each new step I take, I feel this love.

I ask myself, have I really ever been able to receive? Receptivity is so symbolically female. I have always been the "doer." But if dreams are any reflection of my internal life, it looks to me as if I have begun to allow this receptivity.

The aspect of my being in a white bathing suit, white denoting purity, and that it was a "bathing" suit could mean that I am cleansing the doing side of myself—the male. The action side. Those kisses from John show me that my male side is at last working in tandem with the female side. Somehow I am beginning to balance myself.

I cannot tell you how this makes me feel.

Thank you, Angels!

Dear Trinity and Grace,   March 24, 1996

I come, once again, with news of dreams. My world has opened up, so completely. I have to share this with you.

I dreamed I saw a woman walking toward me. She came from quite a distance, as if she were only a speck on the horizon. Everything was bright about her, even her clothing. She appeared beautiful, but I could not see her clearly. We kept approaching one another until I recognized her. This woman was me.

I began to cry when I realized I saw myself in a "perfect light." I knew that she had come to tell me we were the best of friends. We spoke through our minds. As I approached her we blended into one another—our bodies just became one.

I have never felt such complete happiness. Never, ever, ever. . . .

How can this get any better?

I V.
FINDING

MIRACLES

April 2, 1996

Dearest Angels, Gracie my love, Trinity,
and the Holy Spirit,

I had a wonderful day yesterday. I know that so much
is about to take place. I feel excited somehow. I pray that
Margaret's book will get published, as I am sure it will.
Thank you for my dear Amanda. I love her with all my
heart. Please watch over her and bring her love, Gracie.
She needs to realize how special she truly is. I will help
where I can.

I also ask that you watch over John. He needs to know

that he can also be creative, should he choose to be. We both can. It is the biggest gift to realize this. I would wish that we could have a family that loved what they do—who are doing what they truly want. I have this wonderful jazz on now. I feel just wonderful! Guess what? No tears! Just smiles!

I ask that you guide my sister, Liz, as she has her new baby. I will be at the hospital with her. I wish her the best. Now I am crying. Oh well, so much for the smiles! I guess you can have both—happiness and tears. Is there anything that I should be aware of?

We speak of writing here, Mary. Let us examine this writing. What is it you want the world to know about your love for your daughter?

That all continues. That love transcends time and space. That I have learned so much on this journey with Grace. That I am a better person to myself because of my love for her. That having you and Grace and the Holy Spirit in my life has made it worth living. That we maybe cannot understand all, but that there is a reason for everything. We just may not see it at the time. That love is all there is! I feel it! I am living proof of it!

You are right, Mary, when you say that love resides within you. This is important. Keep this in mind always. Love is within you. Always. Love is transforming. You know that is what we speak of here. All the judgments of the past have gone. You speak of how hard you are on your selves on this physical plane. This is what we speak of here. The freedom to choose not pain but joy! To choose joy! This can be done. Others need to understand that this can be done! You can show them and help them with this lesson, this journey. The journey of choice! Do not forget that you can continue to write. You can still guide people with this knowledge. The knowledge of choice. We will be here for you, dearest. We love you so.

And I all of you! Kisses to you and my angel daughter! I just saw a highlighted file with Messages in it, with a story that I had written or started. Is there something that I should know?

We speak of your story now. It is true that you have gotten the message—the message of love, dearest. Do not fear. This is to let you know that we are here beside you, within you, to help you should you need help with the rest of the story. This is a big step for you—the act of revealing. This act alone will set so much in motion.

You feel now the comfort of love. You see this revealed in your family. You see how you look at John differently because you look at yourself differently. You notice Amanda in a different light because you see yourself in a different light. So much has changed for you through this love. This is the transformation we speak of.

Thank you, my angels. I depend on you for all of this. Please help me when I write. I really need you to be close to me, guiding me all the way. If I get a little nervous, know that I need you to help me. I know that I can count on you. I know that you are with me always. You are in my heart.

This is an open invitation to let you know that we are here for you! Do not forget that. Realize, Mary. Realize, dear one. The spirit is free.

Thank you for the invitation. I will need you this weekend, if not sooner. Can you help me with this writing? We can work together. I love you my dears!

April 5, 1996

Dearest Angels, my Daughter, Trinity,
and the Holy Spirit,

I want to thank you for tonight. It is Good Friday and I went to church with Margaret. Although I was not raised Catholic, I found the music, which I think was sung in the ancient language Aramaic, to be beautiful. I found myself crying—not needing to understand the words but only to hear the sounds. They were beautiful. I found that church to be so human in that people worship so openly. It just seems as if nothing is hidden. The reenactment of taking Jesus off the cross was so moving.

When we left the church, I looked up to a beautiful dark blue sky with stars. You could tell that spring would come soon. The air held a warmth to it for me. I thought, when I was at church, of Grace's name and how in Spanish it would be *gracias,* meaning "thanks." I thought of how I had been born on Thanksgiving Day, and how thankful I was that Grace was in my life. That is all that matters. Grace is in my life. . . .

Later that night . . .

Dearest Trinity,

I am back again. I could not stay away—for some reason I could not sleep. I want to thank you for the good news Margaret had from a publisher about her book. It is wonderful and we all felt the joy last night. Deb, Margaret, and I celebrated and toasted and laughed. Well, I am sure you were there! I have been happy today, and then I get a little wistful. And then I think of the book and I get excited. I had told Margaret she could name the book *Grace* if she wanted to. Now I feel wistful about this.

Mary do not fear. Follow your heart. Your heart will lead you. You have these thoughts because you miss your dear daughter and feel, Well, this is all I have of Grace—her name. *But she is so much more than a name, dearest. It is this that we speak of. She is Grace! The Grace of God! Could she not have a more perfect name? John named her. This name came to him for a reason. Your story will be told, dearest. It is with this love that you will see. You have been so selfless to share so much of this with others. This pain. This tragedy. This love! It takes much to be able to do this. Grace feels all of this and knows what you go through. How you have struggled to share your only child. The child you cannot hold. Grace knows all of this, Mary.*

Trinity's voice becomes silent. My fingers hover over the computer keys waiting. I listen. The pause continues. I then hear a completely new voice that says,

"Mama, I love you so. . . ."

And I begin to cry.

GRACE

I continue to listen to the words of this voice. Tears begin streaming down my cheeks. My hands begin trembling. I try again to understand. I have never heard any other voice but that of Trinity. Yet I cannot stop writing.

My mind wants to tell my fingers to stop, but I can't. I keep recording what is being said. . . .

I am with you. We are bound together through the cord of love. This will be for always and eternity. Do not fear, for I am with you. I stand by you now. The light that you have seen has been me. I, too, could not be parted from you. We are together now. And always will be. Oh,

Mother of mine, how I know you long to hear me call your name. I have. I have. I have called your name!

Thank you for the time we had together on this earth. I saw all the love you were and are! I saw how much you cared. I saw you grieve. I saw it all, Mama! Do you not see how we are not parted? How our love has kept us together? That the strength of your love came through? That is how powerful this love is, my mother. You know only love with me and I with you.

I begin to answer. . . .

Gracie, when I look at your photograph, I cry because I remember all those tubes. It was so hard for me, so difficult for you. To see you like that. [My tears are dripping down to the computer keys, on my hands. I try to blow my nose. I keep writing, and I don't know why.]

I know we are together Grace. The power of my love for you . . . I would have done anything to find you, to know that you were safe. I would have climbed the highest mountain for you. [I keep attempting to grasp what I have heard. I continue writing.]

Gracie, this is all about love and you have taught me that, darling. I love you so very much and I am so proud of you. Look at how you have affected so many people and how many more will be affected. This is what your love has done for people. Given love. Stay with me, my little girl. Because I will never leave you. It's just you and me. Me and my baby. Please stay with me. . . .

I then kiss the screen of the computer.

Dearest Trinity and Grace,   April 6, 1996

I do not understand. I don't know why this is happen-ing to me—this experience of last night left me with the exact same sensations as that time when the computer scrolled. I feel as if my mind is reeling. How can this be?

Please, Trinity and Grace. Help me. I am in no-man's land here. I need guidance fast. Please help me.

                                              April 7, 1996

Dearest Angels, Gracie, Trinity, and the Holy Spirit,

Thank you for this Easter. It has been wonderful to be with my family and with John. This is all that matters to me. I loved the conversation around the dinner table today when I could talk about this stuff, the stuff of angels and life and love and what it means to be human. I am so proud of Margaret and the book. She does have a true gift in that she can write such beautiful words and collect all the concepts with such detail. I am not cut from that cloth. But I can talk! I can spread the word of love to all! Just give me a chance and I will! John calls me "bunny" now. The rabbit in Native American symbolism means conquering fear. Boy does that sound good. And you know what? I am! I am conquering fear!

Gracie, I still wonder about what went on the other night. I can't help but wonder. Was that really you?

I will write later.

Dearest Gracie,   April 8, 1996

I am going to attempt to speak with you again. I have so many questions.

Gracie, you know that I miss you. You know that I am trying to understand this. Sometimes it is so difficult when I miss you. If you can hear me, please could you explain any of this? What is going on with me?

Mother, dearest one. Do not despair over your emotions. This is the way in which you recognize your humanness. This is a very big step for you to come to me and cross the barrier of infant to spirit. Yet your love brings you here tonight. It is with love that we can speak to one another. You have so much to give the world. There is no need to blame yourself for anything. Ever. There is no need to blame. Your spirit is free. You know this now. This is a time for celebration! My dear Mother, how I love you! Realize that without belief we could not be corresponding. You would not be able to hear me. But you do hear me. This is what Trinity meant when he said to listen. And you did! You can hear! We will continue these conversations. This I know. All it takes is love, my dearest.

You say to self, "But how can this be? How can I speak to my daughter who is in the arms of God?" But it is so. This is as real as what you can see. You can hear. This is real, my Mother. For so long you did not trust what you saw with the computer. This is real, my Mother. With love so much can be seen! We are together. Let your spirit go with this realization. Do you not feel lighter now? Do you not feel that we are together? For we are together. Do not fret that this is unusual to understand. Love has brought you to this place. And with love we will continue to grow.

There is no limit to the love we feel for one another. Do not put limits on your love. Your gift to the world is your love. Your love is so vast, like the oceans. Rejoice, Mother. When I say rejoice, you know that I speak the truth. I am surrounded by nothing but love. And when I see your love, I sing! Just as when you see the love of Amanda or my father, you sing! You really do! If sadness touches you, know that love is there also. It is there. You can choose to love, my Mother. You can choose.

But Gracie, what about the aspect of duality? Why do we have that? I know it is to learn from, but . . .

The duality, or opposites, can be but an illusion when one sees that all there is is love. You know this to be true with the oneness. When you have transcended a certain issue in life, there is integration. What was fragmented becomes whole. One. You move above the two. It ceases to matter. Day/night, darkness/light, good/evil, all revolves around love.

Grace, this is hard to understand. I have read that we have duality on earth because we have time. Are you saying that we can get to a place where there is no time, no opposites?

Time and duality are both illusions. In time, there appears to be past and future. In reality, this is experienced simultaneously, as one entity, the Eternal Now. This state may be reached by stepping "out of time," by going to the stillness of being—by cascading inward, for all your riches are truly inside, not out. Duality, or opposites, is illusionary. For life in reality cannot be "in opposition" to itself. This would totally negate life. In spirit, there are no opposites. Everything that appears in opposition has become one. The illusion is that there was ever two to begin with. When you see love in hatred, you have risen above the opposites. When you see the light within the dark, you have risen above opposites.

Mother, this is in the stillness. It is in being. It is in the sacred space of knowing. There is transcendence. There can be heaven on earth. This is what humankind strives for. It is peace on earth. You have felt peace in your heart. There is nothing sweeter in life—to know all is at peace within.

Gracie, I feel calmer by talking to you. Can we do this again? I thought that I was losing my faith, when really I was trying to understand this phenomenon, this ability to speak with my infant daughter. This has really helped me, darling. Has it helped you?

Oh, Mother, all your love aids me, feeds me, nourishes my spirit! This is what I have waited for! To be close to you! To have you know that I am here for you!

Things have been so intense for me at work and person-ally, lately. I may just have to rest for a while. I have to also take care of myself. And Liz is having her baby. Can you be there if you are not too busy? It would mean a lot to me. You, too, dearest Trinity! Gracie, this has eased my loneliness for you a few minutes ago. Thank you, dear daughter.

Your mother and friend, kisses to you, darling. Just like I used to do at the hospital.

April 11, 1996

Dearest Angels, Gracie, Trinity, and the Holy Spirit,

I want to thank you for bringing Margaret and Julie to me. Without them, without their love and support, I could not have made it as far as I have. Thank you.

Today Margaret told me to be human. I realized that the only time I had no shame with my sadness and anger was when Grace was alive. I had no shame. When I said those words, I realized that I had so much shame about being human now, even in my own eyes. When Liz had her baby, I felt so much sadness, and I was trying so hard to be happy. Oh, I get all mixed up sometimes.

I guess I still feel a little sad. I think part of this is anger. I just asked my anger what I could learn from it, and I heard "compassion." That made so much sense to me. Compassion. Will you help me with my compassion for self? I really need some help, if you feel this is for the higher good.

Mama, I hear you. I am here near you now. Let us talk. Do not despair. There is so much that you have been through and are trying to integrate. Do not despair!

First, let us speak of motherhood. This issue has weighed heavily on your mind. First and foremost, you are a mother, a mother now. Think of what you have with this motherhood. I speak of Amanda now and how you have opened her up. So much of her trust of self stems from the fact that you have helped her to see the light. Continue to do this. This is your gift to her. This helps her to love herself. This helps you to love yourself. You both need this love. Now!

GRACE

Mother, love the fact that you love. And you love so sweetly. You bring so much joy to others. Why do think you have gotten so much love back in this time of need? Because of all the love that you have given so selflessly for years. This is all being reflected back to you. Now!

My Mother, you are breaking free of the chains that have held you. Celebrate, my dearest! You are free. Today when you spoke with Margaret and Julie, you had an epiphany. You realized where your pain and sadness stemmed from and, hence, your anger. Without this capability, you were unable to move on.

Now let us speak of what it means to be a mother in the future. Where will this take you? Are you ready for this, Mama? Where would you like to go with this? Envision yourself there. Envision yourself with a baby, a beautiful baby. Let this vision take you into the future. Let this love await you there! Yes, you are so right to see a woman pushing her child in the sun. In white! With love! Laughing, yes! All you want, my dearest! This is you! This is you!

Mama, your fear has kept you in a place of not being able to choose. But there is always choice. Know that you can always choose! I chose you and you chose me. We wanted to be together and it is still this way. Nothing can part us. Not now, dearest. Not with faith.

Mother, you know that your thoughts have been my thoughts for so long. That you have recognized my voice from a place of love. That you have heard me in your thoughts. That in so many ways I am your thoughts. You know that none of this was punishment meant for you. This was a road of choice decided long ago. With love. You said, "I will remember," and you have! You have remembered to love, always love.

You know that on the day of my death, your dream was sent to you. To give you hope. Pure hope, my mother. And it did. You could not forget the dream. The feeling of the dream. The divinity! This is what we speak of. Although my father held me in his arms with so much love, you felt what I felt. In death. You have felt that love, Mama.

So do not despair! You know the love of the divine! I want you to know that with this love, you will always choose love. For there is no other way. That is the way. When in doubt, ask one simple question: "How can I love myself?" And your road will be clear, your vision will be filled with joy, your ears will hear the songs of angels. For, dearest mother, you are such an angel. I mean this from my heart! Such an angel. As you unwrap the things that have bound you and cast them aside, you will notice that your movements become filled with ease. Already you have picked up the flow and how that has been part of your life. You will see this everywhere. With love, dearest.

Enjoy your life! Take time to play, and I mean play! Do what makes you happy! Live and love! Do you not see how this has affected your love with my father? With Amanda? Can you not see how this has touched so many parts of your life? And it always has. All aspects of life contain lessons. Now is your time to enjoy the lessons of love. So love! And I will love right beside you!

Thank you, darling! Gracie, I feel that if you were a grown woman or my friend we would naturally be so close. Is this so?

Mother, there is a reason that we were mother and daughter. There is a huge reason. The first being choice—the choice of love. Our love runs so deep, Mother, it has come through the physical world to the divine to express itself. The second reason is that our lessons were so needed, and we chose to learn them together. There is often more than the obvious in

194

terms of how one learns, how one reflects one's purpose. You say, "But my daughter died." How do you know that you have not chosen to help others on their path? From one incident that you judged yourself so strongly about, how do you know that you might not have had a divine purpose? Things unfold in their own time. You have always sensed something so right about yourself. And this is what kept your belief, your faith alive. When others may have doubted, you did not. There may have been moments when you faltered, but you got right back on the path.

Gracie, I know I chose you. When you were just a little dream in my mind, I knew I would have an angel—I love you darling.

April 12, 1996

Dearest Angels, my Gracie, Trinity, and the Holy Spirit,

I want to thank all of you for helping me and for helping Margaret and Julie. There was so much love and happiness in the workplace today! Julie had a dream in which a barrier was being taken away, with Margaret at the wheel of a rental truck. And I have been able to feel compassion for myself. I have been able to speak to my dear daughter Grace. This makes me so happy. Gracie, I am so in awe and so happy for this. That we can communicate! It means so much to me. And the song that Julie heard, "Hail Mary, Full of Grace," that is how I felt—full of Grace.

Gracie, you know that as I drove home I had thoughts that this is enough—to know that we can communicate. That if there are no other children for Dad and me, I have had you. And that makes me so happy. You were everything to me and still are. To think that we can still communicate brings me such profound relief. That I do not have you in physical form does not mean the love stops there. It feels alive.

And so are we, even if, maybe, in different dimensions. Can I thank you enough? Can I thank Trinity enough for helping with this process? Can I thank the other Angels who are so important in helping me to balance and helping me to forgive and reclaim lost parts of myself? Can I thank the Holy Spirit for bridging the way for all this divinity to become manifested in my life? My heart thanks you.

Dearest Mother, we stand beside you now. Our hearts blend with yours in this moment, this moment of realization and love. It is truly an honor to be a part of this, we all feel this! Your journey has been one of strife, at times, yet you survive to tell this story—this story of love and growth. We view this and feel the pride of knowing you know, the love of knowing you know and can assist others on their way if you so choose. This is such a monumental time for all. For Julie, who has connected through love, her barriers are down. She need not worry any longer. For Margaret, whose strength and belief have surrounded both you and Julie. This time brings joy to all! And all of you feel this! Do you not think there is a reason that all of you have come to this point of joy?

Let us speak, my dear Mother, of suffering, which you have been considering of late. Why, you ask, is there suffering? What purpose, you ask, does it serve? Why must humankind go through this suffering? These are such enormous yet simple questions. You have lived this question, my mother. Do you not see?

Why did you go through suffering? To learn. Does one choose suffering? Yes, but not in the way you may imagine. Suffering is chosen when one feels one has no choice. That this is how it is. Everyone chooses.

But Grace, why? How—with your life and death, with natural disasters, things of this nature, how can people choose this?

People choose which lessons they want to learn for their evolution. Is it love they want to learn? Compassion? They choose. One is constantly evolving on all planes. You are so right when you say that we all keep evolving even after death, one can go higher and higher, always.

But Grace, if, as you said last night, things are not always obvious in terms of the big plan, that someone may offer themselves, their life, for something they are unaware of at the time, then how can they choose suffering? I mean, even though they may have had to suffer. As I think of myself, I ask, did I choose this? Because I had no choice? Or thought I had no choice? What?

It is both, Mother. You felt you had no choice and you also wanted to serve. You felt you had no choice on the physical plane. But on the spiritual plane, you wanted to serve. You have always wanted to serve others, and you have—so nobly. You came to the physical plane to learn. You have learned and will continue to do so. On the spiritual plane, you have known what your destiny has always been and is: to serve with love. To be with love. You are integrating both worlds: the physical and the divine.

You know, Grace, that I have trusted you and my love for

you as no other. I know you know that, but I had to tell you. This trust is what really clued me in as to how deep our connection is, because I have never trusted as I do now, until I had you. It started with you. I have never had the ability to love, really love, until I had you. I came close with your father and my family but you know how relationships add that other dimension of learning together. And then you were born and died and I had to live on this trust.

But what really astounds me is that our love crosses all barriers of time and space. And that you heard me! Gracie, Mother loves you so! I do so much darling! I think of you as this wonderful spirit angel. And you have come to me with so much love. We must have really loved one another. And still do. But this seems like such a miracle to me!

It is a miracle, Mother. All miracles occur through love. Remember this! You know now that you can choose. And in so doing can have love in your life. All of you can have so much love in your lives.

I feel that there is much we can discuss here on these pages. That these pages are filled with love. That I can learn so much, that maybe this can help others. What do you think, Grace?

Mother, I think that we are always learning, growing—on these pages, off these pages, in our hearts, and with love. One grows through love. One transforms through love. One knows through love! This I know!

All I know, dear daughter, is that I am so happy to be able

to do this. I am so grateful to be able to do this. It is such a big relief for me to be able to do this. Thank you!

You know, today, when Julie told me she had heard that song, "Hail Mary," and I had signed my name to you last night as your mother, Mary, I knew that to be a sign that we truly were in communication. I saw this great connection. You know that sometimes I do not remember what I have written on these pages when I talk to angels. The impact is felt days later. So when I get those signs, it helps so much. Thank you for that. Please thank God for me for you. I know that God knows, but for the record—this has meant the world to me. Oh, dear Angels! Thank you for coming into my heart! Thank you, Holy Spirit!

Gracie,   April 22, 1996

I am having problems. I don't want my confusion to alarm you. You know that I have been trying to get all this straight in my mind, with my being able to talk to you. I hope that you understand all this. I love you so and I am trying to understand, and I do; I keep reading your words. I miss you, Grace, although I know that you are with me. Thank you for this.

Mother, this is an honor that we speak together. I understand your confusion. Know that I stand by you always, should you need me. I am here for you. I love you so very, very much, dearest. Nothing can take that away. We are here together for a very special reason. That reason is love. Can I tell you that the amount you miss me is the amount of love you will feel—even more. Your heart beats with a pureness and openness that makes me sing. I see you and I smile. I see how you make others laugh and how you bring your gentleness into their hearts. Dear Mother, how can any child want more from a mother? How can any child not say with pride, "This is my Mother!"?

Gracie darling, I am crying so hard I can hardly type. My head hurts now. When I was a little girl, my mother used to say that we could put a cold washcloth on our eyes so they would not look so red after we cried. If you were here with me in human form, we could do that. But I will not get into that. I wish you were in human form sometimes, but what can you do? I am just glad that we can speak.

Mama, listen to me. When you are outside with the flowers and the ground and are just thinking, I will be so very close to you. You will be able to feel me. Think of this the next time you are outdoors. Why do you think that Amanda brought up the name of Persephone when you were looking at the flowers last August? I will be so close. You think now of the robin in the tree last spring—this also was a sign for you. Only for you, my dear, dear Mother!

Gracie, what do you think of these letters? Are they okay for you? What do you think?

Mother, this is wonderful, incredible, so miraculous—you will see how miraculous this truly is! I will help you! We will do this together. Just me and you, me and my mama. Do not fear, for it is done. We will do this together.

Thank you, Grace. I still struggle when we speak. You know that this all seems so very huge to me. And yet I have to be close to you, in any way possible. If this is the way, then this is the way. Dear girl, dear angel, I love you so much, Gracie! I keep crying, even now. I know that someday we will be together and this will all seem like some dream, but until then, my angel, know that you are the best thing that ever happened to me. Gracie, you have opened my heart up so much.

Will you please, if you can, help your father? He seems so confused about what he wants with his music. If this is for the highest good. Let him know that I love him.

Mother, this is done. It would be an honor to help my father. Know that he will be fine. He struggles, as you have in the past. But he is on the road. He will find his way. Do not doubt that for an instant. I am part of this family too! We all work together to stay together. Do you feel better now, my dear one?

I do, Gracie! I feel happy that we have been able to do this, sweetheart. A kiss for you from me. Know that I adore you.

And I you Mother!

Good night, Gracie and my Angels and Trinity. I love you all! Thanks!

April 23, 1996

Dear Angels, Gracie, Trinity, the Holy Spirit,
and the Universe,

I just reread the above passage. I look at those words and they evoke so much feeling inside of me. Me talking to Grace. I am so grateful, please do not get me wrong. It is just that I have doubted some, these past days, because of this. Because I had a baby and now I can talk to the baby. What does it all mean? Here I am, talking to my daughter who died. She was so tiny, and now she is giving me advice and wisdom. Why do I doubt at times and yet cry when I read the words?

Same day . . .

Dearest Angels, Trinity, Gracie, and the Holy Spirit,

I took today off from work. While I was out in the flower garden, I saw this little red thing glinting up at me. I had already raked this area last evening, but I looked more closely and I saw that this thing glinting at me was a shiny plastic heart in the dirt! A heart! A heart in the dirt, in the ground, just like Grace said: "I will be close to you by the flowers and the ground!" Thank you, sweetheart! It really made my day! Please realize that all this helps me to understand and to see! You know that I need encouragement now, so that really means so much. Thank you for this love!

I seem to be wondering what to do now. Amanda told me earlier that she wanted me to go to her dance rehearsal tonight, but now she is with her mother and has not called to tell me where or when it is. But maybe I can use this time to read or something. Dad just came home, Grace, and he seems to be in a bad mood, so I will just be who I am. Help me to send love to him.

Mother, you try so hard. Do not deny your humanness. This also makes you who you are. Be, dearest. Just be. This will assist you in this new phase of life. You are full of love, so be full of love. You sense the energy of my father and this frightens you, because you feel you cannot be as you are. This is not true! You can be who you are at all times. Think, now, of how beautiful things can be for you. And then you will be there. You need not take on anyone else's energy as if it were your own.

I have done this for a long time, have I not?

Yes! You will see. Mother, taking on other people's energy has injured you in the past. But you will see. This lesson has crossed your path for a specific reason.

What can I do, Grace?

Be human. Know this is fine. Let this show. You need not argue if you feel this would not benefit you. Just be, dearest. Calm will come. The quiet will come. Do something for yourself. My father needs his space and time. Do something for yourself!

Okay, I will. I think I will go to my mother's for the night. Amanda has not called. I will see you—I mean, write to you—soon.

April 24, 1996

Dearest Grace, Trinity, the Angels, and the Holy Spirit,

Hello! I am back at home and feeling much better. Thank you. I went to my mother's and actually got a great sleep there. It was so needed. I came home and John was still somewhat in a tizzy about things, but I was able to not let this affect me. I thank you again.

Mother, you took such good care of yourself last night. We know how easy it would have been to defend your position in all of this. The spirit was with you and you acted with it. See how easy this can be when you follow your heart? This has been revealed to you. Mother, when you see, you respond and you show the world how things can be with spirit. With knowing. With humanness.

Grace, I am feeling so much more comfortable about talking to you. I want you to know this. Having you in my life is so important, and to know that we are not really separated means even more. I think that I have crossed some type of line in belief. That I know we are together. I treasure this.

Our love has always been so very strong, my Mother. These bonds are not created overnight, so to speak. This has been proven throughout time. We came to human form to show, to reveal, this love. And it has been revealed through you and me. Know that we love with totality, with pureness, from both our hearts. Stop and know that our love has been with you since you were a little girl. You have heard my voice and I yours, through time.

Thank you, Grace. Thank you for your guidance tonight and last night. You knew just what to do. I feel that I need help when I am changing my behavior and showing it in more loving ways. You know that I have a problem with being human and all that, and also with being a perfectionist.

You are doing fine! We know that you will do all that needs to be done. And we, of course, will be there should you need any of us. If you have any questions, you know where to turn, do you not?

Yes, I do. In thanks, I say this. It takes me a little time sometimes with this. To have it all penetrate. Well, darling girl, good night.

Good night, Mama, good night.

Good night, Trinity, my sweet angel guardian.

Gracie,   April 27, 1996
   Can we talk?

Always, Mother. I am here for you. I love that you want to be so close to me during these times when we are so connected. I thank you for these times, my dear Mother. You are blessed with these times. I want you to know this.

Thank you, Gracie. The blessing is in that we are together through time, that this can even take place. I don't want you to feel left out when I struggle with things, because you are always in my heart. There is not a day that goes by in which I do not think of you in some way. It has been hard for me to understand how I can do this. How I can talk to you after so many months when I never heard your voice. But I am so grateful. You see, I cry every time we talk because I miss you so. I think that you would have been almost two, and we could have gone out today and raked or something, or you could have run errands with me.

I know that you are in spirit form, but sometimes it is just plain hard for me. I have seen two newborns recently, and I get all welled up. I thought this would be such a perfect time to be a mother, such a good time of life for me. I am older and more settled down, and I have gone through a transformation of sorts. I like myself better, or at least understand myself better, but it gets tough. I am running out of time. I know I do have Amanda. I do not know what I would do without her.

I guess I simply miss you, honey. My mother said the other day how beautiful you were. And you were. Just a perfect child. So you see, I do live in two worlds. The one of knowing you as you were and the one of knowing you now in spirit. I am so glad that I have something of you. My mind is wanting to catch up to the rest of me, to my heart. I want you to know these things, dearest.

I say to you, my dear, dear Mother. Live! I want you to live! I want you to be in life. It is an honor that you remember me, a tremendous honor. But I want you to live. Participate! You look back and say, "But what if this?" or "What if that?" I say, live! All of life gives you wonder. With or without me in physical form, you will still have wonder in your life. Treasure these moments because they bring you closer to me. We are together now! We dwell in these moments together. I am in your heart. In the perfection of God's love for you! You look to the past, dear Mother. It is time to look at what is right in front of you. LIVE! BE! CELEBRATE THIS WONDER!

I do, Grace. I want to live. I thought I was living, that I am always living. I thought that I felt the wonder of things. That . . .

Mother, feel the wonder of this. Feel that you are speaking to me NOW! That we are together NOW. Feel this. Please feel this!

Gracie, have I been denying that you were in spirit form?

Mother, this is right in front of you—this wonder. You can choose to believe whatever you choose. But you know this. I am here for you, telling you, from the arms of God, that all is well. That all is as it should be. I am here. Right here. What holds you back, dear one? You can examine this.

Grace, help me to believe this. I do, and then my mind gets all funny on me. I talk to you here, and then I doubt at times. Why?

Mother, you cry tears when we speak. You are moved by feeling. You are moved by love, the love of the words that are so close to you, in thought, with me. This is belief.

You have felt this love for so long. It is in looking at what Is that you are having a miscommunication. This IS! I was always more spirit than human in form. This is the reality! Spirit is the reality, dearest! When you are most true to yourself, it is in spirit that you are able to realize this.

You say, "But the body, what of the body?" Well, what of the body? You struggle with the concept of the body. You struggle with what is not seen, may not be real. But you know.

You know that love is not seen. Trinity is not seen. Thoughts are not seen. But there is belief that all of these exist. The material world brings only that which is material. The spirit world brings that of the spirit. You are crossing into that which cannot be seen. This is a marvel! You struggle with what was once seen and is no longer seen through the physical eyes.

Because you have known me in physical form as a child, you ask now, can it be both? Yet realize the essence is always there, dear Mother, our love is always there. If you hold that close to you, you will see. You will see that it does not matter in which form we come together, be it spirit or physical.

Gracie, thank you. I know you are with me. Thank you for being so patient with a mother who loves you so and yet struggles with this reality. I will hold our love in my heart and let it guide me. I can really see when I keep that in focus. Thank you for that. Can you fill me with your love?

We could not be talking here, my dearest, if our love lights, our spirits, had not combined as one. You are filled with love! Do not fret, nor worry. Live! Be! Let this day be filled with a happiness you have never known. Mother, realize how special you truly are. That is all I will say. How truly special you are!

Grace, I feel almost drowsy now. Thank you. I think that I will rest.

Dearest Grace, April 1996

I come to you tonight because I don't know what else to do. All my thoughts center on what is happening here—right here at the computer. I don't know how to say this, but I am having such a hard time with all of this. I feel as if what little faith I had in all that has transpired is ebbing away or being challenged. I come, Grace, once again, with despair in my heart.

You are my daughter, first and foremost in my mind. I have had to understand things I never thought I would. First your life, then your death, and now your life again.

I have to tell you this, because from the first I trusted you as I have never trusted anyone. You were a miracle to me. And now I question how this can even be happening. How is this possible?

Grace, first I had to get my mind around the computer that glowed, then a computer that scrolled with shimmering letters, then a computer that would not write—all of this is part of my physical world. And God knows, I have had feelings every inch of the way with this, but I have accepted it.

When I asked if you would come to me before, I thought it might be in a dream or vision. I have had to understand your death, Grace, and now you ask me to understand your life. I ask myself if this would be easier for me if you had died as an adult and this had happened? But you were my baby. Gracie, I have had to go through so much with your death, so much pain. I cannot stay away—I have to write to you. But how far can a human mind stretch?

I ask myself why. When I read Peace's words or hear Trinity's voice, I don't doubt. Is it because they are more abstract to me? Gracie, I look at Margaret and see her faith in the angels and God, and I admire her faith so much. Then I sit here and wonder how this can be possible. Please forgive me, darling.

When I heard your voice that first night, it was as if I were remembering a conversation of yesterday and recalling the voices of my sister or mother—there was that much of a distinction between your voice and Trinity's. I cried so hard that night, sweetheart, I had to hang on to the computer—I even kissed the screen. But Gracie, I have stretched more than I ever wanted to. More than I ever believed was possible. I pray to you, to everyone who can help me to understand, if it is possible, please help me to see how this can be. I know you are an angel—I know this. I just never thought it would be this way. I thought that you would have wings or something, that I could see you. Darling, please forgive me. You were my baby—I mean are my baby. Don't you understand? I'm even having a hard time trying to put these words on paper. I guess I don't even know what to call you, angel or daughter. I believe in the spirit—I just never thought it would be quite this way.

Dear Angels, Trinity, and Gracie,   May 1, 1996
I got up out of bed tonight. This crisis in belief continues. Why is this? Can you help me with this? I am doubting everything. Everything. How can this be happening? Why is this? Please, if this is for the highest good . . .

Mama, I stand by you. Thank you for coming tonight to speak with us. You hear the words to the music on now: "Two branches of one tree. God bless our love." Is this not so? You worry so about faith and yet you turn to us when in doubt. This is the truest faith there can be. You turn to me and have since the moment of my birth, in faith and love. How you have trusted this love! And so blessed is this love! Oh, Mother, if I could only make you see. It is for you to realize. But let me tell you that you will see! That this will bring you to such a place of comfort. Your honesty brings you to such a place of knowing. This you can trust. This trueness, even in the face of doubt, is what we speak of here. Your being true to self shows that you believe in who you are, that you have the courage to be who you are! Even in doubt, you are who you are! Oh, Mother of mine, celebrate this huge step. Once again, you trust who you are! Do you not see that you can see? Now sleep. I will be with you. I love and adore you so.

Dear Angels and Grace,   May 1996

I worked in the yard tonight. I keep hoping that something will come to me. If I have a problem, I have to get outside to sort it out.

I have worried constantly, Grace, about this situation, about hearing your voice. I don't know where to turn.

In my dream of last night I saw a file cabinet. In the drawer that was open was a file labeled "Effort." The scene switched rapidly, to my looking at a female physician bending over a child, an infant. I was looking at the doctor from behind. She was caring for this child, and I could sense that she was very desperate. I kept watching this scene. When she turned to look at me, I saw in anguish that she was me. I saw that my eyes had welled with tears. I saw the deep pain in my eyes and my heart just broke. Have I been trying to save you, Grace? What have I done to myself? God help me. . . .

Dearest Gracie and Trinity,   May 2, 1996

I woke up today feeling out of sorts. This crisis continues. What is going on? Is it because I have doubted? Is it because I do not know who I am? Who am I, anyway? I feel like just a body now, as if I have no past, present, or future.

Mother, thank you for coming and wanting to communicate again in this time. You struggle and yet there is no struggle. There is nothing to worry about. I do not want to diminish your perceptions, but this is illusion. You find yourself in this place—this place of questions. Have you not asked questions before? Have you not become someone new before? Did you not move from singleness to a married state with my father? Did you not move from childlessness to motherhood with Amanda? Have you not questioned before? This is what this is about. Questions. And it is as it should be. It is fine to question who you are, who you might want to become. In spirit form, you are always timeless. You question now what it is on the physical plane.

But Gracie, have I ever known who I was, or was I just pretending? Did I think I knew who I was when I really did not?

You question now with honesty. This is something you had a more

212

difficult time doing in the past. Now you want to be who you are and this feels foreign to you. This is that feeling of emptiness that has arisen. Yet you breathe easier. Do you not find this interesting?

Grace, I find this interesting and somewhat hopeful. Please know that I believe in you but this place is difficult for me. I know that you see so clearly and, in your eyes, I probably have muddled vision. Yet this seems big, somehow, to me. Can you just bear with me?

Thank you for all that I have. Even if I doubt, I want you to know that you are the best thing that could have happened to me. So I will just trust that all will be fine, somehow. Okay? I have to go to work. Simply, thanks. I am just so very confused.

May 1996

Dearest Angels, Trinity, Gracie, and the Holy Spirit,

I ask now that you help me with these letters to you, Grace. I ask that you help me with this confusion, this disbelief I struggle with. . . . And yet this love in my heart, this love for you, Grace, is so real. I feel this, this realness.

Mother, thank you. It is with honor that we see the love on these pages and know that this lies within your dear heart. This will free you. This writing will free you. Your breathing comes with ease now. This is so reflective of what IS. Do you not feel the lightness coming into being? I am close to you now. Very close. You feel my energy. My light. We are as one as we speak here. We have been as one inhabiting the same body, the same energy. Feel strong in this knowing. You may write now.

213

KNOWING

Dearest Grace,   June 1996

You know that I have been struggling with my faith,
with trying to understand all of this. I had to run to write
to you this morning, because I woke up with an intense
sense of relief. I know that I dreamed of having faith—
that what I felt I lacked was already there. But thoughts
are rushing from me even now as I write. I realize that I
could not have faith or believe in all of this unless I felt I
knew what it meant. The Greeks have a word called *gnosis,*
meaning "self-knowledge" or "self-knowing." I kept getting hung up on *what* things meant—the questions—

rather than what I *knew.* First let me define *knowing* as "per-ceiving or understanding clearly and with certainty."

Let me try to explain. On a very basic level, through *physical* union, your father and I *knew* each other, and we had you. We *united* by *knowing* each other. This *uniting* happens all the time. Even with thought. For instance, when someone understands an idea, he or she may say, "I get it!" meaning the person *sees* and *understands clearly* and with *certainty.* To do this one must first *unite* with this idea. The idea becomes a part of that person. You *become* the idea through *uniting* with it.

I united with you as a mother *physically.* I *knew* you as a mother. However, I resisted the idea that you, as an angel, were in spirit form. To me, you were still my baby. Yet, you were teaching me that if I could come to *know,* to *see,* to *understand* and *perceive* reality, I could unite with you in spirit.

When I *knew* you in spirit, Grace, I *knew* God. When I *knew* God, I *knew* my *self.* I somehow became united. How many times did Trinity tell me I *knew?* This was my key to unlocking the part of me that had become confused. But let me go on.

Grace, I have tried my whole life to control outcomes. I did this by being good, or trying to be good. When you died and I could not control that, I reasoned that my worst fear had been revealed—I somehow was bad. I justified your death by making myself wrong, and to be wrong you must be flawed. I viewed death as a punishment, the final scene, often painful and full of loss. Then the events began happening.

First, let's look at the comforter being tucked around me. I *knew* when this occurred that it had something to do with you. I never questioned that. I just *knew*. If one were to comfort a loved one, tucking them in bed would be such a gentle indication of this. It worked. I was comforted. Then there was the glowing computer—once again, I *knew* that this had to do with you. The computer had never glowed before you were born, and I only used it to write to you. This is the *one way* I could feel close to you. It was our *connection*. I *knew* this.

Next, your father told me to be *natural* about my out-of-body experience—that it was nothing bad. This opened me up to seeing *(knowing)* that if I was *out* of my body, then my real self was something other than my body. If not a body, then what? I kept stumbling into answers revolving around the spirit. Or *was* I stumbling?

We now come to the aspect of the computer scrolling. I was so deeply affected by this event that I literally fell to my knees and prayed—and I was crying. This was more than a knee-jerk reaction, that of praying. It was something I *knew* in the deepest part of me to do, like breathing. I think now of other men and women who have fallen to their knees when touched by the divine. No one teaches you that. You do it because it feels natural, because you *know*.

Grace, when I think of the burning bush that Moses saw, the tree that bloomed in the dead of winter for St.

Francis, I realize that these experiences happened using familiar landscapes to convey divine messages within the *physical* world. The computer was *my* landscape and a means for me to connect to you in my mind and heart. What had I witnessed? And how had I *known* so completely that this was divine?

Yet, my mind kept telling me to reason. Figure it out. More questions, always questions. *Why? How? It is not possible,* were all familiar thoughts. What we do not understand, we fear. This fear kept cropping up for me. It was an illusion that kept me in a state of confusion. When you hang your hat on illusion, it becomes impossible to *see* love. This fear is now gone.

I reasoned that divine experiences were only for others. That I somehow was not qualified to *know,* to see clearly. I was not holy. I was way too ordinary—and bad at that. But events kept occurring, each ultimately revealing a message of love.

I was open to angelic communication—to the messages of Peace and the teachings, in my case, of Trinity. I began slowly to heal through Trinity's words and to *know* myself. I began to *see* and *understand.* Yet, these angels remained somewhat abstract, seen as divine messengers coming from another place.

When I *heard* your voice, Grace, I went into another tailspin. I trusted what I *saw* on the computer, such as the crosses, shimmering letters, as being more valid than what I *heard*—your voice. I kept trying to reason that a baby could not talk, that you were still my baby. I was playing by earthly rules and chronological age—you were telling me there was a much larger way of looking at my life, that spirit is ageless. Although I *knew* what I had heard, I kept waffling. My mind told me I could not be truly faithful if I questioned.

Grace, you could never remain abstract for me—ever. Once again, for a person such as myself, the fact that you came to me as you did shows me how the divine is at work. You have been the single most altering experience of my life, and I have never loved more. God *knew* that. You *knew* that. And I *knew* that.

This was revealed to me through you. I kept hanging on to the thought that you had died. And with that, a part of me died. But you encouraged me to live.

My abstract view of angels and all things holy was reinforced by seeing God as something distant and far away. I saw heaven as a place to go to rather than a state of being. With you in my heart, I realize God is there also. But the real miracle is that I have moved somehow to seeing God as *living,* because of your continued life in spirit.

I see so clearly that what I know, I *knew* all along.

Grace, you have become my doorway. Seeing your divinity, I *knew* God not as something out there, but as alive and working in my life. And through you, I have been able to see my own divinity, as coming from my humanity, from acceptance, love, and forgiveness. What began as a baby journal now has become a type of prayer book for me. These letters really are prayers to God, through you and through Trinity.

I see how my dreams were my gateways to comprehending and integrating lost aspects of myself. They assisted with this vision, giving me comfort all the way. I see how I used them as my guideposts toward a deeper understanding.

I see so much now. I see this great plan at work. Almost as if it were some great dance, everyone having a part. I see how both Margaret and Julie were not coincidences in my life; that both of them, each with her own brand of love, entered my life for a reason. Margaret, who was the first to speak to an angel, was a writer and could capture divine messages beautifully on paper; she helped open another door. She was the first to see these letters to you, and she told me immediately that these letters were beautiful and needed to be shared so that they could help others. I see that if the computer had been operating correctly, I would not have even asked Margaret for help, nor you, later in my prayers.

I see Julie as having opened my heart with her incredible tenderness and *feeling,* and propelling me to a place of forgiveness. I could have shut down forever. But she became my greatest comfort. Each of these women had a part in this story—this healing. Each of us became *united* somehow with our own particular spiritual journeys. And somehow we had created a kind of "church" by sharing our lives.

I see your father having the strength and understanding that I so desperately needed. Our marriage may not have survived had it not been for him. I could have run away as I had from so much in life and hid from myself. I see how he encouraged me to be *natural,* and that spirit is the *natural* state of being. I see Amanda drawing me out of this shell, this armor that I had surrounded myself with, telling me to live as you were—it is all so perfect.

I see my mother as the ultimate listener—always giving of herself when I called, crying. I see my father, after I told him that I was talking to an angel, as telling me that I should always "follow my heart." I see your Grandma Love, who probably never believed that I would end up speaking to angels, sending me an angel book after you died, causing me to *look* in that direction. Everyone had a divine role. Each member of the family, each friend.

I see now how I thought I was in control. I awkwardly thought that I could control aspects of my life by *trying* harder with everything. This was revealed in my continuing conversations with Trinity. How can one *see* anything if one is always *trying?*

I had put myself in a state of perpetual deprivation. This was my ultimate illusion. I had a false sense of security that kept me emotionally and spiritually deficient and exhausted. For years this has been such a burden to me. I thought that *everything* rested on my shoulders, that I rose and fell with how much effort I put into things. I release this to you Grace—to God. It is such a relief.

KNOWING

I see how the pain of your death also kept me grappling in some type of emotional desert. I saw only pain. I was tied to the pain. I had *united* with the idea of pain and therefore lashed out at myself to create my own personal prison. As Trinity told me continually, you can choose to think what you want. I had chosen hell, because I thought that was the only choice available. And yet, you were merely moving from one state to another in love— *painlessly.*

Just as we can be connected to someone here on earth through pain, we can also be connected to someone in spirit through pain. If I really believed in your *death,* how could I then believe in your *continued life in spirit?* This pain was erased when I realized that you actually lived. This seems miraculous to me.

In reality, it is our love that remains constant. That was what you were trying to tell me. I *know* this now, Grace. I also see how this *knowing* has always been a part of me. That this knowing was my faith, *even if* I questioned.

Grace, I see these ripples coming out from my heart, from all of this. I see how we all love our children, wanting safety and beauty for them, within their hearts. I know now that you are safe and that you have found the beauty you sought. I see that this is what God wants for all of us: safety, love, and beauty.

Gracie, I think that I am on the path. I really believe that everyone in the human condition has come to the earth to learn how to love, that we are all visitors for a short while, and then we leave. In reality, we are some-how more than our bodies; we are all of the spirit. For me, it is so comforting to *know* that there is no pain in death.

I see now that you did not need to stay any longer than you did. Your life was complete—even at five weeks. You did what you came to do, what you were meant to do. I say this in humbleness. When I see how you have hon-ored me by loving me so deeply, by coming to me to show me only love, this alone moves me to a place of pro-found gratefulness.

Thank you, darling, for this message of love. I have the courage now to be who I am, as I am. I know now that everything is possible.

EPILOGUE: INTEGRATING

A door opened, and I went through it. That door was communication. I moved from a place of disbelief to a place of total knowing in my communication with Grace. I walked through this door only because of my love for Grace. Grace and I have continued to speak to one another and I have continued to heal.

The lessons I learned from Trinity and Grace became integrated into who I was. For so long, so much of my life surrounding the birth and death of my daughter had centered on loss. And so much of my healing revolved around finding. These concepts appeared as separate

GRACE

entities for me. Loss had entered my life as some savage intruder that destroyed all that I loved. Finding Grace became a balm that healed my wounds.

However, one question still lingered in the back of my mind. I did not realize this until I turned the key in my back door one day and had a memory of Amanda asking if she could talk to me one night, two months after Grace had died. I told her yes, and she crawled into bed with me where I had been reading. Amanda was having difficulty asking me whatever she needed to know but finally she simply said, "Did Gracie die because of me?"

I was astonished. Amanda went on to say that she thought Grace had died because of a story she had read to her in the hospital! Tears stung my eyes. I told her no, this was impossible. She asked how I knew. I told her I was Grace's mother, and mothers always know. I told her that Gracie had been sick and it was no one's fault. I held Amanda and felt that familiar wooden feeling grow in me again. What I did not realize was that I, too, was asking the same question about myself.

I realized all of this as I turned the key in our back door, two and a half years after my daughter's death. As I turned the key I heard the words: "You are absolved." I felt jolted into a new reality. I saw how ridiculous it was for Amanda to have felt that way, and yet I understood in her humanness how she could ask this. I knew then that this is how God saw me—as a child asking a question for which I was sure guilt and fear were the only answers.

224

These were the exact illusions that Trinity and Grace had spoken of: guilt and fear. I saw the impossibility of what had driven me for months. I had brought light into fear. And fear dissolved into thin air.

I realized how shame and guilt were so closely tied to loss. It became so clear for me. When we say, "I lost my temper," "I lost my job," "I lost my child," what are we really saying? The implication here is that if something is lost, it is gone and cannot be found. But by the same token, is finding not the opposite of losing? So often we stop at loss and believe that is all there is. What we had is gone. We totally blew it. Our chance is gone. We do not perceive of the connection, the lesson of duality that Trinity and Grace both spoke of.

We divide completion, or the ability to heal, when we think in terms of opposites—and therefore we extinguish the opportunity and potential for uniting and becoming whole within ourselves. We say what is lost cannot be found. We stop at loss, because we do not believe that being found is part of the same equation. But are loss and finding not one and the same? Is the circle not the beginning and the ending at the same time? Is this not the exact lesson, or way of seeing, that unifies rather than separates and destroys? We do not believe at the time of loss that what we seek is there.

This is exactly what the concept of duality does to us. It separates instead of unifies. I am sinner or blessed, up or down, straight or crooked. But reality is not this way. In the union of what appeared to be in opposition to itself, I found love. When I lost, I found. Pure and simple. It was there all the time, the whole while. When I said that Grace had died, I had no idea that I—or God—would be found, let alone Grace. I had no idea that being found was part of losing.

This is the message Grace left me, to see in terms of wholeness, not division. To love all of me, not surgically remove any of who I am. This is the greatest connection that there may be.

FINDING PEACE

I cannot part from these pages without telling one more story from my journey. On November 1, 1996, which happened to be All Saints' Day, my husband John and I went out to dinner. We were talking about the miracle of this book and how it could even have come to be—simply from letters to our daughter.

For some reason, John, who has never asked anything of me, asked, "Can you write about Grace's death; can you put that in the book?" I got tears in my eyes and said, "John, tell me what it was like." John began to speak softly and slowly, never hesitating. I began to cry as he told me this last part of the story. . . .

"Grace was in my arms. She had her little fingers wrapped around my thumb—just like Amanda used to do when she was little. I was in the rocking chair with her. And then it was as if time expanded into some great arch and Grace went into it. She simply moved into this place. There was total silence, and yet the room was filled. I had just been speaking to your father about why people have to suffer as Grace did. And then she was gone. I knew that God had heard me. I was so amazed that God had listened. It was so beautiful, and such a great honor to be there. . . ."

I was crying so hard. This was such a gift to me, to hear these words. John held my hand and neither of us spoke. I hung on to John's words. This was the only memory I have of Grace's death to cling to, because I had not been there.

I could not shake the feeling of that evening. It stayed with me the whole next day. That night, I asked Grace about it, still needing to hear. I finally had the courage to ask.

This is my last gift of Grace to you, the words of her death. . . .

My father, John, was holding me in his arms. There was no pain and no greater safety. My father spoke of suffering. He was telling my grandfather of my suffering. At the time, I wondered why, for I felt no pain. I knew this to be how they felt suffering in their hearts. My mother's spirit was with me all the while. She could be in spirit form only in a dream state, and so she came to me, to help me, as she felt she slept.

It was all predestined to be like this, that she slept while I left the physical world. This was not meant to bring grief, but to have her close to me. It could only be done as she slept.

My father's words of suffering were heard by God, for there is no greater appeal than that of a parent. There were many, many angels, many to see me to the higher realms—there was light everywhere. It filled me. It filled the room. It filled my father and grandfather. And yes, there was an arch; this is the passageway I traveled in love. And there were many to greet me, to KNOW me, to celebrate in love!

Time, as my father sensed and my grandfather knew, was nonexistent. We were all out of time, in eternity. We had risen above duality, pain, and fear, and in those moments we touched God.

When my father said that God had heard him, he heard God! And in this he is blessed, as my grandfather is blessed and you, my mother, are blessed.

For mother, it was you who guided me to the light. . . .

And so I leave you here, at the end of this love story. I want all of you to know, in gratitude, what the making of this book has done for me. It has healed the deepest part of my soul and left me so complete. I thank you.

I give you these letters now in love, from Grace, in total peace.

Sincerely,
Mary Kathryn Love

ABOUT THE AUTHOR

Mary Kathryn Love lives in St. Paul, Minnesota, with her husband, stepdaughter, and four cats. She enjoys gardening and conversation, and has a deep appreciation for the quiet solitude that books and reading offer. She grew up in South America and attended high school and college in Minnesota. Love continues to write, having found this to be one of the aspects of life that contains her joy. She is currently a Program Associate in the ISP Executive Study Program at the University of Minnesota. She can be contacted through the web site of The Grace Foundation: http://www.gracezurilovefoundation.com

PEACE

PEACE

MARGARET PERRON

Shannon —
Peace be
with you —
Margaret Perron Nov. 1997

■ HAZELDEN®

Hazelden
Center City, Minnesota 55012-0176
1-800-328-0094
1-612-257-1331 (FAX)
http://www.hazelden.org

Library of Congress Cataloging-in-Publication Data
Perron, Margaret, date.
    Peace / by Margaret Perron.
        p. cm.
    Final work in The Grace trilogy, of which the first work was titled
    Love and the second work was titled Grace.
        Includes bibliographical references.
        ISBN 1-56838-158-1
        1. Perron, Margaret, date. 2. Spiritual biography—United
    States.   I. Title.
    BL73.P47A3   1997
    973.72'092—dc21
    [B]   97—23172
                                                               CIP

Cover design by David Spohn
Illustrations by Randy Scholes
Text design by Nora Koch/Gravel Pit Publications

Editor's note
Hazelden offers a variety of information on chemical dependency and
related areas. Our publications do not necessarily represent
Hazelden's programs, nor do they officially speak for any Twelve Step
organization.

Ten percent of the author proceeds from each sale of *The Grace
Trilogy* will be donated to The Grace Foundation, an organization
established in remembrance of Grace Zuri Love. The Grace
Foundation has as its mission *Creating art and sacredness from the ordinary*.

For more information on The Grace Foundation, visit its web site
at http://www.gracezurilovefoundation.com

Peace is dedicated to my husband, Donny Deeb, who brought peace to my life by becoming Father to my children; to Joe Perron, my earthly Father, who all my life told me, "Peace be with you"; to my heavenly Father, who all my life gave me Peace to be with me; and to Peace, who has always been with me.

And to you. Peace be with you.

CONTENTS

ACKNOWLEDGMENTS

In gratitude for Peace...

I want to say thank you to all those who were so considerate of the space I needed to leave unoccupied in order for this work to come to be. To all those I love who allowed me to be elsewhere so that this work could be completed. To all those who encouraged me and all those who believed in me, and especially to my family who supported me. And thanks to my Thursday-night dinner guests, Ed and Katie Deeb, who gave me the only excuse good enough to give up a night in front of my computer: that of pleasing my husband. And to my goddaughter, Alicia, who was a special gift in the final days of my editing.

In addition to the blanket thanks above to everyone in my family, I must mention my mother, who was just a little sensitive about some of the feelings I have revealed in *Love* and *Peace,* and who, despite that sensitivity, has been my champion every step of the way in this endeavor. Although the sometimes sad and confused thoughts I expressed when I spoke of her were true in a time and place that is past and gone, they didn't then, and don't now, obscure either the love she has for me or I for her. I hope my children, Ian, Mia, and Angela, know the same is true concerning them.

Thanks, too, to my spirit sisters, who have become such a large part of my peace, to my birth sister, Susan, and good friend Lou, whose companionship and words of wisdom were largely deleted from this book but not from my mind or heart, and to Ann Mulally Reilly, who always brought peace to my writing.

To each one of you I can only say that I have felt you start upon the road of Peace with me, I have felt you join me, and your companionship has sustained me through the quiet inward journey, bringing me back to you as surely as it has brought me back to myself and to God.

Thanks also to Dan Odegard for recognizing the value of *Peace,* for being affected by the Way of Peace, and for speaking of it to me in my own language: the language of words. No one says it more beautifully.

Much appreciation goes to Cathy Broberg, who realizes the power of words—both the keeping of them and the deleting of them.

If organizations have a soul, Hazelden's must be one of healing. My appreciation goes out, too, to Hazelden, the healing entity, for realizing the healing power of Peace.

And finally, thanks to Steve Lehman, my editor, who was willing to let *Peace* become part of him, who came to my table and said, "I cannot separate my emotions from this work," who gave me the gift of his tears and with those tears the reassurance that *Peace* was at the right place and in the right hands. In giving *Peace* to Steve, I received peace in return, the peace of knowing that he was the one who would bring *Peace* to the world in the way it was meant to be.

For all I am truly grateful.

INTRODUCTION

The spiritual experience is all about choice. How we choose to live our lives. How we choose to see ourselves. How we choose to relate to the world and the people around us. The spiritual experience seems, at first, to be about making many choices. But it is all about making one choice.

The spiritual experience is the choice—the decision—to do whatever is necessary to discover who we are so we can be who we are. I did not realize this was what it was all about when my journey began. But I had intimations.

I had reached a place where I felt my life was pretty

1

much in order: I had a religion I was happy with, Catholicism, and I had a sense that I could find what was missing in my life by bringing my religion and my life more together in some way—making my relationship with God more than just going to church on Sunday. So I began to pray in a way that was more personal to me than the way I had been taught—I began to pray by talking to God, in a journal format, on my computer. I also began to read books about spirituality. And I began to discuss what I was reading and thinking with two friends with whom I worked, Mary Love and Julieanne Carver.

Only a few months after opening a prayer file on my computer, I began a dialogue with an angel named Peace. This book recounts that dialogue.

What became immediately evident through this dialogue was that my life was not in the order I thought it was. Instinct took over as soon as I had this angel, this *authority,* to consult, and I did not ask weighty spiritual questions but the questions I really wanted answers to. It was only by Peace's tenacity and skill as a listener and as a guide that I learned anything at all. Because he saw into and through my questions to what was in my heart, and caused me to look there as well.

Hidden beneath each of my requests to Peace were some variations of the questions, Who am I? What am I to do with my life? and Why am I in pain? The answers, in their many forms, simply told me that the only one keeping me from being who I truly was was me. The only one who could free me from pain was myself. And that if I concentrated on freeing myself from pain and discovering who I truly was, the answer to what to do with my life would surely follow.

Peace always provided gentle and thorough answers. But he also always provided the only answer I was ready to hear. His responses to my questions became more sophisticated as my ability to hear became more sophisticated and as my willingness to learn grew. We think our willingness to learn is total until we confront our unwillingness to let go of old ideas. We think our desire to be guided is total until we confront our desire to have things the way we want them or the way we think they should be.

Perhaps Peace, himself, put it best when he said:

I can only guide you. Like a tour guide, I can proclaim the sights outside the bus window, the wonders that can be seen there, the paths that would be best to take and those that would be best to leave unexplored. But I cannot force you to look or to hear or to see more than you are ready for. Like the person on the bus, you see only the choices—so many things to look at, so many ways you could go. And like the person on the bus, you choose your own path—often knowing that it will be the one full of surprises, choosing the surprises instead of the sure thing.

Why?

To learn what you must learn in your own way. Because THIS IS KNOWN TO YOU. Despite your frequent requests for information and detail, YOU KNOW THAT YOU MUST FIND YOUR OWN WAY.

Does this mean that you will never choose to make your way the Way of Peace? It could mean this. But it does not have to. You do not have to continue to look about and see a thousand choices. You can, instead, look within and see one choice: the Way of Peace.

Choice.

It is more difficult than one would think to be asked—to be confronted with choosing to be more than what we are, more than what we have believed ourselves to be. I don't know why it is so much easier to choose to be *less,* but this is the way it was for me. I was willing to accept myself as flawed, guilty, and unworthy. I was willing to accept life as difficult, to see it as one struggle—one conflict—after another. But to be asked to see myself as perfect? To be asked to see life as joyous? These choices seemed impossible to make.

Choice.

Peace seemed, at first, to be asking me to look at reality and ignore what I saw there. Being asked to choose to trust in a distrustful world seemed like folly. Being asked to choose to open my heart seemed like an invitation for more hurt to come my way. But what Peace was really asking was for me to choose a new way of looking. To choose a new reality. I came to see that everything Peace asked of me was an invitation. An invitation to change my mind about myself and the world.

Having an angelic guide seemed, initially, to be the answer to my prayers. But soon, the reality of having a relationship with an angel began to pose its own difficulties. You do not just begin recounting angelic communication in day-to-day conversation. How does one say to one's husband, "I was talking to my angel the other day and he said . . ."? Peace thus became a call to choose what I believed in—a choice I believe we each must make, whether it be to believe in God or angels or ourselves or, preferably, all three.

Talking to Peace was also difficult in another way. It seemed to me that after talking with an angel, life should immediately change in some earth-shaking way. But it didn't. My life was still ordinary. I often went straight from talking to Peace on my computer to washing dishes or doing laundry or painting walls. But these things were not what I would have chosen to do had I seen a choice.

Choice.

There were days I would have given anything to be able to make Peace my life. Days when it seemed the dichotomy of talking to Peace and then going off to work was just too much. Had I been single, I truly think I would have sought a more religious life—say that of a nun. If I had been wealthy, I believe I would have chosen a reclusive life of quiet reflection and left the outside world alone for a while. I fantasized that there might be a grant of some kind that would fund me to stay home and talk to Peace and read books and discover what was sacred about life. But I didn't see any of these choices as real choices. I was part of a family and a household that needed two incomes. I was part of a family whose members' lives were not about to come to a halt so I could take a little vacation from life to seek the spiritual. Yet, it was never far from my mind that something miraculous was happening to me and that I was just going on with life as usual. It didn't seem right somehow. So Peace also became a call to extend the spiritual into my daily, ordinary life, to make Peace my life as much as I could within the confines of that ordinary life.

And I found that as I learned to apply the messages of Peace to my day-to-day life, my day-to-day life *did* change. Choices opened up to me where I had never seen them before. I saw that I could choose new ways of doing things, new ways of handling situations, new approaches to relationships. Little miracles seemed to be happening every day. My spiritual life began to *be* my life. My spiritual life began to *bless* my life.

Not that you'd always know it from these conversations. As I reviewed the Peace writing and found that it contained some of the most beautiful, spiritual, divine writing I had ever beheld, I couldn't believe that I could follow any of these passages with still another mundane question about another mundane detail of my life. I couldn't believe the patience Peace had with me. I couldn't believe how long it took me to "get" things. If you question from where this writing came, you might consider that if I were making it up, I wouldn't have made myself out to be so dim-witted. So *thick*. So unable to grasp the simplest truths. But as Peace would say, "how long" it took me to get something didn't matter in the slightest. The journey itself was just as important as the "getting there."

As I reviewed the Peace writing, I realized Peace and I rarely talked directly about God. Yet I always knew we were heading in His direction. I knew I was being prepared. I knew that even if my questions had not been about myself, my *self* was the starting point. We must start with ourselves because faith in ourselves is the hardest faith to find and until we find it, how can we have faith in anything else?

Perhaps the desire for life to change in some earth-shaking way is a desire to have an external "something" to place our faith in. It was hardest to believe in myself when I saw myself as the same woman I had always been, living the same life, doing the same dishes, scrubbing the same floors. But remaining the same *externally* forced me to look *internally* for change. Remaining the same externally caused me to see that while I might do the same mundane chores, I did them more peacefully. I came to live more peacefully because I became a more peaceful person—*inside.* I became a more peaceful person inside by learning to know my true self and by learning to let go of my false ideas about myself. I became a more peaceful person by choosing the way of Peace.

What is the way of Peace? A choice. A choice to see things differently. *A choice to find your own way.*

PEACE

Peace is a dialogue, an adventure, a journey, a discovery. Peace is an angel, a state of mind, a place of being. Peace is something felt and experienced and eventually known. Peace is an invitation. Peace is a beginning. Peace is a choice anyone can make.

I.
PRAYING

PRAYERS

I t is Lent. In church today, the mood was magnificent. Father Baz in his purple robes, the girls singing in choir. The mysterious sound of the prayers said in Aramaic. The wonderful language of the Mass. We pray to be humble, to be forgiven, to be blessed. We pray for our ancestors and for the departed, the living and the dead. We pray the Our Father together, Father with his eyes raised to heaven.

Today we heard the parable of the Prodigal Son. Father Baz said it was named incorrectly. The lesson comes from the father not the son. The father who waits to welcome his child with outstretched arms is like our Father.

There is so much love and community and family in religion. Even the ceremony and ritual of it. What family does not have its ceremony and ritual, a time for giving advice and a time for giving praise, and a time for giving and receiving forgiveness?

I am thankful to be part of this family. I am thankful to be able to ask for blessings on my children and my goals from a source greater than myself.

March 23, 1995

This whole process I am beginning—this preparation to buy a new home—has become a reassessment of my life. As I was clearing out some of the junk in my desk, I found, for instance, the paperwork related to my desire for a reverse tubal ligation. It reminded me of all I had hoped a new baby would bring to my family.

But I also found much concerning my struggles with the babies You were so good to give me. Everything related to my pregnancies and my children's infancy seems, in retrospect, to have been a struggle. It is one of the reasons I so desired a new baby. I wanted the chance to do everything right instead of everything wrong. I wanted, just once, to be wholly joyous about being pregnant from the moment of conception. I wanted, just once, to welcome a baby into a family and a home where love was not just a feeling but an environment. I loved Ian and Mia and Angela dearly. But I could too seldom provide them, when they were young, with an environment of love.

Thinking about all of this again has shown me that I do have that opportunity now, something my dear friend Mary will never have. Her loss of her daughter is a constant reminder of how lucky I am. A constant reminder of how grateful I should be.

I need Your help, Lord, in cherishing and providing for the children I have as I would a new child.

As I look forward to beginning a new phase of my life, a childless phase, as my children grow up and leave, I see that it is not they who are associated with the pain of the past but only me. In them I see only goodness. I feel only the joy they have brought, the fullness they have given my life. I know they will continue to do so. I pray there will be grandchildren someday when they are ready to bring new life into the world. But I realize how important the present is and how much of my life I have spent dwelling on the past and planning for the future. I need Your help, Lord, to remain rooted to the present.

There is so much I want to do. In my writing life alone there are a dozen projects I want to bring to fruition. I have no concept of which project is more important, of which You have put me on this earth to create. But I do feel that writing is part of my mission in life. And I thank You for this mission.

I guess the main thrust of today's prayer, Lord, is to help me live the life I would live (or have tried to live) had you given me a new baby. Give me the strength to cherish what I have as much as I sometimes long for what I don't have.

March 28, 1995

Sunday's sermon was about the paralytic and the miracle of Jesus. Father made much of the fact that Jesus did not just say, "Get up and walk," but, "Get up and walk. Your sins have been forgiven." Meaning that we are often paralyzed by our sins. He talked also about confession in this sermon—using the parallel of confession forgiving us for our sins and the miracle of the paralytic man to suggest that we can be healed not only in mind and soul but in body by confession—by seeking forgiveness.

I am more and more impressed by how my readings on spirituality so often mirror what is going on in Mass. I am comforted that my new spiritual teachers are Catholic. They draw often on their Catholic beliefs and especially on Catholic symbolism and ritual.

I thank God that I was raised in this wonderful tradition and that I have been given the opportunity to raise my children in this faith and in a loving environment—a community such as Holy Family.

I look forward especially, this Lent, to the symbolism of Lent and Easter, of the death and rebirth. As I feel myself being transformed—going from one phase of life to the next—this message is especially powerful to me and I know there is much I can learn from it, that it can teach me, this year.

March 29, 1995

I am stupidly envious of my friend Mary's spiritual experiences which have grown out of great sadness and pain. There is no great sadness and pain in my life right now—not even any great conflict. There is busyness, ambition, creativity, but nothing exceptionally good or bad. And in some ways, it is difficult. It is so new, perhaps.

It is difficult in that sometimes I cannot talk about my "things" because there is always someone with a greater need. But more than that, it is difficult on some psychological level not to be in the midst of something that is so personally moving. I, like Mary, have turned to spirituality in my quest to fill the role that pain and strife so often filled. I am not fool enough to want pain and strife back in my life. And my life is very full, but all in a normal sort of way. It is full of family and work and writing and planning to move, all but the writing being on a more physical than mental/spiritual/emotional level. And even the writing has not lately been writing on my book—the creative writing that fills me with my own personal bliss—but a form of writing convenient to the small amounts of time I have to spend on it.

So, the spiritual journey. I don't mean to portray it as second best, as "I don't have anything else going on in my life, so I am going on this spiritual journey." It has called me. It has captured my mind and my imagination. It has led the direction of my thoughts and my writing. And I guess I can only envy Mary if I don't see this as miracle enough for me. I have been envious because her journey is filled with a different kind of miracle.

I guess I had to write this to learn that that sort of journey is not my way. That this is the one appropriate for me. A journey in words. A journey of reading and writing and slow revelations.

And I may have had to write this to see the need to get back to my book. That, too, is a part of the spiritual journey I should not forget. Following my bliss is doing what God wants me to do and it is how I can bring myself closest to the divine.

Thank You for this gift and this miracle and for making me who I am. Help me to appreciate those things and use them to the best of my ability.

April 2, 1995

I want to say it's Easter because we celebrated Easter today as Mom and my brother Ray are leaving tomorrow for a trip to Georgia. Only goes to show how the ritual holy day and the celebration of it are linked in our minds.

First we went to Mass. My brother Michael arranged for the 10 A.M. Mass at St. Matt's to be said for Grandmother Ivie. It continues to give me a good feeling when prayers are offered for our ancestors, especially Grandmother Ivie, who was so tormented in life by mental illness. The time during the Mass when we remember our ancestors, the living and the deceased, is one of my favorite times. I list everyone in my head, from the grandparents right up to little Gracie Love. It is one of the only reasons I feel guilty when I miss church. The church rules don't bother me nearly so much as missing the chance to remember and pray for those I love.

I like Father Adrian, the pastor at St. Matt's. Today he talked about compassion. It was the sermon of the accused adulteress brought before Jesus. It was His famous "Let he who is without sin cast the first stone" line. Father commented on how the woman did not ask forgiveness and how Jesus didn't grant it.

The line I remember from the sermon is this: "Refuse to answer." Father Adrian talked of how Jesus refused to be baited by those who would follow law without compassion. He even used the Thomas Moore definition of compassion: *com* (with), *passion* (suffering). "Suffering with." "Putting oneself in another's shoes."

He talked about the recent murder of a young girl in the neighborhood, a girl whose grandmother was a parishioner. He used this story to illustrate how we cannot "fix" things. How we cannot make things better. We can only be there. Like Jesus. Be present. In compassion. An easy lesson to see in relation to a death, a more difficult one in relation to life. We have to refuse to "fix" things, he said. We have to refuse to give advice. What he suggests doing instead is asking how the situation has made the other person feel. Being there. Listening. Being compassionate. Things I hope I have done for Mary Love, things I have tried to do. Things I wish had been done for Grandmother. I couldn't help wonder how Grandmother's life would have been different if only she had had compassionate people around her. I pray that she is peaceful now. I can only believe my grandmothers must be angels in the afterlife, with little need of my prayers, with a desire only to be remembered, honored, and perhaps to comfort and guide.

April 8, 1995

I am reading, reading, reading, psychology and spirituality. Today reading one of the Emmanuel books, Emmanuel being an angel who speaks through a woman named Pat Rodegast. The messages of all the books are self-love, self-knowledge, self-acceptance.

I am also thinking about how difficult it is to do the right thing for your children. To love them is not always to be in accord with them, even if it is to always show your love for them, to accept and love them unconditionally. So what do you do about behavior you can't accept?

I see mainly the good in my children, and I believe that is as it should be, that is, their goodness is what *is*. They cannot be bad. They can only be misguided. I want to guide.

It is amazing how the spirituality I am reading about permeates everything. In my most casual encounters with people I hear messages from the readings (or from my own heart) to be kind, to be ethical, to let fate take its course.

Almost as relevant as my readings on spirituality was my annual birthday reading from the astrologer, Pat. I never really believed in astrology, but people I knew kept going to this astrologer and kept coming back with the most wonderful words. It was her way with words that attracted me to her, just as I am attracted to authors who weave incredible spells through the way in which they put words together. Pat's main message for me this year is about letting go, and it, too, is there in my readings. How you cannot willfully make things happen. That it is in letting go and accepting what *is* that you find release and freedom.

And it's all stirring around in me—random thoughts, not yet concrete—about how to live my life more fully. I already find myself breathing easier, being less stressed as I drive to work, being less rushed. Pat said this year would be like walking through water and it is beginning to seem that way. Even as I work and pack and write and fill my days as much as I ever did and more, there is a feeling of slowing down. Of letting go.

But I am still unsure of how to integrate this into the everyday world of raising children. I want to act in kindness and love; I guess I am being told in my soul, in my intuitiveness, to act with kindness and love, even toward the disciplining of my children, maybe especially toward my children. But I do not yet know practically how to use that kindness and love to instruct and guide. Will I be taken seriously if I act in kindness and love instead of in anger? And I can answer myself too, now that I've asked the question. Absolutely I can. But how do I get the point across about behavior that is unacceptable?

Lord, show me the way to make Your will my way.

April 10, 1995

I think we've found our new home. Donny is excited about it, which means he will move on it. And there's a peacefulness about it that I like. There's a sunporch that will be mine all mine! For my office, for my meditation, for my reading room, for my soul!

Lord, if it is Your will and thus my will, let it work out.

April 17, 1995

I'm retyping my second mystery novel, *Who Killed the Mother?* into my Macintosh computer. I'm doing it for several reasons. One is to get it on a compatible, more up-to-date disk. One is that it is something I can do in between preparing for the move. One is to get it fresh in my mind again so I can finish it.

I just finished typing the scene where Mai, who is a fictionalized version of myself, has to deal, in a very public way, with her guilt over the way she raised her son. It's a catharsis of sorts, for her, and for me. To put it out there publicly, to *let it go.*

According to all my readings of late, our true selves are able to be revealed only when we surrender to truth and love. When we quit willing things to happen. When we accept what *is.* Our ISness.

A scary thought out of the Emmanuel books is that we are always ourselves—into the next world, into the next incarnation, into eternity. There are many starting overs but only one soul. Which is why we have to love ourselves.

Lent and Easter seasons were meaningful this year as they came at the same time that I have been reading so much about spirituality, the same time that I've been trying to let go, the same time that I've been trying to be more peaceful with myself, the same time I've been trying to let the rain fall and walk as if through water in my slowed-down physical life, while my soul life gallops along with its own power and speed, both slow and fast, both a rushing into the light and a retreat into the material world.

I had a truly divine experience on Holy Thursday. I went to Mass for the Washing of the Feet. My little nephews, Daniel and Tony, were among the boys who represented the twelve apostles and who had their feet symbolically washed by Father. That was why I went. To see them, to see the ritual reenacted. But I found, to my surprise, that the Blessed Sacrament was to be revealed and left out on the side altar. Parishioners were to stay with it, guarding it, being with it, in meditation and silence and prayer.

And I stayed. I wasn't planning to stay long. But tears started to stream from my eyes. I had to keep taking my glasses off to dab at my eyes. I felt lucky that the church wasn't full and that no one was looking at me. I couldn't understand why I was crying and I couldn't stop. It seemed as if every time I would think of leaving, the tears would start up again.

But I was not unhappy at all—I was overjoyed to have this wonderful opportunity to sit in this quiet holy place, to have the church empty out, to have the light dimmed and the music (classical) play from a tape player. I kept thinking it was what church was supposed to be like and never was. That a church should be a place for quiet meditation where the feeling of holiness could fill you. I can't remember how many times I've wished that there were more than thirty seconds given during the Mass for our personal intentions. Time to talk to God. Father would say, "Bow your head and pray for your intentions," and you'd just get started and he'd be talking again. And I was thinking about all of this, my eyes teary, my sight blurry, when the candles burning beside the Blessed Sacrament gave off a wonderful light. I'll never forget it. It was as if all the flames of all the individual candles came together. I even imagined, for a few moments, that the waves of light came together in such a way that they formed a face and that it was a sign to me. A sign that I was not alone, that someone was with me. I could not quite convince myself that it was just a trick of my eyes.

I stayed for hours.

Then there was Good Friday. It has always been, to me, the most compelling religious day of the year. Even as a child, I liked the mystery of it. The mystery of it drew me. And still draws me. Maybe even more so now because of this church of my husband's. Before marrying Donny, I had never seen anything like it. The way the crucifixion is dramatized. Jesus is taken off the cross and laid on a black shroud. When parishioners enter the church, they bring flowers and lay them beside the crucified Jesus. Later we all file up and kiss his feet. Then six men, like pallbearers, are called up. They raise Jesus over their heads and follow Father in a procession through the church. We follow to the sounds of a grief sung by Father, by the men, from the choir loft, but especially by the women that is so real it breaks your heart. The song is sung in Aramaic, the language of Jesus, but you do not have to know the words to know it is about the lament of Mary crying for her child, her *habeebee*. Because of my memory of this moving aspect of the service, I had invited Mary Love to attend.

I had turned the day into my first pilgrimage, something Pat had advised me to do, defining pilgrimage as a day I create for me, for my spirit, for my soul. I went to early Mass; went to one of my favorite places, the conservatory, to be among the flowers and the light; went to my favorite bookstore; brought the books with me to my favorite restaurant; went back to church. My daughter, my Angela, carried in baby's breath as a symbol of Mary's daughter, her Grace, and laid it on the crucifix. I carried flowers of my own. There was, once again, the Lebanese music, the chanting.

I wondered at my decision to invite Mary. This service always brought me to tears. It had the same effect on her but I could not do more than squeeze her hand, than whisper, "Are you okay?" She nodded. It was a sharing of grief. A primal, spiritual, ritual sharing of grief. I had never realized it so fully before. Then a burial. Jesus, in his bed of flowers, laid behind a stone.

Then Easter. The stone rolled back. The pain of death and grief followed by the joy of rebirth and celebration. Flowers handed out, the same flowers that had lain with Jesus. Eggs from the Maronite Youth Organization, watching my Mia give them to the other children of the church, to the old ladies. To old and young alike, a symbol of rebirth.

All of it happening together for a reason.

Easter Monday, back to church, a Mass said for Donny's grandma. His father, Ed, in and out of the hospital. The house we would like to buy still in limbo. My girlfriends at work into dreams and spirituality and the coming and going of Grace Zuri Love.

I sit, Easter Tuesday, and retype the passage of Mai's confession. Thirteen pages being typed as fast as my fingers can move, being moved by what I'd written.

Knowing this is the place of life and death and rebirth for me. Right here. In the words that somehow come out voluntarily here and nowhere else. In the forgiveness that happens here and nowhere else. In the fiction that is my way of examining my nonfiction. In my prayers. In my way of praying. In my way of synthesizing, with my heart and soul and not my mind, what has happened and is happening to me.

Here is where I let go. Here is where I am in my ISness. Here I am, the soul that will walk through eternity getting to know myself and accept myself and forgive myself.

Even the talk around the table at Easter with my husband's family . . . the gossip of babies born out of wedlock, and welfare moms and smokers . . . talk that goes into the heart of me and causes me to walk away with my humiliation fresh again.

But to come here and examine it. To have Lent and Easter. And to begin to let go.

April 24, 1995

I have entered a quieter time in my soul. It may be the passing of the holy season, it may be the passing of daily updates on otherworldly signs of Grace, it may be that I needed a quieter time. I am coming to believe that we are where we need to be.

And yet I keep reading. I picked up a novel again today, thinking it was time to get back to fiction, but it could not hold me. I went back to Thomas Moore, to *Soul Mates*, to read more about living the soulful life.

What amazes me is that I feel as if I have had the right idea all along. Part of the love affair I have with Thomas Moore is his ability to tell me that. To make me feel that I am on the right track. That before I knew anything about soulfulness, I was a soulful person. The giving of validity to those feelings can only help them to grow. For that I am thankful.

I am also continually astonished by the connectedness of everything I have been reading. It is as if all the things I've needed to hear are suddenly available to me. How can I help but be thankful?

April 25, 1995

Besides reading Thomas Moore, I have been reading the Emmanuel books. When I first heard of them I thought they were sex books! Not so. But they are books written by an angel, so in their own way just as embarrassing—or almost as embarrassing (at least around certain people)— to be reading. Yet Emmanuel's message is incredibly soothing and forgiving. *ISness* is an Emmanuel term, as is *oneness*. All things are one in love is what this basically means.

His teachings are the same as those of Jesus: Love thy neighbor as you love yourself. Yet he goes into the more complicated aspect of loving self more than I have known of Jesus to have done, perhaps because it is more what we need now. He talks about how we can have made no mistakes because everything has a reason, a divine reason. How releasing that is! He talks of fear and guilt as the ultimate in destructive forces and urges us to let go of them. He preaches love and kindness, which is very literally the same as Moore's discourse on soulfulness and manners. Both speak to the integrity of the individual. Both talk about a kind of surrender and letting go of willfulness, bringing me full circle to my theme for the year of *letting go.* And interestingly, Emmanuel talks about our forgetfulness and urges us to let memory come back to us. Memory of other lives, memory of our divinity.

These readings have imbued in me the consciousness to slow down and *breathe*, to quit rushing. To take my time and smell the first hint of rain on the spring air. To be kinder to people. To look at others, even—and maybe especially—those I see on the street, and think, *There goes an angel*. The readings are reminders. Perhaps this is what Emmanuel means when he urges us to *remember*. A remembering that he and Moore both speak of when urging us to be present in the moment.

Finally, Emmanuel says visualize what you want and you can make it happen. Last night I began visualizing a publisher just finishing my book and calling my agent, Dan O., who will then call me. It did not happen today. It may happen tomorrow. Pat thought by the 27th, which is Thursday. Wouldn't that be something! But what did happen today was a call about the home Donny and I want. We missed the call, yet it has occurred to me that although I did not get the phone call I consciously asked for, perhaps I got the one I needed. We shall see.

April 28, 1995

The fated April 27 has come and gone. In the afternoon, I received a letter from Dan O. Its very appearance signaled to me that it was not going to be good news. Good news would have come by phone. Nothing in me expected the news I got, however: that Dan has taken a job with Hazelden Publishing and is leaving the agenting profession. It was a cruel irony coming on that fated day. *What does it mean?* I ask myself. *Why did it happen?*

Why do we even ask such things? Is it the mind trying

to explain the unexplainable? the unknowable that only God knows? Or do we all "know" our life plan, as Emmanuel suggests, but have just forgotten it?

I suppose "why" is a way we lead ourselves into feeling better or worse instead of just accepting or feeling the "now," the "present tense" of what has happened. If we can give some historical reason, we explain it for our mind even if our heart doesn't understand it any better. I can conjecture that it was meant to be because I was meant to find a better agent or because I was meant to concentrate on the house right now, but I would only be guessing.

For now I have chosen to believe that this ending is not definitive, that when Dan follows up on the manuscripts he has sent to publishers before ending his contractual arrangement with his authors, mine will be accepted. Until I am sure that that will not be so, I can put the matter of how I feel about it—the "whys"—aside. I can be in the flow a little while longer, letting my faith in Dan and in my writing be my guide.

April 29, 1995

The girls are in Chicago and Donny and I are alone, as we will be often the rest of our lives. We had a very nice, very sexy evening, and in the middle of it I found myself feeling very happy and realizing that Donny and I both had chosen to be happy—that there had been many instances, when we could have chosen to be miserable, irritable, finding our passion through dissent rather than happiness. And I know that we consciously chose happiness, just as I can see that some people have chosen unhappiness. For many, of course, there are temporary phases of unhappiness with divorce or other problems, but I can definitely see that some have chosen unhappiness as a way of life. Thank You, Lord, for helping Donny and me choose happiness. Please help my family and friends choose happiness too.

It also occurred to me last night that if I must find a reason for Dan O.'s flight from agenting that is personal to me, it may be that I needed to be centered in home and family in order to realize and appreciate the happiness I have—including the purchase of our new home, which today became a reality. I may have needed to understand that my home, family, and especially my marriage is as important as my writing. And I can see that I may not have fully realized this had I received word that I would be published, and had my thoughts centered mainly on myself and my creative life. So, thank You, Lord, for my blessings, in whatever form they come.

THE IN BETWEEN

Have I mentioned that the girls are in Chicago? I was apprehensive before they left. It seemed to me that it was going to be some kind of a test. How was I going to handle it when my girls were gone (for good)? What was it going to be like living in a household of two? What would it mean for my marriage? How would it feel?

I now admit the anxiety was stronger before the girls left than it is now. I have always been one for anticipation, for both the best and worst of what life has to offer. Some of the things I discovered were good sex, pretty good talk, and good eating with Donny. It was nice not to worry about having to fix meals for anyone but ourselves. It was nice not to have the phone ringing or tied up. It was nice to have rooms stay the way I left them, to have only myself to blame if I couldn't find my comb. In short, the girls physical presence was not missed and I learned valuable things about what life will be like when they're gone, that is, that I'll probably like it. This seems significant because it has scared me—as if there will be this horrible void when they are gone.

What I do miss is their love and their personalities, their spirit, their souls. I had a wonderful conversation with Angela before she left. She was talking about her memories in this house. One was how her window always rattles. Another was coming in from outside on a winter day with the smell of snow still lingering. Sound and smell. It made me realize how soulful she is. And when I have such thoughts, I feel as if I'm being a little disloyal to Mia, who I know is soulful too, but who has a harder time expressing herself.

I have never doubted my son's soulfulness, although it has been a constant flirt with the shadow side of things. I know Ian is a tremendously "feeling" individual and much like me. While he literally ran away from things he did not know how to deal with as he was growing up, I ran away also, but to an internal world. You would think, understanding this, that I would be able to help him more, and yet I have always felt helpless to assist him. His running away seemed merely to bring my powerlessness with him to the surface. There was no longer even an illusion then that I could parent him. And it seemed almost that this was why he ran. To show that Donny and I had no control—that I had given up my right long ago and that Donny, as a stepparent, had never had any. In the absence of a consistent father figure, Ian had filled in as man of the house for too long to ever accept parenting again.

Mia, too, I think, is more like me than Angela is. Angela, as young as she is, is the most accepting of who she is and the most ready to let things come to her. She is less wounded by life, I think.

Mia hides her soulfulness with an outward display of fun-lovingness. Ian hides his with his dark side—the side where all his passion now (still) lurks. I hope, I pray, Ian will find a passion for the bright side as well. And Mia, I hope, I pray, will find a way to channel her energies into soulfulness. She, I think, is least familiar with herself and so, in a way, has the most growing to do. At the same time, however, I think she is the one of my children best equipped for daily life. She works hard, plays hard, and doesn't spend too much time trying to figure things out like the rest of us do.

It is now 2:20 P.M., Donny has gone to work, and I am alone. I had looked forward to being alone this weekend. To me, there is something almost divine about alone time, and with the girls actually out of town, the alone time took on even more of an appeal. Friday, Donny was supposed to work until 6:30 P.M. He didn't. I left work at 2:00, saw the girls off on their bus, came home, and he was here. So I painted the garage.

All weekend we worked very companionably together, the roofers were here putting on the roof, people were in and out constantly.

This morning Donny's boss called and said he didn't have anything for him except some couple-hour-long job. So he stayed home and pulled down the ceilings upstairs until twenty minutes ago.

I am, at last, alone for a few hours but I'm in the middle of painting the hallways. And yet, it's no big deal. There was a time, not long ago at all, that planning a four-day, alone-time weekend and ending up with less than four hours alone and having to work during part of them would have driven me wild, made me really frustrated and angry.

So, I think, I'm growing up, not having tantrums when things don't go the way I had planned. Besides, I've had enough small doses of alone time that I'm not in desperate need of it; I've got a house to sell and the reality is I have to work; and anyway, I enjoyed being with my husband.

One of the things I like about being alone, even if I'm working, is setting my own pace. I work a little, have a cigarette break, work, have a reading or writing break, etc. I'm getting more comfortable with setting my own rhythm, even when Donny's around, but I'm always aware of how much time I'm taking and what he's doing, and wondering if he'll think I'm loafing or whatever. I also get to listen to my classical music when I'm alone, which is also a treat, and smoke wherever I want, which is also a treat. This is my first break.

I've been reading recently that it may be possible for people to talk with their angels and I think on my next break I'll attempt that. There's been a feeling in me, ever since Holy Thursday, that something "more" is awaiting me, somehow. All these wonderful, miraculous things have been happening with my friends at work. Mary has actually received messages of a sort through her computer. Julie heard a divine Voice and has been having these epic, detailed dreams that often connect her to Mary. It may only be wishful thinking, but it makes me feel as if something miraculous awaits me too.

Dearest Angel,

I think I have felt you with me since my earliest childhood, certainly in my most tormented times when you would tell me I was special and a part of me believed you. Thank you. That voice that said I was special kept me living as much as I could live. Feeling as much as I could feel. There has always been a wonder in me, something that embraced mystery. It is this part of me that is willing to believe I can talk to you. It is this part of me that says it makes sense. Will you talk to me?

Smell the sweetness. You are sweet. Don't try to force it, to will it, just let it come. It is there in the in between, between thought and feeling. Breathe. Feel your heart.

Why does it feel so heavy? As if it will break?

It's trying to open. To let joy in.

Is that my next lesson?

Yes.

Thank you. What shall I call you?

Peace.

Thank you. You are there in the in between?

Yes. Like white. Like space.

Space between the letters and words?

Like space. Like smoke.

Is it okay that I smoke?

Everything you do is okay.

Really?

If you give thanks for it.

Count my blessings?

No. You are blessed. What you do is blessed. No counting. Look in between.

In between the numbers there are no numbers?

35

Something like that. You're getting it.

Will you help me with my writing?

I am always helping you.

I want to know if my writing will be recognized. I'm sorry it seems so important to me but it is.

Look in between. This time is in between. Time is in between. Don't worry about time.

Will you help me do that?

Of course I will.

Do you mean that in time I will be recognized, but that there is not time? That's hard to understand.

Everything is. Don't worry about time. This is a very important message. Relax. Smell the sweetness.

I never realized how often time comes up. I was just going to ask, Do you mean smell the sweetness of this time?

Forget time. When it is important that you not be disturbed, you won't be.

Thank you. I like your name.

You gave it to me. It has always been my name. Dearest. Remember to rest.

I left my computer screen just the way it was and went off

to paint some more. It seemed almost goofy to leave an angelic communication to go paint but I could not let the brushes and rollers sit too long, and I felt a need to have accomplished a certain amount by the time Donny got home. I also didn't know what else to do. If I hadn't had the painting to do, what would I have done? What did one do after one talked to an angel? I hadn't thought that far ahead. I hadn't thought what it would mean. I hadn't thought to ask certain questions. It had been an impulsive act. Now I wasn't certain how I felt about it. But it seemed as if, as I painted, I kept getting messages. I didn't feel alone the way I always had. Someone else was in my mind, in my thoughts. I spent about an hour painting and then went back to the computer:

I was just going to come back and say thank you, Peace, for talking to me, but since I left here, you have been with me and I have received a couple of very clear messages:
1. Listen to my sister. Really listen. Not just to what she has to say about me but to everything she has to say.
2. That my painting is just as important as anything else I'm doing today, which also means, I would think, that whatever I am doing at the moment is what is important, but also,
3. That it's important to leave this house better than we found it. To leave it with love, in good shape, well taken care of. Because it's going to be important to the people who buy it. I almost have a feeling that the people who

PEACE

buy it might end up being our friends. But perhaps it is the feeling that all people are friends whom I should do my best for.

Peace, has that heaviness in my heart always been joy waiting to come in?

Yes.

I'm already really hearing what you said. I'm sitting here reviewing what has happened, worried about the time and that Donny will come home and find me taking a break when I'm not as far along as I should be. Why have I set him up to be such a censor? All I'm doing is cheating myself out of these minutes (time again) when I could be enjoying my aloneness. Thank you for making me aware of this. I'm thinking that you have something else to say that has drawn me back here. Here I am, wanting to wrap up and summarize, and you are still there to talk to me. This is also a lesson, I believe. To quit wrapping up and summarizing prematurely. Was that your message or is there something else you would like to tell me?

It's in between. [The cursor is flashing erratically]

In between what?

Don't will it. Let it come. You're doing great.

In the spaces in between breathing in and out? Is that where you are?

I am inside. In the blood flowing through your veins.

I keep willing it and I keep thinking about time. And this makes me wonder if I need meditation exercises or if this is an okay means of communication as it is.

Both. Relax.

I am feeling that there is some symbolism for me in the letter *X*.

Good. It is in between yet connected. Study it.

It is two lines going off in different and opposite directions. It is two *V*s one right-side up and one upside down. It is a cross. It is like the shape of an hourglass.

Good. What else?

It is in the word relax. *Lax* is associated with laziness, something I fear being.

Leave fear behind.

Help me. I'll try.

Trying is all that matters. Go back to painting now. There is something about white *also.*

I realized several things while I painted. The first came to me almost immediately: *White* is in between, neither here nor there, not a color but not not. It is the color of Peace, I think. Next, I realized what I was doing with the white paint: I was covering over the bad spots, erasing them, so to speak. Along with that thought came the "white" of baptism, holy communion, in short, sacrament, purity. Then I thought of painting over in white as being a fresh start, a blank page, a new beginning. I made my series of Xs on the wall, something my sister, Susan, had taught me to do, and her words about how to paint came back to me: "Make an X and then fill it in and you don't miss anything." Sounds kind of profound now.

X is the number ten in Roman numerals. The number ten in numerology is a transition number between the roots and the compounds—an in between number.

And as I filled my Xs in, I realized that the Vs it makes are not only right-side up and upside down but crosswise. Four Vs each reaching out into infinity.

Now I do feel it is time to sum up. From my first conversation with my angel I learned its name: Peace. I learned of a symbolic color that represents him: white. I learned what my symbol of our connection will be: the X—and I have seen a lot of symbolism which I can spend some time thinking about. Wow!

Thank you, Peace.

You're welcome.

Now—am I sure I'm talking to an angel? Yes. Maybe one that is part of me, in the sense of all things being one. I guess I could say I'm talking to myself, and it is a little like that. But I did get tears in my eyes and feel them fall down my cheeks when I was told my lesson now is to learn joy. I didn't feel finished until I was finished. I did feel what I wrote about—the heaviness of my heart. Is it gone? No. Is it there all the time? No. It wasn't before either. But it is occasionally. When your heart is heavy, you know it. I know I wasn't thinking of *peace* or *white* or *X* before I sat down. I had been reading about angels and was hoping some name from the readings, like Uriel, wouldn't pop up. They didn't. Peace did. It may seem more of an expression of a feeling than a name but that's fine with me and fine with Peace, apparently. The *X* was something Susan had said in relation to painting, no reason for my conscious mind to bring it up in relation to an angel. So all in all—yes—I think I was talking to my angel. Amen.

I looked up *X* in my *Webster's* dictionary:

the twenty-fourth letter of the English alphabet
to indicate one's choice or answer by marking with an *X*
an unknown quantity
a mark shaped like an *X* used to represent a signature of a person who cannot write
to mark a particular point on a map
a symbol for a kiss in letters
the Roman numeral 10
a person or thing unknown or unrevealed

an abbreviation for extra
an abbreviation for Christ
the power of magnification (in optical
instruments)
x-ed: to cancel or obliterate, usually with a series
of *X*s

Dearest Peace,   May 2, 1995

Since I talked to you, I have been censoring myself. I think of a question I want to ask you, but then I think that I already know the answer to it (as in, Was that you with me in church on Holy Thursday?) or that the question is superfluous and I don't need the answer. Yet I don't want my conscious mind to mislead me. And time is still almost impossible for me to release. And finally, I think I should be satisfied with what I got yesterday, that to expect you to speak to me twice in two days would be expecting too much. Yet I know I am censoring and shouldn't be. The heaviness is back in my heart. Are you with me?

I'm always with you.

I don't want to ask questions then. I just want you to talk with me. What do I need to hear?

The music. What is there right now. Smell the sweetness. Close your eyes.

I am being too willful.

Quit censoring yourself. Love yourself.

Is there something else the painting has to teach me? Do we need to talk about the research I've done? The *X* seems particularly meaningful.

It is. It is multiplication, duplication, more than one.

Meaning I am more than one?

Meaning I am with you and more, much more. An infinity. Center. Go to the heart of yourself. X marks the spot.

My heart.

Your spirit, your divineness. Your in between.

In between being where you are. Between the physical and the divine.

I am the physical and the divine. It is all there. Within. Go within.

I am too into my mind right now. This feels stilted. I'm not sure you're talking to me.

Go paint.

Later—

I painted and now I'm taking a break. Here's what happened while I painted.

After just a few minutes, I realized that I wanted to listen to the Moody Blues. At once I knew that the Moody Blues were perfect: celestial music, vocals, and words. Every song spoke of a spiritual quest, I'm sure of it. Soon

I was singing along while I painted the hallway going up the stairs (relevant? ascending?). Then "Tuesday Afternoon" came on and it made me smile because it actually was *Tuesday afternoon*. While I was singing along with the song, another voice, another breath, came into me. My voice echoed and filled the stairwell. At first it scared me, and I coughed, almost as if there was too much breath in me. Then I sang out again and when I realized it was still there—this other voice—I opened my mouth wider to let it all come out.

Later—

I'm back, Peace.

Another Moody Blues song, "I'm Just a Singer (In a Rock and Roll Band)," came on after I had heard song after song that spoke to me with such clarity about the desire for a spiritual life. And I found myself thinking, *No. They're not just singers in a rock and roll band.* I thought, *They're messengers of the angels.*

Right.

And I wondered if there was a double message for me. A message in a message.

In between.

Yes. Is the message about me and my writing or is it just my hopes that want to make it so? Every time I ask a question about my writing, I'm afraid of the answer and I think I block it.

44

I am with you, writing or painting.

You're going to have to be clearer with me about the writing. Please.

I am also with you when you are blocking. Relax and the answer will come to you. This computer isn't the only way we communicate. Don't strive so to make the answers come in this format. Listen and you will hear.

But I did hear. I heard that song title "I'm Just a Singer (In a Rock and Roll Band)," and heard how limiting it was. And I thought, *I am just a writer* and thought it was the same.

You're right.

So I am also a messenger?

Of course you are.

And so my message will be delivered?

Of course it will.

When? Can I ask how soon?

Forget time.

I'll try. But this has greater import for my coming books doesn't it?

You are growing aren't you? Your growth will be reflected. You don't have to get it all at once. Relax. You don't have to go it alone.

45

Will you help me see the way in book number two?

I am helping you. It's there inside you waiting to come out.

Let go. Let God?

Relax.

I'm not sure I know how.

I'm not sure, either. Learn how.

May 4, 1995

Today is Thursday, the last and fourth day of what was going to be a three-day "work on the house" vacation. Everything takes longer than I think it will and I am finishing up work in the kitchen. First, however, I needed to get my car tabs, and then I wanted to go to church as I usually go when I'm off work.

While I was driving, the morning wisdom came to me. What I clearly realized is how afraid I have been about the book I've been working on. I can barely get the words out to ask for blessings on it, can barely pray for its success. The words always seem to get stuck. And then there was my older notion that I could only pray for a limited number of things, and I must always pray for the health and happiness of my family first. So out of that, I came up with calling the book my offspring so I could include it in my prayers for all my offspring. Now I have realized that I don't have to limit my prayers, and still it was hard for me to ask for my book. This morning I discovered why.

Fear.

In the Emmanuel books especially, fear is talked about as the greatest enemy. As I read this, I found myself thinking that I don't fear that much. I don't live in fear. I am not afraid to walk out on the street at night, not afraid of death, and so on. Then as Emmanuel talked more about fear, I realized he was also talking about things like fear of humiliation, fear of failure. Still, I didn't think it was a big problem for me.

And yet, I have known for some time that I am fearful concerning the book. All I had to do was think about calling an agent and I was seized with fear. All I had to do was attempt to write a book proposal or letter concerning the book to know—to be overcome by—fear. In a way, I thought this was good. The fear felt a little like excitement, and I thought there should be those things we care so much about that we get fearful and excited about them. Excited, maybe. Fearful, no.

So when this occurred to me, I tried to examine where the fear came from. There is some fear of failure, fear of humiliation, but the main cause of the fear, I think, came from feelings of unworthiness. *Who am I to think I can be a published author?*

This wasn't real conscious stuff. Consciously, I could tell myself I worked hard, but even now, as I try to finish the sentence, it catches a little: I worked hard and I deserve to be rewarded for my labors. I deserve recognition. And just at this instant it is occurring to me that recognition may be the other scary stuff. *Recognized* implies being known. Fame does not scare me, but being known is a little scary. Letting anyone read my book is scary because it is so much me—it is like inviting them to know me. And is how can I invite the world at large to know me if I am not worthy? I know some people would read the book and think it is autobiographical and think what a poor mother I am/was—but that isn't the worst of it. The worst of it is what I think. I need to get to the place where I do not have to defend myself or my work because I am at peace with myself/my work. PEACE.

So beginning today, thanks to my angel, I am letting go of my fear. I am saying out loud: "I have worked hard and I deserve to be published. I am letting go of my fear regarding my writing. I am worthy to become a published author."

The other thing that was incredibly apparent this morning is my need to become peaceful with doing what I am doing when I am doing it without worrying about time. I am also worthy of my breaks.

Dearest Peace,

I have come to many realizations since our talk. And I have many things to work on. Thank you for pointing those things out to me. And thank you for steering me to the Moody Blues. I've listened to them all day and could go on listening to them.

I also told my "spirit sisters," Mary and Julie, about you.

I am so honored that they want to come over tomorrow and share with me what has happened. Yet it worries me a little bit. I don't—

Want to seem special. You are.

Thank you. I also don't want to minimize the experience or make it grander than it was. And there is some fear (sorry about that) about it. I'm not sure what it is.

There is nothing wrong with you. You are getting my messages. What more is it you want?

Can I see you?

I am there in the in between. Like a reflection, a shadow, a flower, a flame.

Like the wick of a candle or stem of a match with a golden glow on both sides?

Yes. And like the smoke that rises from it and like the sky.

ON THE THRESHOLD

Dear Peace,   May 5, 1995
      Julie and Mary just left. Thank you so much,
Lord, for giving me friends to share this experience of Peace with. Peace, I am sure you were there with
us as we talked about you. As Julie said at one point, the
whole group of you—all of our angels—were probably
getting a laugh out of us. I like that image.

So do I. It was quite accurate.

I've been listening to more Moody Blues. The CD title is *On
the Threshold of a Dream.* Is this a message?

Threshold *is an accurate description of this place.*

Yours or mine?

Both.

Am I on the right track, giving up my fear about writing?

You are always on the right track.

I have a feeling releasing that fear is the first step in my journey as a writer.

As a messenger.

This is a beginning for me then, isn't it? I've found you and the path is getting clearer.

That's what I'm here for. To clear the path. To clear your fear. To clear your mind. To open your heart to joy.

I have a hard time remembering joy. I know I'll need help experiencing it.

You'll have help. But you must let go and open your heart in order to experience it. You're still blocking. Your skepticism is okay. Fear must go.

Am I fearful of opening my heart as well as fearful of time and of sending my writing into the world?

You know you are. All those lessons you learned when you were talking to your diary as a young girl closed your heart. It has been closed a long time. Your family has been trying to open it. Listen to them. Let them in. They will not hurt you.

Another fear—fear of being hurt.

51

It is the same fear as all the others. Fear is pervasive in you. It has you locked up tight. It makes you unrecognizable to other angels who could help you. Your light is blocked. It all has to do with opening your heart. I promise you will not be hurt if you do this—when you do this.

It's a process isn't it? Not something I can do in one day?

If you choose to make it a process, it will be a process. If you choose to do it in one day, it will be done.

Fear is making me want to make a process of it, isn't it?

Let go of fear. Breathe. Smell the sweetness. Open to it.

My friends were so sweet today. Yet I do feel slightly removed from them, from everyone—the closed heart?

The closed heart.

What is a beneficial way for me to see you?

Only you know that. I will be as you choose me to be and who I am. You cannot change me or my love for you. I will always be with you. There are others for whom this is true also. Nothing you can do can make them not love you. You see, it is safe to open your heart.

Just what I want to be I'll be in the end?

Exactly. If you want an open heart, you will have an open heart.

I want an open heart.

No qualifications?

No. I am ready to be recognized.

Then I am very happy.

I can feel that.

Trust what you feel. Nothing you think or write is wrong, or not from me. You are from me, I am from you, we are one.

Thank you. I needed that permission to accept what comes out here as the truth.

There won't be any lies here. I assure you of that.

Thank you. Thank you. Thank you. I am truly grateful. I love you.

Then you love yourself.

Love has made me uncomfortable, even in the songs. I need to accept love too, don't I?

That is the most important thing. The most important. Self-love. Self-love will get rid of the censor for you, the time demon, the fear.

Is there a shedding I need to do?

Only of your fear and your closed heart.

The Moody Blues' lyrics still go through my mind, lyrics about stepping to the other side of life. Is that what I've been doing with these conversations? Stepping to the other side?

To the in between. To the threshold. To the precipice. Once there you must make a leap of faith.

Isn't that what this is? A leap of faith? Believing that I am talking with an angel named Peace?

That has taken you to the threshold. Now you must leap.

How? Figuratively? Literally?

In your heart.

Leap in my heart. I don't know how to do that.

Yes you do. Let your heart rise up. Let it be your voice. Let it leap from you.

By opening my heart?

By opening your heart.

I said I want to open my heart. What else must I do to make it so?

Open it. Imagine a door that keeps feelings in and keeps love out. Here is the key. I am handing it to you. You see, the light was just seeping out the cracks before. Now it is brilliant. You didn't need to be afraid to open it.

Now what?

Now prop it open. Here is a brick, as heavy as your heart used to be. That's right. You can keep the brick for a while until you learn to keep it open on your own. See, no process when you let go of fear. You replace process with action. It's done. There's no going back. I'll be the keeper of the brick. You aren't to worry about it. When you're ready, I'll remove it. Meanwhile your heart is open. Everything happens for a reason. Remember that, dearest. And remember to rest.

One more quick thing. I know you are there in my dreams. And more. How can I remember my dreams?

With your open heart. They will flow in and out of your heart. Pay attention to your heart when you awaken. Listen to your heart. Listening is very important right now. You don't have to listen for that door to your heart slamming shut. Remember, I am the keeper of the brick. It is open for good. The dreams will cross this threshold of your open door where you will have access to them.

Thank you so, so much. I will carry my open heart with me as I work today and as I interact with others today and get used to how it feels. Thank you, Peace.

You're welcome.

Dearest Peace   May 7, 1995

Please remember how literal I am (which I didn't even realize before now) and give me clues or aides to help me be less literal—or I guess you probably already are, because I got it. I got, from your mention of my diary-keeping days, a true message about the time when I closed my heart.

I had such good parents, Peace, such a good family. I've never understood why I turned out so bad or why I felt so hopeless so young. Truly, by the time I was fourteen, I was so certain I was unlovable. Oh sure, my mom yelled at me a lot, but I deserved to be yelled at. She had a hell of a

55

time with me, Peace, a hell of a time. I'm sure she didn't understand any more than I did what was wrong with me or why I couldn't make it right. It seems, looking back, that all I wanted was for someone to love me. How could I have thought my family didn't? Why did I turn to boys? And when I did, why couldn't I have found one good one instead of a string of jerks, each one making me feel progressively worse about myself?

Were you bad, Margaret, when you were fourteen years old? Can you honestly tell me you were bad then or that you are bad now?

No. That's not what I meant exactly. When I said I turned out bad, I just meant I was not good. Not a good student, not a good daughter.

Margaret, were you bad when you were fourteen?

No, Peace. I was sad. But I was not bad. I was not what people expected me to be. I was not what I expected me to be. I was a disappointment. But I was not bad.

Thank you, dear Margaret, for finally seeing this. It was only your feeling that you were bad, dear one, that brought to you people who did not treat you as if you were good. You were a neon sign announcing: "Here I am, someone who does not deserve to be treated well." It was as if you advertised and they came. You think that your thoughts and feelings about yourself are private, that they don't send out neon lights. You are wrong. Watch, dear one, as your thoughts about yourself change, how those around you change, how they treat you differently.

I thought my inner thoughts had changed a lot since I

56

was thirteen, since my diary-keeping days. I hope they have. But at least I "got it" Peace, got what you were referring to. And I got the *threshold* too, which is a very clear description to me—both symbolic, as in the open door to my heart, and literal, as in the meaning: a beginning, the outset, a point at which physiological and psychological effects begin to be produced. Wow!

Which leads me to this morning, Monday morning, when I should be at work. I called in with a lie about getting estimates, which I guess is okay but it would have been better had I told the truth. But the truth is that Donny has gone out of town to work at someone's cabin, the girls are in school, and I felt as if I couldn't waste this alone time, this time when I knew I would not be disturbed.

All of which is well and good except that I began immediately wasting the morning by feeling guilty about it and by continuing to fear that I will be disturbed. So now I am trying very hard to be in the Now. I just finished *Emmanuel II* last night and the whole final section was about being in the Now and how it is the most important thing. I am trying to believe that what I am doing now is what I am supposed to be doing. But I also just read, both in *Emmanuel* and in James Hillman's *Insearch: Psychology and Religion,* that trying isn't what it's all about. Hillman says trying blocks getting to know another. Emmanuel says there is nothing but *beingness.* So what I am going to try—help!—what I am going to do is place myself in a state of beingness in the Now, and then I hope you will join me there. Good morning, Peace. What do I want to know today?

Good morning, dearest Margaret. You want to know what you do not already know. But you already know what you need to know. Perhaps you want me to help you remember.

Yes. Please help me remember.

What you are doing, what you are learning, is all you need. To stay in the Now, to let go of fear.

I am really beginning to believe you now that I see how pervasive not living in the Now is, and how pervasive fear is. I almost agree with you, too, that I have already learned and read and felt all I need to know. It is why I hesitate with questions for you. But yet I feel you have much to teach me, and even if you did not, I would want to keep talking to you. Show me the way to put the things I knew/know into effect.

Words mean so much to you. Wordmark. Stonehenge. Symbols. Everything, all are symbols open for interpretation. Look at how one page of writing means one thing to one person and something else to another. Trust that you understand the interpretations that are right for you. Nothing you do is wrong. Go ahead and investigate/research. But trust yourself first. These things only help you see what you already know, as I help you see what you already know. And if a time comes when you see clearly, I will still be here. You may even be able to see me. So don't despair your lack of questions. You can ask me anything.

Do you want to tell me anything about my family, friends, or workmates that will help me or them?

They are symbolic. They will be what they are and what you want them to be. Nothing exists that you do not perceive. Your perception is good. When you live more fully in the Now, it will be better. You can help them with your open heart. They will perceive you—they will see you—in a new way. Every breath you take you begin anew. No one can know your mystery. Your soul is safe. Yet those around you need to know you on a different level than they have. To know you with your open heart. Believe me, they will see that your heart is open and will be gentler with you. They will not hurt you. They will give you gifts for your heart. Hear them.

I know my husband doesn't want to be my censor. How can I remove him from that role?

By loving him. Love is all that matters.

I feel a particular soulfulness in my daughter, Angela. How can I help her?

By loving her. Love is all that matters. Love her. Love yourself.

Will our move be good for us?

Of course it will. Honor the old home. The new home will honor you.

I see myself with a spiritual sacred space on the sunporch in my new home.

This is your sacred space. Everywhere you are is your sacred space. The more you come to live in the Now, the more your sacred space will grow so that you feel it around you wherever you are. When you need not be disturbed, you won't be.

PEACE

Is there a way I have to quit letting intrusions disturb me?

When you need not be disturbed, you won't be. I promise you. When you live more fully in the Now, what will be will be. You will trust that everything happens for a reason and you will not be disturbed. Your peace will be more profound than that. Interruptions will not disturb your peace. Your peace will be with you everywhere at all times.

Are you my peace?

Of course I am. So are you.

My writing. What do I need to do to release it into the world?

Release your fear. You know this. You are trying. But you need to just let it be. Your role right now is not to be active with it. You are doing what you need to do for you and your writing is you. You can say my writing. It is more personal even than that and less singular. When you release it, it is everyone's writings. It is you. Which is why you say my writing. But there is no word to say what it truly is. It is you. It is. You are.

Is there anything else I need to know or need to do right now? Do you have a message for me?

Be in the Now. Smell the sweetness. Remember you are sweet. Rest. Get rid of the censors in you. They are only in you. They are your fear. They don't belong to anyone else and no one else wants them. Be complete in yourself. Don't look for others to judge or censor or praise or blame. They will, but don't look for it. You don't need it in the Now from them or from yourself. You only need to be in the Now without fear. Release others from your expectations and receive them with your open heart. It will feel good.

60

If I can do these things, will I quit wearing a sour expression and quit clenching my teeth in the night and quit being tied up with muscle problems from this fibromyalgia I supposedly have?

Of course. It is already happening. Your sleep will be fuller than ever before when you sleep in the Now. Before you go to sleep, remind yourself that you are living and sleeping in the Now. Empty your mind and just be. When you have done this for a while and feel more rested, you can stop taking the medication. Right now you need to rest. It is because you have been so far from the Now that you haven't been able to rest. How can you rest when you are ten years into the future and twenty years into the past? That is a lot of ground to cover. Remind yourself to sleep in the Now, dearest. And rest.

Thank you. Peace.

You're welcome.

Later—

James Hillman says, regarding religion and theology: "The one studies God and His intentions, the other studies man and his motivations, while the place in between is too often left unoccupied."[1] He describes this *in between* as the place where God and man are supposed to meet. Does this somewhat describe where you are, Peace? Where God and man are supposed to meet?

We have met, have we not? This is the first step toward oneness. You are doing what many would call soul work. But it is not work and it is

61

not soul alone. We have met at the threshold—the experience is not only of the body but of the soul and mind and heart. Of all that is.

Hillman also talks about Jesus "curing souls" in the course of living his destiny—living his life the way it was meant to be lived. How does one know if one is living one's destiny? What is my destiny?

By following one's passion, one's calling, destiny is fulfilled. By living, destiny is fulfilled.

Are you saying everyone fulfills their destiny? Not everyone follows their bliss.

Everyone follows the path they have chosen. This is hard to explain.

Are there choices?

Of course. Good, leading question. You have chosen to follow your bliss—to do your writing—but you don't do this full time. You are living the results of choices you have made. And every day is new and new choices are made. It is never too late to follow your bliss, to answer your calling. And people do it in many different ways. Some by providing opportunity to their children that they were denied or that they denied themselves. Who is to say that this is not the true calling of their lives? No regrets. No one can go backwards and do any good by wishing they had made different choices. Their choices made their destiny even while their destiny was preordained. There is a grand plan—a place, a state, a goal—toward which each individual is heading. How they get there is their choice. But they will get there.

Then is there really any choice?

Oh, yes. The experiences of the journey are as important as the end of the journey.

At work, Mary, Julie, and I have been set on a seemingly similar inward journey of which Grace's death acted as a kind of catalyst. Can you shed any light on the meaning of the three of us being on this journey together?

How is this journey any different than any other? How is it the same? Traveling companions come in many different forms for many different reasons. Yes. Grace was a catalyst. But she was not the beginning. She was a merging point, a joining that allowed you to open up to each other and from there to the wider universe. Each death and each birth is an opening. Like a door that stays open for only a short amount of time, spilling in light, extra light, the light of oneness, a gathering of angels, a crowd that by their sheer number alone can act as a beacon, calling those around the event to join them. Both times are what you would call miracles.

At times of miracles, from the most ordinary (to you), to the most extraordinary (to you), there is more light coming into the world and so more opportunity for it to affect you. These events are true gatherings of angels. This is why every disaster, such as the recent bombing in Oklahoma, has such effect. The opportunity to—the certainty is—that one cannot be near such a gathering of angels and not be affected by it. And the effects are not momentary. Once an individual has been touched by the divine, by the light of oneness, it doesn't fade, doesn't go away, doesn't cease to be. People are changed.

You three, who together were affected by birth and death, are not the same. You are not the same as you were yesterday. This will go on

63

forever. A ripple. And you are turning it into a ripple of love by loving each other. Hurrah for you.

"And since finding means recognizing, we are obliged to go over the simple empirical ground, the very basics, of how we recognize that there is 'such a thing' as an unconscious. We shall not establish its existence, nor the existence of the soul either, by argument, by reading, or by any direct proof. We stumble upon it; we stumble upon our own unconscious psyches."[2]

I've copied this passage from James Hillman's *Insearch* because of the definition of *recognizing*. If finding means recognizing, then recognizing means finding. This "recognition" of my writing I asked you about, this use of a word I do not characteristically use, made me contemplate my use of it. I thought of it as a "knowing," that I was inviting others to know me, something I feared and something I thus blocked. Hillman's definition makes me wonder if I wasn't unconsciously talking about my writing as my means of finding self, for myself. And so I am wondering about the basics of how we recognize self. Can you give me guidance here?

True self is in the in between. What you live day to day is truth. What you live outwardly is truth. What you live inwardly is truth. What you live in between is the greatest truth, the weaving together of the other two. How do you recognize self? From the in between. What is your writing but a meeting place of mind and soul in the in between? There is nothing to fear in or about your writing. Let it tell you what it tells you.

Hillman talks about symptoms, too, saying that what symptoms call for is tender care and attention, and that this is what the soul calls for as well. So it is no wonder, he says, that it sometimes takes an "actual illness, for someone to report the most extraordinary experiences of, for instance, a new sense of time, of patience and waiting, and in the language of religious experience, of coming to the center, coming to oneself, letting go and coming home."[3]

Peace, are the symptoms of muscle discomfort I've had for years coming together in what I'm going through now?

You know they are. You are beginning to heal yourself. Be in the Now. Suspend time and doingness. I'm not saying to be inactive, I'm saying to let your mind be restful. Go ahead and turn off your thoughts, especially the negative ones. You don't need them. Turn away from the mind that reviews your pain. Turn from analysis. Befriend your thoughts. Treat them as you would your good friends. They do not need a review of your pain, humiliation, mistakes, and neither do you. Ask yourself, "Would I share this with my friends?" If not, tell the thought to go away. You have been over the past a million times, two million times. It cannot teach you anything new. It hurts you. It has kept the door to your heart shut. Now with the door open, it is especially important to leave the pain outside.

Is this soul work as well as body work?

They are one. But let go of the work. It is soul. It is body. It is psyche. It is divine. It is oneness. It is space like I am space. It is the in between. It is opening to love more than anything else.

"The symbolic attitude of psychology arising from the

experience of soul leads to a sense of the hidden numinous presence of the divine, while the belief in God leads to a symbolic view of life where the world is filled with significance and 'signs.'"[4]

Can the signs we see be trusted? Julie and Mary and I have begun to see what we think of as signs, sometimes of the divine, sometimes things just calling us to look, to see, to remember. How do we know their meaning? Or if they have meaning at all?

All things have meaning. If you see a sign, it is a sign. Just as if you see a bird it is a bird, a road a road, a rock a rock. If the rock were a sign, you wouldn't see a rock, you would see a sign. Meaning is individual, symbolic, uncontrollable. There is no proof. There is no absolute knowing. There just is. A sign. A symbol. A rock. Trust your heart. Trust your eyes. What does the sign tell you?

What about Stonehenge? Yesterday, when I was looking for you or hoping to see you in the flame of my candle, I clearly saw an image of Stonehenge. The two large side stones topped by the flat top stone, and then on top of that were two orbs—round balls of light.

Stonehenge is an ambiguity. It is a place the purpose of which is only speculated about. This makes it mysterious and symbolic. This not knowing that is so difficult for man is really a symbol of the mystery of beingness. Can something not just be in your world? And yet, without knowing the interpretation of Stonehenge, you placed two orbs over the stones. Do they symbolize the sun and the moon Stonehenge purportedly studied? And if this is so, did you know something you did not know you knew?

But this image had nothing to do with you? I was hoping for an image of you.

Look in the mirror. I am you, you are me, we are Stonehenge, unknown, mysterious, but with a higher purpose. Our purpose is to be what we are. Nothing more except to be what we are with love.

When you speak about forgetting the past, I know precisely what you are speaking of in terms of what hurts me—my relationships with men, my guilt over my early parenting, my fear of poverty and dependency. But I wonder about the more distant past. I find I am uncomfortable with the idea of reincarnation, and yet I am fascinated by the real past, the history of my ancestors, my connectedness to them. I feel that there is much for me to learn there, and that this learning honors my ancestors. I feel there is more to come with this passion, this interest of mine. And I don't want to feel that it has no meaning. I am maybe a little confused by your talk of the past and the things I have read about the past. Help me to better understand these things.

Nothing you choose to do is wrong. How can it be wrong to honor your ancestors? And how can it be wrong to have a past? There is no wrong. There is only all that is and all that was. The connection you feel is real. Can you not entertain the notion that this connection goes back farther than you can trace through genealogical lines? If you go back far enough, you simply find yourself. Again. You find yourself again.

Emmanuel seems to say that it is not necessary to find

who we were in a past life. Is this helpful or not?

Helpful? The sense of connectedness you feel is helpful. It is an important link between you and the all that is. Do not fight the things you want to do or force the things you do not want to do. When you are ready, they will come to you. Do not think too much about why you are uncomfortable with the thought of reincarnation, but be aware of it. When you are ready, it will tell you something. Is it not a fear like your other fears, that when you are ready you can thank for what it has taught you and let it go? When you are ready.

Hillman says that through dreams and through entertaining fantasies and receiving the inner world, it occupies more space in our lives and has more weight in our decisions—that is, that our inner world becomes more real to us. He talks about it as the third realm, a sort of conscious unconscious. I think he is saying that it is something not quite me, but rather, something that is happening to me. I love all this Hillman stuff because it seems to speak to me of what is happening to me. And I guess that is how I see you, something that is part of me, but that at the same time is happening to me. Does that make sense?

It makes perfect sense. It is the duality of reality. On the one hand, humanness in all its physical form and pain and daily habit, and on the other hand, the joining with the divine, that which you cannot see but which, when you believe in it, becomes real to you, becomes part of your reality. I like that Hillman stuff too.

He says the entrance to this third realm of psychic reality

lies between mind and matter and perhaps governs both in ways we do not yet understand. *Between* again.

It is a helpful word for you, which is why I gave it to you. Betweenness, duality, connectedness. *Remember that you do not have to understand everything. You just have to be and to know, and to let the wonders of being and knowing have their way with you. Go with the flow of the in between. It will always guide you truthfully. No lies, no trickery in the in between. When you grasp the in between, know that you are on the right path. And it will not always feel like reality.*

Hillman also says the connection within provides the connecting bridge to every other human, that all images and experiences of the soul are images and experiences of the souls of others. Is this the way the transformation will begin?

It has begun. Let the joy of it fill your heart.

What is my role in all of this? Can you give me some inkling of what my role will be on a more universal level rather than the singular, personal level? Perhaps the question I want to ask is, How can I serve?

You are doing fine. You are serving enough right now. Don't be afraid of what will be asked of you. It will only be what you will ask of yourself. It will never be something you don't want to do. When it is time to do more in the service of humanity, you will know it. Your service to humanity now is service to yourself. In fact, it always will be.
Following your own destiny will serve humanity in the way you were meant to serve it.

Thank you, Peace, for once again telling me things that I know in a way that makes me remember that I know them and feel safe with that knowing. I am growing in love.

May 10, 1995

I am amazed at what has been happening to me. An amazement based on the recognition of something miraculous and yet not. Something in between. I say this because while one part of me is rather awestruck—as in, *Why is this frightening and unknown thing happening?*—another part of me is aware of my belief in the miraculous things that can happen because of belief, state of mind, culture.

But I'm a little troubled. I was thinking, earlier today, that I don't need another thing to distance me from people. Yet, even as I thought it, I felt something like distancing, something like being set apart because of this gift. I see now, too, that the last few days have helped me acknowledge this and accept this as a gift. And I think that a gift must be shared. But I am getting ahead of myself.

Distancing. I was struck again today at the distance between Julie and myself. You would think that a sharing of something like this—this angelic communication— would be a natural bridge to closeness. And I could see it was for her, in some way. I could see and feel her look at and see me differently. This, too, has gone on for several days. Yet the distance remains in me.

I can still remember the first time I saw Julie. She was

sitting at the front desk of the office when I came in. And, at that very first encounter with her, I felt disapproval. She has this look, which is dear to me now, but which, at the time, I saw only as judgmental. It is a look of worry, of strain, of her own inner demons. But back then, she seemed outwardly so perfect, so petite, so well groomed and well dressed. I took one look at her and thought she was the kind of woman I could never get along with. The kind of woman who would always disapprove of me. I had this idea in my mind, then, that there were people whom life hadn't even touched yet. People who could not possibly understand a life like mine, a life that had left such scars that I was sure I wore them visibly for all to see.

I have learned so much about Julie since that day. It was as if I saw her, in the first year or so of us working together, as a paper doll, a cutout of a person, the way one sees celebrities, thinking their lives are so perfect, as if they aren't even human. Now I know that life has touched Julie plenty, dealt her her own hard blows. If I know anything about her, I know about her fragility, her vulnerability. If I know anything about her, I know she judges no one harder than herself. And yet this distance remains.

It is from Julie that this thought of not wanting distance first sprang—not wanting to invite anything into my life that would distance me further, from life or from people.

And I think often of the joy that is to be my next lesson. Sometimes it seems as if Italian or Latin would be easier. I could read a book. I *can* read a book. And I can bring what I read here for interpretation at a level higher than my own. I can use the gift for me first. Thank you, Peace. I needed that.

I keep adding to my list:

> Let go of the fear of letting my writing go.
> Let go of the fear of time.
> Let go of the fear of sharing.
> Let go of restrictions.
> Let go of censors.
> Let go of the fear of being known.
> Let go of the distance between myself
> and others.

I came here tonight to write about the threshold. I came across a section in the book *Fire in the Soul* titled, "The Dweller at the Threshold." I could hardly believe it. It talked about the traditional rite of passage as the transition *between* two distinct states of being.

And before I even ask you about this, I can tell myself a few things about it. For many months—since at least February when I had my fortieth birthday, but I would say for some months before that too—I had been feeling and talking to people about the sense that I was moving from one phase of my life to another. Part of this was the very "transitional" age of forty. Part was Ian being on his way to living on his own, Mia being on her way to graduating, and Angela being only two years behind. I knew that the forties would bring about a childless state—or, at the very least, a home empty of children. As I had never been an adult without children, this would be something new and different. It was exciting, but frightening too, and I've written about some of that here.

The other phase I hoped I was entering was that of being a published writer, which I felt securing an agent was the first step toward accomplishing. Then came the purchase of a new home. The process of sorting through years of memories in packing—literally and figuratively—deciding what baggage I wanted to take with me. Some of this was occurring on a subconscious level, some on a conscious level, and thrown in with it all was the awakening spiritual quest, the sudden unforeseen, unforeseeable, turning away from fiction and turning toward this other of psychology, spirituality, theology. From this writer of fiction who was never without a fiction book came a period of not only not reading fiction but not writing it.

I called it at first being busy, the writing of *Prayers* and the *Teen Book of Days,* a form of writing I could do in my "breaks." Even the retyping of *Who Killed the Mother?* was something I could do without the needed time and intensity of creating. The breaks also became a real and prolonged break from the writing and reading of fiction. A break. I just thought of that. Somewhere in here, not too long ago, I wrote, "I deserve my breaks." And what I am realizing is that this is a bigger and more literal break than I ever envisioned. A breaking open. A breaking in two/into.

And so we come to the mythological meaning of the right of passage of the dweller at the threshold. According to Joan Borysenko in *Fire in the Soul,* that right of passage occurs in three stages: the *separation,* the *liminal period,* and the *reincorporation.* In the *separation,* one is separated from one's previous state of being; in the *liminal period,* one dwells between two worlds; and then, in the *reincorporation,* one finds some new role or status in society.[5]

I believe the many months leading up to this one were a separation from my previous state of being, and that what has happened with you, Peace, is the liminal period of dwelling between two worlds, not here and not there but in between.

I have no teachers or guides but you and my books. I am realizing I am involved in something bigger than myself here, something so much more than I ever would have imagined, a passing from one phase of life to the next that is not about the physical, mental world.

I am here with my open heart, Peace, with my heart and hands outstretched, seeking guidance on this path that I am already loathe to think of as a phase, a phase being something transitory, temporary. I do not like the word *reincorporated,* but I need you. I need you to reassure me that the next phase or the reincorporation or the rest of my life will be . . . what? I am not sure what reassurance I seek, only that I am feeling vulnerable and unsure.

Thankful for your gift but maybe not sure what to do with it, how to incorporate it into the rest of my life, what it means for the rest of my life. Will you reassure me?

Now. Live in the Now. When you try to live your whole life in advance, you cannot be reassured. You are right in the middle of life just as you were before. You go to work, deal with children, garden, and paint. Ask yourself, What has changed?

Everything. Nothing.

Everything. All that is. Don't make this another burden to bear. Don't add it to your baggage. Your rational mind is making you fearful with common sense. Let it be. You will not be asked for more than you can give. This gift is not a heavy stone to wear, weighing you down. It is wings to set you free.

Am I really doing okay?

Everything you do is okay. You will not be asked for what you should not give. Let your own intuition be your guide. And know that if you try to receive that which is not meant to be given, you will go empty-handed. Follow your heart. Be in the in between. You're not ready to reincorporate yet. I don't like that word either. Let's call it integrate. *There is no* re *about it. You are not banished to the in between. You are simply there to learn its lessons. My love is with you every step of the way.*

Where will I find my joy?

Right in front of you. It is not lost. You just need to look with your heart instead of your mind and don't try to talk yourself into and out of things. Leave common sense behind.

My heart is heavy tonight, Peace.

Rest, dearest. Rest in the Now. Don't think beyond the Now. That will keep you where you need to be and closest to your joy. And don't worry about your friends. They will find their way. You will be closer. Your open heart will bridge the distance if you stay in the Now. Don't bring what was into the Now with you. The distance that was will remain in the past if you can leave it there. Think of it as a barking dog. Turn around and tell it to stay away. And rest.

Thank you, Peace.

You're welcome.

Dearest Peace,   May 11, 1995

   I come to you today with several questions. I am learning to talk to you even when my family is home, even when the phone may ring, when I may be interrupted. I still wish I had more true alone time, but this is my Now and I am in it. Thank you for that lesson. I have observed myself today, being open hearted in the Now. Listening to the confusion of my friends, going about my day. I am struck by Julie's fragility, by Mary's inability to get out of the mind—by her trying and her thinking and an analysis that leads from one puzzle to the next instead of to answers. I am blessed as the lucky one. The one who gets answers in black and white. It is so clear how each path is different and how our different paths reveal different things that when brought together form a wholeness of thought. We are all novices, just beginning, unsure of ourselves and our answers. I'm thinking that this weaving together of different events, emotions, clues, signs, ideas is somehow essential for us.

No one is greater than the other. No suffering is greater. No blessing greater. It is not a matter of equality but of beingness. There is no one-upsmanship. There is only one.

I know I've already asked you about the spiritual journey we are on together and you gave me a lovely answer to that question. Thank you for that. But all three of us are wondering if what we have in common is more than the journey. Is there also a destination we have in common, a shared goal, something we are to do together?

You are to help each other back to self. To love of self. Is that not a worthy goal? Let me tell you—it is The Goal.
  If you were a microcosm of the world, would you understand it better? Would you not think that helpfulness and cooperation between one country and another, one politician and another would be beneficial? You are a microcosm of the world. Your helpfulness and cooperation with one another cannot be anything but beneficial.

Beatles lyrics keep running through my head. Lyrics about the love we give being equal to the love we get.

It is not an accident that they do. It's a message.

It is not an accident that Julie, Mary, and I are together, is it?

There are no accidents, dearest. You have much to learn from one another.

When you have learned all you need to learn, you will fly off, free. Free of the old, old, old pains you carry. Free to carry your light to others. Remember, this is a schoolroom. That yours is a small office makes it no less of a schoolroom. But it will not be able to contain you much longer.

Is there a significance to there being three of us? At times we have paired off. Julie and Mary share a closeness from the pregnancies that I don't share. Mary and I share something—I'm not sure what or where it came from—that Julie and I don't share. Julie and I have not been close, although today I felt less distance than ever before. And Mary and I, even while we share an indefinable closeness that is as meaningful and full of love to me as any bond I've ever had, also share something equally unidentifiable that is not necessarily loving. There is a way we butt up against each other in competition, a way we compare ourselves to each other or something. It seems, at least for me, that for every step toward connectedness I encounter with either of them, there has been a corresponding step of resistance, either from me or from one of them.

But the resistance is losing.

Yes. Thank you, Peace. There is, then, a significance to the three, isn't there?

There is significance. You've read of myths and archetypes. There has always been significance in the gathering of three. The significance comes from the three finding oneness. You have made the significance by choosing to journey toward oneness. You have chosen to do it to-

*gether. The tricky part is doing it. The difficult part is doing it together.
You wonder at my use of the word* difficult. *The word* tricky. *They
are of your world. You are still in your world. That is the duality.*

*You will pull each other along not by force or physicality, but by
love and patience and being in the Now for each other. You will help
and you will hinder. You will learn by seeing each other's resistances.
You have already learned. You have laughed. You have seen each
other's foolishness where you cannot see your own. But it will not all be
helpful. You will sort and weave and throw away. You will run forward
and back. You have chosen a difficult path, but a glorious path. The
three becoming one, returning to self, will be more powerful than you
know or can imagine. When one fear goes another will come, what one
has the other will want, and at the same time, when one cries another
will suffer, when one is afraid another will offer safety. It is a wonderful schoolroom. Don't you see that what you will learn will be forever?*

How do we know the way to help each other?

*You each must find your own way, but that does not mean each different
way won't offer something to the other. You may bring Julie words and
Julie may bring you light and Mary may provide the vessel. That is the
sacredness and difficulty of the three. If three can become one, a multitude can follow. Like the ripple. One is one and three is three and three
is one and one is everything. One is. Nothing you can do is wrong.
Don't worry.*

But I do.

*If you listen for the truth and respond to and with the truth, you can do
no harm. Trust me.*

I do. And then I have doubts. I believe and I don't. Is this part of the in between?

It is part of the duality. And it is okay. It is what is Now. Don't worry about the future. Don't project. The way away from fear is through love. You are receptive because you have opened your heart. You have entrusted it to me. To you. We are one. Are your emotions something other than you? Is your fear? Are your fingers when you type these words? Grasp—let in—the concept of oneness. If you believe in your-self, you will believe in me and believe in our communication. The road to self is the road to oneness.

Okay. I'm getting it. Just one more thing about my spirit sisters.

As many more things as you require.

Am I right to concentrate on the group questions rather than just on the self or other things?

You know yourself that the questions you ask are the questions. Not right. Not wrong. You may not know the meaning of the three of you, you may not fully grasp what I have tried to tell you, but I assure you that there is meaning. Wherever there is striving toward self and toward oneness, there is meaning and beingness. Can you find this with others right now? You are where you need to be, doing what you need to do. Trust me. Trust yourself.

This leads me to another question I wanted to ask. It is about accidents. About chance meetings. About tests. Are there such things as tests? temptations? Or should every-thing be considered meant to be? Like synchronicity. If something or someone makes a sudden appearance in one's life, does it mean that it should be acted upon or an opportunity will be missed? Or are things/people put in our path to test or tempt us?

Fear guides your questions here. What can tempt you from oneness?

I really want to know an answer to this question.

There will be many opportunities to meet life with your open heart. Will some paths be presented that you will choose not to take? Of course. That does not mean they were not meant to be presented or that they are a test. You have free will. If there were never any choices, would free will still be free will? There are no wrong choices. The path you choose will take you where you are going. It may lead to painful lessons, and you will sometimes not know if the lesson learned in pain could have been learned without the pain. Is pain then a test? No. It is a lesson. Can you receive guidance on the paths? Of course you can. Can I or anyone else make choices for you? No. Trust your intuition. Trust your open heart to take you where you are going.

Thank you, Peace. Thank you so much. You are so important to me.

And you to me. Rest, dearest.

Amen.

May 12, 1995

I read a little of Thomas Moore and Joseph Campbell tonight, looking for where one of them talks about the vessel, because you used that word and I'm afraid Mary

81

won't see it as much. I recall that one of these teachers had a fairly lengthy discussion using the word *vessel*—I believe as container of the soul. Anyway, while I was reading, I saw for the first time the differences between Moore and Campbell and you and Emmanuel. The Now you and Emmanuel talk about is compelling and I understand it. But I was reminded by Moore and Campbell of the sweetness of melancholy, the ruminating done in the name of the soul, even the value of depression.

I think I have been equating the search for joy with being in the Now, with being in the Now with an open heart, and equating this with a need to be constantly content, happy, kind. It is hard to see how this fits with melancholy and ruminating and depression. Certainly being happy in the Now is a perfection we as humans cannot ask for. Surely life continues to provide us with the bittersweet, the sentimental, all those inward-looking qualities that, quite frankly, I value. Have I been narrowing the vision of yourself and Emmanuel too much?

Being in the Now is being. It is being with self, true self. True self continues to experience the wide range of human emotions. What Emmanuel and I, what the oneness asks, is for you to embrace, without fear, whatever emotion you experience. You are still you, dear one. Everything you value about yourself is still there. Much will be bittersweet in your duality because you will see with your humanness and with the divine. How could it be other than this? Your appreciation of the beauty of dark streets in the rain, your lingering farewell to your neighborhood as you prepare to leave it, these are human and divine at once. These are soulful experi-

ences. These are experiences of the Now. That is all that is required.

Thank you for clarifying this, Peace. I'm off to my shower and sleep.

Good night, dear one. And don't worry about forgetting. You will not forget again.

Oh, and Peace, I almost forgot. I found the passage I wanted to show Mary and now your use of the word *vessel* in regard to her makes perfect sense. Mary's friendship *is the vessel*—the precious container in which our souls are safe enough to go through their operations and processes!

For Mary:

"Jung described the ideal setting of soul-work as an alchemical *vas,* a glass vessel in which all the stuff of the soul could be contained. Friendship is one such vessel, keeping the soul stuff together where it can go through its operations and processes.

"The soul requires many varieties of vessels and many kinds of spaces in order to work day by day with the raw material life serves up. Friendship is one of the most effective and precious of those containers."[6]

I I.

S E E I N G

LEARNING HOW TO BE

SPACE VERSUS TIME

May 16, 1995

Yesterday, for the first time in a while, I didn't get a chance to visit here. I had a full day and, at the end of it, found myself feeling overwhelmed by all there is to do in the next month: birthdays, graduations, dance recitals, spring music festival, getting Mia ready for college, work, moving, two houses to complete. Was late to work. Tried to stay in the Now and not worry about the next month, as I was almost sick from one night of having the full weight of it dawn on me.

Today two things happened. First, when I was at work and we were talking about our different ways of connecting with the angels, I realized why it has been easy for me to communicate here. I am used to coming here and turning off my thoughts. I am creative here—that is what my thoughts are about when I come here, to this computer. My main state of mind when I am here is being here. Beingness. I am with the best and brightest of myself here—no wonder I could talk to Peace here. So that was a realization.

The second thing that happened was a John Lennon and Yoko Ono song running through my mind. It played again and again in my mind before I could even put words to it—it was just a melody, endlessly replaying itself. And when I recognized what the song was, "(Just Like) Starting Over," I knew it was a message. Starting over. Powerful stuff.

So today, I come to you, Peace, with what I was going to call urgency, because I have missed you. But I don't want to be willful. I want to let my mind do what it does here, be at its best. I want to welcome you. I want to feel you more than I have in the past few days. Can I feel you? Can you help me to feel your presence?

You can't make me work too hard right now, Peace. I know I'm supposed to forget about time, but I don't have time to work real hard on this now. Help me see the way to be busy and be with you at the same time.

The music was a way. One way.

I know. Thank you.

You don't have to make time for me. You cannot make time for me. I am outside of time, in the in between. So are you but you are also in the Now of your reality.

Comfort me, Peace. Please, soothe me.

You saw today that getting things done soothes you.

Yes. But I have a few minutes now.

Minutes. When you hang on so to time, you get stuck in it. Can you write your novels in minutes? Perhaps. But you don't try. You give yourself space for your writing. Give yourself space to breathe, to rest, to do what you need to get done. It has nothing to do with time. Time has nothing to do with me.

Start anew. With each breath leave behind what you have completed and embrace what you are doing and forget about what you have to do. Dearest, trust me to give you what you need to comfort you. It is not minutes. It is leaving minutes behind.

How can I create more space?

With your open heart, with that part of your mind you bring here. Bring that part of your mind outside with you. Bring it in the car, in the sunshine, in the grass, in the wind. Let those things soothe you. They are always there, they are not in minutes. Always. Space is in the always. Don't bring your analytic mind here. Leave it behind like fear, like the barking dog. Come here to be. Leave here to be. Be.

It would help me to have more of a sense of you, Peace. Can you tell me something about yourself that will give me a sense of you?

I am for you. I am what you need me to be. What do you need me to be? You ask for comfort, but is that what you really want? Or do you want to get things done and use your time wisely. Am I being stern to keep telling you to let go of time? No. I am comforting you by giving you what you need. That is the kind of angel I am. I love you as much as you can be loved. You allow yourself to feel as much of it as you require right now. Remember, you just opened your heart, and you're doing wonderfully, I might add. Until time caught you up again, you were as open as you've ever been. That is where you need to stay. Think of it as a turning to the sun after a long winter. How can you turn your back on it just to embrace time? Time is gloom, no light. Turn to the light and you will see me. That is what I am like. That is how much I want to comfort you, like sunshine after the gloom of winter. Like the colors of spring.

Spring is. Yes, you heard me. [Wax fell from the candle I had burning and made a clinking sound on the glass candle-holder.] *Do not make a process of rebirth. You are new. Last spring's flower is not this spring's flower. It is not tomorrow's flower. It is.*

I've just come back from trying to get a start on sorting things. Everything that I haven't known what to do with has merged into this very spot where I sit and is stacked all around my desk. The first thing I picked up was a pack of greeting cards still wrapped in cellophane. I was sure I hadn't purchased them and wondered where they had come from. In order to see if I wanted to keep or toss them, I opened them. Each carried a simple image of a cheerful child, each from a different culture, each with a simple saying:

YOU warm the coldest days
Wherever you go . . . God is!
You were born Great
You bring rainbows into my life
God made you lovable
God loves you specially
Hello . . . you wonderful person!
You brighten even the rainy days
You are above the ordinary
Hug yourself . . . you are loved
We walk in His care
The Lord is my Shepherd

Ah, Peace, you card, you. I see I can find you anywhere.

And everywhere. I am here to make you smile. Think of me as the smiling angel. When you smile, I smile. When you don't smile, I smile on you with love.

You couldn't have given me a better image.

Image and reflection. You smile, I smile. I smile, you smile. Let your open heart be light. Turn toward the light. This is your way. Our way. Don't worry about it. It is. Let it be.

Now I've opened the desk drawer and found a Prayer to Saint Jude holy card, undoubtedly given to me by Ma, my father's mother. Almost all of my religious things came from her. She was a holy woman, I think. It reads: "Make use, I implore you, of that particular privilege given to you to bring visible and speedy help where help is almost despaired of." What is this about?

Help. Speedy and visible help. It is all around you. That is the message. Open your drawer to all of it, dear one, little one. Yes, little one. You are as precious and innocent to me as a babe. Don't ever feel you have to go it alone again, even if you have convinced yourself you are tough enough to do so. Why, when there is a multitude available to assist you? Yes, the saints are there for you too. Prayer still matters. And it comforts.

Tomorrow I plan to go to Rosary at church.

I'll be waiting for you. Churches are powerful places for oneness for you. You will see many churches this year. I will be in them all. As God is. As you are. They are ancient and their message is ancient, as you are, as I am. You will feel and fill with the oneness there. Going back is in the mind. Being is of the heart. Be with your ancestors in the Now. History is in the Now. Let history fill you with oneness. Now rest.

Help me get really restful rest? Help me dream?

Okay. Sweet dreams, dearest.

Good night, Peace.

May 17, 1995

Tonight I went to church for Rosary. A Rosary said for Peace. [The cursor has become an arrow flashing up!] I went mainly to thank Peace, my angel, for the help he has been to me. Although I have felt anxious still today with all that needs to be done, I also continued to be with my open heart, and Mary even commented on how she can see that I have changed. Other physical manifestations of my change include my desire to wear softer clothes (I don't think I've worn a form-fitting suit in two weeks), the feeling of smallness, a heightened sensitivity to smell, and, hopefully, a happier looking face.

I really had Mary laughing today when I told her about how I had caught an image of myself in a window as I walked to work and was surprised by what I saw. I had thought I was smiling but I wasn't. I felt as if I was smiling but my lips did not turn up at the edges. I suppose my face looked pleasant enough, but it definitely wasn't wearing a smile. I thought, *I'm going to have to practice getting my lips to curve up.* Mary was just howling as I told her all of this and I ended up laughing too. I guess it is pretty funny. Needing to learn how to smile.

Last night, as I was lying in bed, trying to go peacefully into sleep, Donny brought me a family problem that kept me awake and tossing. Yet I turned most of the unwelcome thoughts away and replaced them with loving thoughts, and as I drifted off, the last image I remember was of going feet first into the light. It just was. Not frightening, not silly, not anything. The light was a flat light with jagged edges. It reminded me of a comic book depiction of light, and my feet were going down into it— so it was beneath my feet. At work today it comes out that Mary had a similar image come to her two nights ago. It's all getting more and more connected.

Then Julie tells of a dream in which I have given her a scrapbook in farewell from work as I did our former co-worker, Kathy. But it is covered in pictures of her from all her past lives and she saw beauty in each of them. Then I come home and the next paragraph in *Fire in the Soul,* the book I am reading, is about how the author was taken to the "kingdom of light" and given a book of her past lives.

So, at church tonight. In the first instants, a feeling of lightness, then nothing miraculous. I tried to get into the "saying" of the Rosary and out of my thoughts, with minimal success. Then at the end of the Rosary, Father Baz began chanting in Aramaic and I let his voice just sink into me. And finally I came home and what was the next paragraph, *again,* in *Fire in the Soul,* but one on the ancient reading of Jesus' last days and his giving the Our Father to his apostles. And the author says that the words lost much in the translation from Aramaic and that there is a book of meditation using the ancient Aramaic language as the sounds of going into a deep meditation! Connections, connections.

So, there, in a nutshell, is the life of my soul from this day. Peace, I came here tonight mainly to say hello, to thank you for the difference you are making in my life, to talk to you. How are we doing today?

We are smiling.

As I am just about to go to bed, do you have any suggestions for me as far as getting into a peaceful sleep or about the light I saw last night?

LEARNING HOW TO BE

You are turning to the light and it will find you even in the dark.
Remember that as you fall asleep. That even in darkness, there is light.
The light of oneness in which you are never alone and never unloved.
The light that is nonintrusive, that gives your soul space in which to be.
Perfect privacy and perfect trust.

Peace, I find that some of the intrusive thoughts I have are about men, men from my past. These thoughts seem to come out of nowhere, their only purpose to shame me. Like driving home from church tonight, a street corner, a simple piece of geography, reminded me of a scene from my teens, one of many scenes, many young men, who treated me as a person of no consequence, as if I had no feelings, no value. These kinds of scenes replay in my mind endlessly. I know that it is *they* and not *me* that are of no consequence. They meant so little then. They mean less now. But still they come to me. Is there some way I can let go of these thoughts?

They are your fear. In this life, men were the road to many painful lessons. You are still afraid of them. But more afraid of your own reactions. That your ego would again follow them into darkness. In the light there is no ego, only beingness. Your specialness comes from within, not from anything you see reflected in the eyes of men. Your light comes from within. Keep turning to the light and you will naturally turn from darkness, turn from ego, turn from pain. When you are no longer afraid, you will follow your heart. When you follow your heart, you will reach a place of perfect forgiveness. Forgive yourself first.

HOPE

Hello, Peace. May 19, 1995

It has been a *getting things done* kind of day. It's Friday, I'm home from work. The first open house is Sunday. I hope you and your angel companions will work together to bring the right buyer to the open house, someone who will love it. Love, I'm sure, is the answer to selling our house. In the new house, Peace, will I reach a better balance between doingness and beingness? One of the things Pat told me was that my chart is about doingness but that it was in not doing that I would find my creativeness. And yet this is not a year for *not* doing. I'm sure us finding a house and moving this year is what we are supposed to do, but I also believe Pat. She said it would be a spiritual year and a year of healing. I believe you are my path to healing. I know it. So how do I balance being and doing in this busy year?

You have accomplished much since we began talking. You will not accomplish any less because you talk to me or continue to pursue enlightenment. All wise people are not inactive. Perhaps by learning to love yourself, you are restoring your vitality. There are times in every-one's lives when they are seemingly too busy for contemplation. But your inward life is going on at all times. You never stop thinking. You never stop dreaming. You never stop being.

I haven't heard from Dan yet. It has been more than the three weeks in which he said he would respond to his clients. I have been hoping you would get together with his angel and counsel him to be my bridge to the publishing world.

How do you know I haven't been doing this? I will always do what you ask of me in love. The time for your writing is coming. It will be here when you're ready.

Am I not ready now?

You are ready for many things now. Trust that the right things will come to you at the right time.

Am I ready to learn about karma?

What bothers you are the injustices you fear believing in karma would open to you. You do not want to believe that all poor babies are paying for something. You are right. That is not karma. In a sense, there is no karma, there is only beingness. Remember, the Now is what is important. You have chosen it, in the beginning and in the previous minute. Can you not allow for the possibility that you might choose life again?

I don't think I would, Peace. I've never feared death. I know already that at the end of my life, I want to come home for good. What must I learn in order to do that?

Everything and nothing. You have to learn to be in love with yourself and the world. Then you will be ready to come home for good. You will have remembered the way.

And you will be there waiting for me?

When you die, I will be with you just as I am now. I will never leave you. For an eternity, I will never leave you.

Had to break to do some more housework, Peace. It is so endless! All my little tricks to get things done faster, like throwing something in the closet or storing something under the bed, can't be used because we'll be having open houses. So I set these little goals for myself, sometimes daily, sometimes weekly, like getting one closet cleaned out, or finding out what is lurking beneath the basement steps, and add them to the day-to-day *stuff!*

But in the midst of it all I keep finding these things that just sing to me, like this quote from *Fire in the Soul,* by Joan Borysenko:

> When the "bottom drops out of our pessimism" we are forced to let go of the idea that we are "doers" who can conquer life by the application of our individual will. The first step of any twelve-step program addresses just this issue of the bottom dropping out. In the case of alcoholism, the step reads, "We realized we were powerless over alcohol and that our lives had become unmanageable." We might apply this attitude of surrender to any area of life in which we have struggled fruitlessly to change.[7]

And this one, Peace. It relates to a question I asked of you earlier, about hope. In it, Borysenko quotes Brother David Steindl-Rast:

> Hope, he asserts, is a patient waiting for God, a stillness that allows us to hear the inner voice of guidance. In *Gratefulness: The Heart of Prayer,* he says, "As long as we wait for an improvement of the situation our desires will make a great deal of noise. And if we wait for a deterioration of the situation, our fears will be noisy. The stillness that waits for the Lord's coming in any situation—that is the stillness of biblical hope. . . . The stillness of hope is, therefore, the stillness of integrity. Hope integrates. It makes whole."[8]

I have goose bumps all over because of this stuff, Peace. I'm not sure I understand it all, but I feel sure this "stillness of hope" is the place you've been trying to get me to. Am I right?

What do the goose bumps tell you? My simple answers just aren't good enough for you, I guess. (Just kidding!) You have been in complication and duality so long that sometimes the long answer is better than the short. Or consider that the passage may have been written because it would someday come to you and you would say, "Aha! I get it!" (qualified, of course).

My desires and fears have been very noisy.

Review what you have written here and you will see that they have. You ponder what questions to ask me, you go off in one direction and another, but what is your steady concern? How, when, who, about your writing. As is often the case, it is your greatest desire and your greatest fear at once. Does looking at the stillness as hope make it easier?

Much.

Then the passage was written for you. Hope, my dear.

It's as if I suddenly know how to *be*.

Yes! Yes! Be. Stay with that feeling. You've gotten what you needed. Start listening to simplicity and finding simplicity in the complex. Simplicity, like the in between, will show you the way.

Thank you, again, dear Peace.

Think of hope as you fall asleep and you will awake, even from this busy day, rested and refreshed and new and in the Now.

May 20, 1995

I am still reading *Fire in the Soul* and continue to be affected by its lessons on hope, particularly by this passage quoting Brother David Steindl-Rast.

> Hope looks at all things the way a mother looks at her child, with a *passion for the possible*. But that way of looking is creative. It creates the space in which perfection can unfold. More than that, the eyes of hope look through all imper-

fections to the heart of all things and find
it perfect.[9]

Hope creates space in which perfection can unfold! Peace,
you told me I create space for my writing, that space is
always, and that I can find more space by keeping my
heart open and by bringing the space I bring to writing
into the world with me. Then I discovered *hope* and went
"aha!" And now I read that *hope* creates *space!* I can hardly
believe it. You are so dear to answer my questions and
show me the way.

Hope is being. Being is trusting the way that will be shown. Space is
where you allow yourself to be. Seek and you will find the answers.

I just read that too. The passage from Jesus in Matthew
7:7, 8:

> Ask and it shall be given you;
> Seek, and you shall find;
> Knock, and it shall be opened to you.
> For whoever asks, receives; and
> he who seeks, finds; and to him who
> knocks, the door is opened.

I don't think there is any way, short of divine interven-
tion, that so many things I need to know are coming to
me in so many ways. What else do I need to know, Peace?

You tell me.

Nothing, probably. As you and Emmanuel have said

before, there is nothing new. Nothing we don't already know. And it's amazing, because when the answers I am seeking come to me in that wonderful "aha" feeling, you are right—they are not new. I just hadn't seen them before.

You just hadn't remembered them.

Thank you, Peace. I retire once again, hopeful once again.

May 21, 1995

I was thinking about compassion today and how I had more compassion for others when I was suffering myself. When I was left with three children to raise on my own; when I had no money, no car, no groceries; when I was renting a dark, dreary duplex that I couldn't afford, it was then that my place was the gathering place. Friends and family were always coming by, most often to talk about their problems! And it would give me such satisfaction that they did so. I remember how I used to turn on the oven and open its door to warm whichever friend or family member had come to my kitchen table. It was as if I was available then in some way. Available to them but unavailable to myself. Maybe they would remember it differently, but it seems to me that I only listened, that I couldn't talk about what was happening to me—about having to return pop bottles for milk money, about not being able to clean because I couldn't afford cleaning supplies, about feeling so horrible and guilty about it all but not knowing what to do.

Perhaps the seemingly insurmountable nature of my own problems could fade for a while in the light of more solvable problems.

I was "present" when I was in that survival mode. I was there. I didn't always have other things to do. But as my situation improved, it seems I got so busy keeping life together that I had to create boundaries. I couldn't just sit and listen to other people's problems anymore. My open-door policy ceased to be.

I recently admitted to my sister, Susan, that I hadn't felt so compassionate lately. And all she said was, "Being busy hasn't kept you from being sensitive and open to people." I hope she is right. From the very first, you told me—listen to your sister. Now I know why.

Peace, I now invite you to celebrate with me that I have gotten this far in the journey. I thank you. I want to know you. I want to know me. I want you to know me. I want others to know me. I come asking for the way. Thanking you and honoring you.

When you honor me, you honor yourself and all others. In smoke you remember me, in everything that rises: the sun, the moon, people, smells, bread, fire, light, all things that grow. In the shadow of things, in the flicker of light outside of time.

How do I release myself from feelings of unworthiness?

Go into those feelings and see what emerges.

Pain. The pain of things I do not understand. My laziness as a mother. My promiscuity as a young woman. My

103

relationship with my mother. My grandmothers come to mind, though I never associated either of my grandmothers with my feelings of shame before. They all seem to be about acting without understanding.

Face them. Be a big girl now. Now. They were all telling you before you were ready. You were full of a rich and powerful dream life, a life of the imagination, that was suddenly, almost irrevocably removed, like surgery, like cutting out a piece of you. And ever since you have fought to return to the dream life, the life of the imagination, without realizing what you were doing. You fought to come home to self and to oneness. Doesn't that explain a lot of the whys? You fought being a big girl, being a woman, being a mother, because those labels took you away from the life of the imagination, away from your soul. Doesn't that make you feel better? Believe me when I tell you—that was the why behind the actions you don't understand. It has taken you thirty-five years to come back to what you had as a child. You have come back! Rejoice and be glad. Let go of the pain and understand that coming back was worth it.

Worth even the pain I inflicted on others?

The worst pain you inflicted was upon yourself. You speak of the pain you brought your children, but let me assure you, they chose to come to you with love, knowing the lessons they would learn. Love them and the pain is gone. It is not something that they wear like tattoos, indelibly imprinted. It is gone. It was then, this is now.

But I have carried unworthiness from then my whole life.

And you have learned from it the way back to self, to soul. I tell you, it was worth it. We choose our lessons precisely for this reason: to lead us back to self, to lead us home. You gave your children what they chose to learn so they could find the way back home. How could it be otherwise? How could you change it? You cannot and you could not. Be at peace with the fact that all roads lead to home.

What about my relationships with men, affairs so fleeting I hesitated to call them relationships?

They were fleeting because you would not let them turn you into a woman. You have felt this in regards to your sexuality—how people thought you were so sexy but you were not. You were in reality and, in men's perceptions, a goddess, but you were not in your perceptions. You played a role carefully orchestrated to shield you from the love and intimacy you knew would bring you further and further into the real world. Isn't that what your life was like? A drama in which you were the lead character but had no idea what you would do next? You don't remember many things because they were not real to you. You existed, waiting for life to happen, the life you have here, the life of imagination and the soul, and oneness.

So when I chose Donny, I began the journey back to self?

When you chose Donny, you accepted the journey away from self. You gave up in defeat and you joined the world. You became the big girl. The good girl. You became responsible. And for a while you were very sad, though you did not know why. You could see the same thing in Ian. When forced into real life, he rebelled, no matter how seemingly better it was on the outside, in the real world. It was his inner life he wanted most to protect and which Donny challenged the most. Donny demanded that you come into the world and you came. You thought all was better and all was lost—both at the same time. You are only now realizing the way back. The way to be a big girl and live in the imagination, in the soul, in the oneness of perfect love. Donny asked you to survive in the real world so that your inner world would be safe. Honor him for this gift. It leads you back toward home. It gave you back your self.

I think you're right. What about my mother?

She tried to do what Donny did. To force you into the real world and to force you to survive. That is a mother's job. She didn't realize she was killing your soul. Not often, anyway. And when she had clarity, she mourned. But she always hoped for you. Don't you feel the love? I know you do. When you are with her, pay attention to your open heart. What does it feel?

Oh, Peace, I think I see—I joined the world to find my way out of it. And the grandmothers?

Ma in her kindness and holiness drew you and repelled you. Ivie in her sweetness and her madness drew you and repelled you. They taught you the duality. They gave you a glimpse of something you didn't understand but you knew the glimpse was important. You saw a lot of yourself in each of them. The "being in the world" without "being in the world." They were images of you because they did not accept the one-dimensional world—they did not embrace it with open arms and say this is all that is. This thrilled you and terrified you. You did not understand this any more than you understood yourself and you knew that these things were linked. You were linked to the grandmothers at a very young age, imprinted by their duality. They helped you find the way to live in the world and still head for home. Honor them for this.

Oh, Peace, I do, I do. This is ringing so true for me. Like bells. Like a chorus. Can I send my grandmothers my love?

We're here.

Grandmother Ivie, can I do anything for you?

Sugar, enjoy your life. And head for home. I can't wait to see you and to welcome you.

Ma?

Pray, Marg. It is one sure way to bring you home. I bless you with my prayers and with my love and with my hope for you. Be good to your father. He needs you. And be good to your boy. He is in the duality as we were in life. Pray for him. I knew Donny would bring you back. I look on him with love, too, like he is my child. Love him, love yourself, embrace life fully; there is more to it than prayer, but I guess you don't need me to tell you that. Enjoy each day and everything in it. I'm enjoying your journey with you, Marg, living again through you. See the sun and the birdies and the grass for me, Marg. See it all. And remember me.

Peace, I had to go into the bathroom to dry my tears, and while I was there, this thought occurred to me: *Donny was the first letting go.* The first surrender. Did that come from you?

From me and from you . . . to help you remember . . . letting go is not so bad . . . huge benefits come from letting go. Remember that.

Peace, I can hardly believe I just talked to my grandmothers but I know I did. Thank you so much, and thank

107

you grandmothers for letting me really feel your presence.

Dear Peace,   May 22, 1995

I've been meaning to thank you for the help you have been to Julie. She is using the words that you and her angel gave her to lead her back to self. She is sharing, and with each new sharing, she seems to gain more wisdom. I suppose there is a lesson there.

There are many lessons in the schoolroom. Julie was ready for those you were able to bring her. You can trust her, you can know her, you can help her and let her help you. Through love and through trust. Let it be. It will grow in you. Remain in your beingness and you will see the light.

And Mary?

You have come a long, long way with Mary in a very short time. From the beginning, you knew each other. You are much alike in the burdens you carry, but she protects her uniqueness. The part of her that wants her journey to be hers alone is in conflict with the part of her that wants to walk with you. Let her be. In her beingness she will turn to the light. Be patient. Be hopeful. It will BE.

Thank you, Peace. I retire once again, hopeful once again.

And I smile.

                                                    May 26, 1995

I was going to meditate before starting but I can't. I'm so

excited to be back! I felt cut off from the spirit sisters this week, Peace. It was because Mary started planning Grace's burial for Sunday and it was clear she didn't really want me there . . . and that she did want Julie. She even asked Julie to write something to contribute, so the experience was painful. I felt, as one of the spirit sisters, that it was my place to be there for the ending of what gave us this beginning.

I think Mary knows she has hurt my feelings, for she has tried hard in other contexts throughout the week to say good things about me. But the wound persists. Mary seems to have a stubbornness when it comes to accepting help or direction from me or from you. Julie is so eager to be guided. Mary is not. A perfect example is that, although she has admitted to being confused about all the road closings and construction that have made getting to work difficult, and although she knows we come from the same direction, she does not want to hear from me the best route to take. She does not want to learn from what I have learned. She insists on learning her own way. And it's not something I can fault her for, Peace. It just is what is, as you say. But sometimes it hurts me.

I know you were with me this week, Peace, as I sorted through my feelings about this. I still feel saddened by it but I chose to tell Mary that I couldn't make it to the burial because of the open house here this weekend rather than to confront her with my real feeling that she didn't want me there. If you have any guidance for me here,

109

Peace, I would love to hear it. Have I somehow caused this problem with Mary? Have I been too . . . I don't know what . . . too authoritative or something in the way I have given my information? When I've shared your teachings, have I made it seem as if, because they come from you, they are *the way?*

Peace, I've kept my heart open to Mary, and I would have even if you had not been keeper of the brick, but there is something about her that gets to me. From the very beginning, from the very first time I met her, I knew I wanted her for a friend. I feel so alive, so complete when I am with her. No one has ever touched me the way she has, has had such an ability to make me laugh and cry and *feel.* She does so much for me that I think my insecurity springs from just this fact. I think anyone would be lucky to be Mary's friend. So why would she choose me?

But there are times when I do feel chosen and lucky and blessed with her friendship, as if it's the greatest thing in my life. And so when she pulls back from me, withdraws from me, into herself or into her relationships with others, I get hurt. I feel unwanted and unworthy. And truthfully, it's always a surprise to me. Both that I can feel so close to her and that I can be so hurt by her. Can you help me see the best way to relate to Mary?

With your open heart. With your love. You are doing fine. You are fine. Mary is Mary, as her angel said. She is living out her play, her myth, in the only way she can. She is consolidating her bond with Julie, this is true. She is giving to Julie something Julie needs, this is true. Did you need to be there? For what purpose? To comfort? To share? Perhaps. Julie needed to be there to complete the circle. Perhaps you need to be at your open house. Perhaps if you had really needed to be at the burial, you would have simply said you would not miss it. But you realized Mary's needs in this case were predominant. You were right.

There are paths Mary must walk without you. This does not make you less valuable. This does not make you unworthy. There will be times when the relationships of the three are not equal. Perhaps Mary is only equalizing them now by giving Julie something you had that Julie did not: the benefit of ceremony. That you were not aware of your soul connection at the time of Grace's memorial service doesn't matter. Grace was aware of it.

What do I do with my hurt feelings?

Cherish them. They are part of what makes you special. Then let them go.

What about the future of my relationship with Mary?

Listen to her. Tell her what she wants to hear and not more. Am I telling you not to be yourself? No. You are always yourself, and never more than when you listen and give what is required rather than what you may want to give. This is part of the lesson you will be more familiar with after you have learned joy. After you have learned joy, less and less will be able to hurt you. You will see what IS.

My heart still feels heavy, Peace.

Because you have been away from self. Because you have doubted self. I never love you more than when you need to be loved. When you are feeling away from love, remember I am with you then, more closely than at any other time, sending you love in abundance if you will only receive it. Remember to be receptive. When others seem not to love you, love yourself more. One positive turning to love negates all the negative turning away from love.

What else do I need to give up to love myself? You have helped me greatly with your understanding of my unworthiness. You have helped me to understand my fears. What else do I need to give up in order to love myself?

Guilt. You may ask how guilt is different from unworthiness. Guilt is a response to what has made you feel unworthy. Give up the guilt you feel over your past. And forgive. Forgiveness is also a response to what has made you feel unworthy. Replace guilt with forgiveness.

I feel as if I have been doing this, but it still crops up fresh all the time. It seems as if I ought to be able to get to a place where guilt is unnecessary because I am no longer doing anything to feel guilty about. But then I have a fight with the kids or with Donny and it crops up again. A cycle.

Perfection is not possible in human form. Your fights are part of your schoolroom. Thank them for the lessons they teach you and let them go.

So much is about letting go. How does one continually let go?

By being in the Now. That is what being in the Now is all about. You are not in the Now when you drag things from five minutes ago or five years ago into the Now with you. Practice. That is all you need. Practice letting go every day in all those continual cycles. When you are more practiced at living in the Now, there will be less need to let go of things because those things—those fights or whatever—will happen less, as you can already see they are happening less. And when they do happen, they will happen in the Now and stay in the Now. Practice, my dear.

I know I would be better at being in the Now if I had more time alone. It seems that I get distressed when I have not had that alone time. Can you advise me on how to make more alone time for myself?

Start by realizing that you are alone even when you do not have alone time. (I say this knowing that you are never alone but addressing you and your physical concerns with the physical concept of alone time.) You are already being able to appreciate alone times you never had before because you were not in the Now before when you were doing them—like driving, walking, preparing for bed. As you get more adept at being in the Now, your alone time will multiply. When you get better at letting go of time, your alone time will multiply again. You are doing fine! You are doing great! You have learned a great deal about these things in a short amount of time. Continue to practice, continue to look for alone time in the ordinary. Make alone time out of folding clothes and making the bed. And if that still is not enough, make more alone time by giving yourself more space at the beginning or end or middle of your day, or all three. This being here with me in front of your computer is not your only alone time. But come here as often as you want. Don't let the clock or the presence of others deter you.

JOY

Dear Peace,   May 27, 1995

I have read much recently about joy being the turning
from despair, and now I'm wondering if my despair is the
pain I've given myself about the past and, if so, can I find
joy now simply by turning away from despair.

You have learned many things that will help you turn to joy. Hope is a
major one of those things. So is space. So is now. So is being in the in
between. So is being here, creating. Have you forgotten as you wait for
your writing to find its place in the world that its place is here? Have
you forgotten that you find your greatest joy in creating? in writing?
Practice all the things you have learned and bring them here, to your
writing, just as you bring what you have here, your divine space, into
the world. The more you learn to do each, the more you will learn about
joy. Joy is.

In a way, I guess I have forgotten the writing that has
brought me so much. When I read "think of a sacred
moment" for going into meditation, I think only of the
joy I have found here, in this basement. Of that vacation
from work when I completed my book for the first time,
when the joy of creating and the joy of completing and
the joy of vacation and the joy of alone time were so
great, I danced a jig of joy. I think I have been afraid to go

back to creating on *Who Killed the Mother?* because I'm not sure it is the writing I should do now and I'm not sure where to go with it. I guess I haven't let go of my fear in regards to my writing.

And when you hold on to that fear, you destroy the chance for joy. For you, writing and joy are irrevocably linked. Can you have one without the other? No. Because, for you, writing is your holy expression of self. You cannot honor the whole self without writing, and you cannot honor the writing without honoring the whole self. Writing and your journey back to oneness are thus linked, integral, integrated. We are both blessed by your ability to use this skill, this talent, this art, in your spiritual quest, your journey home. But it is not the only use for your writing. You know this.

Your writing is a big part of why you are here—of your destiny. One journey cannot replace the other. The journey that is your destiny is also your path to oneness. And you know writing is your destiny. Can you turn your back on anything in this life you know with such certainty? Where else are you so sure of yourself? Where else do you know you can find joy? Obviously it is not in the waiting and wanting to be published. It is in the writing, the doing—for you, the beingness of your writing. Bring your love and compassion to your writing and you will bring it to yourself.

And yes, you have had enough despair. I do not mean you will never have it again, but for now, you have had enough. You can turn from it, if you will, and you can embrace joy, if you will.

I had been thinking of joy like happiness. Like the feeling of happiness you get from doing something fun or having a stress-free dinner with family. But some of my readings by Rollo May in *Freedom and Destiny* have helped me see joy in a new light.

Not only does May talk about the Persephone and Demeter myth—a myth Mary has lived and is still living since the death of her daughter, a myth that has thus touched each of us spirit sisters—as being devoted to the link between despair and joy, but he also talks of the resurrection of Jesus as being the same story, only from the view of Christian theology. The death that must precede the resurrection is like the despair that must precede joy. So it seemed as if he was talking about two current themes touching my life and as if he had linked them, just as Mary joining me on Good Friday had linked them. Only now I see that both link back to my readings about the dweller at the threshold. I'm so darn literal sometimes that I just don't *see*. The rite of passage—moving from one phase of life to the next—is the same myth! The myth of moving from despair to joy after a death is not just Mary's story, because of a literal death, but my story as well because of a figurative death, my own. Julie, too, is likely caught in the same myth, the journey of leaving one self behind and going on to another. It's what we're all doing! Dying and being reborn!

Once again, Peace, another author is causing me to "get it," to *see* the story of my own life. To *see* the story of the spirit sisters and the purpose of the journey—to be reborn to *joy!* It should not surprise you, then, that after "getting" the above, the passages below rang so true for me:

> Happiness relaxes one; joy challenges one with new levels of experience. Happiness depends generally on one's outer state; joy is an overflowing of inner energies and leads to awe and wonderment. *Joy is a release, an opening up; it is what comes when one is able genuinely to "let go."* Happiness is associated with contentment; *joy with freedom and an abundance of human spirit. . . . Joy is new possibilities;* it points toward the future. Joy is living on the razor's edge; happiness promises satisfaction of one's present state, a fulfillment of old longings. Joy is the thrill of new continents to explore; it is an unfolding of life.
>
> Happiness is related to security, to being reassured, to doing things as one is used to and as our fathers did them. *Joy is a revelation of what was known before.*
>
> Happiness is the absence of discord; joy is the welcoming of discord as the basis of higher harmonies. [This was one of my problems, wondering how one could hope to be happy or joyous all the time—this helps explain it.]
>
> The good life, obviously, includes both

joy and happiness at different times. What I am emphasizing is the joy that follows rightly confronted despair.[10]

JOY AND HOPE ARE BOTH ABOUT POSSIBILITY!

"Rightly confronted despair." That seems to be the key, Peace. May is not talking about despair brushed under the carpet, despair that is allowed to make the rest of our lives miserable, but despair that, once confronted, is transformative!

Turning from despair is moving from the prospect of life going on as it always has—filled with all the difficulties and struggles and conflict we have always expected—to a life of possibility, a life where joy is possible. It is just the same as me thinking I have to feel guilty and unworthy for the rest of my life because of my past and not seeing that it can change. It is just the same as me thinking I will retire from the university because I am forty years old and it would be too risky to make a change. Despair is being stuck in the prison of what we have become with no reprieve possible. But, Peace, joy, like hope, is the experience of possibility!

And there are other people out there who "get it"! Sometimes, when I contemplate how it's just you and me, sitting here in this basement, having a dialogue on a computer, it seems as if we are isolated. But then I read someone like Rollo May, or bring something like what I've learned from Rollo May, or from you back to the spirit sisters, and *I feel as if I know something I've never known before!* I realize that these feelings I've had aren't weird, aren't unique to me—that others, too, have struggled to understand joy, to find joy, to experience the possible. I never knew this, Peace! I always thought I was such a loner, such a weird duck, so "into my mind" in a way other people were not. And it's just not so, is it? How funny that talking with you, being on a spiritual quest, has made me feel more *normal* rather than less. More aware of what connects me, not only to God, but to other people. Another thing I have to thank you for, dear Peace.

Your awareness of what connects you to God Is your awareness of what connects you to your brothers and sisters. Your awareness of what connects you to your brothers and sisters Is your awareness of what connects you to God. It is the same thing. And your awareness thanks me as I thank you.

THE POWER OF WORDS

CENSOR

May 28, 1995

I have been thinking of telling Donny about what I am doing here—at least the part about making myself feel better by understanding myself better—and I just realized in an "aha," new sort of way what I am leaving behind with the move. How I am going to go anew to the new home. What a wonderful allegory, what wonderful symmetry! As I leave the old home with tender love and care, I leave the old self as well. I leave with the tender love and care that the two of us, together, have created out of the old patterns of judgment and fear and despair. Oh, thank you, Peace, again and again.

Can I have this time to work here on creating my new self and turn to creating in my writing again when the move and the self are complete? That sounds like such wonderful timing to me! Unless you think I am putting off "creative" writing out of fear. I just don't want it hanging over me like a weight, like a "should do" kind of thing. When it becomes a "should do," I don't believe I could find joy in it. But thinking of this time of preparing to move as a time of preparing myself for the new life—a life that includes the creative writing again—that feels right to me. How about you, Peace?

It sounds like inspiration to me. Just remember to follow your own truth. If you become inspired to creative writing, will you turn your back on it because of this new timetable? That is all I would tell you to guard against. When you set up timetables, suspect them. They may help but they may hinder. Do not let yourself get stuck in anything having to do with time. However, if what you feel now continues to be what you feel until you move, then that is what you should do. Regardless, you will be New when you move to your New home if you continue to treat yourself with love and care. You are new every day you treat yourself with love and care. But with practice, you will be much closer to the new self you are becoming by the time you move.

These things are happening together for a reason and you know that. Trust what you know. Do not be dissuaded from what you know by anything or anyone. Every time you tell yourself, I will do this after I do that—I will quit writing here after this cigarette, I will quit working after that CD has finished playing—stop and ask yourself why you are making rules. Practice being without rules as you practice being without time, as you practice being in the Now. Your greatest censor is still yourself. Think about that word. Look it up. Can a self whose destiny is to be a writer write with a censor looking constantly over her shoulder?

I turn to my *Webster's* dictionary:

> Censor (n): 1. one of two early Roman magistrates whose duties included taking the census 2. an official who inspects printed matter or sometimes motion pictures with power to suppress anything objectionable

> Censor (vb): to subject to censorship

> Censorship (n): the action of a censor especially in stopping the transmission or publication of matter considered objectionable

> Censorious (adj): marked or given to censor; critical

> Censure (n): the act of blaming or condemning sternly, an official reprimand

> Censure (vb) 2: to find fault with and criticize as blameworthy

Holy moly. What have I been doing?

What have you been doing, indeed?

Blocking myself and my writing as objectionable, blame-worthy.

The words that pop into your head do so for a reason. They are words and they are symbols too. What a powerful symbol you have had working against yourself. Censor, like recognize, tells you so many things: what you do, what you fear, what you crave. Rid yourself of the word, the doing, the fear, and you go a long way toward ridding yourself of the negative symbol. The negative.

Unbelievable. Not only do I not see what is right in front of my eyes, I also am unaware of what dwells in my head, what inhabits me.

Seek and you shall find. You are on a hunt. You will find many false gods on the way to the real God. You are on a hunt for the divine and when you take away all the negative false gods inside yourself, you will find the treasure is yourself.

I just can't get over the profundity of what goes on here, Peace. It can only be the divine. Thank you for continuing to prove it to me even when I am not in doubt. Thank you for giving it to my humanness, which needs it in order to continue on the road to the divine.

You give me a lot of help along the way, you know. You are a good student. I give your humanness an A+ for today's work. Welcome back.

WORDS OF COMMERCE

May 29, 1995

Memorial Day. At Dad's for his birthday party and for a day of remembering those who came before Dad. Remembering Ma. New babies on the way. The family gathered on the deck, the day glorious and lush, everything green, Canadian geese families on the lake, my sister, Susan, with a boyfriend, Mia about to graduate, Ian looking different than the last time I saw him, a trip to Mary's remembering Grace. Remembering to be with my open heart, at least and at last, for a moment of the day. Happy Memorial Day!

Now I am back, Peace, back. Back and forth I traipse in the duality. Life and LIFE. Both wonderful, both lovely, both full. Thinking of the new house. Such newness awaits. Thinking of exploring things of the body, the body's connection to the spirit, the spirit's connection to the unconscious mind. A world of possibilities left to explore. One life's journey to turn within and see possibilities and newness. Permission to live an inner life fully. So much to be thankful for. I thank you here and I thank you out there in the world, in the beauty I have eyes to

124

see. But I still want to come home. As beautiful as life is, I am anxious, full of curiosity and expectation about the next phase, the next life. I stand ready to prepare myself for it by using my time in this life to come to fully love myself, to open my heart to love all others. What is the next step on this journey of truth and love?

Joy. You are beginning to feel it but you are right to do some inner work on your body too. The body, as well as the soul, needs to welcome joy. Your body needs to reach a place of restfulness. It is on the road to regeneration. It will want to soar like the spirit. What you are striving for is a lightness of being. Remember that. You are already feeling lighter. When your body catches up to your spirit, think of how it would feel to walk on a cloud.

Peace, as I search for other things to ask you about, I am struck by how little is still bothering me. It's as if I know that things that bothered me in the past are behind me. What that leaves are the issues we are already dealing with or have dealt with to some degree. One of those issues is my fear of intimacy. Is there anything you can share with me about that?

Loss. An overwhelming feeling of loss. Think of the word intimate. *What does it imply? Closeness, sharing, loving, confiding. They are things of the adult world and of the infant world. They are what you start out having in a psychic sense and what you seek in love as an adult—with mind as well as spirit and heart and soul and body. Mind is a culprit here, because it fills with fear.*

Every human must go through the forgetting stage from infant to toddler—that is the first loss of intimacy. But it is in some way okay because the toddler forgets what she has lost. But as an adult, this loss is a wanting, an active longing, to be heard and recognized and understood as an individual, as the unique being you are. One of the things that kept you from intimacy was your inability to define who you were because you were not being yourself and because the self you were hiding was a self that your mind had told you was bad.

The other part, that continues with you, is a thing of quantity. You believe that if you ask for something you need, even if you ask to share something that you are, pray for something that you want, you will be using up valuable favors. You deal with yourself and with feelings as if they are a commodity, a savings account, and you live in dreadful fear of bankruptcy. Take all ideas of quantity and favors and barter and get rid of them. If you can believe that what love you give is returned to you, how can you not believe that what love you take returns something to the one who gave it? Does it not make you feel good to have someone share a secret? to give pleasure? Then why would it not make another feel good to give you pleasure, to hear your secret? In the world of love there is no bartering. No one keeps track of what you owe. You will never go bankrupt! When people talk this way it is only a social way of talking. You can correct them or you can show them the foolishness once you believe it is foolishness. If you are always paying debts, how can you not feel bankrupt?

This is important for you to grasp. Leave numbers, quantity, favors, bartering, trading, all ideas related to commerce in the world of commerce. They do not belong in the world of love. As you came to see, censor was a powerful negative symbol. So are all those words you have related to feeling that are not about feeling at all. Living in love is living in a world of plenty! You never have to go without again.

DEFENSES

May 30, 1995

Dad's real birthday; the choir Spring Spectacular; Mia's orientation for the legal internship program; a drive to Minneapolis; now a half hour to respond to a call on the house, to prepare to leave for the concert, to pick up the video camera, to pick up Mom. And I'm stressed. I have my period, so it's almost inevitable, but I'm more stressed than I've been since I found you, Peace. And I know part of it is my anger toward Mary. She has aligned herself with Julie. And I persist in feeling like a *child* about it. Like, *If she doesn't want to play with me, I'll just show her.* That's what my feelings were about today—they were of the "I'll show her" variety. I tried to get my mind to shut up but I couldn't. I even realized why Mary puts up barriers to me—because she's like me. It's as if neither of us are comfortable with caring about each other overly much, with getting too close, with being indebted to each other. Maybe it's because of our mothers being friends. I don't know. I just don't know.

What childish part of me is doing this to myself, Peace, leaving me with a million things to do but unable to do them until I come here and get rid of this and get to the center of myself again, the part of myself that loves? I almost even felt my door trying to close, today, Peace, over such nonsense. Help! Help me let go and help me understand.

You were right to come here. Let the next half hour leave your mind for a minute. Let yourself feel uninterruptible. Breathe. Hold hope in your heart. Hope for Mary and hope for yourself. Breathe in the possibilities of tomorrow, of the next minute being new. Hope that the next minute will be quiet, that the next minute will be peaceful, that you will enjoy. Go ahead and do what you have to do with hope in your heart. Then go ahead and get in your car and be uninterruptible for as long as you can be. You need silence right now to center yourself more than you need me, although I will be with you. Then come back and we will talk about your inner child and we will welcome that child with love and compassion.

I'm back. Thinking of kids. Those wonderful, spirited, earnest, energetic, soulful young people of choir. I wouldn't have missed it for the world. I did spend moments appreciating the beautiful night. I'm better, not cured but better. Wanting to get back to where love is and stay there. And I'm not talking about here. I'm talking about that place inside which on good days I can take around with me like a shy little sister. I think I'll be better with the Mary situation by tomorrow. It reminded me of the times during the choir concert when I would start feeling competitive for Angela. Why wasn't she doing a solo? Competition. I always hated it. I know Ang hates it. I know I hated it as a child. Angela is like me in that: she's

128

proud. Too proud for competition. Some weird kind of pride I hung on to throughout growing up. What was I proud of? Nothing. But I *had* pride. I guess I could hardly stand rejection of any kind, not even that of supposedly healthy competition. I guess I'm still the same way. Should we work on inner child stuff, Peace?

There are no shoulds, Margaret. Do you want to?

I want to understand self. I don't think I have a lot of things to work on until something like what happened with Mary comes up. And I don't think I understand the readings that say "go into it." Am I supposed to embrace unhealthy things like my feelings of today?

There are no supposed to's, Margaret. And there are no unhealthy things. Every time you chose love, you negated the harder feelings, feelings that were true in what they were, feelings of an open heart learning its way through the thicket of the world.

I like your image of carrying your love around like a shy little sister. I am with you when you grope with feelings of humbleness. They are there when you are in a state of love. The pride is there when you are in a state of defense. This state of defense was the constant of your youth. Do you need to understand what started the war? what made you shore up your defenses? Or do you only need to see that you have defenses, built up over a lifetime, that you will break down, dismantle. Today is only the beginning. Think of yourself turning all the soldiers around and sending them home to their mothers. You will be left undefended, yet victorious. You will be left to be!

So think of this situation as giving you the opportunity to turn one soldier away. You've just granted this one small part of yourself a life-time furlough. How happy that part is! How joyous! Turn every situation where you want to shore up your defenses into a party of homeward-traveling soldiers, soldiers homesick, returning home with all God's speed, rushing to new possibilities, freed! Pretty soon the army will be only a battalion and finally only one loyal private, and even he or she will want to be freed to return home.

If I didn't have defenses, what would happen to me?

You would stand. You would be. You would be free!

I wouldn't be massacred?

Wounded, perhaps. But your wounds would become your badges of glory. Real war wounds instead of imagined ones. YOU would stand or YOU would fall. Why should others stand or fall for you? Because of duty? Because of blind loyalty? When it is you standing up for you, it is real. Your defenses are only imaginary. But if you are going to have imaginary defenses, and you are for a while, why not set them free? It will be a better illusion than that of expecting them to defend the fort against whatever onslaught might occur. See them standing in the rain and mud, and each time you need them you instead send them home to the sunshine. And ask, What am I defending against? Where is love here? Where am I here?

But if I'm walking around like the shy little sister, won't I need defending?

Only from the other part of you that is the solid big sister. You are now both. But you will be one. When you come to love all of yourself. Who told you you had to be perfect?

Thank you again, Peace. *Defenses.* All these words that are symbols I never saw before. It is enough for tonight. Thank you.

Your gratitude honors me—and you. Rest, dearest.

TRUTH

May 31, 1995

Truth:

> In religious literature the word "truth" is used indiscriminately in at least three distinct and very different senses. Thus, it is sometimes treated as a synonym for "fact," as when it is affirmed that God is Truth—meaning that He is the primordial Reality. But this is clearly not the meaning of the word in such a phrase as "worshipping God in spirit and in truth." Here, it is obvious, "truth" signifies direct apprehension of spiritual Fact, as opposed to second-hand knowledge about Reality. . . . And finally there is the more ordinary meaning of the word, as in such a sentence as, "This

131

statement is the truth," where we mean to assert that the verbal symbols of which the statement is composed correspond to the facts to which it refers.[11]

In no circumstances, however, can the study of theology or the mind's assent to theological propositions take the place of what [William] Law calls "the birth of God within." For theory is not practice, and words are not the things for which they stand.[12]

Dear Peace,

I feel as if you have sent me on a search for truth, but for once, my reading has not helped me. In fact, the more I read about truth, the more I am convinced it is not something one can know, like fact, which is what I always believed before, with my literal way of interpreting the word symbols of the mind. More than this, I really cannot say. I'm getting a sense of truth as something that has to be experienced or felt within, but which mind cannot ever truly explain or prove. In what I don't know, am I getting close to the concept of truth as you represent it?

Seek and you shall find. If you associate truth with me and me with something true that cannot be explained or proven, you are close to understanding truth. Now, if you associate truth with yourself, and understand that it Is and yet that you will constantly seek it, you come closer. Truth, as related to God, cannot be explained by the words of man. Like so many concepts we struggle with—like time—there are no words to describe the lack of time in a way you will understand. Living in the Now is as close as you can come to truth. Living in the Now is as close as you can come to love.

I wish I hadn't gone into the readings on truth, tonight, Peace. They captured my mind and confused it at a time when I am not much interested in the mind to begin with. I'm happy with getting away from the concept of truth as fact. Is that an okay beginning?

It is an okay ending. Some travel a lifetime with fact. If you can give up fact, you can be free to be open. Half of the journey is spent getting rid of concepts that keep self closed—in a prison of all it has learned since its birth. The more illusions you rid yourself of, the more space you will have for the fullness of self.

Thank you, Peace, for that high praise, for that acknowledgment. I wonder, as a writer, how I will deal with words in the future—now that I see their illusion and their power. I still can't believe how I have censored myself with a word!

Words are the habits of a lifetime. They are also the experience of a feeling—think of Hope when you get discouraged by words. Hope taught you how to be in this schoolroom.

Yes. You're right, as always. Can we go back to my inner child for a while? It is what I really wanted to discuss when I came here, and I've come to learn that I avoid things for a reason.

You come back to inner child to explain away the whys of pain. You cannot. Like truth, pain can be better understood in what it is not. Is it punishment for having done something bad or having been bad? No. Absolutely not. Is it someone's fault? Only if you believe in fault. If you believe in a divine plan, then there is no room for blame or fault finding. Reasons, yes. The reason for pain is to help you find your way home.

What you told me about my feelings of unworthiness rang so true. I felt as if you had just been waiting for me to ask the right question. So I guess now I'm greedy and I just want you to tell me more about why I am the way I am.

There is a reason questions are answered rather than answers coming before the questions. Your questions represent what you are ready to know. When you say, "Tell me something," I risk telling you what you are not yet ready to know. Be patient and understand that you will ask the right question at the right time.

One of the reasons, Peace, that I am not into my mind tonight, and that I ask again about the inner child, is because of Mary and Julie. You helped me so much, yesterday. Things really were better today. I know my feelings were caused by my insecurity rather than by Mary—even my perception of her not wanting me at the burial. I've let go of my anger and hurt feelings but I am left with a kind of bewilderment about what is going on with these two women and me, Peace. When we are close, I don't even need to understand it; it is just the most wonderful thing. But when the distance between us returns, even though there is still love and respect, even when I have let negative feelings go, it's as if I don't understand it at all again. Why is it them this is happening with? Why Mary? Why Julie? I have a "real" sister. I have friends who have been my friends half a lifetime. Friends with whom I am beyond the stuff that still happens with Mary and Julie. Friends I don't compare myself with, don't compete with, don't wonder day to day whether or not they like me. Why is it these two with whom so much still must be learned? Why is it us three? Three people still learning to be friends, still having to get to know one another. Maybe I really am the misfit, the odd woman out. Maybe it's supposed to be just Mary and Julie. Maybe I am inserting myself where I don't belong.

And yet you know the truth is that this is meant to be. You know there is a reason. A reason much like the difference between happiness and joy: happiness being a contentment with what is, joy being an exploration of the possibilities of what can be. Your friends of a lifetime represent your happiness with what is. The spirit sisters represent the possibilities of what can be. The truth is that you thought it was contentment that brought you here—and you have since discovered it was not contentment but discontent. You thought you were not full of fear but discovered that you have been and are. You are with the spirit sisters because you do not know them, because you can discover them, because through your learning with them, you are learning about yourself.

You are right, as always, Peace. This is the truth. Even I recognize it. Thank you.

III.
PREPARING

THE POWER OF HABIT

RULES

June 10, 1995

Ever since I read about truth, I have been into my mind and my mind is making my husband into a censor again, even though he's upstairs watching TV, and my daughter has come in and dropped her needs into my lap and I once again feel as if I need to run screaming into the night for some quiet and peace. And yet I'm tired and I know I should rest, and perhaps there I will find some quiet. So I ask, How do I turn off the rule maker, the piece of myself that is always saying "After this

I'll get to work," or, "One more question and I'll go rest?" Where did that rule maker come from and how can I befriend this part of myself?

Good question. The rule maker formed in you as a response to guilt. When I mentioned guilt the other night, you did not think that it was much of a problem for you just as you initially did not think fear was. Your greatest source of torment has been what you perceived as your laziness as a mother. I tell you that if you were in the state now that you were in then, you would know to call it despair. You would know to call it a dark night of the soul during which you were lost to yourself. But then you called it laziness and, in response to your enormous fear of laziness and your guilt about your supposed laziness, you have created a rule maker of great power.

How can you rid yourself of the rule maker? Rid yourself of the cause of the rule maker. Forgive yourself. You thought if you understood why, that would be all you would need. It was a great part of what you needed. Forgiveness is the other part. Remember that you are tending yourself with love and care as you are tending your home with love and care so that you can go on to the next guilt free. That is what it is all about. To leave the house with love and tender care, the best it can be for the new owners. To make yourself over, the best you can be, for the new home. Does your home hold on to those days when you did not treat it with love and care, and say you cannot change me? No. You put on a new roof and a new coat of paint and it is new—as good as it can be. So you, too, need to put on a new roof, a new coat of white to be new, to be as good as you can be now. Leave the past behind, put on a white coat of forgiveness and truth.

How?

By letting it happen. By letting go. By surrendering to the Now. Every time you hear the rule maker raising her voice, ask her what she is feeling guilty about now. Ask and you shall receive. Get an answer. Honor that answer for what it has taught you and let it Go. Let it leave and never come back. Eventually when you ask, "What are you feeling guilty about now?" the answer will be nothing. It will be only the habit that remains.

Practice being in the Now with hope. All the rest is merely going to be a matter of answering questions and letting go of the answers and the habits. Now rest. Let me be the rule maker, time keeper, once in a while. Trust me until you can trust yourself. My rules will be ones that make you laugh, and my time will be Now.

Thank you, Peace. Good night.

Dearest Peace,   June 11, 1995

As much wisdom as I have gained in my readings by learned men and women, Emmanuel remains, next to you, my favorite teacher. I can read him any time and be soothed. I am particularly gladdened when I find something that reminds me of our talks. This happened recently with the following passage:

> Live your lives in expanded curiosity,
> wondering "what if?" Censor nothing.
> Mystery is mystery because it cannot be
> understood.
> So follow the mystery.
> It will bring clearing vision.[13]

Peace, I think in my first conversation with you, I said that the mysterious has always caught my imagination. I remember so fondly how I loved private spaces as a child (and still do). How when my father kept his messy garage, it was such a treasure to me. There were three marblelike rocks, almost brick-sized, that I loved just to look at. One was gray, one pink, one white, and they all sparkled like glitter. There were cans—from baked beans and peas to Comet—and I would mix them up like science experiments. I baked mud pies. I loved boxes—like Crest toothpaste boxes I'd find in the trash (in the garage). I had the box memorized. I even liked the little folded papers that came in the boxes. And I liked the dark rooms of the basement. The canning room and the storeroom where the Christmas decorations were kept. Anywhere semistrange, semidark, semiforbidden, where I would find time to be alone with my imagination.

I bring all those parts of me here to you, Peace, because here is where I know I confront real mystery. Because here, for the first time, I am finding my way out of illusion into the light, and surprise—I can still honor that side of myself that is shadowy. This is not like confession. This is not where I have to be good. This is where I am allowed to be. Thank you for that. And thank God for the gift of it even before it brought me to you.

Tonight I tried a new tactic and I liked how it worked. I made dinner, did the dishes, made the bed, did some laundry, and then came here. Donny felt easy with me being here because he had time to talk to me first and because I did my part in keeping the family functioning. Now I can be here without guilt, without rules. I needed that.

EXPECTATIONS

Dearest Peace,   June 12, 1995

I feel better this morning. I feel like ceasing to define everything. You woke me with a thunderstorm. I have lived all my life with thunderstorms without understanding them. If I understood them intellectually, they would lose some of their power and wonder.

This combination of busyness and not feeling well is getting to me. And I think half the reason is because I haven't made enough time here. It probably has nothing to do with time at all—but with space, having space to be. I may be on my way in my head, Peace, and I may be able to carry it over to some degree at work because I am with others on the same wavelength there, and there are times I even feel it here at home, but here is where I feel it the least.

Family life seems to be a life of constant expectations.

Sometimes they are mine and sometimes they are others', and sometimes I make them seem as if they are from others when they are really from me. What is it about expectations that brings out the irritable, the stubborn, the rebellious in me? Or is it just that there are so many expectations, from so many different sources?

Time and quantity are both at work in bringing about these feelings in you. Fear is at work also. Are you afraid you cannot meet all the expectations? Then fear is working against you. Are you afraid you don't have enough time to complete all the tasks that are expected? Then fear is working against you. What does it take to turn the fear around?

Expectations lead to fear too easily. Why? Because they are about outcome. They are the minigoals that make up your days. They are the minigoals that come without thought. And because they come without thought, you have to ask, Whose goals are they? Where did they come from? Where am I here? Where is love here?

If you have to clean your house because it is expected of you, you feel resentment and rebelliousness. If you choose to clean your house from feelings of love, no resentment follows. Choose your goals each day and practice being in the Now with them. Only you can decide when you can say no to things. Perhaps you might ask, What would happen if I chose to say no? More likely, you will get the best answer by asking, Where is love here?

Many of the things you are doing are preparatory, the work before the ritual. The ritual—the graduations, birthdays, the move—are about love, or they would be if you gave yourself space to contemplate their reason for being. The days of acting without knowing why you are acting are quickly becoming the days of the past. When you act out of your own inner knowing, you will act with love.

You might try starting each day with a prayer of preparation. What am I preparing for today? An answer might be something like, I am preparing myself to return to oneness; I am preparing myself and my home for a great change, for a transformation; I am preparing for the day on which my daughter will be honored for all she has become and all she will be; I am preparing to bring knowledge to those who are still in a state of forgetting.

Thank you, Peace. This is very helpful. It's as if we lose track of the good "why" which lies behind what we do. Birthday parties shouldn't be burdens and wouldn't be if we looked at them as a celebration of a life.

Right. If service is only duty without the thought or feeling about the life served, it is a bit of a sham isn't it? Looking for what is real, what is at the heart of something, will always bring that something into the light.

It's all kind of the same thing, isn't it, Peace? The way we look at things and the way we use words?

Yes! Look at what happened when you took away expectation and replaced it with preparation. It is all so simple, really, Margaret. It is not looking at things with optimism, which is the state you used to try to psych yourself into, but looking at the truth of things. It is not only about the "big" questions, Margaret, it is particularly about the little ones, the daily ones. For they are the only ones if you are living in the Now.

145

And if I am spending the Now preparing for the future that is okay?

It is how you live. But yes, preparing for the future might help you to keep from projecting into the future—if, and this is a big if, Margaret—if you know the truth for which you prepare. You cannot go to Italy without preparation, can you? But in order to prepare for Italy, you need to know why you are going and for what it is that you prepare. With Italy you have a good sense of the why, but remember to ask, Where am I in this picture? This is about your truth. Just do not forget, when preparing for the future, that today is what is important. How you prepare, like how you get there, is the essence of the truth you seek.

So, if I prepare with anxiety and hurry, I've lost sight of my truth?

Haven't you? Can you see the truth when you live in fear? That is what anxiety and hurry is about—living in fear. Preparing with thoughtfulness, with lovingness, blesses your Now, even while what you prepare for is about the future.

I guess if I am going to listen to your advice, I should start preparing more thoughtfully for Mia's graduation party. *The Celestine Prophecy* talked about how we learn to be in relation to how we were brought up. That in response to intimidation, we become "poor me"; in response to interrogation we become aloof; in response to aloofness, we become interrogators. All to get the attention we need. I could see that my mom was an interrogator and my dad was aloof, and I could see that I became aloof and Mia became an interrogator. Mia and her questions are incessant.

Look at her. Listen to her. Hear her. Respond to her with love. This is all she needs to go out into the new phase of her life. Fix her in your memory every day. What do her eyes look like, her skin, her hair, her clothing. This looking at her is essential. When you look at her with love, the love reflects back to her and she takes it into herself. Love is the most pure form of energy. Reflection is a potent means of giving it. You can do no harm with a look of love, no harm with an open heart and an open ear. Look, listen, love. That is the way to fill Mia with the energy she needs for her journey. Apply the lessons you have learned to her. Stay away from shoulds. Stay away from fear. Stay away from concepts of limits. Live in a world of plenty. Give of yourself to her. Give, give, give. Be conscious of not draining her energy with negativity or uncertainty. It is not a time for active guidance. She will learn what she learns now. Just be in the Now with her.

Thank you, Peace.

COMPLEXITY VERSUS
SIMPLICITY

June 16, 1995

Hi, Peace! I'm back! Two things occurred to me that I would like to talk to you about. Neither of them are burning questions. They are questions that have been able to come because so many others have been answered. One of the best parts of coming here is not knowing what will transpire, how one thing will lead to another, which may just lead to the one thing I really need to know right now. Now! This keeps our relationship so alive! So vital! Which leads me to my first question, which is about simplicity.

As soon as you talked to me about simplicity, I had to find something to read about it. And, as it happens, as it has happened so unmistakably since we began talking, I have found just the right thing, a whole book on simplicity. *Voluntary Simplicity,* by Duane Elgin. It says this:

> To live more voluntarily means to encounter life more consciously. To live more simply is to encounter life more directly. By its very nature, then, voluntary simplicity can be defined as living in a way that fosters our conscious and direct encounter with life itself. The "life" so encountered extends far beyond that typically acknowledged in the daily social routines of Western cultures. It is LIFE—in its vastness, subtlety, and preciousness—that is the context within which voluntary simplicity acquires its genuine significance.[14]

Elgin goes on to say that life becomes more relevant when we view the universe as our home and death as our ally. Viewing the universe as our home helps us to view the whole and its vastness, and viewing death as our ally helps us to remember what is important. Taking that concept one step further, we will remember what we will take with us—which you have been saying is what or who we are and love.

And so, once again, it all circles around to self-love. I will, of course, keep reading about voluntary simplicity, but I hoped you and I might have a conversation about it, about what you felt I could learn from the concept of simplicity.

Simplicity is important Now because of the world you live in Now. While all life is complex, life within your social structure is particularly complex. X = multiplied. Everything is sped up. The human race itself has doubled in your lifetime—something it has never done before. You have heard that this has happened because of the great evolutionary step that is about to take place. You talked to a baby the other day about his angelhood and he understood that you understood. Julie asked her baby if he remembered and he did. Small, small steps. Giant leaps. What if the next generation were to grow up remembering?

This talk reminds me of a source of my spiritual journey that you and I have never talked of here but that I have not forgotten: the January/February 1995 issue of, *Utne Reader,* perhaps my first awareness that the world was about to change, that an evolutionary step was coming. The issue took one hundred visionaries on every topic imaginable and, just by putting them together, showed what their visions had in common: the need to rethink everything in our culture. In the introduction to the visionaries, John Spayde wrote: "Their revolutionary is the individual human who decides to stop and take a breath—and then, having discovered that she or he lives somewhere called this moment and this place, begins to think the thoughts and take the actions that will help this timespace to live."[15]

What really got me going, however, was a separate piece by Václav Havel, who recognizes that we, as in the whole world we, are in a transitional period where one thing is dying and another being born. He compared this time to the Hellenistic period and the Renaissance and said that what distinguishes these times is a blending of intellectual and spiritual worlds. But he did not leave out science either, noting that both the anthropic cosmological principle and the Gaia hypothesis remind us that we are not alone but an integral part of a mysterious whole.

I've gone back to that article and that magazine many times, for hope, inspiration, vision. What is it all about, Peace?

What is remembering about? It is about love. What is simplicity about—narrowing what is important to us down to the basics. What is important? The shortest and most complete answer is love. You are right when you see that all concepts return to the root concept: Love. And love, in turn, returns to all other concepts because living love means living more completely, loving the universe, even embracing death as a release into love. Everything in the universe is about love expressing itself. It is only humans who do not remember this.

So writing, including my own, is love expressing itself?

Oh, yes. Could it be anything else? All of your actions, whether you know it or not, are love expressing itself. There is no "more." Writing is not more expressive of love than anything else you do, because there is

151

no more. But some actions bring you closer to love of self, and to truth, and you honor yourself and God and all that is when you do those actions. It is hard to explain without the use of such terms as more, *which, in their nature, presume a quantity and a limit. It is perhaps better expressed in terms of energy—those actions in which love expresses itself knowingly and, from the heart, from the desire for truth, create greater and greater cores of love or energy—a ripple effect. Not* more—*a ripple.*

The word *ripple* brings me to the other question I wanted to ask you. It is about the river. I used to say I wanted a job that did not require me to cross the river every day, and I said this because of having to cross icy bridges in the winter. But now, every day I cross the river, it is a reminder to look at the scenery, the greenery, and I feel almost as if there is a message for me in this being drawn to look, to see.

Everything that draws you to look, to see, is a message. Because you are drawn to words, you like these messages—you say, "I can understand them." Because you have understandable messages, you can share them and learn from them and you feel lucky because of them. I am happy to bring them to you, both here and by other means, but unwritten messages are just as important, especially for you because you refuse to see. You are afraid to see.

I am afraid, for some reason, to see things I consider divine, or miracles. While part of me wanted to reach out immediately to my Uncle Nino after his death, another part of me was afraid to because I was afraid I might "see" him. Are you talking about my fear of seeing the divine or a broader fear?

Seeing the divine and seeing are the same. You have defined yourself with words and it is a narrow definition as words cannot contain the wonder of all that is. It is wonderful that you have no fear of words. Because of this, we have this means of communication. But imagine what it would be like to have no fear! To make the rest of the world as open to you as our communication is.

Much of your fear comes from the inability of your words to encompass all that is. You think, If words can't define it, what use is it to me? *You think,* My way is with words *and are content to leave it at that. You think,* My way is with words, *and think if you cannot come back here and put words on an experience, it is of no value to you.*

You must become like the painter who sees beauty where there is no beauty. You do this with your writing, but you do not recognize and value it. What were all those painful scenes in your book The Ninety-Seven Days *about? Beauty! Beauty! Beauty! Who were they about—or I should say who were they for? Were they for that unknown and unseen audience? Yes. But first they were for you. First they made beauty out of pain for you. This is why your writing is valuable and divine and blessed. Not because it may one day bring you fame and fortune, but because it made pain beautiful!*

So what does this have to do with the river and with seeing? Just this: The river is calling you to open up your vision—to see the divine in life and the life in the divine and to bring this to your writing and to your thinking and to you. The river is there to say your way is more than writing. You think, I am blessed with writing, I dare not

153

want more. *And I tell you you must! If you want life to affect your writing, you have to be affected by life! You are just beginning to learn this as you walk around with your open heart. Think if you had learned this all your life as you learned words all your life. Yet it is not that you have a lot of catching up to do; there is no cumulativeness, there is only experience. If you experience the divine once, it is a lifetime of experience. Are you experiencing the divine here? Are you? Or are you experiencing words here?*

I do not mean at all to belittle what goes on here, but to prod you to be open to more! The goose bumps and the tears are a beginning, but still so much more awaits. Joy awaits. I want so much for you to experience Joy.

What is the river telling you? Can you define the river with words? Could you make a being that had never known a river, know a river through words? Could a painting of a river make another understand, know a river? There is something of an observer about the artist. Like the proud parent who is more concerned with a good picture of a child's moment than the child's moment. That is what you are like, standing back ready to take pictures and write captions. And I say delve in! What is the difference between looking at the river and being in the river? Know the difference! To know the difference you must experience it rather than observe it. You could observe the river all your life without knowing what it would be like to be in it. Jump into life! That is your leap of faith.

Why am I afraid to see, to jump, to experience?

Because it is safer on shore. But I ask you, safer than what? You are safe until the moment you are going to come home and then you are more safe than before. Everything in between is life. In between. Go for the in between.

In between birth and death is life.

Yes. YES, Margaret, YES!

Life—which is what voluntary simplicity is all about!

Yes! Everything circles back to what is important.

Thank you, Peace. As always, you brought me to something very significant from something I thought relatively insignificant. Help me Live with a capital *L*, Peace. Help me See. I will try to be more open to experience.

Then experience will be more open to you!

ONE-ON-ONE

June 22, 1995

I have, with your help and advice, remembered more and more of my dreams, and in several of them I am at a retreat center. I wondered if this was a message.

Retreat. Interesting word. Meaning what? Surrender? Falling back to regroup? Go ahead, look it up.

> Retreat: an act of withdrawing, especially from something dangerous, difficult, or disagreeable 2. a military signal for withdrawal; also a military flag-lowering ceremony 3. a place of privacy

> or safety: refuge 4. a period of group
> withdrawal for prayer, meditation, and
> study

In my dream, the last meaning was the most obvious. I was with my work friends at a beautiful place.

You are at a beautiful place with your work friends. This is one clear meaning, but I would not dismiss the others. All are about withdrawing. From what do you wish to withdraw?

If, from anything, it is from the busyness of life — to leave the busyness of life and go to a quiet place. These things have great appeal.

I asked you this because I wanted you to examine the answers. You and I have only recently talked about your need to embrace life and how all of life's moments can be holy moments, and yet you are still drawn to withdraw from life. There is nothing wrong with this, if it is really what you want to do at the soul level—at the level where you know yourself. And it is perfectly normal in times of busyness to want to retreat. But I ask you to examine with your heart the desire to withdraw. You are beginning to understand the difference between choosing what you do and acting out of old habits. Is the desire to withdraw old habit or what your real self wants right now?

Perhaps you went to the retreat center to rest in your dream so that you could have more energy to embrace life in your waking hours. Withdrawal from busyness can be a wonderful embrace of life or it can be a retreat from life. Your dream may ask you to be aware of the difference. One way is about love and one is about fear. And I believe you were witness to some fear in one of your dreams. Let words guide you to the truth. If it is love, then you will be guided in the right direction. If it is fear, you will not be.

Thank you, Peace, for reminding me not to fall into old habits. I also wanted to ask you about the connectedness of dreams and thought going on in the office. Thursday night, Julie and I were both talking to our angels about joy at the same time. Then I had a dream in which the words *one-on-one* came up, relating to children, and *one-on-one* came up with Julie at her counselor's office and caused her to cry. Her angel is Water, and we have all had thoughts and dreams about water. Is this connectedness trying to tell us something?

Connectedness is. And it is important. It is the linking point like the in between. Here is one thing. Here is another. Here is the in between. Where things connect. Isn't it exciting?

Yes. It is. I felt you wanted to tell me something about *one-on-one* also.

One-on-one. *Look at the words. Look at the phrase. Not one and one. Not two separate beings, but one-on-one. ONE. Everything is one. Oneness is the goal, the end of the journey. What then is one-on-one? You think of it as a way of relating. Yes! One-on-one, like hope, can help you understand how to be. Be! Can you relate two-to-two? No. Can you relate one-to-two? Only if you see things and being as separate. It is about relating to one. To oneness. To all that is.*

And more simply, if you think of the usual meaning of the phrase, it is about goodness, isn't it? Relating as one being to another. A personal relationship. A relationship. It implies trust, openness, closeness; it implies being known and knowing another. It does not discriminate. It does not save relationship for a few special people. It implies relationship with any ONE. It is a wonderful phrase. It can lead you and Julie both to oneness if you let it help you remember how to be!

Thank you, Peace. They are wonderful words and it is wonderful that I have you to lead me to their meaning. Thank you. And thank you for Julie. And Mary told me to thank you for letting her know she only has to visit the place of her grief. You are being a wonderful help to all of us.

These words may not seem as much like prayer as they did at the beginning, Peace, but I still like to think of them as prayer—to you and to God. I cannot claim to understand the oneness principle, but when I talk to you, I do feel that it is much like talking to God. And although I do not say, "I pray for this or I pray for that," I know you understand that I am praying for understanding, for meaning, for the way to oneness, and that I pray for it not only for myself, but also for my friends and family and all of the great oneness of the world.

A life lived in the pursuit of oneness, Margaret, is a prayer. And just as with prayer, that life is "heard" and responded to. Don't worry. There is no "one" to misunderstand you. There is only One.

Is there anything you want to tell me about the dream in which I kept returning to my father's and about the rocks?

Even as you typed the words "returning to my father's," you understood. You grew up with God the Father. Now you are learning to think of your next phase as a return home. You are dreaming about your journey home and many of your dreams will be full of the richness of discovery that you will greet on your journey. It is important that you write about your dreams because they help you remember! Dreams help you remember and writing helps you remember. In addition, because of your affinity with words, sometimes you only have to see the thing in words to See. I kept returning to my father's. Yes! And you made rich and beautiful discoveries there. Yes! And you traveled there with your spirit sisters. Yes! All you need to do with your dreams is remember them, write them, and See what can be seen. Avoid extended analysis. Just See.

Thank you for helping me remember my dreams. Is there anything else you want to tell me?

I want you to stay in the Now. Let it be. Everything is a gem. You are a gem. The next step is alchemy, transformation. Let these things be like a promise. You are preparing. For more than you know. I promise you. Smile, dearest. Rest. Remember. Joy is coming.

That's a little mysterious isn't it, Peace?

Yes. It IS.

Good night, sweet Peace.

Good night, dear one.

FREEDOM

June 23, 1995

Had a rough day today. I am probably PMS-ing. It is as if I am wound up tight and anything will make me snap. I don't want to. I don't plan to. I tell myself to stop. I tell myself it is over and then I do it again. Lose my temper. Yell. Get excited. Get frustrated. What can I do?

Remind yourself for what it is you prepare. Remind yourself to breathe.

Why do I have such a hard time making decisions when I am like this? Is there anything you can tell me about making decisions that will help me?

Making decisions is about choices. You have not had a lot of experience with making choices. You have, in the past, let choices pass you by and let life happen to you. When you did this, you associated what came of this as "bad." You had babies you weren't ready for. You did not make good decisions about men and school and jobs is what you think, but it is not that you did not make good decisions—you did not decide at all. You put off choices until there was no longer any room to choose.

Now you are facing choices that have to do with buying things. In the past, you have chosen to buy things you could not afford, to such a great extent that you had to work very hard to get yourself out of debt. And you have set up censors for yourself in regards to spending money just as you have about spending time. Ask yourself if this is not all about the "being a big girl" that we have discussed. Everywhere that you are fearful of "making the same mistakes" and "falling back into the old patterns," you give yourself censors and rules that prevent you from taking full responsibility for your own actions. In doing this, you have robbed yourself of the fundamental value of freedom.

Do I have to add "fear of freedom" to my list?

If adding it to your list helps you rid yourself of the fear, by all means add it to your list. It is much like what we discussed about participating fully in life. What are you afraid of? Your fear is based on old habits and on an old Margaret. You are coming to realize that you are not today the person you were yesterday. Why then can you not accept that you are not today the person you were ten years ago?

Certainly you have to be mindful of what you can afford. Don't be afraid to take matters into your own hands, figure out what you can

162

afford, and spend freely and happily within that limit. If you are going to work with rules, a better rule than using Donny as a censor would be to know how much you can spend and know what you want to buy and then do so. Practice, dear. Practice making conscious decisions daily. Big ones and little ones. You will be amazed at how much easier it gets as time goes on. And practice telling yourself you are free. FREE!

What about the song Janis Joplin sang, "Me and Bobby McGee," that has always been my very favorite song? That has always struck such a chord in me.

You loved that song because it was one of your most bittersweet lessons. You went to that place where you had nothing left to lose and then you associated that place with freedom. I ask you now to think of "nothing left to lose" differently. Think of it from a place of plenty, a place of love, a place where the important things are those which you can never lose because they are within. Be in the Now with these thoughts. See if they don't change how you feel about freedom.

You have written to me about "voluntary" simplicity. "Voluntary" is all about freedom, about making choices with free will. I have told you before you are coming to a place where you will no longer act without knowing. This all goes together, Margaret. The lessons are all intertwined. You are getting them. Don't worry. Breathe. Rest. Remember. Decide. Choose. All with love.

Peace, that place where I had nothing left to lose wasn't free.

I know, dear. Remember that these were not the only lyrics of the song. Feel good, Margaret. You have what you desire within you. Letting go of the past will set you free.

BEING WITHIN CONTENTMENT

VESSEL

Dearest Peace,   June 24, 1995
    I have been somewhat melancholy since last
    we talked. It is hard to describe the beingness I
walk around with. It is a feeling of walking on—no, not
on—but through water. A slowed down feeling, even
when I am busy and my thoughts distracted. I have been
incredibly tired, but mostly what I feel is inner calmness.

In this time of busyness, I am grateful for this sea of
calm, almost like a shield wrapped around me, although
you would probably not be pleased with the word *shield*.

I'm not sure what brought me here, tonight, to examine these feelings. I assume it is part of conscious remembering, being conscious of how I feel day to day, hour to hour. And Mary, who is developing a relationship with her angel, said that she felt he was a teaching angel and we talked about how it is like going to a counselor to examine self—much better, of course—but similar in a way that is draining even while enlightening.

You are creating space, dear one. That is what you describe, for lack of a better word, as a shield, as moving through water, as calm. Think of the eye of a hurricane. That is what the light within is like and it is inextinguishable. I take you back also to the word vessel: *1. A container (as a barrel, bottle, bowl, or cup) for holding something 2. a person held to be the recipient of a quality (as grace) 3. a craft bigger than a rowboat 4. a tube in which a body fluid (as blood or sap) is contained and circulates. Amazed, aren't you?* Vessel *was associated earlier with Mary. It was a good word for Mary. It is a good word for you now. It is almost a stage that you are at—like* threshold. *But where* threshold *implies a place,* vessel *implies a space. A space to be filled, a space to contain and circulate, a person held to be the recipient of a quality (or an angel) such as grace, and a craft to transport you. You are at this moment a vessel moving through space, creating space as you move, filling up and circulating—CIRCULATING all that you are learning and all that you are. You are a sacred vessel.*

You have felt the energy of this space reach out to others and inward to self. Moving, circulating, but always contained as within a vessel, as within the eye of the hurricane. Inextinguishable. Your body is, in a very real sense, a container, a vessel for the soul. While at the same time the soul is a vessel for the self. A container, a vessel that has all the properties of fluidity, circulation, creation, personhood, transportation. You are right to examine how you feel. It does expand your consciousness, your space.

You need not search for joy or happiness. They are there within the vessel. Sometimes, when the space of the vessel is surrounded by the hurricane, it will feel like a shield and it will be protective in nature. There will be other times the vessel will ride high through an open sea, or open space, letting wind be its propeller and its guide, gliding on top of the water, gliding on top of space with pure love and joy.

Thank you, Peace. That is all that I needed right now. Thank you so much for being here for me—like a best friend.

Thank you, sweetheart. Sweet heart.

Dearest Peace,   June 25, 1995

Mia's graduation party is over. It is a huge relief. The thunderstorms that were predicted all week came this morning. They sounded beautiful, because they waited. Mia's day was lovely, she was lovely, everything went well. Today, we have likely sold our house.

When last we spoke, I was a little disturbed or uneasy about the feelings that had come up in regard to freedom. I don't feel a real desire to pursue it at the moment, but trust that you will lead me to pursue those things necessary for me in the Now, and I am happy to do that with the issue of freedom.

Earlier, I had the feeling that Mary's angel would be called Trinity. Then I thought, perhaps her angels *are* a Trinity. So we could look at that, if you like, but I feel no burning desire there, either. I wonder if I have other angels, but I love talking to you and feel no desire for more right now, so we can talk about that or not. Then I found kind of a new good word. I had bought this very weighty book called *Being and the Between,* which is full of jargon I don't know the meaning of. I was looking up *univocal,* which isn't in the dictionary by the way, and found the word *unity.* I loved its meaning:

> 1. the quality or state of being or being made one: oneness 2. a definite quantity or combination of quantities taken as one or for which one is made to stand in calculation 3. concord, accord, harmony 4. continuity without change (~of purpose) 5. reference of all the parts of a literary or artistic composition to a single main idea 6. totality of related parts *syn* solidarity, union, integrity.

Thought I'd look up *Trinity,* too, while I was at it. Capped it means:

> 1. the unity of Father, Son, and Holy Spirit as three persons in one Godhead. 2. *not cap:* triad, a union or group of three usually closely related persons or things.

Peace, I am feeling so contented today that we can talk about anything or nothing. Nothing is leading me to questions or concerns of the Now. Yet I would like to talk to you out of a place of contentment, to thank you for your help in the events that led to this day and this feeling. I am so thankful Mia had a good day and so thankful we have a buyer for the house. I am so relieved and yet almost emotionless. I am content to be. Thank you for my beingness, for bringing me to a place where I recognize it. Thank you for the good friends and family that made up my day yesterday. For my husband and children. For the breeze that blew yesterday, for the thunderstorm that waited, for all that is.

You create as you go, sweet heart. You had as much to do with the events and the feelings as I. More. But I appreciate your appreciation. I appreciate your wanting to be with me in a place of contentedness. Smile. Breathe. Appreciate the lightness of being. It is a good starting place for more. If you want more. When you feel content and unquestioning, you are open for more and more will come to you. You are not feeling like being active now. You can see it in the things you've said and brought me. This is fine. Don't worry that I will request of you something active today. Rest. But in your rest notice what it is to Be; notice the thoughts, dreams, imaginings that come to you. What comes to you in a state of contentedness is untarnished by desires, feelings, fears, active longing. Listen in your contentment to your inner voice, however it presents itself to you. Then, when you are feeling more like looking at and seeing these things, we will discuss them. Now. Go rest. Be. You deserve it.

Thank you, sweet Peace.

Peace, I'm back. I was drawn to a book, *Mavericks of the Mind: Conversations for the New Millennium,* interviews by David Jay Brown and Rebecca McClen Novick, that has been here forever, and I read all these great things that inspired me to come back. They're all from an interview with Carolyn Mary Kleefeld.[16]

And, Peace, this woman talks about everything we just talked about in a slightly different way! She says, "Ideally, all people would develop a self-referencing point to comprehend themselves and their universe well enough to guide their own vessel with awareness." Peace, *she uses our words* and *our meanings.* Everything from *in between,* to *vessel* to *possibility* to *circulation.* But most amazing are the words you just gave me yesterday! Just yesterday you said *vessel* was a good word for the stage I am at. You said I was a vessel moving through space, and she said a new book she is writing discusses the recordings of her "own particular vessel as it rides the waves of existence." You said I was creating space, and she said art creates the space to let what's possible happen. I can't remember you ever using the word *circulating* with me before, and she says, creative expression is a "unique circulation."

She not only used words from yesterday, but words from our first conversation when she said, "The ancient codes lie in the seams *between* worlds. They only await the radiance of our conscious light to be illumined, *recognized.*" (All emphasis mine.)

Peace, I can't believe this! And suddenly I'm here wanting more. And if I can't find it here, I'll go to bed and feel the breeze and listen to the night sound and find it there. I just discovered the word *unity,* and she said, "Notice that the word 'universe' means united verses. When in harmony, life is a symphony of united verses." Peace, I know it's waiting for me! Some alternate universe. Uni-Verse. That's what it is—the something more! And knowing that I might not be able to get here and record it here is all right because I know I will find it, and even if I can't bring it back with me to me, it's okay because it's something more. What is it that makes me want to sing?

Sing! Everything is okay here.

Sing with my fingers. Fly fingers, sing fingers. . . . Weave the universe, invite it in, let it hum.

I'm with you, don't panic. Go with it.

Feel the universe. Let it all come together.

Don't analyze it—smoke it, feel it, breathe it.

What is a trip? A drug trip, a trip trip? A journey in a vessel. A vessel. Riding the waves of existence. Riding. Going moving energy feel it, pump it, circulate, ancientness, authenticity, "I feel as if I'm in touch with what I call the 'ancestral resonance.' This would be a poetic translation for receiving information from everything that's ever happened. Within one's every breath lives every beginning."[17] Beginning, circulating, pumping, ringing, singing, going, moving, pouring, soaring, learning, leaping, authoring our own lives, lives, living, sleeping, dreaming, doing, being, ISness, oneness, divineness, trinity, unity, universe, verse, vessel, More. Peace, water, bridge, dying, changing, transporting, porting, journeying, going, boing, bong, good-bye, buoy, bounty, country, earth, living, oneness, planet, pond, trees, earth, sky, water, soil, soaring, bird, life light, likeness, lightness, beingness, transforming, being, seeing, sleeping, sealing, dolphins, walking, talking, communing, lowering, rising, rising, rising, rising, higher, higher, higher, higher, higher, clouds, spirit, angels, god, god, god, god, energy, all, that, is, is, is, telling me telling me telling me god is god is god is within with in in, in, in . . .

Dear Peace,   June 26, 1995
    What happened last night and what did I do up there?

Dear Margaret,
    What happened last night and what did you do up there?

I don't know. It was a random act of senselessness.

I don't think so. Why random?

The word just occurred to me. It just happened—randomly—there was no reason for it, no design.

Why senselessly?

It did not make sense.

171

But what did you think about it?

I thought it might be some kind of primitive communication; that was what went through my head. Kind of senseless, huh?

Why? Is communication with ancients impossible? You wanted more, you wanted to approach things in a new way. You wrote what went through your head. You were not trying to make sense and you were not trying to communicate. What goes through your head? Where did those words come from? Where do thoughts come from? The brain? The mind? What is the difference between the two? How can you prove that there is a difference? How can you prove that thought comes from the brain? Maybe some thoughts come from elsewhere. And, if so, from where? Where does love come from? From the heart? The heart has been proven to be a mechanical pump. Where is proof of emotion, where is proof of unconscious? Why did your mind, this time, give you a series of words instead of sentences and paragraphs? Or wasn't it your mind? Were you talking to me? to you? or to someone else? Or was someone else talking to you?

I tell you, all of it is true and there is no proof. In your dream you were in the Alps. Can you disprove you were in the Alps? Can you prove it? Your doctor told you today dreams don't have memory. Is he right or is he wrong?

I still don't understand it.

Margaret, it simply was. Words. Words were. Words came to you and you recorded them. You had a stream of consciousness. A stream. A flow. A river. A sea. A peace of the universe, a piece, a peace. Words flow. Where from? From you. From your desire to record. Re-cord. Re-establish. Links, linkages. With all that is. Is this mysterious? Yes. It is. There will be flows you will not be able to record but they will record you. They will become part of your signature. Yourself.

Peace, I feel a need to write my impressions of what has occurred thus far. Am I trying to analyze what should not be analyzed or am I trying to synthesize?

Trying implies analysis. Trying and synthesis do not go together well. I suggest you read, digest, and then let transformation begin the synthesis. You are wanting your knowledge to come together into a philosophy, a way of being. This is transformative. This is more. Just remember to make whole rather than to fracture.

Strum, hum, sing, dance when the universe calls you to do these things. Practice, participate, play. Your fingers tried to play the keys last night. Perhaps they were just not fast enough to catch the light.

Okay, Peace. So when I feel contentment, as I did last night, I am close to a place where *more* can happen. You were right—I knew I was. Then I found this remarkable writing by this woman I'd never heard of before. It was an incredible feeling, more so than with the other things I have read. It felt like a link. What then was I supposed to do?

Feel the linkages. We are all one in the universe. You and she are linked. Link-ages. A link with the ages. It is a living universe, Margaret.

Linkage: the manner or style of being united; the quality or state of being linked; a system with links (like Xs?).

Linkages are the in between, Margaret. Trust the in between.

There is much lately about unity.

Yes. Oneness: unity. It is the goal. It is not just words, dear one. Unity is real, the linkages you feel are real. How else do you explain these words that are so close even though you never saw them before? If Carolyn had written, "I am a woman," that would be different. It would be a statement. But she was talking about discoveries along her journey. You, too, are on a journey. Perhaps they intercept, connect, link. Perhaps you share knowledge in more ways than you know. How does the mind operate? How does it come up with its words and images? Partly it is chemical, but partly it is alchemical.

I want you to imagine the possibility of there being real linkages between you and people you have never before met, such as authors of the material you have read. You do not always know why you do the things you do, but as I told you before, that is changing. Who did you write The Ninety-Seven Days *for? Perhaps for someone you are linked with though you do not know it. There are forces at work in the living universe that cause you to be the instrument and the musician. One day you are playing for all the world to hear, one day you are playing for one other to hear, one day you are being played. And always there are ripple effects. You may right now be writing this as part of a divine plan that will awaken the divine music in another. Nothing you do is without purpose. That you don't always know the purpose is part of being alive. Part of being. But I say again, you will not much longer act without knowing why you act. You are becoming conscious.*

Yes. I am becoming aware. More some days than others.

With awareness comes intentional acting; not cumbersome, not pro-grammed actions, but acting with knowing your intent, your purpose, for what it is you prepare.

What about avoidance? I find myself so often avoiding even things I know I should do or should want to do.

What you call avoidance may be procrastination, it may be not doing something you do not want to do, or it may be avoiding the dance, it may be holding back, it may be turning away from the recurring verse you need to hear to be free. Know the difference. Know yourself. Relax. You are doing fine. You cannot force more to come. But it will come.

Thank you, Peace. I love you.

CONNECTION

July 1, 1995

I cannot believe it is July. My busy season at work. The final month in this home—no longer truly mine. The last month I will write at this desk in this small corner of this universe of my old home. And yet the feeling I have today, that I have had virtually all day, is one of sweet contentment. I am aware of how "right" things have gone for me, and I am so truly grateful and so truly blessed. I feel, in a very real sense, that things have gone "right" because of the journey I am on, because of my being open to possibilities, because of my new inner calm. I feel just as certain things cannot always be so "right," but it's wonderful—full of wonder—this notion that my own "rightness" has caused the "rightness around me." I know I have not chosen the correct word here, Peace, but I thank you again and again, that I have found my way to this place, this day, this contentment in this moment of time or beyond time. This Nowness.

Our last conversation led me directly to *The Tibetan Book of Living and Dying,* by Sogyal Rinpoche. It led me to a course of expanding my connections, my living connections, to encompass those of great spiritual teachers. And it has led me to a study of meditation—of, as the author says, bringing the mind home. *Home.* Now there is a word of many meanings. None of which I will bother to look up in my contented state of mind.

I have done good work today: I have come home and taken a shower and put on my most comfortable clothes. I have bought a bottle of wine. And whatever happens tonight, I am content to be with. I suspect, however, that I will be back.

July 2, 1995

How can I describe the experience of last night with any

words other than pure contentment? My husband, my mate, my love, and I sat on the porch talking, touching. We were content together and if it was for one night, it was enough. We talked much of the new house and some of the old, and then he, sweet romantic, put on *our song,* "Always and Forever," and we made love while the fireworks sounded in the background from Taste of Minnesota. It could have been a movie scene but it was my own.

When we had parted from our lovemaking, Jimmy Buffett came on the stereo, this man my husband identifies with and plays so often that his music feels like background music to my life. It was vintage Jimmy we sat and listened to from the porch. And Donny came out with a gem of wisdom about complaining. He talked about how people didn't used to complain all the time and how it is only fashionable, today, to complain, and this is why people do it; and how he would hope to change that fashion in the people close to us. Perhaps it is our joint mission: to make it fashionable to be content and joyous!

Then, still on the porch, still sitting quietly, he said, "We should go to church tomorrow." He was so right, so wise, for we have been letting work on the house interfere with church. And Father talked about the miracle of Jesus filling the nets of the fishermen, and how He called us all to be His disciples to net men, to bring them the light, the news, the word. And Father talked of how we all have a

177

mission—we just have to find what it is! It was lovely.

And now, today, I get to spend time with my sister. And I get to put money down on my furniture, furniture that came to me as if it were meant to—the furniture that I had cut out of the paper and hung over my desk as my dream furniture. And it just occurs to me now that this is what was said in *Ask Your Angel*. To make a visualization of what you want. I did. And it came to me. At 50 percent off, at a price I could afford. And it cannot even be delivered until after July 31, the exact date of our moving. How can I be grateful enough? I almost fear how well things are going, but I will not allow myself to entertain this fear.

I tried to meditate on the porch before my husband joined me, and when I sat in alignment, it felt right, like a posture I was coming home to. And I realized instantly the meaning of carrying meditation into your *samsara,* your real life, as my husband joined me and we touched and talked and had mostly silence and love between each other.

I know good things are coming to me as I open my mind and heart to goodwill. And if bad things were coming to me, as I'm sure they will one day, perhaps I can remember this time and never let them shake my inner content. Thank You, Lord. Thank you, Peace!

July 4, 1995

The most important things coming to me are the teachings in the books I am led to read. I just read, for instance, in *The Tibetan Book of Living and Dying,* about *bardo. Bardo* is a Tibetan word that simply means a "transition" or a gap between the completion of one situation and the onset of another. *Bar* means "in between," and *do* means "suspended" or "thrown." In between! The natural bardo of this life encompasses the whole period between birth and death—making the period between birth and death a "transition." It says this life is one of constant suspense and ambiguity and that this constant uncertainty contains, by its very nature, gaps, spaces in which profound changes and opportunities for transformation are continuously flowering—if, that is, they can be seen and seized.[18]

I feel I have been led to this book in order to better understand the in between with which you originally introduced yourself to me, and perhaps me to myself. Is it possible that I am currently in one of the natural gaps, in a space between this life and the next, this life being the one of my first forty years and the next the one of the upcoming forty? That I am in a natural bardo state in which profound changes and opportunities for transformation are presenting themselves?

I am only your guide, Margaret. I cannot reveal your life story. You are creating it every day by everything you do. But can you doubt that you are in a state of transformation? Are there not things about you that will never be the same as they were last February? Or even yesterday? Who is to say that it was not the insight that you were in a phase of passage that brought you to me and to the readings initially?

You may see that I am less willing to answer questions—if so, it is only that the questions you ask are growing more farsighted. In the state when your questions are farsighted, your most appropriate counselor is your own heart. You are approaching the phase of synthesis, in which you are to put together all you have learned. Look at the wisdom and insight of your recent writings. They are the goal. What comes from within is the goal.

As my guide, Peace, what then is your role?

To show you the in between so that you can see what can be found there, so that you can learn what is to be learned there, so that you can integrate your knowledge into a whole. You are not outgrowing me but you are becoming ready for more.

Is there another guide, Peace, who is working with me or who will work with me through this next stage of synthesis and transition to wholeness?

There are many, many guides, dear one.

I only ask, Peace, because of this feeling that something new is coming, something different, something to help me with the next stages of my study with meditation and with becoming more fully conscious and because I can't imagine what this something new *Is.* You keep telling me the time is coming when I will no longer act without knowing why I act—perhaps the biggest compliment you could pay me—and I know it will only come with my ability to remain conscious in the present, with my ability to stop and think before I act.

Not to stop and think. To always have an inner knowing that guides you—part of which is me. And it will come from always being conscious of what guides you—part of which is me, but the much larger part is your open heart. It is the integrating of wisdom into a self which is able to accomplish this constant open beingness that you are wondering about. It is the infinite possibilities of this next stage that excite you even in your calm core.

There are two things going on here. One, this something more you seek is within yourself. Two, you are uniquely suited to this means of communication. It comes naturally to you. Meditate to quiet your mind. Come here to express it. Don't get the two mixed up.

You see the light of the computer reflecting back to you—and I tell you, you reflect back to it. Do not mess with this, do not mix it up. You see the smoke hit the reflection and dissipate. This is what your spirit guides are like. A consciousness joined with your own, not separate, not the same. You are the vessel that contains the consciousness. Like a clear glass of water, it can be seen through, but that does not make the water any less real or the glass any less a container or the liquid any less fluid or thirst quenching. If you think of yourself as this clear glass vessel and your spirit guides as being contained within, unseeable, or see-through-able, does this help?

It reminds me a little of the Buddhist description of karma as the consciousness that remains between one life and the next. It is not the individual, not each memory, but the piece of ourselves we only catch glimpses of—the true consciousness (which I am hoping to develop) that continues. The essence. In this sense, then, of your being part of my consciousness, you could be part of the former self?

This is true in a way. Would it be within your ability to understand that you might have a spirit guide who was once yourself? Would it be beyond your understanding to realize that all beings are part of self? The concept of reincarnation accepts that the consciousness, the mind wisdom of a great teacher, may become the mind wisdom of another great teacher, a teacher who has all the wisdom from this life and, within his or her consciousness, all the wisdom of past lives as well.

Is this why I am struggling with concepts of rebirth? Because I am afraid of the consciousness I have brought forward from past lives, afraid of that pain or humiliation or failure?

If there were those things, could you not learn from them? Can you not cease to fear them? Let fear go. The more you seek cannot get through the barrier of fear or self-denial. Accept all of self—past selves and future selves, then you will be ready to know your other spirit guides. Go and rest and contemplate—what can you not accept? When your answer is nothing, when you are open to all that is—to truth—then we will go forward in search of more. It is a great discovery—a great journey—if you let go of your fear.

SERENITY

Dearest Peace,   July 6, 1995
     Mary used a good word for what I felt most of
the day today: *serenity.* Then as the day wore on, the
serenity was pierced by tension. I came home and felt
serenity again, and then an argument with Angela
pierced it again. I have not yet, in the throes of tension,
learned how to pull myself back to the place of serenity.
Can you help me see the way to do this?

The way to do this is to come to all situations from your place of seren-
ity and, when you notice your serenity leaving, call it back. The point is
to notice it when you have it and to notice it when it is leaving. Are

*there times when you should not be serene? No. This does not mean that
from a place of serenity you cannot argue, but you can argue without
losing what you have if you notice that what you have is leaving. Like a
friend whose helping hand rests on your shoulder, notice serenity, and
notice when the hand is removed. Ask it to return. It will return. You
simply have not yet remembered, in times of stress, because you need to
practice.*

*You are becoming better at controlling the stressful situations you
encounter when you are alone, but you are not practicing when you are
with people. You let the energy of the other person pull you from your
place of serenity, like someone shoving away that helpful hand that
rests, RESTS, on your shoulder. That hand is not guiding you or pushing you. It is at rest with you. Calm and placid, something like the
brick propping open the door to your heart. Inactive yet accomplishing
its mission. You have many times visualized your open heart. Now visualize your helping hand as well.*

Thank you, Peace. I know this will help. But what can
help me with the aftereffects of tension that settle in my
stomach and so are carried into the future even when I
would like to return to serenity?

*I would like to tell you to meditate, but I know you are having trouble
finding a sacred place in which to do this. So first, I will tell you to
make a sacred place in which to do this. Make space for it. You cannot
go on forever hiding your spiritual journey. There is a fear that keeps it
under wraps and a habit of keeping yourself under wraps. A habit that
brings you some self-satisfaction, like your smoking. You use smoking to
take a break. You can use meditation also. Quit kidding yourself that*

smoking and break-taking are private things no one knows about—you know they are not. Start thinking, at least, of letting your family in on your secret. It is not something to be ashamed of, and sharing it will not make it less personal. More is more. The more you share, the more you will get back. This is an important lesson about "more" that you need to know and that you need to act upon.

Thank you, Peace. I needed to be reminded of those things, also. It is hard to imagine how I will be in the new home, and I know that how I will be is my own choice and my own making. If I state that I want to meditate every morning in peace, my family will respect my wishes. If I choose a "place" to smoke, my family will accept it. I am still afraid to ask—to make my wishes known.

You were once afraid to make your wishes regarding furnishing your new home known, also. Sometimes wishes come true to show you that wishes come true—if you let them be known. It is like the joke about the man who prays to win the lottery and when he confronts God after many times of not winning, God says, "You could at least have bought a ticket." Contrary to what you believe—or you wouldn't act the way you do—your mind cannot be read, your desires cannot become a burden on others, whether they are known or whether they are not known. Ask and you shall receive. Remember this. And ask. Not just here, not just God, but there—with your family and friends, in your life. Let others bring you joy. More is more. What is brought to you, you will return.

GUARDIAN ANGELS

July 9, 1995

I have been feeling as if the more I search for a "way" and a "method" to reach enlightenment, the farther I am getting from it. Then I read in *Healing Words,* by Larry Dossey, a little story about the writer Natalie Goldberg. Apparently, she had a Buddhist master, Katagiri Roshi, here in Minneapolis with whom she had studied for years. Then she moved away, did a lot of writing, and came back to see him. She asked him for more lessons and he said, "Don't be so greedy." He said, "Writing is taking you very deep. Continue to write." She said, "But Roshi, it is so lonely." And he asked, "Is there anything wrong with loneliness?"[19] He admitted that he was lonely too, and that the point was not to let loneliness get in the way, that anything we do deeply causes loneliness. It just is what is and must be accepted.

I had been reading *The Tibetan Book of Living and Dying* and put it away in favor of *Healing Words*—possibly because the strongest message of the *Tibetan* book is that you can't approach spirituality with a shop-around mentality. You have to find what works with and for you and stick with it.

I did not take this to mean that I should not read, explore, investigate, but I came away with the feeling that I have what I need: writing and Catholicism. I think back to how Thomas Moore and Joseph Campbell and James Hillman started me on my quest by touching something in me that resonated, something that felt profound and right. And how glad I was that these teachers were of my faith. Even many of my favorite quotes from other books were from monks, saints, and Christian contemplatives. Even if it does feel lonely sometimes, I think the moral of the Natalie Goldberg story, as it applies to me, is that my spiritual quest is what it is and I need to accept it. That I know what is right for me: my religion and my writing.

Perhaps they are one and the same.

Yes. Thank you, Peace. Perhaps they are. I guess I *know* that there is no place where I am closer to the divine than here—right here—with you, but not just because of you. Because here is where my higher consciousness speaks. I am not ruling out meditation or any other form in pursuit of enlightenment, I am only opening myself up to the possibility that my meditation takes place here, in the pauses, perhaps.

Oh, yes. You are finding what is right for YOU! You are taking the leap into personal realization.

And I am seeing that I can have desires and have them met. I have furniture, drapes, towels: I am building the house of my dreams, as part of a team with my husband, who is honoring my desires because I have made them known to him, because I decided what I wanted, because I let my desires be known to me. I am beginning to make decisions, to know myself well enough to make decisions. Where furniture might have seemed a simple thing before, it suddenly is not. Or to rephrase that, furniture is simple, but building a home that honors my desires, honors my family, is a holy task—which makes the furniture, the drapes, the towels, a blessing. I am thankful for each piece, from washcloth to couch. And I realize that this is the way it should be. This is how we should live. The spiritual journey is becoming the life journey, part of every facet, every decision, every waking hour and in the hours of dreams.

I was just looking something up in my *Lives of the Saints* book and found the term *Guardian Angel* and the fact that October is the month of Angels and the Rosary. I did not know this before. The feast day of Guardian Angels is October 2. My book says:

The angels are pure spirits endowed with a natural intelligence, will, power and beauty, far surpassing the nature, faculties and powers of man. The angels number millions and thousands of millions around the throne of God; praising Him and serving Him as messengers and ministers, and as guardians of men on earth. . . .

Those blessed spirits who are appointed by God to be protectors and defenders of men are called Guardian Angels. Faith teaches us that each individual has a Guardian Angel who watches over him during the whole course of his life. It is also a generally accepted doctrine that communities, the Church, dioceses, and nations also have their tutelary angels. The Guardian Angels . . . endeavor to keep us in the right path: if we fall they help us to rise again, encourage us to become more and more virtuous, suggest good thoughts and holy desires, offer our prayers and good actions to God; and, above all, assist us at the hour of death.

Prayer: O God, who in Your unspeakable Providence have deigned to send

Your holy angels to watch over us, grant
Your suppliant people to be always
defended by their protection, and to
rejoice in their companionship forever
more. Amen.[20]

Ah, Peace. There it is. My own religion telling me exactly
what I have found in you. And what a lovely prayer, to
ask to *rejoice* in your *companionship* forevermore. Ma would
be happy that I have made use of her little book. The
Word, being passed down generation to generation. This
is such wonderful permission—and it was here all along.
As you were here all along! As my religion, my faith, was
here all along! That you endeavor to keep me on the right
path. *Yes.* That when I fall you help me rise up. *Yes.* That
you encourage me to become more virtuous. *Yes!* That
you suggest good thoughts, *yes* and *yes* again. That you
suggest holy desire. What were we just talking about? *Yes!*
Peace, you are my guardian angel?

Yes, dear, I am your guardian angel.

I am even learning, Peace, not to balk at words like *suppliant*—inactive words that I used to think implied lack of
will and weakness. I now know they mean the opposite. I
now understand what surrendering to a higher will
means. It means to be!

You have been a good pupil, Margaret.

You have opened my mind and my heart. I am eternally

grateful, and I am beginning to think that eternally means eternally.

It does, dear one.

There is so much more I need to learn. Somehow I am certain you will lead to where I can find.

All paths lead to home. All wisdom comes from within. Together we will find your wisdom, layer by layer. Think of wisdom as the petals of a rose. You have been collecting them. Why? Outside of time and space you knew they would connect to your journey. Your layers of wisdom, like shades that block the sun, are being peeled away. Now you might think—peeled away *implies "getting rid of." It is good imagery because much of wisdom is indeed getting rid of*—*getting rid of those things that block your ability to see and be.*

And Angela started the rose petal collecting.

You know she is a visible link for you to view the connectedness of the universe. The two of you can be in tune enough to speak without language. This is not a great accomplishment, however. The great accomplishment is in seeing that as you and Angela are connected, all are connected. As deep as your compassion flows for your children, the world is like your children and your compassion will be as deep as the river. Your prayers are your thoughts and your thoughts come now from a place of knowing within. Your thoughts, thus, when compassionate breed compassion, when angry breed anger. It is very important for you to remember not to act, think, speak without knowing. The days when you did so were like your adolescence. These days are not days so much when you are grown up, when you are big, but when you are open. And just as you are

191

*open to receive, you are open to give. Try sending a message of calmness
and peace to your spirit sisters. Write it below and see what comes of it.*

To Julie—as we prepare for our students' arrival, do let
go of worry, do let go of fear, do let go of rushing, do trust
that you can depend on people, that people love you and
will not judge you. Be. Be in a state of calm restfulness.
Feel your breath come more freely. Feel the tense muscles that hang on let go. Let love embrace you. Believe in
love, including the love of your father. Let it soothe you.

To Mary—as you gave me the word *serenity,* let serenity
now rest on your shoulder. Give yourself permission to
suspend judgment, to be in a place of serene restfulness
with the events of last summer. Let Grace rest within
your heart as she rested in your womb. Be her gentle
mother. Take care of yourself as if you still, in taking care
of yourself, are taking care of her.

May you both bring your restful calmness, your quiet
breathing, your belief in self, with you into our busy season. May you think of it as a time of connection with your
spirit sisters and so with your spirit. May you view these
coming days with an attitude of "what will be will be and
all will be as it should be." Let us all turn from the illusion
of control and let go and Be. Amen.

LIVING IN A WORLD OF PLENTY

We're two days into our on-campus session and there have been two miracles. The first, and I say "first" because it happened to me, was this: I asked Donny to get me one hundred dollars to use as change for student fees because I had forgotten to stop at the bank. I needed the one hundred dollars to be in fives. He said, "The cash machine doesn't give fives." And I know he saw himself running around to different stores exchanging the money he got from the cash machine for five-dollar bills. But the cash machine gave him twenty five-dollar bills. The second miracle was that Mary's step-daughter, Amanda, saw Grace. She saw a toddler sitting in a chair in the backyard and saw her vanish into white light.

I came tonight to have a conversation like we used to have, when you did more of the talking than me! I've been hogging the white space lately! I came without questions in mind. Now I wonder if the miracles are the question. I believe my miracle was the same as the miracle of the furniture and the drapes and the house and all the good things that have been happening to me in my new state of openness. Mary's miracle is different, and perhaps it is hers to hold to her heart and not for me to examine. I just wondered if there was anything you wanted to share about them.

Mary's miracle, like your miracle, is one of the open heart. These are the only kinds of miracles. The Grace miracle was a miracle of love. Grace allowed this miracle to happen through the open door of their love for each other. It happened through Amanda to bond Amanda and Mary with love. Love creates miracles as love creates the universe. It is just that the universe is such a large concept. Does believing that everything is one make it a smaller concept? Are small miracles not miracles?

I get so nervously excited when you tell me things like this that all thought seems to leave my mind.

Your mind is the conduit. Its flow will not always be even. You are not an electric company, after all. You are a dear, open heart.

This makes me think of my dear husband and how when

194

I have been too tired to give him physical love, I have tried to telepathically send him spiritual love, a love I send from the open door of my heart, outward like a wave of light. Does this have effect? Does he feel my love?

Why not ask him instead of me? All love goes out like waves of light. Your visualization only intensifies it, directs it. Try directing it into the universe sometime. Try directing it to the trees and sky. Try opening up even wider—to the all that is. Experiment, practice, and above all have fun. Take joy in giving love—in sending love. You've been thinking a lot about your Aunt Alva. Sending her your love. I won't tell you she knows this, but I tell you that you cross her mind as she crosses yours. Think about it. Crossed minds.

My very first book, a book about Grandmother Ivie, was going to be called *By Heart*—for the process we have of committing things to memory, to remembering. It just struck me, the profundity of those words in the new scheme of my wider understanding. *By Heart* and *crossed minds*. They are very similar. Word symbols that almost give me goose bumps.

Your words. In the beginning there was the Word. You are on the right track, the right path, with your words. You are using them as they were meant to be used: as symbols to express the divine. Words are nothing more than miracles of the mind.

They don't compete with silence do they?

Silence without words can be complete understanding or the totality of loss. Silence is silence. Words are words. There is no competing.

195

When there is competing, as there was at work today, what is the best way to deal with it?

It takes two to compete. If you do not compete, it will not touch you. Your stumbling block away from serenity is people. It is true for many others. Monks withdraw for this reason. Serenity is easier in alone time. Easier is not always better. Practice carrying serenity on your shoulder. Soon it will just be—not easier, not better—it will just be. The goal is to Be.

Healing Words, by Larry Dossey, talked about how surrender is very active—because it has to be done again and again—and about how different it is from giving up. Do you have anything to tell me about surrender? Is that what I'm doing? Is it like having the courage to change the things you can and the wisdom to know the difference?

Your inner view is what creates change. In a constantly changing world, what is change but the status quo, the norm? Efforts to make change are thus a contradiction. You live in change. The only moment is Now. How you view the Now is how the Now will be. HOW YOU VIEW THE NOW IS HOW THE NOW WILL BE. You have felt this. To have experienced this is to know reality. If you surrender to the Now with love in your open heart, you are very close to home indeed.

Peace, is my next step still to find joy?

Are you not finding it? Do you not recognize it? It is not something profound you seek. Do not go on looking. Look within. Open the door to your feelings, smile! rejoice! This moment is joy! Let it fill you.

I am kind of a circumspect individual, Peace. You are right that I have joy in my life. I don't have to be exuberant about it, do I?

You can't clutch it to yourself, either, sweet heart. If you clutch it to yourself and bury it back within, you will smother it. Let it out! There will always be more. You can let it out quietly, sweetly, with your sweet smile, with your kindness. But you can't clutch it to your chest and say, "I have joy now and it's mine, all mine." That is not the nature of joy any more than it is the nature of love. Feel your joy and let it radiate out from you the way you are letting love radiate out from you to your husband. Don't be a miser. Remember to leave all those collecting-of-resources ideas behind you. It is not the furniture that will make the home. It is the love. You cannot collect joy and love and miracles and hold them to yourself. You can only let them be in the moment. The miracles are there to bring you joy to bring the world. Share, sweet heart, share.

A part of me is still fearful of all the good things that have been coming my way. If I were to get a publisher now, all my dreams would be coming true. It is almost as if so much good has happened, I don't dare wish for more, and I fear something bad will happen to balance the scales.

Forget scales! Forget balance! Forget limits! The universe wants you to be happy! Go ahead, be happy! Don't let fear tap you on the shoulder with its whispers of "bad follows good." HOW YOU VIEW THE MOMENT IS HOW THE MOMENT WILL BE. There will be difficulties. There will be struggles. It is not as if you haven't had them now. You are very busy. You have money worries. You have all the difficulties of a normal, busy life, and more. And yet you have miracles and joy! You do not need perfection. There is no perfection in the duality. There is no need to fear.

I cannot repeat strongly enough—the universe, the all that is, wants you to be happy, wants you to realize you live in a universe of plenty. You are doing your part now to make it so. And so it is. Forget change. In your world, nothing lasts forever. Enjoy the Now. When fear taps your shoulder, tell it your shoulder is already occupied with serenity and tell it to move on. There will be challenges that test your serenity, big ones and little ones. But you will be ready for them. Your happiness is safe. It is your time to become safe in the world. Trust this. Trust each moment to be what it will be.

July 17, 1995

I have been away too long. Today I only want to say hello, to say thank you, to say how glad I am you are with me throughout the day, to say thank you for the gift of consciousness which helps me remember that I am a being of love. Thank you, too, for your last message. It is often not until I review my messages that I see how dear they are to me.

Mary, who is now communicating with her angel frequently, has talked with me about this need to review messages. One or the other of us is always coming in and saying, "I got a great message last night," but unless we have it printed out, we can't remember quite what it was, or at least can't *convey* what it was. We both have to go back to the written words to repeat them to ourselves without the interaction. It's as if we really "get it" when we're in the midst of it, but then, until it is reviewed, all we can say is that we "got it." We can't explain what it was we "got." It's as if when we're receiving the messages, we're caught in the power of it all and it all makes sense and it's all wonderful. And yet afterwards, we are left kind of drained—sometimes a joyous drained, sometimes a melancholy drained, sometimes a hopeful drained, but almost always *drained!*

Often, I feel as if I expect too much. Sometimes when I ask something of you, I do not feel, initially, as if you have given me a very clear answer. But when I review your answer later, I recognize that you have given me the only answer, the answer that is perfect for me. Not, perhaps, the answer I wanted. But the *answer.*

Often I await profound wisdom, complex wisdom, instead of being satisfied with the simple. And yet the simple is so profound. Like your telling me that it is my time to be safe in the world or to trust each moment. These are profound simple gifts and truths that I can't be grateful enough for. Thank you for all my messages, for me and for others. Help me to combat things like jealousy, envy, tiredness, competitiveness in my work and my relationships. Thank you in advance. I love you.

Hello, Margaret, and good night. Remember to rest and to smile and to be open. You have much to learn from this wider experience of people and cultures. Don't limit yourself. Don't forget to be open. Don't be afraid to ask. Seek and you will find. Honor your work and it will honor you.

TRANSITIONS

July 20, 1995

I have been very busy but busyness has not diminished my desire to concentrate on this spirituality. The spirit sisters are beginning to plan a day together away from work, and the mere thought of a day to spend together sounds like a feast, a banquet. It seems an amazing thing that has happened to us. Three ordinary women. Three middle-class, married, working, struggling women, about as different, other than as women, as we can be. It may be that we have the ideal environment for what is going on. It may be that wishing for a more ideal environment is folly. Yet I've had recurring dreams of a retreat house.

Perhaps it is your own home—your new home—that will be a retreat for you and for others.

Is there anything you can tell me about the coming direction of things?

I can tell you not to push for a direction. Go with the flow. Rest. Rejuvenate. More is coming. The move is the beginning.

Is there some way I should ritualize the move? Make it a thing of ceremony and beauty?

You will. It is one of your strengths. You will not forget the importance of this time. Look for beauty. When you have a choice, choose beauty. And do not be hurried into acting without thinking. Let ideas flow. But rest and rejuvenate before acting.

July 21, 1995

As our moving day approaches, I live more in the future than in the present. Even disregarding the move, it is the future my thoughts are drawn to. What will be important to me in the coming months? Writing? Learning? Traveling? Homemaking? I had an idea of writing for a grant, using this piece of work I have created with you as a means to request time for a sabbatical for me and Mary and Julie, perhaps with a guide, to show the world what three ordinary women can do and become.

I may not speak overly much of the spirit sisters here

but you know that it is because what happens here also happens there—at the office—when I am with them. It is as if here "it" happens on this computer with *you*, and there "it" happens in conversation, in sharing what has happened here, in *being* together with *them.* As if they are the divine manifested in my daily life.

I think of so many things, all bounded by time, bounded by the job, the move, the trip. I will go with the flow, but I also know these ideas are occurring for a reason. I know ideas are one of the things I need to let flow. I am surprised at how often my ideas are about *us,* as in the spirit sisters, rather than just about *me.* I am more certain than ever that what is happening with *me* is bound up in what is happening with *us.*

My biggest fear, whether about me or us, is that I will not act when the time is right for acting. Time again. I was getting away from time, Peace, and now I am being drawn back in. Some of which I know is the result of the busyness of work. Can you tell me how I will know when the time is right, when I need to act? It is hard to get my ideas around being and letting go and going with the flow and still seizing opportunity. Will opportunity be going with the flow? As I move away from things of the mind to things of action, the concepts we have discussed become less real to me, more ephemeral. Or perhaps it is only being away from you.

Or perhaps it is only being away from you. Remember to ask, Where am I here? Where am I in this moment? In this flow? Yes, you have to

202

live your life, do your busy work, but you do not have to do it on automatic pilot. Being aware in the moment will bring richness to the moment, will make the opportunities present themselves, will let you see them. Will let you seize them or them seize you. If you do not act without thinking, you will not act wrong. But revise your idea of thinking. Thinking is not planning. Thinking is not simply ideas. Thinking is understanding. Thinking is knowing self. Think of thinking as being aware of the moment. Being aware of what you are doing. Being aware of what you are preparing for.

What you are feeling is the end of much preparation and the beginning of a time of doing. Thinking about how to do what you will do will not necessarily help you. Think more about why. Make choices. Do not act on automatic. Act from the heart and the gut. Move, flow, from one thing to the next with love. And as you do, there will be choices that present themselves to you. You do not know that you will be working the same job next year, so why worry about it? You can know only today, and even today is not meant to be worried over. Remember while you do things why you do them, do them voluntarily or choose not to do them. Feel yourself flow with the moment.

Thank you, Peace. More later.

Yes, dear. MORE later.

July 23, 1995

Dear Peace,

I have not had a profound experience of you in quite some time. I have not used candles or incense to invoke a mood, and I have not had time alone in which to approach you. I am now alone for a few minutes, and I would like to return, in feeling, to the closeness and mysteriousness of our earlier encounters. That this form of communication comes easily to me does not, in my heart, make it right that it should come to feel commonplace and devoid of mystery. I ask you once again, with the sincerity of a beginner, of a seeker, to come to me and be with me and speak with me. Not out of any great desire for answers, but out of a great desire for a feeling of the divine to once again come over me.

I have reviewed thoughts in my journals from my past, from a me I can still identify with but who is not the me of today, a me who felt empty and alone, a me who struggled to survive and who searched for reasons to survive and for some cessation of the emptiness. You have filled me, Peace. I went to church today. I heard about the path and about the few who find light in the darkness. Your light has filled my emptiness, yet I return at moments to a loneliness perhaps inherent to being a human being. It is from this reminder of emptiness, from this reminder of longing, from this reminder of loneliness that I call upon you. Will you join me once again, dear Peace, and as my Guardian Angel bring me good thoughts and help me rejoice in your companionship?

Stay steadfast, Margaret, in your turning toward the light. There may be a time to visit the place of emptiness you once knew, but this is not the time. To remember loneliness, to experience loneliness is a primal place, a place of beginnings. You seek a return to the mystery of beginnings. Every day is a beginning. But you need not return to primal aloneness. You have experienced the light of oneness. I am with you. You will never be alone again.

Thank you, Peace. Thank you for bringing me out of the primal beginnings.

To the path. Together you and I have identified the path. A simple path. A path of love and Nowness.

And of communication?

And of a communication deeper than communication. To communion. To union. Out of the duality of beginnings into the in between of union and connectedness. You wanted, today, a reminder of connectedness. You wanted a respite from your human path of busyness. Here it is! You do not always have to rejoice in an active way in our companionship. Quiet communion is companionship of a higher level.

Thank you, sweet Peace. I have wanted to lay my head down in weariness.

To be comforted. To be quiet. To pause in the in between. I know, dear one. Pause. Relax. Ask and it shall be granted. Seek and you will find.

Will you help me find some quiet in the busyness of the Now? Can you assist me in ridding myself of this cough that must sap some of my strength? Will you show me the will of the higher power?

Good girl. Ask and ask. Ask as much as you like. There is no formula I haven't given you. There are no instructions you do not already have. But when you ask, you become open to receive. Do not be afraid to ask.

I am about to move and I will need to contact my agent, Dan O. I have been afraid to ask him for an update, fearing, of course, that he will say go find another agent. I guess I want to ask you to assure me that this will not be his response. But I won't do that. I do ask you to guide me in my communication with him and to guide him in his communication with me. Can you do that?

I hear all your requests and my hopes are your hopes within the path you are bound to travel. Why not tell Dan there is More? He cannot read your mind. Your writing is your truth. Do not be afraid to ask regarding it. Do not be afraid.

Which "more" do I tell him about, Peace?

Simply tell him there is More and let his response guide you. Put your feelers out. Be receptive. See what comes. You will not have to struggle for what is coming next. It will happen. It will flow. If you let it. If you let the universe provide for you, it will return the love you are trying to give. Approach all you do now with your open heart and with your awareness so that you do not act without understanding why you act, what your purpose is, what you prepare for. Then the best that can come to you to fulfill your destiny will come. Pray. Ask. Love. Release.

July 28, 1995

I was thinking about how little I have read lately that resonated within me, and thus, how little I have had to bring to you in regard to thought-provoking questions. I feel in some ways you have dodged my questions regarding my "writing life," despite your reassurances that what goes on here is good and is truth. I have taken this to mean that you refuse to predict my future. But if you can offer me guidance at this time, I would appreciate it. As I just wrote in a letter to Dan, the move is a time of new beginnings and although I do not foresee myself moving in and sitting down to write within the week or maybe even the month, I am hopeful for a direction to present itself to me.

Write what you are compelled to write. Follow your bliss. This is where you will feel the rewards of your writing. Do not think of writing and outcome together. When you think of outcome, your writing will not come from the heart. I have and will continue to advise you—do all you do from the place of your open heart and you will be rewarded. Inspiration will come. Inspiration—to breathe into, to breathe life into. New home, new life, new breath, new inspiration. Leave worry behind like the old home. If you leave worry behind, inspiration will come and with it its own rewards.

Dear Peace,   July 29, 1995

The girls are at the Maronite convention in St. Louis, my busy season is over, Donny is not home from work, we close on the new home in two days. It is time to pack. Perhaps even this computer. It is time to leave behind this corner, this dark, damp, basement room that has given me so much light. I am overwhelmed by the tasks ahead of me and that is why I think of packing my computer earlier than is precisely necessary. I think of this because the time for contemplation here, at this site, is drawing quickly to a close. I am entering a time of action, of packing and cleaning and physically relocating. And while this computer is here, I am drawn to it and to you.

Just this afternoon I had a Grace experience and was able to share it with Mary. I was standing on the loading dock smoking and thinking about a student's presentation on the ethics of keeping children born with serious health problems alive to have a quality of life most of us would think is not worth living. The student had brought doctors in to visit one such home for these children to make them ask themselves if sending a patient home alive was always the most important thing. And I was thinking of telling Mary about this when a brilliant yellow butterfly swooped down before me. I believed it was Grace or a message from Grace.

In this busy time, I have been far from experiences of Grace. But I am at an open place at this moment, in which truly anything can happen. I am without a plan of how to pack and how to move and what to do first, second, and third. Part of me wants badly to devise such a plan, just as I have come here to announce that this will be the last time we talk in this place even when it may not be. I am in a state of suspended animation, even with you, struggling to envision how things will continue. In a week, where will I go to be with you in communication?

And yet while I say I am open, I know that a part of me is not. I do not come here with the open mind and heart of the woman who has been writing to you for so long. I do not know what has happened; perhaps there are expectations where there were none before, fear where there was no fear. For in this state of transition, where and when everything is changing as you have assured me it does moment by moment, all of the time, I am anxious and uncertain. I welcome any message you have for me. I welcome especially the feeling of you. Please come to me in the in between of this time, this time that I am grateful for and yet fearful of.

Hope. Go back to your readings on hope. To your writings. Hope is possibility. Limitless possibility. Your new home will be what you make it, not with a plan and a list but with an open heart. And not only your new home. Your new you. Remember, you are a child of God. Your possibilities are as endless as life itself. Let your spirits rise like smoke, like hope. Feel the lightness of being that comes over you. Smile. Laugh. Be happy. This is truth. When people say "true happiness," this is of what they speak. You have little experience with true happiness. You will have none if you do not lighten up. True happiness is a reward you cannot turn your back on and cover with anxiety. All those times Felicia said, jokingly, "I can tell you're really happy" when you were showing no signs of it, are an example. Let yourself be happy. Let yourself be. Let yourself go. Let go. Shed yourself of fear. Shed yourself of worry. You know things will get done. Allow yourself this.

Your landscape will change. Like life after life, you will still be you. What do you want to be? The essence of you. The real you. The you who has an open heart. Go to the center, the circle, the boundlessness of who you are. To the peace. Go forward from a place of peace. Leave anxiety behind. I will help you and I will be with you. Think Peace is with me *whenever your anxiety awakens. Is this not the Now you have hoped for? Your busy season is over, the move begins.*

It never occurred to me before, Peace, but when you just reminded me to tell myself, "Peace is with me," I thought of my dad and how, when I was growing up, he was always saying, "Peace be with you." It sounds so prophetic now it makes me want to cry. My dad, my earthly dad, telling me all my life, "Peace be with you." And here you are. With me. Part of me. As I'm sure you have been all my life though I did not know it. It makes me feel better as I get ready to begin. I just have to get started. Once the journey is embarked upon, it will move forward on its own.

You have embarked on the most important journey of your life, the journey to the center of the self. All other journeys are a matter of putting one foot in front of the other. Believing you are safe. That you will be on solid ground. Only the spiritual journey requires you to leap. To leave the solid ground behind.

But my journeys are combined. Intertwined. A web. How do I leap across the precipice on the one hand, and take small steps on the other?

One is human life, one is divine, the web is the in between. Think of the in between as being where Peace resides. A foot in both worlds, with Peace in between.

And Peace is both you and a feeling.

And Peace is both me and a feeling, and they both are one and they both are within you. A place, a concept, an emotion, an alternate reality. Truth is in the in between. The in between is within.

Treat me as a child for just a moment and let me ask,
What should I do next?

Begin. We all begin anew once more. We all begin anew. Begin. Dig in. Get into it. Immerse yourself in it. Begin anew. With each step you take, feel yourself beginning anew. Go for it!

You have more energy than I have at the moment, Peace.

You are wrong. Your energy is limitless. Beginnings are limitless. They are energy at her most intense. The big bang. Energy released. Poof! Heaviness gone. Lightness emerging. Begin, begin.

> Begin: to do the first part of an action,
> commence, to come into being, arise,
> also found, originate, invent.

YES! Come into being!

July 30, 1995

Thanks for yesterday, Peace, I felt better after talking to you and had a better day today. My mind is full of concerns like carpet and cupboard liner and paint. Coming here helps me remember why my mind is full of these things and what it is I prepare for. Not just a new house but a new beginning in a home that will honor me. It has, in the waiting, almost become a presence, and I do feel as if it is waiting to welcome me. Please be with me, tomorrow, Peace, as I open the door and cross the threshold for the first time. Be with me in my activities—activities that may not include this computer for a while. Be with me in

211

my cleaning and painting and gardening. Be with me as I turn preparation into action and still my mind for moments of peaceful reflection. Help me to create, especially in my sunroom, a sacred space full of mystery and light, calmness and energy. Guide me to those things of beauty that will endure, that will be part of the simpler, less consumptive life in years to come because they satisfy and lend contentment to my life. You have taught me to ask, and I am asking, dearest Peace.

Hello, Margaret. Welcome back. Today you are once again open and receptive in your asking. You are asking without fear because you are asking from a place of knowing. When you get to that place with your writing, you will be ready to ask and receive. Your path with your new home is clear. It is about combining the earthly and the divine. It is about accepting the duality of this life in a place of serenity in the in between. Take your time. Give yourself as much space as you can. Look at your home not as spaces to fill but as space in which to be. Let yourself Be in it as much as possible. Let it fill you with its presence—a living energy that is unique to it. Combine your uniqueness with its unique energy. Meld, web, integrate, transform. It, too, has a spirit. Place has spirit. Yard, grass, trees have spirit. They will welcome you. Recognize them.

Dear Peace,   August 6, 1995

I have been almost a week in my new home. I have scraped wallpaper, scrubbed floors and woodwork, shampooed carpet, painted. David cut the grass and I pulled a few weeds. Angela has been my constant companion. Mia and her boyfriend, Chuck, come in the evenings. Donny's parents, Katie and Ed, spent one day with us. New carpet and wallpaper are ordered; the furniture will arrive at midweek. I spend my breaks with a cigarette on the back steps. The freeway already bothers me less. I want Father to come and bless the house.

I think most about you and my spirituality when I am taking a break in my yard. Yet the empty "spaces" of the house work on me. The neglected smell of six months of emptiness is leaving, the smell of paint and Lysol replacing it. We have pushed back our move-in schedule by one week. It is for the best.

Tomorrow I am to return to work. The busy season seems aeons away. Work itself seems unimportant. I have noticed the single-mindedness with which I go about my work at the house. I set a goal and it is all that's on my mind. It is almost therapeutic, as is the physical work. Sometimes, especially when I am cleaning up after others in the new house, I get a feeling for my new role, and it is one of "grand" mother, in the way of powerful mothers of the past—the one about whom the family centers and gathers itself, the one who holds together the life of the family.

My spirit sisters have been absent from my dreams but my dream life has been rich, including everything from wallpaper to Jimmy Smits to Jack Nicholson. Each time I come here feels as if it may be the last, Peace, the last in this place. And as my reading has become uninspired and close to nonexistent, so has my questing for answers. I come to talk to you almost not expecting an answer—our connection seems weak, as does my connection to the spiritual. And yet, I know my life is forever changed by the events of the first half of 1995, and I do not want the journey to stop.

Please return to me, dearest Peace, and grant me your assurances that when I leave this place for good, I will still have access to you.

I am with you. Dearest Margaret. You cannot escape me. There will be times when you will try to turn aside your spirituality. You cannot. It is within. Think of the word channel.

> Channel: the bed of a stream; the deeper part of a waterway; strait; a means of passage or transmission; a range of frequencies of sufficient width for a single radio or television transmission; a usually tubular enclosed passage: conduit; a long gutter, groove, or furrow.

You worried, when you asked for Mary and Julie, about the power of being a channel and about the responsibility. Think instead of the beauty, the symmetry, the flow of it. Honor it. Be grateful for it. Pray. It is a flow. From you to me, from me to you but both at the same time, like a river flows, always there and always moving, a place, an idea, a movement. Like thoughts that can't be grasped or proven, but surely are. The communication is always open, dearest. You can block the flow but you cannot stop it. Moving with it is the safest, surest way to navigate

214

it. You are always there. It is always part of your actions, from the simplest to the most complex. Transforming the mission as you move to fulfill your destiny.

Thank you, Peace. I love you, and I am forever grateful to you and to this communication.

You are welcome, Margaret. Go in Peace.

Dearest Peace,   August 8, 1995

We are *really* packing today, Peace . . . me, Mia, Angela, Chuck. And it's happy. We're getting along, listening to Creedence Clearwater Revival; the mood is just right. Thank you to all who are watching over me and have been watching over us in this move. Donny and I had our first almost-fight yesterday. It has blown over. The new house is taking shape. The transition is almost complete. I'm overjoyed to feel this close to you and to be feeling this good about the move. I think I needed to feel close to you again before I could move with *peace* of mind. To feel close to you is to know you come with me. Despite what you told me, I had to feel it in my innermost being. Now I do. Thanks. Do you have any advice for me, dear friend?

Don't pack all your memorabilia away. Put it on display. Don't worry about where it is to go now—just think of its storage as temporary. It is time to surround yourself with the memorabilia of your life. Let it be open. Share it. Most of all, don't worry.

I like the idea of putting my things out. In fact, it gets me kind of excited. Thanks for the idea.

215

Let go of your worry and the things that will please you will become apparent. Also the things that will please your husband and children. Don't try to control things. Let them flow and everyone will feel better. Rest when you're tired. Work when you have energy. Laugh with your children when the mood is carefree. Enjoy! It is time to enjoy! Remember that joy is your lesson in this time. Good things are coming to you. Accept them with joy. It will all come together in a way that pleases you and your family if you do these things. That's a promise. Yes. Smile. That's what pleases me the most.

Back again . . .

I can't believe how much *stuff* we have. Consumption has to stop. There is only so much stuff one house can hold. Even one like our new house. I know I'm supposed to leave worries behind, but the thought of having all that storage space and not having enough storage is ridiculous. I must have forty suit jackets and I don't even care to wear suits anymore. And yet, can I part with them? I don't know. It seems so foolish. Both having them and parting with them.

If I had something to eat, I think I'd just sit down and eat and then go to bed. Tomorrow will come and we'll move and I can't worry about it. I'm writing here now just to have an excuse to sit down. I know you don't mind. On to folding clothes, packing CDs, finishing the kitchen. Then pick Ang up at work and get something to eat, and bed. Thanks for everything today, Peace. And thanks for the dreams!

You're welcome, Margaret. Rest well.

Dearest Peace,   August 16, 1995

Well, today is the absolute last day I will talk with you from here. The last of everything comes *home* with me *today.* Last night, Donny and I shared what felt like our first night in our new home. We finally got the drapes up, and afterwards, about midnight, sat outside together. It reminded me, as it does each time I sit out there, of traveling. The nights have been humid, the air is full of the sound of crickets chirping, and in the background is the noise of the highway—just like at the many motels at which I have stayed in my travels, both as a youth on the way to and from my grandmother's house in Georgia, and as an adult, as in last year's vacation to South Dakota. Those memories are all wonderful to me and so are the memories being made in these first days at our new home.

We sat together in the cool humid air, Donny shirtless, and I leaned against his cool skin and we talked quietly and had moments of intimacy and relaxed for the first time.

As I walked in the nearby park this morning, I thought of you telling me to look for beauty, and it's there in the paths and on the lake but no more so than in my own backyard. Thank you for all of it.

The kids are going to be here any minute. Is there anything you want to say to me—any last words—from here—before I disconnect?

PEACE

Go in peace, Margaret. Go about your life and your spiritual quest in peace. These are words that have been with you all your life. Remember them. Yes, a spiritual quest can stir waters that have been long still. But the object of the stirring is to come to a peaceful rather than complacent stillness. A peace in the Now, in whatever you do, with whomever you're with. A peace of spirit, a peace that comes from the center of the being, from the center that has been forever and will be forever. A peace to carry forward into the next life. A peace to carry outward to others. But a peace, mainly, that fills the being. The limitless being. Go in peace, Margaret. Carry the Peace of me within as I carry you. We are all interconnected in peace. Go in Peace.

IV.
BEGINNING

IMAGINING

August 27, 1995

I am writing from my new office—my new home. It is in a corner of a damp basement (if you can believe it, I let my husband appropriate the sunroom for the TV) and I don't care. It feels so good to be back. I sat down, pulled up the Peace file, and there it was. It felt almost miraculous to see it here, in this new house. In this new house where everything has come together so beautifully.

I have learned to find a simple grace and quietude in the smallest things: winding extension cords, cleaning or cutting endive, things I do with my hands. But this is the biggest, the grandest, the happiest. Peace is here! I have read the whole Peace file, and I am moved by it, by my own innocence more than my knowledge. I haven't thought of myself as innocent since I was thirteen. There is a sweetness about the Peace file—from the first day when I was told to smell the sweetness. It is the sweetness of innocence, of teacher and pupil. To read it is like learning to read all over again . . . the knowledge, the excitement, the adventure. The love of words! I cannot begin to say how much it all means to me.

And so, here I am, about to ask Peace to join me once again, putting it off only so that I can wait until I have a quiet hour with no pressure to do other things. Because I know Peace is my still, quiet voice within and I know he has led me and will continue to lead me to breakthrough moments of higher consciousness and greater creativity.

I have begun to say affirmations from a book I just bought, *Higher Creativity: Liberating the Unconscious for Breakthrough Insights,* by Willis Harman and Howard Rheingold. Those affirmations are:

> I am not separate.
> I can trust.
> I can know.
> I am responsible.
> I am single-minded.
> I have no other desire than to know and
> follow the will of the deepest part of
> myself.[21]

And I realize that this is letting go. Turning events over to the higher self, the unconscious, surrendering, if you will, to the will of God.

And this is where I am at. This is my beginning in my new home. Happily, contentedly, surrendering, letting go. What a relief!

I cannot wait any longer. Welcome Peace! Welcome back! Welcome home! It's me, calling you home. Will you answer?

I am here and I am happy to be with you. I am smiling. We are not Home, but we are home on earth, home in the physical, home in well-being. Safe, comfortable, surrounded by beauty. Home. Peace on Earth.

Thank you, Peace on Earth, for bringing Peace to my little piece of it. For bringing yourself here. This, too, is a relief. You're here! My eyes fill with tears of joy to have you here, to have what we have here continue. Thank you. Welcome.

You have learned much in our break.

I have tried (for want of a better word). I have been mainly involved in the physical, but as I said before, as it comes together it has risen to a higher level.

Yes! It has living spirit. Like the words that come together to form a beautiful philosophy, a living message. Everything is coming together.

Is it, Peace? Is everything?

Everything has come together for you to the point of trust. Why trust?

Because you have decided to let go. No. Not decided. You have let go. With your innermost being you Know, you Trust, that you can let go. I could not force it upon you with my words. You were the only one who could make the choice. And you did it now, today, on this time of our rejoining. Hurrah for you, dear one. You are one step, one giant step, one leap, closer to Home.

I didn't even realize I was going to surrender until I did, until I had, and the relief flooded me. I think it was an unconscious decision as much as it was a conscious one. I think this is the way it is supposed to be.

That is the goal. To let go and let your highest self, your connection to all that is, do the planning, the deciding, the choosing for you. It is not not you. It is the best you. It is us. It is from oneness. You and the all that is connected. Linked. Xed. Joined.

This is so new to me. Now what do I ask you, dearest Peace?

If surrendering has lulled your curiosity, it is only so that you can rest in the relief. Rest as you have never rested before. Rest, and in your resting will come the stirring of the still, quiet voice, the voice that asks for more out of a whisper of calmness rather than the raging of necessity, desperation, frustration.

I have no other desire than to know and follow the will of the deepest part of myself. . . .

Look deeply and there I am, reflecting back what you are.

What is the will of the deepest part of myself, Peace?

Curiosity already? Before rest? All right, dear Margaret, I will give you something to think about in your calm restfulness: What is relief? Where does it come from? What emotion is it? Is it from your head or your heart or your soul? Or is it a relief that spans the entirety of your being? And if so, what more is there to your being than head and heart and soul? That is the plane we will be on now that you have surrendered, now that you have let go. Sometimes I will have to remind you that you have let go and we will need to spend some time unraveling the ties that have bound you up once again, but when I am not reminding you, we will be communicating differently. On a higher plane. As if from a mountaintop with the sun shining on us and a clear lake reflecting the image down in the valley. Visualize a new reality from which your relief springs. Leaps! Rejoices! Be light in being, as in the opposite of being heavy, and be light, as in luminous. Let your light shine. Let your relief be like a beacon. A safe haven in a stormy sea. You will see that others will be attracted to your light. You will learn from them and develop a new curiosity about service to others and to the universe. You will sing, you will write; released of burdens, you will float. The higher Will will reveal to you the next steps, the next leaps.

Are you my higher will?

I am, you are, and so much more. You Know this, Margaret. I am your comfortable companion, your guardian angel. There are so many more to guide you, dear one. Now that you have surrendered, you have announced to the universe that you are Ready! Ready to be taught and aided, ready to teach and aid. Ready to be a light to all, both heavenly and earthly beings. You are now connected on your journey to all who

225

have surrendered on their journey. Arms linked, you could circle the globe. Light linked, you could circle the universe.

Can we bring this down to a more earthly level for a minute, Peace?

You make me smile and laugh out loud. Hear the heavenly music. Is it your daughter and the stereo or is it a choir of angels? I tell you it is both. At this very moment a choir of angels is rejoicing in your surrender.

But you wanted me to come down to earth. I smile and smile. You have made me so happy tonight. Just imagine, dear one, a life without struggle. I know you are thinking to yourself, No, that cannot be, but I ask you to imagine it. I ask you to imagine waking up and doing what you want to do every day. I ask you to imagine your children as happy and healthy as you could hope for them to be. I ask you to imagine your marriage continuing as happily as it has been but on a deeper level. I ask you to imagine your relationships with all your friends being on a deeper level. I ask you to imagine your dreams of being a published writer coming true. I ask you to imagine a car that will be like a transport to the clouds. I ask you to imagine an international trip filled with love at every turn. I ask you to imagine intimacy beyond any you have ever known. Is that earthly enough for you, my dear?

It is more like heaven.

Exactly. Imagine a heavenly life on earth. Nothing less. And go on to imagining this heavenly life on earth coming true for all those dear to you. And imagine the number of those dear to you growing infinitely greater. To bless is to increase. You will go through life blessed, increasing the capacity for life in all of those around you. Again, you wonder, a dream too good to be true? Do you not trust the universe, the collective power of beings such as myself? I have told you many times the universe wants you to be happy. Imagine it and it will be so.

Okay, I'll imagine it. But I am still only human. I still have the day-to-day, hour-to-hour "stuff" of life to deal with. I don't mean to rain on your parade, I want everything you mentioned, I love that you want it for me, I even believe it has a chance of happening, but I still don't see myself having that deep inner stillness as a constancy. I can come here and hear all these wonderful things and feel wonderful and feel relief, and then I go upstairs and act the same way I always have.

You have only just made the choice, dear one. Give yourself breathing room. Give yourself space. Give yourself relief and restfulness as a gift before you think of the minutiae of life. Do you think you cannot have all the happiness and success I described and still be human? And still be crabby occasionally? Yes, you will increasingly find a calm center. But it will come from your relief. Don't block the relief, the huge relief, with small worries.

Okay, Peace, I will *be* with my *relief*. I will imagine with my relief. I will leave the minutiae of life behind for a while. I will float through water instead of walking through water. I will be grateful for the relief. I thank you and all that is for it. Just help me achieve my calm center, okay?

Let relief calm your center, okay?

The dictionary defines *relief* as removal, lightening, release from duty, elevation. Okay, Peace. Why do I feel like one step forward, one step back?

Because you are not accustomed to relief, to joy, to imagining having what you want. It seems too easy to you. It seems beyond belief. You are trying to will yourself to believe instead of staying steady in your relief. But it is a momentary setback. Let it go and go back to relief. Stay there as long as you want. Rest there. It does not mean you can't come back here, that we can't continue to explore marvelous things, inner things, outer things. You are worried, aren't you, that I have taken away the quest that has become something fundamental to you, something you enjoy? Dear one, this could not be further from the truth. While you are resting in your relief, your unconscious mind, your higher self to whom you have surrendered, will be doing your work for you.

This is a foreign concept to you, I know, which is why you have struggled to let go. But you have let go, as you have opened your heart. I am the keeper of the brick and, if you will, the keeper of your surrender. I didn't think I would have to remind you of your letting go so soon, but I will remind you as often as you need. You have turned your burdens over—not shirked your duties. There is no law that says you must struggle. It is only the conditioning of your upbringing, the illusion your unconscious mind will help wake you from. This is the lesson of joy we spoke of at our first meeting. Let the relief grow in you and it will turn to joy. Be at peace with your relief, sweet heart.

Remember the sweetness of the journey you read about here only today. Imagine all you can imagine without struggle. But first rest in the relief. I cannot say this strongly enough. Give yourself space to rest in relief. Do this, dear one. Then we will talk again. Believe me, you will get used to it. You will say, "Why would I struggle to hang on to all that struggle when Peace was telling me all along I could let go?" Now, go rest in relief in your new home.

August 29, 1995

I am crabby, crabby. It is PMS. It is wanting to control things in the new house, to have others take care of it the way I want them to. It is not having my own space that has a door, that has privacy. It is wandering around the house wanting to smoke and having nowhere to go now that it is so buggy out at night. I have gotten lovely rest and lovely dreams. I go to work and stay mostly un-crabby. I come home and I am crabby again. The systems aren't functioning smoothly yet. The girls don't clean as I'd like, Donny doesn't pick up after himself, the garbage people didn't come, we haven't figured out the recycling, the cats shed hair everywhere and get on my furniture. I just want to stay home and take care of my house. I want to hear from my agent. I want to rest in relief. Yet I continue to struggle. And, of course, it's hard not to feel guilty about being crabby when I have this wonderful new home and this wonderful spirituality and wonderful sleep and dreams. Peace, HELP! What's the matter with me?

Your body needs to catch up with the rest of you. You, the real you, are inspired—you have received the breath of hope and spirit and freedom and divinity. Your body is still living with the old you. Your body is demanding some attention and you're not listening. You don't want to

229

listen. You are afraid of what its demands may be—from quitting smoking to getting exercise to meditation. You are happy to work on your mind and soul but the thought of body work bores you. You're in a time of manifestation. Wanting the inner you to become the outer you. You're being directed in this just as you have felt inner urges that directed you to begin this file, to pray, to read. Listen to the still, small voice. Otherwise it starts to scream.

That's how I feel, as if I could scream—about everything, everything that doesn't go the way I think it should.

You may hate the thought of body work but you love the investigative process, the discovery of new knowledge. I'd like to propose something. Why don't you tell me a few words about how your body feels and tell me why you think it feels the way it does, and then we'll start trying to find ways you will like to have your body catch up with the rest of you. You don't have to worry that I'll ask you to give up smoking. I won't ask you to do anything you are not ready to do, and I can perhaps give you suggestions.

All right. It's as if everything inside me is under pressure and, although you have told me I've released, I feel as if there is no release valve. Just pressure. That's the main thing.

First of all, wear purple tomorrow and as often as you need to in the coming days. Purple is the color of manifestation. It will remind your body of your new spiritual state.

Remember to breathe. Breathing deeply will help release the pressure and will remind you of your inspire-a-tion. Go and buy those foods

you want to eat now. Get your new contacts. Your clear vision is impor-
tant now. Spend as much time as you can among the trees; you need
their energy, and if you breathe deeply when you are with them, they
will use yours as well. Look for the Aramaic book of meditations. Listen
to soothing music. Repeat your affirmations. Imagine having the body
you want. That is enough for now. To imagine it is enough. By imagin-
ing it and giving it to your higher consciousness, some ideas that you
will like may come to you. And some miracles may take place!

Thank you, Peace. I feel better already. I do. Whether it's because I had alone time with you and smoked five cigarettes or because of what you told me or a combination, I don't know, but I feel better.

Today is the anniversary of Grace Zuri Love's death, Peace. I dreamt of a baby last night. I wonder if this anniversary of her passing has anything to do with either the tension I feel or the dream.

You are feeling some of Mary's tension. Because you are connected,
you have taken on some of her energy as your own. Tomorrow will be a
better day. Believe this. The cycle is complete now. Mary's relief is
coming. You can always call upon Grace to help you through difficult
times, as you can call upon anyone, living or spirit, if you call with an
open heart and are open to receive their aid.

It is hard not to think of Grace as a baby.

At our core, we are all the same: ageless and eternal. Grace's personal-
ity was strong and sweet and loving; that it did not have time to reveal
itself doesn't matter. As a baby, she was strong and sweet and loving as

she is now. Spirit is what goes deeper than personality. Smoking may be part of your personality now, but it is not part of your spirit. You will not smoke in your spirit form. And you will not miss it, I promise you.

Okay, I read you. Thank you so much. I forget to be grateful sometimes with my personality. My spirit is always grateful. Good night.

I smile upon you in your sleep. Rest in relief, and imagine!

Dearest Peace,   August 30, 1995

It is the end of another very long day but one in which we at least had dinner. We even sat around the table after dinner and discussed music and Jimmy Buffett and dreams and what inspires. Thank you, Lord! We needed to eat dinner and have table talk. It has calmed something in me that all the spirituality could not calm—it calmed my humanness.

I probably would not be here tonight if it weren't for Julie. Today she asked me to ask you what the heck is wrong with her. She very humorously tells of her steps backward—the tension and gritting of the teeth, the strain she is under. And she asks: How do I get out from under it?

So I took her request and stored it away in my brain and, in the late afternoon, at cigarette break, I started getting messages, I think. They went something like this: When does Julie have time to be Julie? That the answers have to come from Julie but they can't while Julie can't connect with Julie. I heard that she needs time free of responsibility on a regular basis. That she is a systematic and organized person and needs a systematic and organized way to go about her quest. Things to that effect, anyway, after which I know my own mind got in the way and embellished your basic guidelines with thoughts like, *Yeah, she should get some time to herself, a baby-sitter, more help from her husband.*

So I'm here to see if you have anything clearer, more direct, more inspirational to say to her than my, "Yeah, you should get some time to yourself." I know that the "When does Julie have time to be Julie?" came from you. Is there anything else?

Tell Julie to have a dialogue with herself. What is at the center of Julie? Who is she? In the busy life of a young mother, it is a lot to ask. It is almost impossible to detach self from mother. But ask her to try. Ask her to make space for herself in which to be just Julie and then to have a conversation with herself. What can Julie say about Julie's nature, wants, desires, dreams that are about Julie alone, separate from everyone else—not just children and husband but mother and father and work and friends.

This may sound confusing because I am always going on about our connectedness. But the connectedness works best when each person is fulfilling her unique individual destiny. It is like a net where each filament is intricately bound to the next, and in the end it is one piece and serves a different purpose, with each part holding its weight and none stronger or weaker than the other. None stronger or weaker than the other. In trying to be the strongest link, Julie may actually make other links weaker or become weaker herself!

Tell her to think of the universe, the all that is, the angels that pro-tect and guide her as her safety net through which she cannot fall, can-not escape, cannot become lost, cannot be hurt, and upon which she can rest as on a swinging hammock under the open sky. The universe is here to cradle her. She need only lay down her burdens and rest.

However or wherever Julie can find her restfulness is the beginning point from which she must befriend herself and find out all there is to know about herself, as she would want to know all about a new friend. Think of it almost like a courtship. Each discovery will only cause her to fall more in love with self. When she is in love with self, she will have made half the journey and will know the path to complete it. Tell her I am aware that this is not new advice, not the timeless wisdom she seeks. But the timeless wisdom she seeks will be found on the journey inward.

Thank you, Peace. As always, you say the simple things with beauty and profundity.

September 3, 1995

In four months, we've written two hundred pages, Peace. Makes me a more prolific writer than I have been on my own. But I'm about to get back to it—to *Who Killed the Mother?* It's Labor Day weekend. Angela goes back to school Tuesday, Mia and Donny go to work, and I have a day off! I'm hoping *Who Killed the Mother?* will just sing to me on Tuesday, Peace. I'm feeling very ready to get back to it, very hopeful about it, and yet pretty peaceful as well. Whenever I get anxious about it, or more specifically,

The Ninety-Seven Days, I try to remind myself I've turned it over to my higher power. My subconscious agent, my agent in the sky.

I slept for fourteen hours yesterday! I must have needed it. I know you keep reminding me to rest! Today I'm going to take care of a few practical matters, like getting myself a chair. And at the first opportunity—a family dinner, the *next* family dinner—I'm going to talk about the help I need from the family both to keep the house clean and to get my office ready—that is, to get a room with a door. I keep thinking it was part of the bargain on buying this house, and I will remind myself that bargaining has nothing to do with love, and this is to be a labor of love like everything else having to do with this house, this home. There is still much to do in everyday matters, as there is in my spiritual life.

I have been without something compelling to read the last few days, which is probably good, as it gets me back in the mood for writing. But I do hope to buy a book today. I have thought a lot about imagining. When you were telling me the wonders that awaited me upon surrendering, you kept saying "imagine . . ." At first I took you too literally, as if you were saying these things will come about, not "imagine" these things will come about. You were giving me something active to do, not saying these things would be done unto me. And I've found how important imagination is in a different context. I remember reading something by Sam Keen in which he talked about how he goes along day to day and then something like seeing a father cradling his dying son in Bosnia on TV will make him stop and imagine how it would feel. And because I was thinking of *imagine* in a new way, I suddenly saw how imagination is the start of everything. If we cannot imagine how another feels we cannot have compassion. If we had no image in our minds of Africa, our knowledge of Africa would have no impact on us. If we could not imagine there would be no discovery, no invention, because humankind would accept what *is* totally.

And so, while I've come to a new understanding of *imagine,* I've also come upon some messages of duality. First, I have surrendered and given over my desires to a higher power. Then you tell me to imagine. I'm not sure I know how to imagine without will, without worry, without turning imagining back into desire. Second, we are told to be in the Now and to accept that everything *is,* yet if we stayed completely in the Now and accepted everything in its ISness, we would not imagine and discover and invent—would we?

Everything Is. This does not mean that human beings are aware of all that Is. Accepting all that Is does not mean denying that there are things we cannot see. It is accepting and embracing the mystery. Imagining Is. Like Knowing. Like Trusting. It does not come automatically in its true form because of the illusion and habit of culture and upbringing. I told you before, in your childhood you had a rich life of imagination. Being forced to grow up too soon altered your ability to imagine. In writing, you

236

have forced your way back to a life of imagination. But it is still not the imagining of your youth. The imagining of your youth was innocent and pure. Imagining for the sake of imagining. Imagining for fun! You invented stories and whole worlds for the sheer joy of it!

You are still a novice at joy. You are still unsure of your footing in the world of joy. Perhaps it is because of your old view of imagining. Imagining is not about will or about willful desire. It is about joy, first. It is about going back to the lessons of childhood when you saw with fresh eyes and you saw equally as much with your imagination as with your sight. When I told you your sight was going to be important, I was not kidding. Because you are being asked to go beyond "regular" sight. You are being asked to imagine with fresh eyes, with youthful, innocent eyes. How can you See possibilities with eyes so grounded in reality? Go back to hope—hope being the loving and limitless possibilities a parent feels for a child.

See the possibilities. Imagine them! This is very important. You wonder how imagining is different than Seeing the possibilities. And yet when you heard the word Hope used in this way, as a way of see-ing limitless possibility, you thought you understood how to Be! You said yes! You were excited. If you cannot get your thoughts around the word imagine, it is only because of the pain of childhood and the for-getting that childhood pain caused you to do. If you cannot imagine, See the possibilities. Imagine the possibilities. Sight and imagination.

You talked about being able to imagine Africa. Can you see Africa with your eyes, with your sight, without the benefit of television or pho-tographs? No. But you can see it in your imagination. Open up your idea of sight to include imagination. It will enrich all of your senses and your compassion as well.

You want me to be less literal.

I want you to Be. To rest in relief. Leave literal behind for a while. Leave reality where it's at: at the body level. Let your spirit soar! That is all I am asking, all that I am trying to get you to achieve. And yet you hang on so tightly. You cling to your reality. You look to science for verification. Fine. Do so. But come along with me too. Don't be forever letting it pull you backward. Make a leap of faith. If you do not believe, how can you surrender? What do you surrender to? I know you believe. You know you believe. In the God of your youth, in the All that Is. Is it only my teachings you chafe against? Or is there something you are afraid of? Meditation? Then don't meditate. But do open your eyes, imagine, see, believe. Have convictions. Believe. Believe what you believe. That is all that is required. Just as I say "be who you are." That is all that is required. It is all one, isn't it? I can tell you a million things but when I say "be who you are" it is all the same, all one.

Perhaps that is the problem. Perhaps I am not in tune with myself at the moment. Perhaps I am just in a state of flux. I have lost the tension or most of it since I got my period. And I am restless because I haven't a good book, something new to sweep me away to the next idea. I am so darn greedy, Peace. I am always after more. And what I like best are books that condense it all for me—take all these teachings and put them together and then say, see what it all points to? That is what I like. Not to be told this is the way, or I've disproved \this way, but the openness of all the teachers I've encountered. I'm uncomfortable with those who say this is or this isn't. I'm comfortable with possibilities. You were right about me there. Does this mean I lack *conviction,* the state of being convinced; belief?

Sweet heart, relax. You are doing fine. You are content in the mystery. That is enough. You can believe in the mystery. I only ask that you remain open to it. That is exactly what I ask and you have led me to a good way to describe it. You believe in the mystery and, therefore, you believe in staying open to the possibilities of the mysterious.

Like the other day at work, when the radio came on by itself? All three of us spirit sisters were standing there when it happened. When it came on, it was nothing but static. Mary went to the knob and fiddled with it and we got a religious song about surrender—about putting oneself in His hands. And Mary and I looked at each other, sure that it was a message. (We had to tell Julie it was a message.) We were open to the possibility of the mysterious, and I told Mary, "Well, Peace told me he was going to remind me I had surrendered." Is that what you're talking about?

That's exactly what I'm talking about. Yes! Yes! That is all you have to hang on to—your openness to the mysterious, to the possibilities. That is all the spiritual quest requires. That is your conviction, your belief. I think it is a good belief. How about you?

Yes. It works for me. I understand it. It fits where I am at this time. It fits my Now. Thank you.

NEED

September 12, 1995

Today is my wedding anniversary. The day began with a dream. In it, I was floating on a raft in the sky, waiting my turn to fill the bird feeders there with birdseed. The teenage boy who was filling them ahead of me was walking on air. He was sweating and obviously finding his task both trying and exhilarating. It was a sacred duty and he was fulfilling it. He was to make two trips and then it was to be my turn. While I wanted to do it, I was afraid of doing it. I saw his effort and I thought, *I am heavier than he.* When it came my turn, I could not step off the raft. He made one more trip. Then when he came back and I was going to step off the raft and complete at least the second part of my task, we were only three feet off the ground. I had missed my opportunity.

It was a dream of deep feeling and poignancy for me. It also followed a day behind Mary Love asking me, "Have you asked Peace about your writing?" She asked this in the context of me talking about the Dan O. situation. I responded, "It seems as if I ask him all the time and his answer is always elusive, something like, 'It will happen when it is time.'"

And finally, Mary returned the books she had borrowed. One was the James Hillman book and in it I read: "Curiosity about fact and detail gives way before the open contemplation of what is, just as it comes."[22] And I feel slightly "wrong" about my curiosity, or better put, I feel as if I have been going about it the wrong way: with curiosity rather than contemplation. Curiosity, I now see, is about the details, while contemplation is about the whole. And so, while I am seething with questions: What did the dream mean? Does it relate to my writing? Am I missing out on some opportunity by not taking action? When do I know that taking action is right? How do I know? And how do I meld it all with the truth of having surrendered? I already know—just in this minute—that surrender is not about curiosity but about contemplation. And this new way of seeing gives me *hope* once again, because it helps me see how to *be* once again and particularly how to be within my surrender.

So I come to you with what I hope is a state of contemplation—a state not active but open—to hear what you care to share with me about this time and the questions, rephrased in the language of contemplation to be questions not of detail, but of how to be. I sit, my heart open to contemplation, prepared once again to listen. I await your voice.

The only movement is circular. The gold ring falls into the porcelain bowl and spirals. Its sound is clear and singular. It is an image borrowed from your reading. Reading that stays within you waiting for the moment at which it can be of use. It exists within you until it can be of use and when it is used, it is transformed. It becomes something other than what it started out to be. This is analogous to the godliness within you. It is there, waiting to be used and thus transformed. This is your writing, also, waiting within to be used and transmuted. The circle of life, death, rebirth is constantly occurring within you. Constantly. It is. No beginning. No end. No thought ever dies. It exists once it is thought. It is. But constantly changing: living, dying, rebirthing as needed.

My need to accomplish something with my writing seems to be greater than any other need I have. It comes up again and again, circular, unstoppable. Is it only ego, Peace? This *need?*

If you could meet your own needs, you would not be human, and yet you are the only one who can meet your needs. This is the divine. The divine may come in the form of another person, in the form of an angel, in the form of new thoughts, in inspiration. The one who meets your needs is the divine One no matter what form it takes.

242

Peace, I ask here, as I may not have asked before, for help in fulfilling my need.

Can you define this need for me, dear one?

Please, Peace, Lord, Ancestors, help me to meet this need. Is it a purely human need, Peace, as I was about to say it is? Is there no divineness in my cry to be heard? I want to say it is not about ego, and fear that it is. I want my writing to be wanted. That is what I want. I want that comfort, that security, that validity. Is there something inherently wrong in that? Is that why my need goes unfulfilled? Please tell me truthfully, Peace. Is it that the writing in and of itself is supposed to give bliss and comfort and security and validity even while going unwanted? Am I missing something important here?

My dear, you have stated your need. It needed to be stated. You want your writing to be wanted, you need your writing to be wanted. You have expressed your need for the first time, for the first time. Why do you now want to find something wrong with it?

Need has never been comfortable for me, Peace. I have not liked to need. I have particularly not liked to give expression to what I need. I resist it at every turn. Why, Peace?

Fear, sweet one. Fear is not a simple thing. It is not a pat answer. It is. As circular and unending as everything else. Need is tied up, for you, with survival. It is ancient. One needs air to breathe to survive. One needs food to eat to survive. Expressing a need is as ancient and eternal as the will to survive. To live is to need. To be present in human form is to need. Can you deny yourself food and air?

Had to break to take Angela to her guitar lesson. Then my sister, Susan, came over. Then Donny came home with some friends. I realize I can't control things. I'm frustrated and I have to let it go because I can't control life, I have to accept what comes, but . . . where do you draw the line between acceptance, letting go, accepting noncontrol, and being Milquetoast? More on this later. The following occurred in my car while I waited for Angela. It was written in a notebook and transcribed here.

What do I *need* to know about needing? Once again I feel as if I'm missing something.

There are those who equate divineness as a cessation of human need. There literally is no such thing. To be human is to need—air to breathe being an example. Divineness comes in part, then, from trusting that there will be air to breathe. It would be difficult to function at all if this need being met were in doubt, as it is imperative that those who do not have food to eat make meeting this need their main function. This is one reason the meeting of basic needs is seen by all sane governments and people of power as an inalienable right. Because it is recognized that one must be free of this basic striving if one is to be more than this striving.

Your thought then, I need my writing to be wanted, *is an expression of your will to survive. And it is. It is set in its circular motion. It lives. But it lives the life of one who must seek each day the food necessary for survival because it does not trust that this need will be met. Needs are needs. They are not right or wrong. There are only needs and the degree to which we trust they will be met.*

The Catholic joke you brought up earlier about the man who didn't buy the lottery ticket now comes back to me. How do I know when to act and what actions to take? I am trying to tell myself this isn't the detail seeking of curiosity, as it probably is, but looking at it in as big a way as I can, in as whole a way as I can, I know I must write, I know I must trust, but then mustn't I also do? I had such a strong feeling that my agent Dan O. was going to be *the one* to bring my writing to the world. How do I know when to let go of that and seek elsewhere?

If your need is for people to want your writing, they first have to know it exists, don't they? Let it go, as literally as you have let go of other constraints and fears. Send it out into the world. Let it be known that you have a need to be filled and see what the universe sends you. Buy the lottery ticket and have faith. Trust that your needs will be met. Believe that they will. If your need remains a secret, your writing will remain a secret as well. People who can help you are in your life for a reason. Let them help you. Don't be stingy. Tell the world as you know it. There is someone in it who will be the right one. I will show you the way if you have faith and let go. The answers are waiting to come to you.

Am I to do anything with this writing, Peace?

You need your writing to be wanted. All your writing? Don't you think there are those waiting for this writing just as you wait for those who want to read your writing? It is a circle, dear one, a living circle. Like your supply and demand, though I do not like to use words of commerce. Build it and they will come. Write it and it will be read. Sweet heart, it is as simple as that.

What about all those writers who never are published?

Trust that what needs to be will be. Think of the authors who have touched you. Their words were there to fill your need, your need was there to fill theirs. A circle. A golden ring falling into a porcelain bowl. A natural law of gravity causing it to spiral and sing. It is a golden ring until it hits the bowl. Then what is it?

Dearest Peace, thank you for your wisdom. Please hit me over the head with the map I must follow, the instructions on how to proceed. Peace, Lord of all that Is, ancestors, show me the way.

Dear Peace,   September 13, 1995

I spent a lot of time today thinking about needs. First I thought I had to voice my needs and that a failure to do so was a failure. Then I thought again. It is all in the approach we take, isn't it? Contemplation rather than curiosity, for instance. It seems to me that with almost all my needs, approach, the right approach, rather than the actual voicing, is what matters. Take, for instance, those small things around the house that drive a person crazy: if approached, as you have taught me, with the thought of "what is it for which I prepare?" the feeling changes.

And so I am looking for a way to respond to needs that doesn't come from voicing them. This may be a cowardly way of avoiding my "need to voice" but I do want to think it through nonetheless.

Even if some needs must be voiced, how must they be voiced? I know that I have voiced my needs concerning my writing, when I have voiced them at all, with fear. Fear of failure, fear of not being worthy, fear of ridicule, you name it. And I can't help but wonder if the same fear doesn't pervade everything. It is basically a fear of asking and being denied.

I remember when my sister, Susan, would come home from college and ask Dad for money and he would make her jump through all these hoops for five dollars. She was probably nineteen or twenty, and I was fourteen or fifteen, but I remember telling her that I had already learned it wasn't worth it. By that young age, I already thought that almost anything was better than asking. Independence seemed the most prized thing in the world. But I'm getting away from myself. Or maybe I'm not. Expectations, too, which you and I have talked about here, were, by my early twenties, something I had learned not to have. It seems as if, in sum, I grew up believing in a world of scarcity where my needs would not be met or the price was too high.

So, if I take it as a learned behavior, can I do anything substantial about it? What my original thought was, thinking more of relationships than writing, was that if I acted always out of love, if I remembered love in every situation, I would be open to having my needs met. That in a thought environment permeated by love, the meeting of needs would be more of an exchange—the circle you spoke of—or the cycle of give and receive. Creating an environment for needs to be met.

Not that I have found this easy in relationships, certainly not much easier than voicing my needs, but maybe a step I can take while waiting to see just how I come to voice. Teaching myself how to voice the important things. I have learned to do this in my work environment as part of leadership and professionalism, as part of becoming more knowledgeable and being able to speak from a knowledge base, from a fair certainty—in other words, that what I speak won't be foolishness. And, because of my work environment, I feel fairly certain that what I say won't be ridiculed and that it might even bring change.

And I am going to take a class called "Ways of Knowing," and I am going to be expected to participate in class discussion and I am going to participate. This journey has made me so excited about learning, Peace! And as you said yesterday, everything you learn stays inside you waiting until you need it. So I am taking steps in almost every direction.

But I don't know how to translate this optimism to my writing. Which leads me back to what I am looking for by becoming a published writer and it brings me back to ego because I want—what do I want? I want to be proud of myself. How's that for laying it on the line? I want it so that I can hold my head high. So that my mother and father can introduce me as their daughter the writer. So that I can bring the authority of that title to all my dealings in the world. So that people who have never read a word I've written will nonetheless think highly of me. I'm looking, Peace, for respect. I think of my former teacher Kate Green reading tarot cards. And I think, *She got herself enough respect through being an author that she can now do what she wants!* (This is the way I look at it—not necessarily the way she does.) That is what I want, to feel that I have enough respect that I can do what I want and still have that respect. This is as truthful as I can be. This reminds me of how the astrologer, Pat, defined power: the freedom to do what you want. And she predicted that I would become a powerfully compassionate woman in this second half of my life.

But I just can't build that circle out of all of it, Peace. I know the veil of illusion is lifting; I know I am seeing more clearly; I know coming at life from an environment of love cannot possibly hinder anything and will likely help. But I still can't translate it to my writing.

You must respect yourself first. At work you do a good job and you respect that you do a good job, so much so that you can defend your right to do other than your job on job time, and do so confidently. You have learned at work that it doesn't matter how much time you spend getting something done as long as it gets done right. This was a

PEACE

fantastic accomplishment! Why can you not bring it forward into other areas of your life? One reason is that the work of the wife and mother is never done. No matter how much you do, you feel as if you "steal" time for yourself. Steal from whom? The family. Where did this come from? From your shame about your early parenting. You tried to write it out of yourself in The Ninety-Seven Days. *But it lingers and I say it matters a great deal.*

Why can't you translate this confidence to your writing? Because you have not gotten the recognition you need and because you are less certain of your skills. Is work the only place where you are an expert? To yourself, I think the answer is yes. You trust that you know at work. You TRUST that you KNOW.

It doesn't matter, dear one, that you want respect. What I mean by this is that it is not a bad thing. You can want this. You can have this vanity. And if this "respect" sets you free, how can it be a bad thing? You are simplifying matters when you feel that this accomplishment of a published book will grant you all the respect you will ever need, but so what? It matters not. You will learn the lessons you need to learn from it. Do not fear your reasons for wanting to publish what you have produced. Of course you want to share your creation with the world. You would not be normal if you did not. For heaven's sake, give yourself a break! Why shouldn't you want this?

Because it is a need—that is what it comes back to. You do not want to need. Your aversion to being needy is so strong. It is as if you think you should be able to fill all of your own needs. You operated under the illusion that you did almost all your life. Even when so few of your needs were being met that you barely survived! Don't you See? Peel this layer of your persona away and see the gem beneath. You are

250

not in control. Independence does not mean superhumanness. You are not a cartoon character. When so few of your needs were being met that you barely survived, it didn't matter to you. All that mattered was that you weren't asking anyone for anything, you weren't expecting anything from anyone. These have been the driving forces of your life. You would rather have starved to death than appear needy. Oh, sweet one, you have chosen a hard road. But tomorrow you can choose a new one.

This is what is so hard about writing, Peace. I can write. If I had all the time in the world, I could write and write and write. I don't *need* anybody to write. All I need is myself and time. But to publish what I write, I *need* somebody. I can't do it alone. I must seek help.

And that is perhaps the lesson writing has come to you to teach you. Seek and you shall find. Ask and it will be given unto you. This is one of the greatest teachings of your God. You cannot avoid it and attain enlightenment. You cannot avoid it and attain joy. It is part of the one-ness, sweet heart. You are not the One, the singular, the independent being you have always supposed yourself to be, you see. You are part of a whole. It is as if a ring of hands circles the globe, one clinging to the other and here you are refusing to join hands, insisting you must go it alone. You never have to go it alone again, dear one. You are not alone. The one you need is available to you. For every need you have, I promise there is a corresponding being whose need is to fulfill your need. It is a circle of interdependence, of humility, of hands going empty until you clasp them.

MIRACLES

Dear Peace,   September 15, 1995
The spirit sisters are getting a day together. A whole day. Even a night. I have shared so much with them. I will approach this gathering with love and with my open heart, but if you can believe this, I wonder already how it will go, what I will be able to share of myself. Whether I can close the distance and *connect*. I want to connect with people. I want to let them touch me and be touched by them. I want bonds, Peace. I want things to grow around me and to become more than what they have been. I really do.

*We will help, dear one. Do not worry about it. Hold on to your feeling
of hope, of limitless possibility. Let go of all else. And rest.*

Dearest Peace,   September 18, 1995

I have become immersed in the preparations for the trip
to Italy. And as I plan, I feel and see it more and more as a
pilgrimage. It is the holy sights I want to see most, then the
family, then the beauty. I realize this preparation is important and plan to devote myself to it—extending my spiritual quest to include my pilgrimage, ceasing to think of
them as separate. This will allow me to prepare without
feeling as if I am neglecting my spirituality and, more truly,
to prepare for the purpose of the journey, making a physical journey part of the spiritual journey. I have only now
thought of this and it brings me a certain Peace!

It also makes me think about the journey to this house
and how little time I have really spent making the journey here and the getting here connect. In the busyness, I
forgot about coming new here. When I surrendered, I did
not think of it as becoming new in my new home, as the
rebirth I had anticipated. This, too, is only now coming to
me. It must be in the time away from actively thinking (in
letting go?) that the actual integration of ideas comes
together. Thank you for helping me see this today.

Peace, it is uncanny how talking to you opens up my
eyes, even before you have shared a word with me. And as
I say this, I realize what perhaps my spirit sisters do not:
that it is the oneness of this process (which I was about to

call a two-way-ness), meaning that we both give to it equally, that makes it work. And I think that is probably the key to the work my spirit sisters want to do at the cabin: the realization of the oneness, the giving as well as receiving, the flow. And this also helps me to see what a process this is, or to put it better—as you yourself also put it recently—what a cycle it is: give, receive, integrate, give, receive, integrate. And to add another spin to the cycle: give, receive, integrate, share, and all its possible permutations. Am I on the right track, Peace? (I know I am, but I ask you to share in my discovery of what you have given me and what I have made of it.)

You have it! Yes! Yes! It is a living cycle, and the more you can make the cycle of your spirituality spin and spiral, the closer you will get to the goal you seek: to all the goals you seek, if you look at all aspects of life as part of the cycle. Can you think of your writing this way? Your journey? Your work? Your family? The more you can think in terms of the living cycle, the more your living will cycle to the rhythms of the universe. And how about adding love to the cycle?

Yes! And imagine!

Yes! And believe!

Yes! Oh, thank you, Peace. I'm off to another worldly chore and I'll be back.

When I return . . .

There is another cycle that works as well: work, write, think, regener-

254

ate, imagine. They really aren't separate: family, writing, spirituality, travel. They are part of the whole and part of the cycle. Every act is part of the cycle—or can be. It is stress, worry, rushing that breaks the rhythm of the cycle, and more than this, it is the otherness that you have for these things in your mind: Spirituality is for me. Writing is for me. Work I do for the family is for them. *Not so. All is for the whole, the oneness, of you, your family, your community, your country, the universe—because they are all joined just as your activities are joined.*

Thank you, Peace. I think I'm getting it. It's funny how some ideas have to sink in on a purely intellectual level, some on a spiritual level, and others at the level of humanness, of day-to-day life: doing work, making love, needing. I had a couple of wonderful messages from you this week: one, an otherworldly chime while Donny and I were making love, reminding me to love, and two, a message in a song. Listening to the radio in the truck with Donny, I knew the next song was going to be a message. Imagine my surprise when it was "Inner Sweetheart" by Soul Asylum, from a CD titled *Let Your Dim Light Shine.* (The kids gave me the actual name, I thought it was something about your *dome* light—maybe because I was riding in the truck!) And finally, there is the Beatles song that has been running through my head for weeks: "All You Need Is Love," which I thought was a message about love and realize now may be a message about need. How am I doing, Peace?

Excellent, as always, sweet heart.

I have been reading in *The Power of Place* about possibilities. It says:

> Great achievements, such as Angkor Wat or Chartres Cathedral, give us a sense of the possible.
>
> Equally important, however, is to know that the same *possibilities* lie within the scope of our own actions. Few of us has the power of a Khmer king, the real estate of Yosemite, or the honed skills of a Zen master. Yet what each of us has *is enough*. There is opportunity in every action to show what we love and hold sacred. [Emphasis mine.][23]

This all brings to mind approaching the spiritual retreat I will share with my spirit sisters as one would a sacred place—that this would increase the possibilities for all of us.

Your purpose will make it a sacred place, not only in that sacredness will occur there, but most particularly if you can feel your connectedness with the sacred, your connectedness with the universe. Remember always that you are not separate and the sense of the whole will come to you, and from that sense of the whole, the sense of oneness.

Thank you again, Peace, for another hour of connectedness with you and the whole. Anything else we should think about?

First, go beyond thinking. Be. Feel these things with your inner being. Try not to spend "time" thinking in the usual sense. And don't forget love. Bring love and an open heart with you. Bring love as you would bring a friend in from the rain. Bring it inside and radiate it outward like sunshine.

That leads me to my final quote of the night, Peace: "An open heart will embrace any new place and bring to it what is needed for a good life. It will find and make in it the 'wholiness' that brings us to hold our places sacred."[24]

Thank you, Peace. Good night.

Sweet dreams, sweet heart.

Dear Peace,   September 23, 1995

Just was putting away another box of stuff—photo albums—and, of course, I got to looking. I then found, out of a thousand possible photos, the ones I took in the conservatory, including a photo of the St. Francis statue—something I can give to Mary, that she'll appreciate because of her interest in him.

I've propped St. Francis up here in front of my computer—the St. Francis I was going to give Mary—and I had an interesting thought. I thought, *I like having St. Francis here.* I know I have two of these photos, and I could go back and find the other and give one to Mary and keep one for me. And for just an instant I thought, *No. Mary wouldn't like that. She would like St. Francis to be her symbol alone.*

257

And then just as quickly, I realized that I was putting thoughts into Mary's head. I can't explain why. And I thought how if we both had St. Francis by our computers, it would connect us. Maybe it is me projecting thoughts onto Mary that sometimes keeps her and me from connectedness. I will guard against this.

The retreat with Mary and Julie was wonderful, Peace. When I spoke to you, during the retreat, asking for messages for Julie and Mary, it was so overwhelming. It was such a miracle, Peace.

You have also just picked up A Course in Miracles, *out of a thousand possible books, and you knew it was the one for you. You have been thinking today that what happened at the cabin was a miracle. It was. There are no degrees of miracles. No almosts, no halfhearted efforts or results—only miracles.*

Thank you, Peace. This is the most peaceful I have ever felt about sharing your messages. I'm not sure why, perhaps because I have accepted it as a miracle and, with your help, have accepted that all miracles are what they are with no degrees of miracle-ness. I thank you particularly for this gift of peacefulness with this kind of communication. I felt it even yesterday, before reading about miracles. At the end of our day at the cabin, Mary and I walked down the driveway (Julie had to leave a little earlier) and it was truly the most beautiful day I can remember. The leaves, the sky, the bluffs all had a clarity to them. Not only was the angelic communication miraculous, but the day. And then what I read about miracles really made sense, because it was said that miracles bless the ones who are the channels for the miracles equally as they do those who receive the miracles. I did feel blessed, and in moments I still feel it. Thank you for the miracle of the day and the continuing feeling of blessedness. Help me to carry it forward. I am amazed that I ever forget about it, for even a short time, yet I do.

But it is within you. Feel the deeper peace that resides in you. Linger there. When you reside in Peace and feel that peace also resides in you, the duality will no longer take the memory of it from you; it will walk with you through your days.

I feel, Peace, a very loving atmosphere surrounding me, like an undisturbable light. I feel even as if you are being gentler with me.

As you join the ranks of the blessed, this feeling will grow. Your preciousness to me and to the All that Is has increased in a way that has nothing to do with More. (Because it started as perfect love it cannot grow.)

I went to church today. I was glad to be back. Once again I heard everything new, new as in *new* since I found you, Peace. When Father said that if the whole world could love God the whole world would know peace, I understood. *I understood!* He said this is the season of the Holy Cross, and it is here to remind us to pray and to love. I know now that they are the same, that every act of love is a prayer. He also mentioned how October is the month of the Rosary. And just now I feel, in remembering this, that he was talking to me. That his message linking prayer and love to the Rosary and to this time was a message that came one-on-one from him to me, as well as a message that he gave to the whole congregation. And I see how when you have said an author speaks to *me,* meaning *me* particularly, it is the same as this feeling I had of Father speaking to *me,* and it is true. I see how, somehow, someone can speak to me individually—making the message implicit to me—and still be talking to the whole. That this isn't contradictory. That it can be. That it is. Even though I can't really comprehend how it is. Thank you, Peace, for helping me accept what is. Thanks for everything.

You are welcome, dear Margaret.

THE SCHOOLROOM EXPANDS

SAFETY

Dear Peace,   September 25, 1995

As I was leaving for work today, still trying to define the new feeling of peacefulness I have been feeling since our retreat, the word *safe* came to me. Safe is how I have felt the past few days. And almost as soon as it occurred to me that safe was what I was feeling, I saw a sign that said "Safety First." It was a *sign*. Then I went into work and I told Julie how good I have felt and

PEACE

that I have felt safe, and she got that "this is unbelievable" look and she said *safe* was exactly how she felt about being with Mary and me at the cabin. How to her, feeling safe, with me especially, was a Yes that negated many No's. And we both had felt an immediate longing to hang on to the feeling. And it's so weird, because the word *safe* had never even occurred to us before, and here it had occurred to both of us at the same time. The power of what happened at the retreat has stayed with us, Peace, I know it has. Thank you so much for everything. Especially for allowing me to receive messages for my spirit sisters.

The interesting thought that came to me out of rereading the messages was the talk about access points. Julie was told that hers was through her skin, through her body. Mary was told that hers began with being affected by the everyday. And it was mentioned that my access point was through my writing.

With Julie, knowing comes to her by her being accessible to the elements, open, seeable, because through letting others see her, she will learn to love herself. For Mary, knowing comes to her by the way that she is affected by the beauty of dailiness, and by taking care of herself, in treating herself with tender, loving kindness; in seeing the daily beauty of herself, she will learn to see the world; to See. And so for me, I suddenly see writing differently too. I see that it is through writing that knowing comes to me, and it is through writing that I will

262

learn to love myself. And maybe that by letting others know me through my writing, I will learn to love myself and to *see* and to *know*. And I just got goose bumps about it. It's one of those things that was right here in front of my eyes all along and I didn't quite see it. I'm still goose bumpy, Peace. What does it mean?

It means I am smiling. It means you are learning Truths. It means that you are beginning to See. It may even mean that you are beginning to smile.

I am smiling. And I feel your tenderness for me. Everything seems just a little bit different.

Your perceptions are shifting.

I think I am actually feeling this bodily.

Yes. What is talked about in the Course [in Miracles] *as levels, levels of perception, are beginning, quite literally, to shift. Let go and ride the waves. There is no need to try to hang on to feelings like those of safety. Once you begin to try, the naturalness of it ceases to be. Let nature take its course. The sun doesn't try to rise in the morning or set in the evening. The sun knows its purpose. As your purpose becomes less and less divided, there will be fewer and fewer levels of perception until, finally, you know. Trust what is happening within you. You are being guided now in a much more literal sense because you have surrendered and because you are closer to the Truth, the all-knowing of oneness. Leave doubt behind. Stay safe.*

WAYS OF KNOWING

September 28, 1995

I started my "Ways of Knowing" class Tuesday night. Its approach was accompanied by what I hesitate to call fear, and could be more accurately described as nervousness. Finally, I reminded myself I was safe and directly afterwards saw another safety sign. I felt better.

The feeling after the class was one of exhilaration and one of worry. I worried about my performance in the class, feeling as if, as when I spoke with Dan O., I was entirely too gushy about my excitement for the class and too timid to come forward when I had an idea. What was my idea, you might ask? What we were talking about was knowledge (or epistemology—the theory of knowledge). More specifically we discussed "What is knowledge?" What I heard that came closest to an answer was that knowledge has what it takes to be shared—that it is shareable.

Sharing, of course, made me think of the spirit sisters. And my idea concerns how interesting it will be to contrast how the three of us have come to believe we know things with what is happening in class. It may also be interesting to contrast what I'm reading in *A Course in*

Miracles, which also talks about how we know. In whatever context I examine it, however, knowledge needing to be shareable makes perfect sense and maybe even makes the most sense in the context of the spirit sisters.

I want to return to the issue of safety, which Mary and I discussed in relation to my writing and the writing itself in terms of my life goals. Because something is different. If I were to be asked two months ago (perhaps two weeks ago) what my ideal future would be, I would have said being able to write full time. Period. No hesitation, no doubt. And now, suddenly, I realize this is no longer entirely true because one of the major things that appealed to me about being a full-time writer, besides writing, was the idea, thought, image of myself locked away from the world in my own little room, where no one and no thing would disturb me. And that image no longer fits. (As of . . . this weekend?) I realize that there must be a service or sharing component to my work/my writing/my ideal image. I am no longer willing to take myself out of the world; rather, I am at a stage of putting myself back into it: thus the class, thus the sharing with the spirit sisters, and, perhaps, thus the sharing of my writing, my thinking, myself. And as I talked to Mary, it suddenly occurred to me why the shift has occurred, and here it is: because I am now safe. Because I am safe.

And so, I can only hope that, "Now that I am safe" I am also "Ready" and something will happen with my writing—the something that is meant to happen—either within me, as in a new and better writing, or something outside of me, as in someone wanting to publish what I write.

And so we are back to hope, Peace. But a hope that is different, in one way less active and one way more. Less active in that I truly feel that if I am open, the answers/the way, will come to me. And more active in that I am taking my hope back into the world.

Peace, Mary, too, got "safety" out of the weekend. Each of us can hardly work. We are full of energy, but a directed energy—an energy that is for *us*. It will be much appreciated if you can help us get our work done (work-work) as well as our "real" work (spiritual work).

Thank you, Peace, for all of it. I know it is a lot. I know you are not only keeping up with me but are way ahead of me. Now that I have safety on my side, I hope you will feel free to guide me in even more ways than you have. (I greedily ask.) And I can hear you telling me to rest. So I'm going. Good night, dear Peace.

WANTING

The day started out with a dream. In it, I'm walking in front of Grandmother Ivie's house in Georgia. A television is on inside and I can see a mom, dad, and toddler sitting within. I am unclear about my feelings here, but I'm aware that what I have come for is to touch the stones of the house.

Then at work, Mary announces that she found the most wonderful new shop and it's called Stonehenge, significant in itself because of it being something you and I have talked about, Peace. But in addition, the whole store is dedicated to stones, or at least that is its main attraction. What struck me was that Mary should come in talking about stones immediately after I'd dreamt of touching the stones of Grandmother's house. Not the bricks, which is what her house was built of, but the *stones.* It just got me all nostalgic about Grandmother and thinking about the writing I had done about her. I went through my "personal" file in my desk drawer and unbelievably, I actually had a copy of the first chapter of the book I had begun about her. I started reading it and began to cry. I felt so touched and so connected to Grandmother, for the first time in a long time. And I felt connected to Mary and Julie too. I started to tell them about the book and the dream and how the book was going to be called *By Heart,* for the process we have of remembering or memorizing things. And it just felt so powerful to me, Peace. I was feeling really sensitive and as if I was getting messages I didn't quite understand. Then Mary suggested that since Stonehenge was only about a mile away, we should go there during our lunch break. It was pouring rain and as Mary drove, I read aloud from the first pages of *By Heart.* We were all feeling misty by the time we got to the store.

It was a wonderful little store, with stones of every kind and with books, jewelry, CDs, and incense. It was a small store with just one little shelf of books, but what should be on it, facing front and center, right at eye level, but a book called *Circle of Stones.* I opened it up. It asked how things would have been different had we had a place to go to be with the grandmothers.

When I got back to work, I was still feeling this incredible connection. I took my *By Heart* chapter outside and read it again, thinking of it as spending a few minutes alone with my grandmother. When I was done, the song "Amazing Grace" ran through my mind. I couldn't help but wonder if the song, the chapter, the stones, the whole day was telling me I had been blind and that this writing on my grandmother was what I was supposed to be doing.

Amazingly, when I got home, no one was home. I put on my Enya CD and just sat and listened. But I didn't only hear the music, I started to hear messages. Messages about wanting. It was almost as if Grandmother Ivie was trying to tell me that her life had been one long wanting for everything she didn't have and that I should quit wanting and Be. It made me see that writing and wanting are one and the same in my life, and that it's probably not a good thing. But what am I to do about it?

What do you want to do about it?

I don't know, Peace. I want to see *The Ninety-Seven Days* published. I want to finish *Who Killed the Mother?* and see that published. Then I don't know what next. I thought I had my third book figured out. I know that I am to write with the wisdom I have gained. I always thought that I would finish Grandmother's book someday. But I want a linear world where B follows A.

Wanting isn't what it's all about, is it? If you stop wanting and Be, what then will you do?

If I had all the time in the world I would write Grandmother's story and my story and your story. Your story is most difficult because I fear admitting to it. I know I'm not supposed to fear and when I fear I am being separate. I told my friend Kathy about you the other day and it was wonderful. I suppose the more I share, the more I will get over the fear.

It is your fear that concerns me. Because you are perfectly safe. You know you are safe. No one is asking you to tell anyone you are talking to an angel. So what are you afraid of?

I want—and I will use the word *Want* with a capital *W* because that is what it is—to be a published writer so badly. I realize it is in my wanting that I am losing the ability to write something publishable. And I did even give up the fear for a while when I *let go* and when I felt *safe*. But the idea of returning to my writing about Grandmother brought back the yearning, the wanting. I feel this even though my grandmother has warned me not to want and not to throw away happiness, which is not exactly what I'm doing, because I am happy, but not perfectly happy because of this wanting. So I guess I should give up my wanting. But I don't know how.

Okay. Give it to me. I'll take it. Sweet one, do not chastise yourself about wanting, just give it up. If it makes you feel better to give it to me, then give it to me. The lesson of your grandmother is that no one can give us what we Want and we can't give it to anyone else either. Let's instead try to turn your Want into something else.

270

Like what? *Ambition* is the only other word I can think of for it and it is really just the same old thing.

Look, you know every painter who paints a painting would like to have people praise it and say they would give anything for it. But that is not why the painter paints. If you had no talent for writing, you would be wanting it and still no one could give it to you. You are a child of God. All things are within you. All the talents you could ever hope for are there. You have come a long way to believing you have talent. You have had it confirmed in several ways. You are only one person away from having your writing published. But in your wanting, you are forgetting why you write and for whom you write. You write because it is you, it is who you are, and it is you for whom you write. And when you are not separate from the whole, you write for everyone. But when you separate yourself with fear, you write for no one if you write at all.

What you wrote about your grandmother was some of the best writing you have ever done. It came pouring out from within. Not because it was from your grandmother, but because it was from within. As your grandmother is within, as I am within. There is no separation, dear one, unless you create it with your fear. Fear and wanting have much in common. They feed on each other. They are predicated on believing that the universe will not give you what you need. Want as opposed to abundance. Look up Want. *It is not something that you* Want.

> want: to fail to possess, lack 2. to feel or suffer the need of 3. need, require 4. to earnestly wish
>
> want: a lack of a required or usual

amount: shortage 2. dire need: destitu-
tion 3. something wanted: desire 4. personal defect: fault

wanting: not present or in evidence:
absent 2. falling below standards or
expectations 3. lacking in ability or
capacity: deficient

wanting: less, minus 2. without

You're right. I don't want *Want*.

*Then give it up, sweet one. I will help you keep it from your mind, as
will the Holy Spirit. I am glad you have called upon the Holy Spirit.
The Holy Spirit is the most powerful of allies. You have such strength,
such wisdom in your corner now! Do not despair. Believe! The universe
would like you to have all that you desire. Believe, and it will be so.
Cease to worry about it. Just write! Write from the heart. Write to
know yourself. Write to know what you know. Is that not what we have
been doing? Slowly revealing what you already Know? That is what
writing is, dear one. Is it not a worthy aim in and of itself, and does it
not stand to reason and to spirit that the more you know and the more
you know you know, the more beautiful and full of knowledge your writing will become? Just like you! Let me remind you, your writing is
you—and it is beautiful!*

Thank you, sweet Peace. I am sorry to be so dense. But the
message to go back to the writing about my grandmother
seemed to come from you, from the Holy Spirit, the
unconscious, the dream. Can't you just tell me yes or no?

WANTING

Can't you tell me what I am to do with it?

You've already done something with it. You got a message you needed from it. You must write what you must write because it is coming from within.

Then, I guess, for now, this is what I must write. It's just that I w___—okay. If I give up wanting to be published, I know this is what I want to write right now. Okay. Thank you. I'll stay with that. If I give up the *W* word, it is clearer. It is perfectly clear. Thank you again, dear Peace. I love you and I can't thank you enough for what you do for me.

You are welcome and welcomed, as always, dear one.

PEACE AND GOODNESS

November 15, 1995

I have just returned from Europe and am so comforted to be here with the things I love about me—my husband, my children, my books, my computer, my "things." I am going to have to do some thinking about the difference between a *Care of the Soul* way of cherishing certain items of significance and the less positive attachment. But for the moment, I am glorying in the simple joy of being "home." It feels unbelievably good to be here.

I always marveled that people could return from Europe and not be profoundly changed. Have I been profoundly changed? I don't think so. I don't know that I needed to be. I do know that I have come home with a new appreciation for many things—first and foremost Home! Also Family! And by family, I mean perhaps something new. The journey to the ancestral home, the pilgrimage home, was important, but the new appreciation is of the living family—and the living family is here! It is in how we live that family truly continues. In our remembrance, our values, our culture. In, perhaps, those things we cherish, from items to memories. In, assuredly, the continued communication between family members. It is this, more than any place, that is important. It is the living, more than the deceased, who constitute family.

This became particularly poignant to me as I visited grave sites of both saints and family members. Rather than being struck by the presence of individuals there, I was struck by the lack of presence. Again, it is in the living that spirit resides. The living who visit those grave sites are what makes them places of holiness. So, certainly, it was important to go. Important to *see,* to *visit,* to *pray.* Important to the living. Important to Mom. She felt her dad would have been proud that she made it to Sutera. I agree. But again, the importance is to the living and the living connections that will continue. Instead of someday saying, "Our ancestors came from Italy but we don't know exactly where," our visit will help keep the family alive. Help one living being to know another—keep us connected.

Hello, Peace.

Hello, Margaret.

You talked to me at Assisi. I was anxious, and so I said, "Peace, stay with me" (this as I approached the church, after having seen many signs of your presence), and you said, "I'm with you." And I am sure it was you who then calmed me as I repeated the words, "Let Peace be in my heart." I referred often to my motto for the trip—not something that came specifically from you, but from *A Course in Miracles*. There were two mottoes actually. One was "See every human encounter as a holy encounter," and the other was "See the glory of God and know it is my glory as well." I would think of people, not as angels on this trip, but as God. And I saw so many glories, Peace. Man-made tributes to glorify God and the glory of God's creation. God and man together.

Yes, Margaret. There lies the message of your journey. God and man are one. Their creations are one. Space does not separate. The mind does. All are connected.

Welcome home, Peace.

Home is in you, Margaret. Home is in God and God is in you. The peace of your earthly home is God and the peace of His home is you. As happy as your husband was to see you, so is God. When you reside in peace, you reside in God. Reflection, Margaret, it means so many things. Now is the time for reflection. The glories you have seen are in you and of you. Now is the time for reflection of these glories.

Keep me peaceful, Peace. Let me remain peaceful in my enjoyment of home and God and all that man and God have created. Please help me not to start making rules and time lines for myself again. Help me to reflect the peace and glory I have seen.

They are within, dear one. Hold on to that. Do not worry. Know yourself in your glory and that you can do no wrong. Know yourself and your rules and time lines will be unnecessary. Belief. Faith. These, too, are messages of your journey. Did you not see these things? Did you not feel them? Did you not ask, "Why?" "Why are these people here?" "Why are they called the faithful?" Full of faith. You saw the creations of faith. You saw what one individual of faith can do. You saw what you can do. You can do miracles. You can do anything. You need not worry about what to do. You need only have faith. You need only believe you can do what you are here to do. Know that you and God are one and you cannot know otherwise.

My main enemy, Peace, seems to be time. When I am rushed, I cannot or do not remember who I am and what is important. I know you will say to forget time, but in modern life, it is next to impossible to do so.

Simplify. It is what you are thinking and wanting anyway. Each time you think about adding to your life or your property, ask yourself if what you are adding will simplify your life or make it more complex. Handle things one-on-one. Do one thing at a time—the thing you most want or need to do. And ask yourself when you are rushed or have things you do not want to do, what the consequences will be if you do not do those things. The world will not end, I assure you. Be. You have asked often for inspiration. Breathe it in during quiet moments. Reward

277

yourself with quiet moments. Reward your family with quiet moments.
Call on me as often as you need and when you think of me, when you
think Peace, be at Peace. Gather it around you.

Quiet your mind. It is your own mind that is noisy, and you can con-
trol it. When it is noisy, tell it to be quiet. When things are rushed,
take one thing at a time. Remember for what it is you prepare.
Remember to enjoy what you are doing when you are doing it. Rest.
Relax. Smell the sweetness.

Ah—the sweetness, Peace. I never smelled such sweetness as I did entering the tomb of Saint Francis. I almost
forgot about it. It was incredible. It was lilies, but it was
more, wasn't it?

You are sweet, dear one. In your peace, your reverence, your quiet,
smell the sweetness. Saint Francis was very sweet, very dear. So are
you. We are all one in God, you see. We are all sweet.

Thank you, dear Peace. I don't seem to be able to stay
away from here today. Somehow, the continuation of
things holy is linked with my expression of them here. I
feel the holiness of making bread and cleaning house, of
organizing and puttering in my home. Yet it all feels like
a bubble that can be burst by the pin of "real life." I don't
want to talk on the phone or think about bills or
Thanksgiving or Christmas. I just want to *be.*

You control your mind. Don't think about those things you do not want
to think about. There will come a time when you will want to think
about them. Wait for it.

To get back to the trip, I do believe we honored the family with the trip. We were an event in the little towns of Sutera and Milena, especially. We said, "You are important to us" by our being there. At least I hope that is what the relatives knew from our visit. And without the visit, the unexpected wouldn't have happened—spending our final night in the House of Smiles, the home for homeless boys, surrounded by Friars and Fathers and their good works, by the happiness of our cousin who has devoted her life to the boys. Was there some special significance to this, Peace? To our final night . . .

surprising you with its goodness?

Pax et bonum. *Peace and Goodness. Saint Francis's message. Reflected in the world. The one you live in. The day-to-day one you fear will infringe on your Peace. Your trip was about finding the meaning of your life. It isn't something you can decide on. But you can reflect. It is time for reflection. Peace and goodness. You will share both with the world, your world. There is much good that can be done in it. Peace and goodness are meant to be shared. This is what you are striving for—your way of sharing with the world. It is that part of you that yearns so to be published. To be published is to share. It is not only recognition but reflection. Reflect. Reflect on all that occurred on your journey. It will lead you to yourself and to what you can share with the world.*

Dear Peace,   November 17, 1995

Mary said on the phone today she is getting answers— it is all coming together. Perhaps my reflection will do this for me as well. But I come today with questions. Or I come, at least, hoping for answers. I do have faith. I do believe I will find what I have come into this life to do. But I, like Mary, would like answers. Yesterday I asked for peace and time to Be. Today I ask for answers. I'm sorry, Peace. It is only that I seek direction. Yesterday you said to reflect on the journey. Reflection is always revealing to me.

Today's lesson in *A Course in Miracles* concerns the meaninglessness of life and the fear that meaninglessness breeds. Is that my problem? That without clear direction concerning the course of my life, I fear it will be meaningless? And yet, if I have faith, which I say I do, I know meaninglessness is impossible. To accept that this world is illusion and we are all godlike beyond that illusion is a difficult lesson. I do believe it, because I know Donny's body, his physical form, is not the true Donny I love. The true Donny I love is godlike, is more than his physical form. And I saw in Europe that the tombs of saints are not the point—not the place of spirit. I saw that it is in the living that one finds the godlike. But it is also in the creations of the living—which, according to the *Course,* are all supposedly part of the illusion. It is hard to say Saint Peter's is meaningless while, at the same time, I realize it is the emotions, the spirit stirred by Saint Peter's that are the important thing.

So, I come seeking guidance. I do have this wonderful time before me. This time of being home and appreciating

my home and family, this empty time in which to reflect.
Just steer my reflection in a direction. Lead me. Take my
hand and point me where I need to go. Please?

*Smile, Margaret. Be happy. You are headed in the right direction
whether you know it or not. There is no meaninglessness where you are
going.*

Where am I going?

*Toward the real you. Toward your real meaning. All is as it should be.
Trust me. You are where you should be and you are heading where you
should go. Each time has its purpose. This time is not meaningless. You
do not have to produce to be meaningful. The time of Being is very
important. The time of resting and reflecting is as important as any
other. Do not be in a hurry to move on. Be peaceful and in your peacefulness, listen.*

LEARNING TO LISTEN
IN A DIFFERENT WAY

CREATING

November 21, 1995

Y ou seem quiet to me lately, Peace. Is this an illusion? Is this true? And if it is true, is there a reason
for it?

*You are learning to trust yourself, a very important step along the path.
I am here. I am with you. I am helping you learn to listen in a different way. You may not hear me as loudly but you will hear. Do not
worry. All is as it should be.*

It is becoming harder and harder for me to believe that I am doing all I should do. I keep expecting to wake up one morning and *know* that I am to finish book number two, or to publish this writing, or to do Grandmother's book. Jesus keeps talking about our creations in *A Course in Miracles*, as if they are pleasing to God. But I am not sure what He means by creations. I know the mind is holy and the creations of the mind are thus holy too, but is He referring only to creations of the mind that see the Truth in all God's children? Or, if everything we see is something we create, is He talking about how and what we see? Or, is He talking about creations in the way that I would, the producing of something with this wonderful gift of the mind? Or, is that only the human way of thinking of creation? Can you help me here?

Everything you do is holy, one thing no more so than another. Only to you is producing something more important than your interactions with your brothers and sisters. But you should be hearing something else loud and clear from A Course in Miracles. *The Holy Spirit speaks to you through your brothers and sisters, and it is in giving that you receive—blessings and everything else. So producing is no longer a solitary act. Can you begin to look at producing as a gift to your brothers and sisters? Take the ego away from your thoughts about producing, particularly your writing, and you will begin to see the true purpose of what you do.*

Everything you do is creating. For whom do you create? Turn your creating over to God, over to the Holy Spirit. You will be guided if you do not fear and if you do not have ego standing in your way. The Holy

Spirit cannot answer a question you are afraid of receiving the answer to. You do not think you are afraid. See how fear and trust are linked. If you trust absolutely that the answer will be the right one for you at the right time, you will receive it. Your impatience is, in a way, a symptom of distrust. Would God withhold from you that which you need Now? That which you are ready for? Don't you see how you are learning in this time of quietude?

You are preparing for God's work. Remember our lessons on knowing for what it is that you prepare. You prepare for Thanksgiving to take place on the day of Thanksgiving. Not before. You do not try to rush it. You do one thing one day and one thing the next. And on the day for which you prepare, it all comes together and is as it should be. So it is with God's work. Every day is a preparation. Do not despair that you do not know the day on which you will be called upon. Every day is as important as the next. All are God's work.

You do not know which interchange may change a life. You may be doing God's work tomorrow when you encourage someone. Every action has a reaction, every act of giving returns something, not only to the giver, but to all God's children. It is the ripple effect. What you do to one you do to all. This is literally true. So it is important to be mindful. Start each day knowing for what it is you prepare. Be mindful. Be still. Listen. Smell the sweetness.

Thank you, sweet Peace.

GRATITUDE

Dear Peace,   November 26, 1995

I started out realizing I wanted or needed to write about resentments. This is because of how often I have been full of them. Resenting that I have to work instead of being grateful that I have such a wonderful place to work and such wonderful people to work with. Resenting my housework or, even worse, resenting others in the family because I am the one doing the housework. Resenting phone calls or anything else that interrupts what I think is more important to be doing. The list is endless.

However, although resentments seemed to permeate my days when I look back, once I recognized that resentment was what I was feeling and saw how illogical it was, it has not reared its ugly head, or not much. It is hard to keep track of all the nonsense the mind comes up with in a given day. I hope *A Course in Miracles* will help me change this last statement. One thing it helped me see, after a few words with Donny, was how when we feel we are being attacked, we attack (I would have called it defense before). And how you cannot attack if you love. It made me realize how, if when I feel Donny has attacked me, I

285

stop and say, no, he couldn't have attacked me because he loves me; I won't attack or defend in return. And it's so true. I realize how many little interchanges I can change with this one thought. It might be the simplest thing, like walking in the door and having Donny ask, "Are you just getting home?" and me immediately thinking he is attacking me or judging me or suspecting me, and so instead of saying, "Yes, I had a lot of work to do today. How was your day?" I attack—if not with my words, with the tone of my words. "Yeah, I'm just getting home. It's busy at work, you know. I had things to do." Practical life lessons. It is an amazing thing about the spiritual, how it gives one all these practical life lessons.

I read something today that may have taught me about why, once I recognized it, resentment disappeared. It said how you cannot change something by fighting it, that fighting it only gives it more power. Pride was the example the article used. The trick, it said, rather than fighting pride, is to learn its opposite—humility. Something I should probably give some thought to. But my thought of the moment is that maybe the opposite of resentment is gratitude. And thus, my gratitude outweighed my resentment and got rid of it for me. Kind of neat. What do you think, Peace?

I think you're swell, Margaret.

I am learning, Peace. More this year than I could have imagined. Now I tend to want to quit my "Ways of

Knowing" class. I want to stay home. I want to enjoy home. That's all I want for Christmas. I don't want to *want* anymore at all. I'm trying to avoid the papers and the sales and the stores. I want to stay in contentment and not let myself be drawn out of it. And like a dieter, I know better than to put tempting things in front of me, for a while at least. Until I am more secure in my contentment.

Peace, I went back to work today. Julie mentioned your earlier words about how the office could not contain us much longer. I am content, but I would be so much more content if I could stay home. But that's wanting, isn't it? So I won't ask you questions about the future that I would like to ask. I will remain content in the Now. But I will ask something for Julie. She had a profound experience in Milan. She hadn't been feeling spiritual or thinking about things spiritual when a work of art seized her with emotion. Again it involved music. She was in a room of a museum that was dedicated to music, I believe she said. But she wonders at the source of the feelings that rose up in her. Can you or Water help her?

Peace replacing anxiety. That is what music is about for her. It will soothe her. It will lead her out of the woods of fear where she has been so long. Tell her it is not important why it is so. It is important that she let it lead her, that she follow. Turning to what makes her feel good is not self-indulgent. It is necessary. Water and art and music are expressions. She feels them. It is necessary for her to feel. It is better if she feels good. She no longer needs to feel bad. Tenderness. She can feel tenderness toward herself now. Not judgment. Not fear. Water, art, music will bring her to tenderness for herself and give her the means of expression she so needs.

These things affect her because they are expressions and she has no means of expression of her own. It is all locked within her bursting to get out. Tell her to get a fountain, fish, music that rains like water falling, paint brushes that dribble water colors like rain. Her expression will flow. Fluidity of expression will lead her to God and to self and to tenderness. It is expression she finds so beautifully painful she can hardly stand it. Because it is calling out to her. She wants to share herself so badly but she is blocked by fear of expression. At every turn she wants to make herself known but is unable. She is crying out to be heard and no one can hear. It is so lonely.

I am still full of tenderness for Julie and will always be, even after she learns to be tender to herself. I call out to her to express herself. I ask her, beg her, plead with her to let go of her fear and let herself flow. I do not want her to be lonely anymore. She need not be. Tell her to do it for her children if she will not or cannot find a way to do it for herself. Her children cannot be the sole expression of her love because they have to be for themselves. But they will try if she does not find a way to begin, to try for herself. Tell her in her selfless love for her children, she can perhaps find the courage to let go.

To let go is to expand. To express. To give. To share. Julie wants to do all these things. She wants to extend. To encompass. Yet she withdraws. And with each withdrawal, she feels diminished. Ask her to be on the lookout for these withdrawals. If she can begin to recognize them, she can turn them around. Every time she feels the need to withdraw, tell her to expand instead. To think of herself as water flowing outward rather than like a raisin shrinking into herself, wrinkling and *growing hard. Take the raisin and puff it out into a grape. Make it into wine. Let it flow.*

Thank you so much. I will tell her.

Thank you. I will be with you, with her, when she reads the words. When she hears. I will surround her with love and the space she needs to feel what she needs to feel. And I will be with her when she chooses to begin. To be reborn. Julie, think of Christmas as a time of birth—for the Son of God, and for you as well. Be reborn to a life of joy. Begin.

HOME

Dear Peace,   November 30, 1995

I still want to talk to you, but my husband is upstairs sick and my overwhelming feeling, as I sat down to write, was that now is not the time to write, now is the time to surround my love, my husband, with the love he needs. My other thought, although this sounds cruel in a way, was that maybe his illness is there in order for me to take care of him and for him to let himself be taken care of. Perhaps it is there because he needs to feel more of my love. Perhaps because I need to learn to start with him, the one I have learned the most about love from. And as

I write it, I realize how true that statement is and how much I want to love him, not only as a wife, but with God's love, a love to strengthen and enhance him—and by reflection, myself. Family is the greatest place to learn about love, of this I am sure. It is the kindergarten and the graduate school of love. So upstairs I go. Back to the classroom of love, where I need to be. More here later.

Dear Peace,   December 8, 1995

I just want to write a little about what has been taking place. First of all—Julie. Julie has begun, because or with the help of what happened here. Thank you. She felt her angel's presence. She heard his voice. She heeded his call. When I brought her the words of her angel, before even seeing them, she decided to take them to the hospital chapel or meditation room to read (something she had never done before). Then, before she had even gotten to the last paragraph, where Water said he would be with her, she said she felt wrapped in something protective, as if a cushion of light were surrounding her. It was all very moving, for her and for me. She is becoming more and more dear to me as I know her more through this extraordinary communication. The one way that she *is* truly open is in her wanting to know. I've not known anyone to be as open in an appeal for guidance. I know none with a more sincere desire. There truly is a tenderness about her.

Second—me. I read about guilt. I read how guilt takes

up all the space that love would occupy. And I gave my guilt to the Holy Spirit. And I felt my breathing immediately come easier. How much more room I will now have for love!

I also am going to try to "give up" my ambition for my book, as in "give it up to a higher power." I hope you guys will take care of it for me. And I have received a message: Awaken—Behold—Rest.

Every time I have sat down here recently or felt I had time to write, other things drew me away—as they will tonight, it's trim-the-tree night. But I know it's time to come back, whether to you, Peace, or to me, I am not sure. I know this time is different somehow. Perhaps because I returned with an openness for joy and, having glimpsed it, want it. Perhaps because I am grateful for what I have. Perhaps because I have given up guilt and ambition. Perhaps because it is simply time for a different kind of learning, a different season. Or perhaps it is all of the above. Home and family may be my learning circle for the moment. I'm just not sure. But I think coming back here, talking to you, talking to myself, talking to God, will help make me sure. Be with me, Peace. Help my thoughts be prayerful. Prepare me to return here with an open and receptive mind and heart. Now—back to the family and the tree.

MESSAGES AND MESSENGERS

Dearest Peace,   December 12, 1995
It is time to talk together once again. I have been away from you—both for practical reasons and for familial ones of the highest order—and I have been away from you at times on your insistence and at times on mine. But I am content. I have been fighting getting sick and at the same time flirting with it. As with all or most ill-nesses, I feel a part of me must want it. That part is the part that needs some rest. Awaken—Behold—Rest. Messages.

I asked Mary to ask her angel, Trinity, about my writing. I say this sheepishly because part of me felt this was going around you or going around my vow to give you my ambition for my writing. But it really wasn't, Peace. It was me sincerely continuing my search for my destiny. I am not certain I am "supposed" to continue my search, but a part of me still wants to be active in defining it. And more important, I felt there was something connective when I asked you for help for Julie and Mary, and so I thought asking Mary for a message for me now might be a way of giving something to her as well as one of receiving something for myself.

I invite you now to share with me in my contentment, to update me, to guide me as you always have, to share with me what is right in this time or space for you to share. Will you visit with me?

I am with you. I have never left and never will leave. I am merely with you differently, as you have recognized. Why? Partly to show you how well you do without this communication. Partly to give you space in which to enjoy your joy. To dwell in the house of the Lord. The new house will honor you as you honor it with your contentment. You do not have to be sick or unhappy. You have the power to honor your decision to embrace contentment. This is a time for contentment and for the sharing of it. You can rest without being sick. It does not have to do with time. It has to do with peace.

Your peaceful contentment is more important than your Christmas cards and gifts. It is your preparation for Christmas. For the birth of your savior. Of the birth of your salvation. Of your birth. Of your freedom from guilt. Continue to go with what you feel in the Now and you will not go wrong. When you question what you feel in the Now, it is

293

only so that you can be sure of how you really feel, so that you can free yourself of the shoulds and oughts of the duality.

Thank you, Peace. I admit I am feeling out of practice. You are right, of course, and having you is part of my contentment. The discontent, which is really too strong a word, comes from wanting what I do not have—more, answers, and I almost said guidance, but I do have that from you. Is there a way I can feel and understand your guidance through the waters of contentment to the meeting place with my destiny?

Let go of want. You want answers I cannot give you. Ask me for what I can give you.

What can you give me, Peace?

Assurance. Assurance that you are where you need to be, doing what you need to do.

If I wasn't, would you tell me?

You will not ever be in such a place, for no such place exists. You cannot fall off the path. Doesn't that reassure you?

Yes. But how, then, can you guide me?

I see the path clearly where you do not. That does not mean I can tell you where it leads. But I can illuminate the road beneath your feet—if not the next hill.

So you can make the Now clear but not the future?

There is only the Now. The future is of your time and your time is not real. In eternity there is no time. All is one. Learn the lessons of A Course in Miracles. *Who you love now you will always love. Some things are for always. It is the things of impermanence that concern you when their very impermanence should signal you that they are of no concern. Dear one, dear one, seek and you shall find.*

Peace, I seek my destiny. Can't you help me find it?

Sweet heart, you know it. You are living it. Your sweet contentment is part of your destiny or you would not be experiencing it. You had to find it before you could share it. What is it you want to share?

I guess it is myself, Peace, and the writing I lament so over is just one part of that self.

Do you want to share a self of guilt or a self of contentment? A self of love or a self of fear? You are preparing for this sharing of self. You are being blessed with health, more time, more money, love. Trust that these things will grow the more you share of them. This is a time for consolidating and learning to believe in the permanence of your goodness and good fortune. You have not been idle in your journey to fulfill your destiny. You are learning to give just a little more than you are comfortable with and finding it doesn't hurt you. This is a lesson. You are learning that giving up guilt doesn't hurt anyone. This is a lesson. You are learning that if you give up competition, it will cease to exist. This is a lesson. You are trying to learn that if you give up ambition for your writing, it will free you. You are struggling with this lesson because you feel the writing is more a part of your destiny than the love and kindness and compassion and givingness of your self you are learning to share. You can only learn by teaching. You can only receive by sharing.

295

Yet you wait patiently (??) to share your writing. Why? Is someone else giving you divine advice to sit on it? Give and you shall receive. What is it you hope to receive and how does this affect how you share?

I would hope, eventually, to receive money, or a "living" for my writing so that I could write more and more, so that I could learn more and more and share more and more.

I tell you you must reverse your thinking, you must share, learn, write, receive. Give and you shall receive.

Thank you, Peace. I know you are giving me guidance and I thank you for it. May I ask you now, is there anything I can offer?

Offer your joy. It fills the heavens with laughter and music. Share your joy. Give of it. You have an odd idea of selfishness concerning joy. But you cannot share joy if you do not feel joy. Feel joy daily—for you, for us, for the universe. Joy is shared automatically with all that is. It is enough in and of itself. But you can also consciously choose to share it, which will only make it stronger.

Thank you, Peace, for pointing that out to me. I'm sorry it took me so long to ask you what I could give in return.

There is no "so long," there is only Now. I am the Way, the Truth, and The Light, said the Lord. Follow him and you will know the Way, the Truth, and The Light.

December 15, 1995

Mary asked Trinity about my writing and she read his response to me. It was about sharing. It was about unfolding. It was about dreams. I wonder if you have anything to say to me about this.

Listen to Mary. You are a star. A being of light. Share. Let your light shine. Only you are holding yourself back. There is nothing in you that does not deserve to be a star. A bringer of light. Let your fear go. Dare to share. You are the researcher. Mary keeps telling you this. Research means to search, to seek. Seek and you shall find. Write. Make phone calls. Look in books. Follow the signs. They are before you. Before. The past is not in you but before you. Open your eyes. The future is Now. That's why what you want is Now. Do not worry about your impatience. Patience can be active as well. Surrender is active.

Give your research to the Holy Spirit and He will guide you. He sends those to guide you. Nothing takes as long as you think it does. Forget time. Doing and being are complementary. Do not make lists. Do. Do what feels right to you. You are being guided. When it feels right, do it. Rest. Rejuvenate. Go on. Eternity awaits.

December 16, 1995

In my dream, I am biking from Minneapolis to St. Paul over a cobblestone bridge. When I reach the St. Paul side, I run into two classmates, women, who proceed to get in a discussion with me about who my writing reminds them of. I say it most resembles Veneer, and I spell it, because I am not sure I'm saying it correctly. One of the other women says, "No. It's like Susan Sontag's." Then we

PEACE

go into a classroom where others are discussing my
writing and comparing it to the works of other
authors—and I wonder why? What is the point?

Peace, someone is speaking to me in my dreams. First of
all, me saying my writing is like *Veneer* shows a layer of my
fear I have not contemplated previously. Do I think it is
superficial? A glossy finish on something cheap or of little
value? Second, others are telling me it is worthwhile.
Although I barely know Susan Sontag, I know enough to
know she is a respected writer. Finally, I'm wondering
why this need to compare at all.

So, Peace, help me here. Is there something "real" of
"real" value waiting to come forth instead of this work that
is veneer? Or is the work I've already done "real" work?
And do I carry this fear I had not defined in these terms?

All right. Let me give it a try first. I don't think I feel my
writing has no value. I think it is as good as much of the
writing that is published. But I suppose, then, I would
need to ask myself why I have avoided finding a new
agent. I'm not sure it was any great subconscious thing at
work. First I was busy with work, and at the same time I
was giving Dan time to make some response. Then I was
busy with the move and the trip. Now I am busy with
Christmas. Yet I know that these have not been good
enough reasons for someone whose every other thought,
as reflected here and elsewhere, concerns my writing. If it
were so important to me, so paramount in my life, so
integral to my happiness, why didn't I make time for it? I
made time for this writing.

Psychologically, I was unprepared for what happened to me, for Dan's quitting agenting. I had thought the need to sell myself was behind me and that I could simply write, and I thought simply writing was what I really wanted to do. But I have not written much other than this. Would I have if things hadn't happened the way they did with Dan? I don't know. I only know that this has been the writing I have wanted to do. I keep saying that I want to get back to my "creative" writing, but the crux of it is that I *don't* want to. There. I have finally admitted it. I am admitting it to myself as I write it. If I had really wanted to get back to it, I would have. If I had really wanted to pursue it, I would have contacted other agents.

This is the writing that has meaning for me now. Whether the writing of mysteries will ever have meaning to me again I do not know. This is what I have been afraid to admit. Because I do want the life of a writer. I do want writing to be my life. And I came so close to making it so with the mystery writing. Will I ever come so close again? Can I really give up something that has for so long held out the promise of giving me the life I want?

What has all my lamenting about my writing really been about? It has been about not knowing what to write while the whole time I have been writing away and finding more solace from it, more wisdom, more peace than I have ever found before. My lamenting has been hanging on for all I am worth to ideas that belonged to the old Margaret, to the Margaret who did not know

Peace. Ideas that turned writing into a false god. Ideas that told me all could be achieved through being a published writer instead of that all could be achieved through God. I wanted the life of a writer so I could be proud of myself. I wanted the life of a writer so I would have respect. I wanted the life of a writer so I could share. But what have I been doing? Spending my year taking away all those things that made me feel I could not be proud of myself. Getting rid of all those ideas that said I was not deserving of respect. Sharing.

Even as I write this I am close to tears. Not because of all I have gained, but because of even contemplating giving up what I have thought I have wanted all this time. Grandmother said to give up want. Peace said to give up want. Yet even now, even as I begin to realize how much of what I have wanted I have found, I cannot believe I am even contemplating giving up the goal that has been my goal for so long. It feels like giving up my right arm. It feels like cutting out my heart. It feels like taking my identity away from me. But it also feels like what I must do. I can't even bear to think about it. I don't know what to do.

December 20, 1995

I've got it now. I couldn't hear the message that this message is for the universe because I couldn't bear to give up my fiction. So I asked the Holy Spirit to make my decisions for me after reading in *A Course in Miracles* that He would answer immediately, quietly, with the decision that was right for everyone it touched (which is everyone, not just me). And yesterday, in the midst of my despair, in the midst of my not knowing what to do, Mary Love came to my house, to my table, and told me that what we have lived is the story, our journey is the story, the spirit sisters are the story. She said she had awakened to a message: "This is the story." She came to my table and gave me back my life as writer.

"This is the story." *Our* story—the story of how three ordinary women have shared the journey to oneness—is what I must write. As she told me about it, about how she knew this was what I was meant to do, she went back to her spirit bag and retrieved her journal and read me Trinity's message one more time.

> *As you see you share, all of you do, this unfolds.*
> *The story unfolds. You trust, you share, you grow.*
> *This is life. This is what dreams are made of. This*
> *is LOVE.*

Her voice echoed in my kitchen. Like a shadow on her voice, her words took on added meaning. "This is the story."

I called Julie at work after Mary left and told her what Mary had brought me—told her that we both knew that my next writing was meant to be our story—and asked her if it was all right with her, and if she, too, would participate in the collaboration. She got goose bumps. It's going to be, Peace. I have my answer! I know what I'm supposed to write!

The Holy Spirit, using you and Mary and Trinity as His messengers, has answered me. Mary and Julie and I will collaborate on *our* story. Nothing is stopping me now.

Even one of Gracie's first messages concerned my first book and Christmas. When Mary's computer first started malfunctioning, the file in which Mary had written her note to me concerning her thoughts on *The Ninety-Seven Days* was the only file she was allowed to enter. The cursor went to the word *christmas*, which she had noted as a typo because it was not capitalized, and would not stray from it. It is Christmas. Was Gracie trying to be a messenger too? Was she trying to tell us that by this Christmas we would be working on a book together? Will *our story* be my first book? I do not know but I thank you for this Christmas gift.

December 27, 1995

Peace, I want to thank you for tonight and ask you to help me in keeping this peace. It was my first day back at work since the holidays. Everything went well. I got up and had time before work. I shared the writing I have done on *our story* with the spirit sisters. I did some work. I came home, started salad. Donny came in, made pasta. Angela's boyfriend, Matt, was here. Mia came home from work. We all sat down to dinner together. We laughed like crazy. Donny was at his best lampooning choir and orchestra directors. The kids held their own. They made fun of each other, teased each other, and laughed about it.

After dinner I washed dishes. Mia picked up the table and the pans. Both girls dried while Matt pulled up a chair and strummed his guitar. Donny's nephew, Nick, came in and he and Donny went into Donny's room to play his new Sony system. I came here.

We are all happy, Peace. We are all comfortable. The girls have each other and nice friends and boyfriends. We have our house! We are happy *together*. Thank you to all the powers that be. My life feels as near to perfect as it has ever felt. I have everything I've ever wanted, it seems, and purpose as well.

It is this purpose I want to ask your help with. The writing of this book between the three of us is going to be difficult. Most difficult, probably, for Mary. But also, in a different way, for me. I am used to writing here. I am not used to collaborating. I have left all the garbage stuff behind with the spirit sisters. I know this book couldn't be written while Mary and I still held even the least bit of competitiveness—and luckily we gave that up after Europe. I can't remember right now what, if anything, precipitated the change, but it was there when I returned to work from the trip. I knew, and Mary knew, and Julie knew, and we each knew the other knew, that the old garbage was gone.

This project is not worth bringing it up again. Help me keep it behind me. Help me bring nothing but love here.

Help me stay away particularly from competition, from envy, from comparison. Help me to assure my spirit sisters that they are more important even than the project. Help me stand ready to abandon it in favor of friendship and love if that is what is required. Help me to share my strength with Mary through it if that is what is required.

Peace, Holy Spirit, you started me on this road and I will not fail the right outcome if you stay with me. Don't let me lose you. Don't let my writing ambition rear its ugly head. Let this purpose stay pure, even while I know I don't even realize the extent of my part in this purpose or the extent of this purpose in the world. I want to say, don't let anything mess with my happiness, with my peace; but I know it is my peace that brings me happiness and it is my sharing of my peace that brings much of the happiness to my home and my table.

What a wonderful thing a table is, what treasures we bring there. Please help me to stay in gratitude for my table and its fullness. I am proceeding. I am taking the advice in *A Course in Miracles* literally, and I am not looking back, I am not hesitating or reconsidering. But it wouldn't hurt to feel your reassurance, Peace, your blessing on this course, this purpose. If you have any advice for me on the best way for me to proceed I would love to hear it.

Tell Mary what you just told me. Reassure her. Wait for her to catch up. Take your cues from her. Listen. I believe you. Believe yourself. Your open heart is bringing you wisdom to share. The way is being shown to you. Listen and you will hear.

I will, Peace. I truly am at peace with this project in whatever way it turns out. I know you have told me to proceed and I am at peace with proceeding. But I will be equally at peace with waiting. With giving Mary time. With doing what is needed. I think at my core, at my center, I am truly without ambition in this purpose. It is only at my extremes, on the outer reaches of myself, my old self perhaps, that I worry it will regain ground, that the ego will fool with my peace. That is why I ask your help. Keep my ego out of this project, dear Peace, dear Holy Spirit. Then I know it will proceed as it should proceed, according to God's holy plan.

Thank you for asking, dearest Margaret. Your request has been accomplished.

Dearest Peace   December 31, 1995, New Year's Eve

The year is coming to an end. THE YEAR. Since May 1, I have lived and breathed this year with you. Sometimes I think I have come so far. I have learned so much. And when I do, some old teaching tells me not to praise myself, that it is bad manners. I still have much unlearning to do. And much sharing. But I have come far. So far I am hardly the same person. I am not the person full of shame. I am not the person full of guilt. I am not the person full of resentment. I am not the person full of envy and competition. I am not the slave to time. I am safe. I am beginning. I am new and living in the Now. I feel love almost all the time. I feel gratitude almost all the time. I

305

am often peaceful. I am very often content. I am more into being than searching.

This last has made my communications with you less frequent. This last and love—being with my family and particularly my husband. This last and purpose—working on the goal given me by the Holy Spirit.

Yet I still need your help. I am not full of these negative things anymore. I am happier than I have ever been. I only need a little help, I think, to go the rest of the way. Am I right, Peace? And can you give me the help I need to proceed?

Dearest Margaret,
The year that begins tomorrow will be the first of many years of a new life for you. You do not go into this year or any others unaided. You cannot fail. You cannot go backwards. You carry this Now forward with you. Smell the sweetness of this Now. You are sweet. You are lovely to the heavens. Your happiness brings happiness to the heavens. Let go of illusion. You do it here. You can do it everywhere.

Things are happening for a reason. This you have taught me. Everything happens for a reason, for what it is meant to teach us, bring us. Now today I read in *A Course in Miracles:*

"In any situation in which you are uncertain, the first thing to consider, simply, is 'What do I want to come of this? What is it for?' The clarification of the goal belongs at the beginning, for it is this which will determine the outcome."[25]

I know my reading this today was not an accident. I have seen how you have helped me reach my goals: from my home to my furniture to my car to less stressful periods. Now I know it is time to set a new goal. It is important for the purpose the Holy Spirit has made clear to me, and it is important for this day, this hour, this year—for every situation. For everything that happens that disturbs my peace as well as for everything I want to happen, the question is, "What do I want to come of this? What is it for?"

How seldom we ask these questions! And how difficult to answer. What do I want to come of this? What is it for? I feel it is imperative for us to answer this about *our story,* to set the goal and then have faith. I will work on this with the sisters.

For my own answer, I am uncertain except that I know it is my purpose, given me by the Holy Spirit. Is that goal enough?

That goal is more than enough. That goal is The Goal.

I don't need to define it further?

Do you think the Holy Spirit's goal is to have you embark on this purpose for your own fulfillment alone? Trust that the Holy Spirit sees the grander plan, the picture you would obscure by worrying about the frame. Leave your goal as it is. Do not worry about it. Do not reconsider. Begin. Proceed. Do. Be.

Thank you, Peace.

January 1, 1996

We have been talking at work on how to proceed with writing our story. There has been no lack of permission for me to begin. Mary and I both have journals to draw upon and Julie has an incredible memory. We recently spent an afternoon typing up some of her important dreams and experiences from this year. Her recollection of dates and detail is truly amazing.

It is becoming clear that I will write and that Julie and Mary will guide me, helping me to remember the chain of events that linked our year. Toward this end, I asked Mary if I could read the journal she kept on Grace. I had asked her for it not without tact and gentleness, but with a writer's dispassion. I wanted to see it as a researcher, to know how she felt so that I could bring it to our story.

She had typed it on her computer and printed it out months and months ago. It had been "collecting dust" beneath the bed in the room that would have been Grace's room but which had become Mary's writing room. No one had ever seen this writing.

It has a cover page that says *"Grace's Life* by Mary Kathryn Love." I have now read it.

I seemed to go into another place while I read. I didn't cry, although I felt I should have. But it was as if it emptied me out. It was as if it was so full of feeling, it drained me of feeling, made me numb. But it stayed with me like a vice around my heart. It stayed with me until the moment I returned to work and saw Mary sitting at her desk, a scene I had seen a hundred times, day after day, month after month, and yet, in a way never seen. Mary.

That was when I broke down. I didn't intend to. I didn't know I would. I didn't know something in me had been waiting for the moment of seeing her again. As if I couldn't break down without her. Couldn't shed the tears without sharing them with her. I just hugged her and cried on her shoulder, saying over and over, "Mary, I never knew. I never knew."

I had never known. Never had even the faintest knowing. I thought I had been compassionate. But I had not understood her grief. I had been there. Had thought I had seen. But I had never seen. Some part of me had thought that I could understand her loss in a way that any mother could understand. That I could understand because, as a mother, I could imagine what it would be like to lose a child, because I had almost lost a child. But I hadn't even come close. Now I had. Now I had come close to Mary. Because this writing was Mary.

I told Mary it was the most beautiful writing a mother had ever done about her daughter. It was. It was also the most beautiful writing a woman had ever done about being a mother, about being a woman, about being human and vulnerable. It had everything. The joy of the beginning, the uncertainty, the loss, the ending. It was a tribute to Grace. But it *was* Mary.

It was almost too much. I am not going to be able to be a dispassionate writer, Peace. This is going to ask more from me than I ever imagined. What have I gotten myself into?

January 3, 1996

I try not to worry about writing the spirit sisters' story. I try to just be in my willingness to proceed. Yet I wonder how to proceed. I worry about time. I worry about energy. I worry about Mary. I worry about the responsibility of it. I worry about my relationship with you.

What is your role now and what is mine? Can I still come to you for answers or is your quietness a sign that the time for this is waning? I am peaceful in comparison to my general state a year ago. I am not peaceful in comparison to my general state a month ago. I feel I know the way now, but not how to get to the starting gate. I hope for the Holy Spirit to illuminate the way and then wonder—again. Peace, I am worried that where I don't get answers, don't get communication, I will get fear. I don't need much to keep me going. I would be happy just to feel you. Mary thinks I have given her some of my peace as I offered her on the phone the other night. I teased today that I felt as if I was having a brain drain.

I worked on our story last night. We're thinking of calling it *Love.* We talked about it at work. I am being very careful with it, not letting fear intrude upon it. It is more "me" that fear is snapping at. Can you help?

I remind you that it is when you are feeling most away from love that I love you most. When fear calls you, ask, "Where is love here?" What has taken you away from feelings of love? It is not me, sweet heart. I am sending you love in abundance. Are you open to receive it?

Have confidence, dear one. We will not let you down. Envision not disaster. Envision not strain and stress. Envision not trauma and uncertainty. Go boldly forward. You are only doubting self. Yet, remember that self is not one. You are not alone. Do not let my quietness or any other thing convince you that you are alone or unworthy of your calling. You have answered The Call. Do you think all of heaven will not rise to answer yours in turn? It will come together. That is what it is all about. Coming together. You are wanting structure before the time for structure. The foundation is taking shape. The structure will follow. Perhaps what you perceive as your weakness will allow others' strengths to emerge.

But you are not weak. There is no weakness, as you perceive weakness, in you. You are very strong. You are not your body. Trust. Trust that the Holy Spirit is doing His job and that He will help you to do yours. Your Peace is with you and you will never lose it by extending it outward. Do not confuse your feelings of weakness and your extension of your peace to Mary. Only know that the answers are being given to you even when they seem not to be the answers. Trust. Have faith. Rest. You have gotten good at extending your love and light. Now practice receiving it. Be a sponge. Drink it in. Feel it. Be grateful for it. Remember the happiness of gratitude and love. Go rest. Feel my love tomorrow. Feel the love of others. You will feel better.

January 5, 1996

In further preparation for writing *Love*, I asked Mary to share her "angel talk" journal writing with me and I have just finished reading it. It is so lovely, so sad, so bitter-sweet, so human, so very human. These fears really are universal, aren't they? And this writing does need to be shared, doesn't it? I read Mary's writing and I think, *How could it fail to move someone, anyone?* No one could be immune.

I realize how little she talks of things that trouble and disappoint her. I can see how when she feels bad, she wills herself not to feel. I understand. I understand her imperfections and they touch my heart. It is such a knowing. It is such an honor.

And yet, in her writing, she is much as she is in life. Her dramatic way of talking, her sweet way of showing her happiness, her silent way with her sadness. Absolutely nothing there not to love. The innocence of it all. The wanting to be good. To know that the self is lovable. It is hard to fathom that she does not know how lovable she is. How good. How sweet. How kind. How giving.

And I wonder, in retrospect, what my writing sounds like. I am not about to compare myself anymore. But Mary sounds so real. So absolutely true. I thought her writings about Grace were "pure" when I read them, so totally uncontrived, so full of her *self* and all that she was. A pure nakedness of being, feeling, all her pain, love, humanness exposed, vulnerable, pure. What it was. The way you are always saying we *are*. That something *is*. That is what her writing is like.

And I just don't know if I have that pureness in me. And again, I am not saying this in a judgmental way toward myself, only in an acknowledging way, and it is because I am a writer and being a writer is my greatest fear and joy. Can I be uncontrived, can I be just who I am, can I be as pure when I bring all these longings and expectations with me to my writing? I do not know. Perhaps this is my greatest lesson, and how appropriate that I should learn it from Mary. What you have been trying to tell me I needed Mary to learn. I am only realizing this as I write it. The reason I can't fear my writing, can't project, can't bring all the garbage of longing to it is because then it isn't me in all my selfhood; it isn't the essence, the pureness I would like it to be. I realize all writing doesn't have to be all that. And I realize I cannot strive for that. But I also realize I have to drop all the extraneous stuff I bring to my writing.

I hope there has been some pure writing here. I think there has been. But I ask your help, dear Peace, in a way I haven't asked your help in a long time, to bring me back to writing from the heart, and only writing from the heart, because I know that is where truth lies. And I want to bring that heart and that truth to all my writing, but especially to *Love,* Peace. I owe it to Mary and Gracie and Julie and to the heart and truth of the writing Mary shared with me. Will you help me?

You have finally asked the right question. I knew you would. I have been readying everything for this moment. It is done. Rejoice! Let your lingering sadness fall away. It is not only the last barrier with your writing, but also your last barrier with Mary. You would wonder

313

sometimes why your feelings would change from sheer happiness, when you were with her, to nothingness, to feelings of lack. You were no longer competing. You were no longer comparing. But what was it? It was her genuineness, that self that was so purely self, and you wondered, though you did not know it, could not define it, where that genuineness was in you. You have lived with a false front so long, so unknown to self that you became self-conscious. Self-consciousness has today fallen away. Rejoice. You are pure. You are what you Are. Finally, dear Margaret. You can Be. Without pretense.

I assure you that you did not carry pretense here with you often. You never carried it here consciously. Only the longing to overcome it, though you did not know that pretense was what you longed to overcome. Now you can rest. Now you can truly relax with who you are. No need anymore to fool anyone. No need to cover over something unworthy with a veneer of goodness. Your goodness is genuine, dear one. It was only the veneer that tarnished it. Rejoice that you do not need it anymore. It is over now. You can truly rest. You can find joy now. No more need to polish the silver. You are gold! Nothing to work on anymore. It is done. All you have to do is BE. The work has all been in the polishing what was already a jewel you only thought was coal. Go and be the jewel you are. But first get the rest, the first real rest, the rest of the completed, the one, the finished, the united. The work is done. Rest.

Dearest Peace,   January 6, 1996

When I finished here last night, I went up and wrote in my dream journal about how important your last message and the moments with you here were to me. How grateful I am. I did rest well. I didn't wake up fully until

11:30 this morning. I have had a lovely day cleaning and puttering and putting away the Christmas decorations. Preparing, finally, for the New Year and all its possibilities. I am just so grateful, Peace, for everything. I love my home so much I even love cleaning it. I love just being with my family. I would like it to go on forever—it is heaven to me, right here, right now. And I know this is where you have wanted me to be all along. Thank you for getting me here, Peace, and for all the help you've given me and sent me on the way.

I wanted to call Mary and be with her and share what had come to me from her writing. Do you realize, Peace—of course you do!—that she even had a dream the night before last about trying to solve a mystery and the mystery concerned me finding someone? It was me, wasn't it, Peace? The *me* hidden behind the veneer. Not just the writing—as in my dream—but *me!* I was lost and now I am found. I AM FOUND!

I went to sleep last night, Peace, repeating to myself, "I am who I am, I need do nothing. The work is done. I can rest." It was so sweet, Peace. Such a gentle place. I think I may even have relaxed.

I've been typing the rest of Mary's journal. This is the one she kept when she was unable to get into the computer to write. I thought by typing it, it would be available for use in *Love* and it would also really get it into my head. I was right. I was only going to type sections. Only those things I thought might be useful. But I cannot exclude

315

anything. I'm continuing to type not so much for *Love* as for a gift for Mary. And perhaps for me. I am still with her today even though I did not call her and we did not get together. I know it is a weekend when her stepdaughter, Amanda, is with her and I did not want to intrude.

My body is getting tired of typing, and yet I want to finish. I will break in a little while until tomorrow—don't think I'll finish tonight—and I know it's not important to. I can wake up to Mary again tomorrow. Peace, I have been hoping there would be a Christmas miracle and Mary would get pregnant. She desires it so greatly. It is to her what my writing is to me—her greatest desire and her greatest fear. If my prayers are being heard, Oh Lord, let this happen for Mary. Bring her this joy. I hope we are both now open to having our dreams fulfilled. I feel in my heart you have brought us to this place—together. It would be such a sweet bond, to seal our growth with the happiness of our heart's desire. If it is Your Will.

Peace, I have no questions for you tonight. No pains. No frustrations. I bring you only my gratitude and my greetings. Do you have greetings for me, dear friend, best friend, friend of my heart and soul?

What a lovely greeting, dear one. Your happiness is assured. Happiness is enjoying the Now. As long as you remember what you have felt and seen the last few days, you will be happy. You will know your heart's desire as you have never known it before and it will be. You no longer need anything to make you happy. You need nothing and you need do nothing. Do not begin again to strive and plan. You know your immedi-

ate purpose. You are preparing for it with love. You will complete it with love. No striving or planning are required. LET IT BE.

I must say thank you, also, for the music of the Beatles. You know I thought of their song "Let It Be" last night in connection to Mary. I don't know if they are guides or their music tools for you, my guides, but I thank you for it. I am just so grateful for everything. I cannot tell you enough, thank you enough. Any parting words, my friend?

The world, the universe is your friend tonight, dear one. All is friendship and love. All is right with the world. Your corner of it is expanding. The beauty of your home is yours to keep and to share. Trust that what will make you happy will come to you even if it is not what you thought it would be. Think of your striving for happiness this way— think of all the "things" you have striven for in the past. Did you know then what would make you happy? If you strive for red shoes, you may not find the blue that will make your feet dance. Just LET IT BE. And rest. Leave it all to me and the Holy Spirit. We know God's plan. God's plan includes more happiness for you than you can imagine. LET IT BE. And we will take you there.

Thank you, dear Friend, dear Guide, dear Messenger of the Divine. All my love, Margaret.

EPIPHANY

D earest Peace, January 7, 1996
I went to church this morning. It reminds me
of how I began this writing. With a trip to church,
with the residual awareness that comes from that hour of
contemplation and ritual.

Today we were celebrating Jesus' baptism and the feast
of the Epiphany. The moment Jesus was identified as *who
He was.* Again my life is mirroring my faith, my religion,
my God, and the calendar year. I looked up *epiphany* in the
dictionary today while Mary was here with me, sharing
with me the wonderful occurrences of the last two

318

days—my identity, my becoming *who I am*. Here is what we found together, with the accompanying goose bumps, of course:

> epiphany: from the Greek *epiphaneia,* appearance, to show forth, manifest
> 1. an appearance or manifestation of a god or other supernatural being
> 2. in many Christian churches, a yearly festival, held January 6, commemorating both the revealing of Jesus as the Christ to the Gentiles in the persons of the Magi and the baptism of Jesus: also called twelfth day [Mary told me as in the twelve days of Christmas.]
> 3. (a) a moment of sudden intuitive understanding; flash of insight (b) a scene, experience, etc., that occasions such a moment

Peace, I had my Epiphany! With the church's Epiphany! With Jesus! and with Mary and you. I had it here, I had it inside. I am identified. I am without my veneer, my covering over. I am Me.

I can only say thank you again. I am grateful again. All over again. Fresh today. Freshly grateful. Freshly *Who I Am.*

It was a blessing to be able to share it with Mary, who

gave me the gift of *Who She Is* so that I might have this gift of *Who I Am.* And although Julie wasn't with us, there was another part of it, Peace, a part that pulls her in (because of her angel being Water and water being such an important symbol for her). Today was also the day that holy water is blessed. The holy water of baptism: of rebirth. I got holy water for Julie and Mary and will give it to both of them tomorrow.

> baptism: from the Latin Christian baptism, a dipping under
> 1. a baptizing or being baptized; specif. the ceremony or sacrament of admitting a person into Christianity or a specific Christian church by immersing the individual in water or by pouring or sprinkling water on the individual, as a symbol of washing away sin and of spiritual purification
> 2. any experience or ordeal that initiates, tests, or purifies

Oh, Peace. It purifies! Of course. And that is the gift you and Mary and God have given me: the gift of being newly purified—not only my writing—but me.

Is there anything further I need do to purify my union with Julie? Something still seems to stand between us at times. Was it only my veneer or is there something else?

Can you guide me, either here or when next I see her, as to how to leave the barriers behind?

The barriers are gone from you. Do not even remember them. See Julie only with your open heart and give her space in which to open to you. She is still just a little bit afraid. Seeing what Knowing each other has done for you and Mary will help her. This helping each other and giving gifts to each other is what it is all about. Be gentle with her while she unwraps her gift. I assure you when the gift is opened, it will be one of love, and the bonding, the transformation, will be complete.

THIS IS THE STORY. This unfolding. It is not over. The work is done but the story continues. For a lifetime. This is how destiny is revealed. How the talent, the uniqueness, the special gifts of each are brought to the open. Are given space to be. This is only the beginning. A lifetime of happiness awaits. Do not delay. The time has come. You are in it. The time is Now.

Thank you, sweet Peace. I will not delay. I am IN IT.

EPILOGUE

Whaen this work was first being considered for publication, it was suggested that the passages concerning my desire to become a published writer would need to be deleted. "Writers don't talk about writing unless they are writing a book on writing," I was told. I think this mandate also had to do with the uncomfortableness of my publisher, Dan Odegard, in being included in the content of a book he would publish.

But after the more careful consideration of my editor, Steve Lehman, it was decided that my desire had to be included. Because what we desire is at the center of our lives—is our own central theme when we are considering who we are. If everywhere that I talked about my writing you inserted your own desire, you may have learned a lesson similar to the one I learned. Whether we desire power or wealth, talent or the recognition of talent, children or grandchildren, the perfect relationship or the perfect occupation, what we desire is the grand determiner of how we see ourselves in relation to the world around us. It can be the key that unlocks all the rest or the locked door that bars our entrance to everything beyond it.

My journey with Peace was one of taking my desire and identifying its true nature. Of finding the truth within my desire. My original desire to write was not about this writing. The choice to share this writing was a difficult but necessary one. That choice being to be who I am. Because by the time I had finished *Peace,* I was no longer a mystery writer. My desire no longer had to do with writing mysteries.

The decision to share this writing was a difficult one because I was afraid of admitting I was talking to an angel, afraid of admitting I had chosen a spiritual life, afraid to change the image of myself as "mystery writer" that I had held on to for so long. I was not afraid to write mystery novels that dealt with tortured souls and the darkest hours of life. But I was afraid to write about the real mystery of discovering that there was something beyond myself that could help me bring my own tortured soul to the light.

EPILOGUE

Dan Odegard was the mysterious "link" between the person I thought I was when I began my journey and the person I have since become. The link that eventually brought the Peace writing to the light. When Dan was my agent, I looked to him, especially in the early days of my spiritual quest, as being as much an answer to my prayers as Peace later became. He was going to be the "agent" who provided me with the means for doing what I wanted to do with my life: write. And I quite simply had faith in his ability to do so.

But then the day came when I received his letter saying that he was leaving the agenting profession for a position in publishing at Hazelden. The letter came two days after I had begun visualizing his finding me a publisher. The letter came on the very day on which my astrologer, Pat, had predicted I would have a publisher.

I thought Dan's leaving the agenting profession was terrible news. I did not, of course, know then that Hazelden would become the publisher of *The Grace Trilogy* or even that *The Grace Trilogy* would be written. I still thought of myself then as a mystery writer.

But for some reason, despite the "bad" news, I continued to have faith in Dan. I continued to believe, as I told Peace, that, "He would be my bridge to the publishing world." He was.

Was this a small miracle? A divine coincidence? I prefer to think of it as the natural outcome of faith. There were many more divine coincidences that led to the publication of *The Grace Trilogy*. It was as if some unseen force was moving around the puzzle pieces of many lives, bringing them together to make this work available to you. I have no doubt, any longer, of what that unseen force was.

This is the final message I leave you with. What we have faith in becomes an agent to bring us what we truly desire. What we truly desire, when given to God, brings God to us. Because what we desire was given to us by God to bring us to Him.

Peace.

NOTES

1. James Hillman, *Insearch: Psychology and Religion* (Woodstock, Conn.: Spring Publishers, 1994), 40.

2. Hillman, *Insearch,* 50.

3. Hillman, *Insearch,* 56.

4. Hillman, *Insearch,* 65.

5. Joan Borysenko, *Fire in the Soul: A New Psychology of Spiritual Optimism* (New York: Warner Books, 1993), 154–57.

6. Thomas Moore, *Soul Mates: Honoring the Mysteries of Love and Relationship* (New York: HarperCollins, 1994), 94–95.

7. Borysenko, *Fire in the Soul,* 154.

8. Borysenko, *Fire in the Soul,* 154–55.

9. Borysenko, *Fire in the Soul,* 156–57.

10. Rollo May, *Freedom and Destiny* (New York: Bantam Doubleday Dell, 1981), 241–42.

11. Aldous Huxley, *The Perennial Philosophy* (New York: Harper Colophon, 1970), 125.

12. Huxley, *The Perennial Philosophy,* 131.

13. Pat Rodegast and Judith Stanton, *Emmanuel's Book III: What Is an Angel Doing Here?* (New York: Bantam, 1994), 237.

14. Duane Elgin, *Voluntary Simplicity: Toward a Way of Life That Is Outwardly Simple, Inwardly Rich* (New York: Morrow Quill Paperbacks, 1981), 137.

15. John Spayde, quoted in *Utne Reader* (Jan–Feb 1995): no. 67, 56.

16. David Jay Brown and Rebecca McClen Novick, ed., excerpts from an interview with Carolyn Mary Kleefeld in *Mavericks of the Mind: Conversations for the New Millennium* (Freedom, Calif.: The Crossing Press, 1993), 157–72.

17. Brown and Novick, *Mavericks of the Mind,* 167.

18. Sogyal Rinpoche, *The Tibetan Book of Living and Dying* (New York: HarperCollins Publishers, 1992), 102–3.

19. Larry Dossey. *Healing Words: The Power of Prayer and the Practice of Medicine* (New York: HarperCollins Publishers, 1993), 22.

20. Rev. Hugo Hoever, ed., *Lives of the Saints* (New York: Catholic Book Publishing, 1955), 386, 387.

21. Willis Harman and Howard Rheingold, *Higher Creativity: Liberating the Unconscious for Breakthrough Insights* (Los Angeles: Tarcher, 1984), 226.

22. Hillman, *Insearch,* 40.

23. James A. Swan, ed., *The Power of Place: Sacred Ground in Natural and Human Environments* (Wheaton, Ill.: Quest Books, The Theosophical Publishing House, 1991), 324.

24. Swan, *The Power of Place,* 333.

25. *A Course in Miracles* (Mill Valley, Calif.: Foundation for Inner Peace, 1993), 366.

ABOUT THE AUTHOR

Margaret Perron majored in English at the University of Minnesota where she won the Jean Keller-Bouvier Award for literary accomplishment. She has been a public relations director in the nonprofit sector and has worked in administration at the University of Minnesota while pursuing her interest in writing. She grew up in St. Paul, Minnesota, where she continues to find sustenance from her faith, her friends, and her family. Perron is currently a Program Associate for the ISP Executive Study Program at the University of Minnesota. She can be contacted through the web site of The Grace Foundation: http://www.gracezurilovefoundation.com